Prospects of Democr

Prospects of Democracy focuses on 172 contemporary states and provides a vast comparative study on the state and conditions of democracy to be found there. The analysis includes the use of historical data and variables from 1850 to the present day. Tatu Vanhanen demonstrates that the most important factor in the data he presents is the level of resource allocation and that this can be used to explain the emergence of democracy in a particular state.

The book contains five major chapters, followed by statistical data, and concludes with five critical essays on the analysis from five regional experts. The work sets out the theoretical interpretations of democratization, has a research hypothesis on democratization which is tested by empirical evidence and finally analysed and explained. There is also an analysis of democracy, and its prospects, in each of the 172 countries. At the end Mitchell A. Seligson, Ilter Turan, Samuel Decalo, John W. Forje and John Henderson provide a critical commentary on the sources, analysis and findings.

This is the most extensive comparative survey of the state and condition of democracy yet made. It contains important new findings regarding the factors influencing the process of democratization and gives forecasts for democratic change. *Prospects of Democracy* will be essential reading for those studying comparative politics and democracy.

Tatu Vanhanen is Docent of Political Science at the University of Helsinki and Emeritus Associate Professor of the University of Tampere, Finland. He has been studying the problem of democratization since the 1960s. This is his thirteenth book in the field.

Prospects of Democracy

A study of 172 countries

Tatu Vanhanen

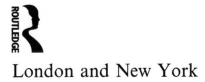

London and New York

First published 1997
by Routledge
11 New Fetter Lane, London EC4P 4EE

Simultaneously published in the USA and Canada
by Routledge
29 West 35th Street, New York, NY 10001

Typeset in Baskerville by
Pure Tech India Limited, Pondicherry
Printed and bound in Great Britain by
Mackays of Chatham PLC, Chatham, Kent

British Library Cataloguing in Publication Data
A catalogue record for this book is available from the British Library

Library of Congress Cataloging in Publication Data
Vanhanen, Tatu.
  Prospects of Democracy: A study of 172 countries / Tatu Vanhanen.
  Includes bibliographical references and index.
  1. Democracy – History.   2. World politics – 1945–.
3. World politics – 19th century.   4. World politics – 20th century.
I. Title.
JC421.V29   1997
321.8 – dc20   96–26285

ISBN 0-415-14405-1 (hbk)
ISBN 0-415-14406-X (pbk)

Contents

Part II Comments

Figures

Tables

Contributors

AUTHOR

Tatu Vanhanen is Docent of Political Science at the University of Helsinki and Emeritus Associate Professor of the University of Tampere. He was Associate Professor of Political Science at the University of Tampere until his retirement in 1992. His recent books include *Democratization in Eastern Europe: Domestic and international perspectives* (edited with Geoffrey Pridham) (1994), *On the Evolutionary Roots of Politics* (1992), *Strategies of Democratization* (editor, 1992), *Politics of Ethnic Nepotism: India as an Example* (1991), and *The Process of Democratization: A Comparative Study of 147 States, 1980–88* (1990).

COMMENTATORS

Mitchell A. Seligson is Daniel H. Wallace Professor of Political Science and Research Professor, University Center for International Studies, University of Pittsburgh, USA. His recent books include *Elections and Democracy in Central America, Revisited* (edited with John Booth) (1995), *Development and Underdevelopment: The Political Economy of Inequality* (edited with J. T. Passé-Smith) (1993), *Elections and Democracy in Central America* (with John Booth) (1989) and *Authoritarians and Democrats: Regime Transition in Latin America* (edited with J. M. Malloy) (1987).

Ilter Turan is Professor of Political Science at KOC University, College of Administrative Science and Economics, Istanbul, Turkey. Until 1993 he was Professor and Chair, Department of International Relations, Faculty of Political Science, Istanbul Unversity. Much of his work has been in the field of comparative politics, focusing on political behaviour and political institutions. Among others, in English, he has co-authored *The Legislative Connection: The Politics of Representation in Kenya, Korea and Turkey* (1984).

Samuel Decalo is Professor of African Politics, University of Natal, Durban, South Africa, and Visiting Professor, University of Florida, Gainesville.

He is author of several books and articles on military regimes, African politics and democratization, including *Coups and Army Rule in Africa: Motivations & Constraints* (1990) and *Psychoses of Power: African Personal Dictatorships* (1989).

John W. Forje teaches political science at the University of Buea and University of Yaounde, Cameroon Republic. He has also worked as a Research Fellow at the Institute of Human Sciences and at the Centre for Action–Oriented Research on African Development in Yaounde. His recent books and publications include *The Failure of the Nation-State and the Return to Functional Democracy in Cameroon* (1993) and *Democracy and Democratization in Cameroon: A Case Study of Rapidly Changing Political Landscape* (1991).

John Henderson is Senior Lecturer and Head of the Department of Political Science, University of Canterbury, New Zealand. He is a specialist in politics of Pacific island states. He has published several articles on politics in Oceania and edited (with others) a book, *Towards a Pacific Island Community* (1990).

Preface

The problem why some countries are democracies and some others are not has interested me since I read S. M. Lipset's seminal book *Political Man* at the beginning of the 1960s. My attention focused on deviating cases like India, wealthy Arabian oil states and socialist countries. I wondered whether it might be possible to invent explanatory principles that could apply to all countries more satisfactorily than the economic development hypothesis. The first time I formulated my idea on the crucial significance of resource distribution was in my licentiate study on the distribution of political power in India (Vanhanen, 1963). I noted in the conclusion of that study that one cannot claim with certainty, merely on the evidence of India, that the success of western democracy presupposes rather the division of the population and élite into different social basic groups and an even distribution of economic and intellectual power than a high level of economic development. I continued that if we could show that such an assumption applies not only to India but also to other countries, the future of western democracy in economically underdeveloped countries in particular would look significantly brighter than in the case that democracy would be regarded as a political system suitable only to countries that have achieved a high level of economic development. Since then I have developed that idea and tested it by empirical evidence. I became fascinated by the prospect of detecting so strong regularities in democratization that it would be possible and plausible to make predictions on the chances of democracy in single countries on the basis of their resource distribution.

This book, which summarizes my earlier studies and extends the analysis to the contemporary states of the 1990s, may be my last extensive comparative study of democratization. I leave it to the future to test my predictions and the usefulness of the theory of democratization formulated in this book. I would be happy if other researchers could find some useful ideas from my study and would like them to test them by new empirical evidence and improve them.

I want to express my gratitude to many persons and institutions who helped me in different ways in this research work during the past four years. Especially my thanks are due to Hung-mao Tien and James Myers, who discussed my paper on the chances of democratization in China in the Sino–American–European conference on contemporary China in Taipei in August 1992, to Vucina Vasovic and Palle Svensson, who discussed my research project in a special session at the IPSA World Congress in Berlin in August 1994, to S. D. Muni for his valuable comments covering South Asian countries and to Samuel Decalo, John W. Forje, John Henderson, Mitchell A. Seligson and Ilter Turan for their commentaries published in this book. I am also grateful to the anonymous reviewers of the manuscript whose critical comments helped me to pay attention at least to some defects of this study.

I am grateful to the Institute of International Relations, National Chengchi University (Taiwan), for a travel grant to the Sino–American–European conference on contemporary China in 1992 and to the Academy of Finland for a travel grant to IPSA World Congress in Berlin in 1994.

Finally, my warm thanks are due to Routledge's Politics Editor Caroline Wintersgill, Senior Editorial Assistant James Whiting and Copy Editor Janet Goss for their help in getting this book published.

Tatu Vanhanen
September 1996

Abbreviations

AP	agricultural population
CIS	Commonwealth of Independent States
Com	Competition
CPE	centrally planned economy
CPS	concentrated private sector
CL	civil liberties
DC	degree of concentration
DD	degree of decentralization of non agricultural economic resources
DER	Distribution of Economic Power Resources
FF	family farms
FIS	Islamic Salvation Front
FLN	National Liberation Front
FRUD	Front for the Restoration of Unity and Democracy
GDP	Gross Domestic Product
GNP	Gross National Product
GNU	Government of National Unity
HDI	Human Development Index
ID	Index of Democratization
IKD	Index of Knowledge Distribution
IOD	Index of Occupational Diversification
IPR	Index of Power Resources
ISI	Index of Structural Imbalance
IPRI	Index of Power Resources and Structural Imbalance
KANU	Kenya African National Union
MOE	market oriented economy
MPLA-PT	Popular Movement for the Liberation of Angola-Workers' Party
NAP	non agricultural population
Par	Participation
PPP	People's Progressive Party
PR	political rights

Pre	Predicted value of ID produced by the regression equation of ID on IPR
PSD	public sector dominated
RAP	representation, accountability and participation
Res	Residual produced by the regressive equation ID on IPR
ROC	Republic of China
SWAPO	South-West Africa People's Organisation of Namibia
UAE	United Arab Emirates
UNITA	National Union for the Total Independence of Angola
UP	Urban Population

Part I

Comparative analysis of democratization

Introduction

Democratization of political systems is a theoretical problem that has fascinated me since the 1960s. The collapse of authoritarian socialist systems and the emergence of numerous new democracies since the 1980s have intensified the quest of researchers to explain democratization and to evaluate the prospects of democracy in the regions of the world still ruled by authoritarian regimes. Scientific knowledge on the causes and conditions of democracy is urgently needed. Karl Popper says that scientific knowledge starts from problems. According to him, 'a theoretical problem consists in the task of providing an intelligible explanation of an unexplained natural event and the testing of the explanatory theory by way of its predictions' (Popper 1992: 3–4; see also Popper 1983: 191–205). That is just what I am trying to do in this study.

The great variation of political systems from the perspective of democracy is the problem tackled in this study. How to explain the democratization of political systems that has taken place since the 1850s, but which has been a very uneven process? Why have some countries democratized and some others not? Further, is the number of democracies increasing or decreasing and on what grounds? What are the chances of particular countries establishing or maintaining democratic institutions? Is it possible to make reasonably accurate predictions on the prospects of democracy in a particular country? Is democracy spreading over the world, or are there social, economic, cultural, or other constraints that make democratization very difficult if not impossible, in some parts of the world or in particular countries? I am trying to provide a theoretical explanation for democratization and to test that explanation by empirical evidence. A satisfactory theoretical explanation for democracy as well as for its lack would be useful because it could help people to formulate conscious strategies of democratization and because it would provide a theoretical basis on which to make predictions of democracy in particular countries. The predictions given in this study will test my theoretical explanation in the future.

One could ask at this point: why should we be interested in democratization instead of some other aspects of political systems? Does democracy make any difference? I think that the level of democratic governance is a very important aspect of political systems and that it makes a difference from the perspective of people living under a particular political system. The difference is that it belongs to the nature of democratic governments to take care of the many, to serve their interests in the endless struggle for survival in this world of scarcity, whereas it belongs to the nature of autocratic systems to serve the interests of the few. This difference is an inevitable consequence of the fact that all those who have power tend to use it for their own advantage. Because power is shared by the many in a democracy, power is used, or at least attempted to be used, for the advantage of the many, and because power is concentrated in the hands of the few in an autocracy, it is also used to serve the interests of the few. This is the reason, I think, why subjugated and common people living under autocratic systems dream of democracy or something like it and why they start to struggle for power and democracy as soon as they are able to challenge their rulers. It is reasonable to assume that a democratic system provides a better framework for the good life and human dignity of the many than an autocratic system, but this is not a sufficient reason for the ruling few to give up their mono-poly of power and to share power and the fruits of power with the many. As a consequence, democracies do not emerge easily, and it is often difficult to maintain established democratic institutions. The many have to struggle for democracy and defend their democratic freedoms and rights against the few who would like to establish their own hegemony. It is difficult to know the results of such struggles in advance. In fact, most political systems may be somewhere in the twilight area between the rule of the few and the rule of the many. It is exciting to explore the causes and conditions of democratiza-tion and to evaluate the chances of democracy in particular countries.

Prospects of democracy in the world will be explored in this study on the basis of an evolutionary theory of democratization formulated in my earlier comparative studies (Vanhanen 1984a and 1990a). We could also call it a resource distribution theory of democratization. Hypotheses derived from that theory will be tested by *longitudinal and cross-sectional* empirical data covering nearly all independent states. The purpose is to find out to what extent it is possible to explain the variation of political systems from the perspective of democracy by a theory that is expected to apply to all countries and cultural areas. The idea that the same explanatory variables could explain a significant part of the variation in the degree of democra-tization across all cultural regions is based on certain axiomatic assump-tions on the similarity of human nature and on the existence of approximately similar politically relevant behavioural predispositions among all human populations. To the extent that empirical evidence sup-ports theoretical assumptions on the regularities in democratization, it becomes possible to make predictions on the chances of democracy and democratization in different countries.

This study is built upon my earlier comparative research on the regula-rities in the process of democratization that I have carried out since the

1970s, but it is also intended to develop the theory by experimenting with alternative ways to combine explanatory variables. The empirical analysis of this study will be focused on the contemporary states of the 1990s, but the principal regression equations providing the criteria of predictions are based on the observation units of the whole period of my comparative studies since the 1850s. In this way it becomes possible to take into account the relationship between dependent and explanatory variables over the period 1850–1993. The axiomatic assumption on the similarity of human nature makes it plausible to hypothesize that the relationship between dependent and explanatory variables was the same in the 1850s as it is in the 1990s. The results of empirical analyses indicate to what extent this assumption is historically correct. If the pattern of relationship between political and explanatory variables has remained approximately the same since the 1850s, it is reasonable to assume that it will also continue in the next decades. The more constant the relationship has been, the more confidently we can make predictions on the basis of this relationship.

Part I of this book contains five chapters and five appendices. In chapter 1, some theoretical interpretations of democratization are reviewed. Because my own theory of democratization is related to many earlier and contemporary studies and theories of democracy, it is appropriate to begin this study by a review of alternative theoretical explanations of democratization and of empirical comparative studies of democracy. However, because I have discussed various studies of democracy in my previous works, I do not refer to all relevant studies and theories in this book. My attention is limited to some contemporary theoretical explanations and comparative studies of democratization. They provide points of comparison for my own study. After reviewing alternative approaches to study democratization, I will introduce my own evolutionary or Darwinian theory of democratization and explain how it is derived from the principles of the neo-Darwinian theory of evolution by natural selection. According to my central hypothesis, democratization is expected to take place under conditions in which power resources have become so widely distributed that no group is any longer able to suppress its competitors or to maintain its hegemony.

The research design of this study is introduced in chapter 2. I try to explain how the hypothesis on democratization can be tested by empirical evidence and how the results of empirical analysis can be used to make predictions for the prospects of democracy in particular countries. At first, theoretical concepts are operationalized. Empirical indicators intended to measure the level of democracy and the degree of resource distribution are defined, and various ways to combine political and explanatory variables into indices are discussed. Research hypotheses are formulated on the basis of operational indicators. Finally, the units of observation and the period of comparison are defined, and the methods of statistical analyses are specified. I have divided the 172 contemporary states of this study into seven regional groups on the basis of geographical and cultural differences:

1 Europe and North America
2 Latin America and the Caribbean
3 North Africa, the Middle East, and Central Asia
4 Sub-Saharan Africa
5 South Asia
6 East Asia and Southeast Asia
7 Oceania.

Chapter 3, on the empirical analysis of democratization in 1850–1993, includes the results of correlation and regression analyses by which the research hypotheses are tested. I have carried out these analyses separately in two major comparison groups. The first comparison group is the total longitudinal group comprising 1,139 decennial units of observation over the period 1850–1993. The second comparison group is a cross-sectional group comprising 172 countries for the period 1991–3. These 172 countries are included in the longitudinal group, too, but only from one point of time. The results of correlation and regression analyses in these two comparison groups indicate to what extent the relationship between political and explanatory variables has remained the same over time as hypothesized. It is plausible to assume that the relationship based on the longitudinal comparison group provides a more reliable ground for predictions than the relationship observed only at one point of time. Therefore, the results of longitudinal statistical analyses will be used as the principal grounds for predictions. Correlation analyses are used to indicate the strength of hypothesized relationship between operational indicators of democracy and resource distribution. Negative or weak positive correlations would falsify the research hypotheses on the dependence of democracy on the degree of resource distribution. In this chapter, I also compare the results of correlation analyses based on my explanatory variables to the results produced by some alternative explanatory variables (GNP per capita and Human Development Index). Regression analysis discloses to what extent the general relationship between political and explanatory variables applies to single countries. It is used to test the research hypothesis, according to which all countries tend to cross the threshold of democracy at about the same level of resource distribution. The results of regression analyses will also help to differentiate between the countries whose level of democracy is approximately in balance with the degree of resource distribution and the countries whose level of democracy is significantly lower or higher than expected. Further, the results of regression analyses for single countries are used to make predictions on the prospects of democracy in particular countries.

In chapter 4, the prospects of democracy in single countries are analysed in greater detail by regions and predictions on the prospects of democracy for single countries are made on the basis of explanatory variables and of the results of regression analyses. It should be noted that these predictions are based on the relationship between political and explanatory variables in the whole world group because I assume that the theory of democratization applies equally to all cultural and geographical groups of countries. For various reasons, there may be considerable differences in the strength of relationship between political and explanatory variables from one regional group to another. A purpose of regional analyses is to find out whether there are any systematic differences between regional groups. The arithmetic means of political and explanatory variables are used in the comparison of regional groups, as well as the arithmetic means of positive and negative residuals produced by regression analyses. Predictions on the prospects of democracy in particular countries are based on the results of regression analyses because the purpose is to see to what extent it is possible to predict the chances of democracy in particular countries on the basis of the explanatory variables used in this study. In some cases, however, it is reasonable to also take into account some theoretically relevant local factors that are not included in my explanatory variables. However, I do not try to list all possible relevant factors because my intention is to test the explanatory power of the common explanatory variables of this study. It means that some part of the variation will remain unexplained and some of the predictions given in this study will be incorrect.

In chapter 5, I summarize my central arguments, the results of empirical analyses, the regularities in democratization since the 1850s and predictions on the prospects of democracy in different parts of the world. I hope to be able to show where we can expect the survival or failure of existing democracies, the emergence of new democracies, and the persistence of autocratic systems. I shall also discuss various strategies of democratization, including the role of institutions. My point is that we could use theoretical knowledge of the conditions of democracy to formulate appropriate social reforms and political institutions. All types of social structures and political institutions are certainly not equally appropriated to support the establishment and consolidation of democratic politics. Furthermore, I shall refer to some incalculable factors that may affect the chances of democracy.

Because my theory of democratization differs from other theoretical explanations of democracy in some important respects and because my empirical data on political and explanatory varibles may include various errors, I asked some area specialists to check my data and comment on the results of this study. They were to examine the method, the results and predictions of my study critically, to indicate on which points they disagreed, and to present their own possible interpretations and predictions. Unfortunately some of the invited experts were not able to complete their contributions in time, but five scholars – Mitchell A. Seligson, Ilter Turan, Samuel Decalo, John W. Forje and John Henderson – sent their commentaries, which are published in Part II of this book. I think that their critical comments complement this study in a remarkable way and provide interesting reading. They enliven the study by many details missing from my

statistical analysis. Contributors also refer to several possible defects in my
methods, variables and data, and make suggestions of alternative variables
and approaches to study the problem of democratization. It should be
noted that their comments are based on two earlier versions of this manuscript, not on the final one, so they were not able to take into account all the
details of the final text. The five commentaries are quite different, which
tells us something of the alternative ways to study democratization and to
look at the results of this study. I let their comments speak for themselves
without arguments. I only introduce them briefly and try to point out some
characteristics of each contribution.

Mitchell A. Seligson examines the structures of IPR and ID indices and
the significance of particular variables. One of his interesting comments
concerns the lack of political culture variables and the absence of income
distribution data. He argues that the Urban Population variable may be
theoretically misleading and should be re-evaluated. It may be so. Further,
he refers to findings that show that land concentration may be higher in
Latin American countries than census data indicate. It is a very noteworthy
observation. Seligson seems to agree with my predictions on the prospects
for democracy in Latin American countries, at least in major points, but he
pays attention to several anomalies in IPR and ID values as well as in
values of some other variables, particularly in the cases of Costa Rica,
Argentina and Uruguay.

Ilter Turan focuses on democratic anomalies in his contribution covering
the region of North Africa, the Middle East and Central Asia. His question
is why democratization has not taken place in some countries in which
social conditions are, according to my independent variables, ripe for
democracy and why some other countries have democratized in spite of
unfavourable social conditions. Such democratic anomalies are most frequent in the Middle East, North Africa, sub-Saharan Africa and East and
Southeast Asia. He argues that the path to democracy may not be as linear
as I assume in my study and that I have left out a set of critical political and
socio-political variables. Some universal factors that have not been taken
into account in my study might explain a part of the unexplained variation.
He refers to colonial legacies, to the lack of political community, to the
characteristics of the international system and to the economic interests of
the ruling élites. Ilter Turan emphasizes the need to study deviant cases.
According to his argument, the significance of socio-economic relations is
secondary compared to the role of socio-political structures in many deviating countries.

Samuel Decalo comments on my study and predictions for the prospects
of democracy in sub-Saharan Africa from the perspective of qualitative
analysis. He argues quite convincingly that quantitative data on some
variables do not provide a sufficiently detailed and correct picture on the
nature of political systems and their social environments. Many non measurable variables should be taken into account, including political culture.

He refers to several factors and circumstances that affect the chances of democracy in Africa in his colourful article. Decalo's contribution illustrates inevitable tensions between quantitative and qualitative studies, between the generalist and the specialist, and between the comparativist and the case-study expert. However, he does not seem to disagree with my predictions in general, or express his disagreements in particular cases.

John W. Forje's major argument seems to be that differences between sub-Saharan Africa and old European democracies are so great that it is difficult, if not impossible, to compare them within the same framework and by using the same indicators. So he disagrees with one of my basic assumptions. He refers to many failures of African countries to establish and maintain democratic institutions and tries to find explanations for these failures and gross violations of fundamental human rights from colonial legacies and local circumstances. He emphasizes the significance of specific conditions of each country and the significance of political institutions as well as the rule of law. Forje's contribution includes valuable information and observations on the contemporary nature of politics in sub-Saharan Africa, including his own country, Cameroon. He does not comment on my specific predictions on the prospects of democracy in particular African countries, but he comes to the conclusion that democracy presupposes a pluralistic society. It is also my central theoretical argument.

John Henderson's commentary on the prospects of democracy in Oceania adds many details to my statistical analysis of those countries. Following his suggestion, I changed the name of that region from 'Australasia and Pacific' to 'Oceania' in the final text. Henderson focuses on my predictions and says that he disagrees with my optimistic predictions. It is interesting to note that he refers to the possibility of military coups in Papua New Guinea, Solomon Islands and Vanuatu and of the re-emergence of traditional political structures in all Pacific states. Let us see what happens. These three countries have been problematic in my study because of their large positive residuals. In addition, Henderson's article provides information of other small Pacific island states that were exluded from this study.

1 Theoretical interpretations of democratization

The variation of political systems from the rule of one to the rule of many has interested political philosophers and political scientists since Plato and Aristotle. They have attempted to unravel the origins of autocracy, democracy and other political systems, to find out what kinds of social conditions are connected with various types of political systems, and to clarify causal relations between political systems and environmental conditions. Many of these studies have concerned the conditions or prerequisites of democracy. There are numerous theories and explanations of democracy and democratization, but it has been difficult for researchers to agree on the most appropriate theoretical interpretation of democratization or on the causal factors of democratization. Thus this crucial research problem is still open. Various theoretical approaches compete with each other.

I am not going to review the long history of democracy studies, and I would not be capable of doing it comprehensively. Besides, there are many good reviews of contemporary studies of democracy and democratization (see, for example, Pennock 1979; Sartori 1987; Arat 1991; Whistler 1993; Diamond 1992 and 1994; Diamond and Marks 1992; O'Regan 1992; Almond 1992; Sorensen 1993). I have reviewed the history and some aspects of contemporary democracy studies in my earlier works (see Vanhanen 1971: 12–23; 1979: 3–13; 1984a: 9–15; 1990a: 36–47). In this connection, I refer only to some contemporary theoretical approaches, which provide alternative ways to study and explain democratization, after which I shall focus on my own approach to tackling the problem of democratization and evaluating and predicting the prospects of democracy in the world.

VARIOUS APPROACHES TO EXPLAIN DEMOCRATIZATION

Contemporary political scientists and sociologists have explained the problem of democratization from many perspectives and have come to different conclusions on causal factors of democratization. The development paradigm proposed by Daniel Lerner (1968) and S. M. Lipset (1959 and 1960), which connects democratization to economic growth and modernization, seems to have been the most influential approach in the field. According to Thomas A. Sancton, most political scientists agree that certain preconditions are necessary. Among them are 'a fairly high level of economic development, a strong middle class, a tradition of tolerance and respect for the individual, the presence of independent social groups and institutions, a market-oriented economy and the existence of élites willing to give up power' (Sancton 1987). Sancton's formulation reflects the central arguments of the development paradigm.

However, many researchers disagree, at least partly, with these arguments. The Latin American dependency theory of Andre Gunder Frank (1967) and others challenged the theses of the development theory in the 1960s and claimed that global capitalism was the cause of underdevelopment in the Third World countries and, implicitly, of the lack of democracy in the Third World (see also dos Santos 1993; Wallerstein 1982 and 1993). It transferred attention from domestic factors to external ones. Guillermo O'Donnell's (1973) bureaucratic authoritarian model challenged the development theory by claiming that modernization coincided in Latin America with the emergence of a new type of authoritarian regime (see O'Regan 1992). Some other researchers have emphasized that democratization is connected with different causal factors, including historical factors, social structures and conditions, economic development, external factors, political culture, and political leadership (see Dahl 1971; Diamond, *et al* 1988–9). Raymond Gastil (1985) argues strongly that democratization may depend on the diffusion of democratic ideas more than on any socio-economic factors (see also Fossedal 1989). Guillermo O'Donnell and Philippe C. Schmitter (1986) pay attention to the crucial role of political leadership in the final stages of transitions from authoritarian rule to democracy. It is clear that researchers do not yet agree on the nature of causal factors or on the direction of causal relations. Let us examine some of these studies in greater detail.

S. M. Lipset (1983: 469–75) refers to several other social scientists who have found a positive relationship between economic development and democracy. Their studies have confirmed the findings of his original study (Lipset 1959) on the association between stable democracy and indicators of national wealth, communication, industrialization, education, and urbanization. He explains this association by a hypothesis according to which 'the level of a country's economic development independently affects the orientations conducive to democracy of its citizens.' It means that democratic attitudes and beliefs serve as intervening mechanisms between economic development and democracy. It should be noted that Lipset stresses, in addition to economic development, the significance of political culture, legitimacy, and suitable institutions as conditions of democracy (see Lipset 1994).

In a new study, S. M. Lipset *et al* (1993) reconfirmed Lipset's original hypothesis on the association between economic development and democracy, but they emphasize that economic development alone does not produce democratization. Other relevant factors including 'national idio-syncracies, the play of historical, cultural and political factors and the behavior of leaders may advance or prevent democratization in any parti-cular nation-state or group of them.' However, they still regard economic development as the dominant explanatory factor. According to their find-ings, the relationship between levels of per capita income and democratiza-tion in the late 1980s was even more striking than in the 1950s. In addition, they refer to the possibility of N-type relationship between economic growth and democracy, but they do not reject the linearity assumption of the original Lerner–Lipset model. They assume that the relationship between economic development and political democracy will be linear over extended time, although there is 'the possibility of negative relationships at inter-mediate ranges (i.e., the range of GNP per capita between $1,500 and $3,500)' (Lipset, *et al* 1993; see also Diamond 1992: 109; Moore 1995; Fukuyama 1995; Rowen 1995).

Larry Diamond and Gary Marks (1992: 6) refer to evidence that shows, 'with striking clarity and consistency, a strong causal relationship between economic development and democracy'. They assert that the level of eco-nomic development 'continues to be the single most powerful predictor of the likelihood of democracy'. Larry Diamond's (1992) article 'Economic Development and Democracy Reconsidered' includes the most comprehen-sive recent review and discussion of the research based on Lipset's seminal study and hypothesis on the relationship between economic development levels and democracy. Diamond re-evaluated Lipset's thesis and tested it by new empirical evidence. A cross-tabulation of per capita GNP in 1989 and regime type in 1990 for 142 countries shows again a strong relationship between economic development and democracy. The relationship between democracy and development was even stronger when the Human Develop-ment Index (HDI) constructed by the United Nations Development Pro-gram (1991) was used as the development indicator. The HDI had a substantially higher correlation (0.71) with the combined index of political freedom than GNP (0.51). Diamond argues that a country's mean level of 'human development' or physical quality of life predicts its likelihood of being democratic and its level of political freedom better than its per capita level of money income. He explains this difference between the HDI and per capita GNP by an assumption that although 'per capita national income appears to be the one independent variable that has most reliably and consistently predicted the level of democracy, this is likely a surrogate for a broader measure of average human development and well-being that is in fact even more closely associated with democracy.' Consequently, he decided to reformulate Lipset's thesis into a new form: 'The more well-to-do the people of a country, on average, the more likely they will favor, achieve, and maintain a democratic system for their country.' Diamond's reformulation of Lipset's hypothesis seems to make it stronger. Diamond concludes on the basis of his extensive review of the evidence that Lipset was 'broadly correct both in his assertion of a strong causal relationship between economic development and democracy and in his explanation of *why* development promotes democracy' (Diamond 1992; for Lipset's thesis, see also O'Regan 1992).

I do not have much to say on dependency theory in this connection. It has been difficult to test its assertions because hypotheses were never clearly stated. As Anthony O'Regan (1992) says, 'dependency theory was unable or unwilling to create, develop or even define testable hypotheses.' Its popularity was based more on its political appropriateness than on its theoretical ability to explain development or underdevelopment. It seemed to liberate national élites from responsibility by blaming external forces (global capitalism) for underdevelopment, poverty, inequalities, and the lack of democracy in Third World countries. These theorists argued, as Larry Diamond notes, 'that the dependent capitalist developing states were captured by élites in alliance with and serving the interests of dominant countries and corporations abroad. This exclusionary alliance required political repression of popular mobilization to maintain low wage levels and high profit levels.' They posited a negative relationship of economic development to democracy (Diamond 1992: 114). Some researchers have attempted to test this implicit hypothesis by empirical evidence. The results of some studies support the hypothesis slightly; some other studies indicate that there is no clear relationship, and some results clearly contradict the hypothesis (see Bollen 1983; Muller 1985 and 1993; Arat 1991; Hadenius 1992). Results have been confusing and partly contradictory. It may be due to the differences in observation units as well as in indicators that have been used to measure dependent and independent variables. It seems to me that dependency theory cannot help to explain democratization or the lack of democracy in developing countries, but I do not want to claim that all external factors are insignificant from the perspective of democratization. In some cases, external factors may be highly relevant. They represent types of power resources that have been used both to further and to obstruct democratization.

The problem with Guillermo O'Donnell, Philippe C. Schmitter and Laurence Whitehead's study on *Transitions from Authoritarian Rule* (1986) is that it does not test any clearly stated hypothesis nor produce such hypotheses. O'Donnell and Schmitter make this quite clear: 'We did not have at the beginning, nor do we have at the end of this lengthy collective endeavor, a "theory" to test or to apply to the case studies and thematic essays in these volumes' (O'Donnell and Schmitter 1986: 3). Their 'Transition School', as Anthony O'Regan (1992: 21–4) notes, shifted attention from generalizable political development theory to individual nation monograph studies and upon the tactics and organizational skills of individual élites and élite groups. Their study clarifies the final stages of the process of democratization, although it does not provide any theoretical explanation for democratization.

Ronald H. Chilcote *et al.* (1992) attempted to apply the concepts of a Marxist class theory of state to transitions from dictatorship to democracy in Spain, Portugal and Greece, but their country analyses did not produce any clearly defined and testable theory or hypothesis on the transition to representative democracy. In fact, they were more concerned with the problem of why transitions to socialism did not take place in those countries. As Chilcote (1992: 201) says, their objective was 'to analyze why Socialists in those countries favor political accommodation and therefore have reached an impasse in the long-range process of a transition to socialism'.

Robert A. Dahl argues in his influential book *Polyarchy* (1971) that democratization cannot be explained by any single causal factor and that several different conditions should be taken into account. He differentiated between seven sets of conditions (five of which I discuss here) and assumed that if all of them were favourable for polyarchy, a country had very good chances to establish and maintain polyarchy, and vice versa. Dahl continues the same line of argument in his later study *Democracy and its Critics* (1989). He connects the chances of democracy or polyarchy, as he says, to definable environmental conditions, but not to any single dominant explanatory factor. The first favourable condition is that the means of violent coercion are dispersed or neutralized. The second condition concerns the nature of a society. A modern dynamic pluralist society, in which wealth, income, education, and status are dispersed among groups and individuals, provides a favourable condition for democracy. Such a society disperses power sufficiently to inhibit its monopolization by any single group, although it does not necessarily eliminate significant inequalities in the distribution of power. Third, cultural homogeneity facilitates polyarchy, whereas subcultural pluralism is unfavourable for polyarchy. According to Dahl, subcultures are 'typically formed around ethnic, religious, racial, linguistic, or regional differences and shared historical experience or ancestral myths'. However, he notes that 'under certain conditions polyarchy can survive, and even function fairly well, despite extensive subcultural pluralism'. The fourth condition concerns the beliefs of political activists. A country is very likely to develop and sustain the institutions of polyarchy 'if it possesses a political culture and beliefs, particularly among political activists, that support the institutions of polyarchy'. Finally, foreign influence or control forms the fifth condition. The intervention of a more powerful country may prevent the emergence or function of the institutions of polyarchy in a dominated country, but foreign intervention can also be used to implant the institutions of polyarchy. All the conditions listed by Dahl may be relevant for democracy, but the problem is how to operationalize them and how to weight the significance of different conditions. Besides, some of these conditions (cultural homogeneity and foreign interventions) are not equally relevant for all countries (see also O'Regan 1992: 31–6).

Larry Diamond, Juan J. Linz and Seymour Martin Lipset focus on the struggle for democracy in their large twenty-six-nation comparative study *Democracy in Developing Countries* (1988–90). They 'seek to explain whether, why, and to what extent democracy has evolved and taken root in the vastly different cultural and historical soils of these countries'. They did not think it possible to base their study on any coherent theory on democratization because 'there remain huge gaps in our understanding of the factors that foster or obstruct the emergence, instauration (establishment), and consolidation of democratic government around the world.' Like Dahl, they assume that many different factors can facilitate or obstruct the establishment and survival of democratic institutions. Therefore, they left it to each author of country chapters to offer 'a summary of theoretical judgment of the factors that have been most important in determining the country's overall degree of success or failure with democratic government' (Diamond, *et al.* 1990: 1–4). As a starting point, they referred to the ten theoretical dimensions that various theoretical and empirical works have associated with democracy:

> political culture; regime legitimacy and effectiveness; historical development (in particular the colonial experience); class structure and the degree of inequality; national structure (ethnic, racial, regional, and religious cleavage); state structure, centralization, and strength (including the state's role in the economy, the roles of autonomous voluntary associations and the press, federalism, and the role of the armed forces); political and constitutional structure (parties, electoral systems, the judiciary); political leadership; development performance; and international factors.
> (Diamond, Linz and Lipset 1988 vol. 2: XV)

Later, on the basis of the twenty-six country studies, they listed the following facilitating and obstructing factors for democratic development: legitimacy and performance, political leadership, political culture, social structure and socio-economic development, associational life, state and society, political institutions, ethnic and regional conflicts, the military, and international factors (Diamond, *et al.* 1990: 9–34). Their list of relevant factors does not constitute any clear theory of democratization, although it implies that democratization cannot be explained by any single factor in all countries (*cf.* Cammack 1994: 176–7). It would probably be very difficult to operationalize these factors, to measure them, and to weight their relative significance.

Samuel P. Huntington (1984) does not consider it possible to explain democratization by any coherent theory because too many factors can further or obstruct democratization. He refers to Dankwart Rustow (1970), who criticized studies that focused on 'preconditions' of democracy and looked at them primarily as economic, social, cultural, and psychological, but not political, factors. Huntington admits that various socio-economic conditions affect democratic development, but he also emphasizes the significance of the political process of democratization. Concerning preconditions, he points out that the emergence of democracy is helped by higher levels of economic well-being, the absence of extreme inequalities in wealth and income, greater social pluralism, a market-oriented economy, greater influence *vis-à-vis* the society of existing democratic states, and a culture that is less monistic and more tolerant of diversity and compromise. However, he notes that 'no one of these preconditions is sufficient to lead to democratic development', although a market economy may be a necessary condition. With respect to the political process, he says that 'a central requirement would appear to be that either the established élites within an authoritarian system or the successor élites after an authoritarian system collapses see their interests served by the introduction of democratic institutions.' It is a very good observation. Huntington's conclusion on the prospects for democracy in 1984 was pessimistic. He assumed that, 'with a few exceptions, the limits of democratic development in the world may well have been reached'.

It has always been difficult to evaluate the prospects for democracy in the world. Six years before Huntington's article, Ralph Buultjens (1978) had presented even gloomier predictions on the future of democracy. He regarded democracy as an endangered species and argued that, 'in the modern world, democracy is fast losing out to other political orders, and there is little indication of any mass movement toward the full restoration of democracy where it has been lost or even its revitalization where it exists.' It seemed to him that 'ours is the declining phase of a brief historical era of about two hundred years'. Buultjens concluded: 'In summary, this survey does not offer any serious and near hope for a major expansion of democracy outside those areas where it presently functions', and he finished by noting, 'we must reluctantly conclude that it is not an encouraging vision and contains little evidence that democracy will be the wave of the remaining decades of the twentieth century.' Buultjens seems to have failed in his predictions. The next two decades will disclose the worth of the predictions given in this book.

In his recent book *The Third Wave* (1991), Huntington analyses the three waves of democratization since the last century and tries to explain 'why, how, and with what consequences a group of roughly contemporaneous transitions to democracy occurred in the 1970s and 1980s and to understand what these transitions may suggest about the future of democracy in the world.' He reiterates his thesis that the 'causes of democratization differ substantially from one place to another and from one time to another' (Huntington 1991: 30, 38). Therefore, it is hardly possible to find a common independent variable that could explain democratization in all countries. The following propositions summarize his arguments:

1 No single factor is sufficient to explain the development of democracy in all countries or in a single country.

2 No single factor is necessary to the development of democracy in all countries.

3 Democratization in each country is the result of combination of causes.

4 The combination of causes producing democracy varies from country to country.

5 The combination of causes generally responsible for one wave of democratization differs from that responsible for other waves.

6 The causes responsible for the initial regime changes in a democratization wave are likely to differ from those responsible for later regime changes in that wave.

(Huntington 1991: 38)

Huntington explains the third wave of democratization by referring to many different causal factors, including declining legitimacy of nondemocratic rule, economic development, the role of western Christianity, external actors, demonstration effects or snowballing, and the significance of political leaders. Particularly he pays attention to the positive correlation between economic development and democratization and makes a difference between broad-based economic development involving significant industrialization and development based on the sale of oil. He says: 'In contrast to patterns in the oil states, processes of economic development involving significant industrialization lead to a new, much more diverse, complex, and interrelated economy, which becomes increasingly difficult for authoritarian regimes to control' (Huntington 1991: 65). This is an interesting observation. It directs our attention to structural consequences of economic development, to the fact that the control of economic resources becomes diversified. However, a list of assumed causal factors does not constitute any theoretical explanation for democratization.

Raymond Duncan Gastil (1985) argues that socio-economic preconditions are only secondary factors in the more general process of the diffusion of democracy. He evaluates the future of democracy largely in terms of a struggle for ideas. Gastil considers 'democracy to be an idea, or group of closely related ideas, that spread in recent centuries from a very few centers'. The future of democracy, he says, 'will be related to the continuing strength of this diffusion'. In the Comparative Survey of Freedom by Freedom House, which Gastil started in the 1970s, the existence of democracy 'in a particular country will be seen as primarily the result of the relative effectness of the diffusion of democracy and its supporting concepts'. So his approach contradicts 'more than a generation of political scientists who have stressed cultural and situational factors in the ability of peoples to accept or institutionalize democracy'. Gastil's theoretical explanation of democracy is a really different one, but it has not been tested in *Freedom in the World* reports, which have concentrated to evaluate the level of political rights and freedoms in the world (see Gastil 1988). In *Freedom in the World 1991–92*, R. Bruce McColm attributes the democratic changes of the past decade 'to a wide-range of impersonal historical factors such as the integration of the global economy, the cross-boundary appeal of new information technologies and the growing desire of nation-states to become re-integrated into larger regional economic and political communities' (McColm 1992: 49). However, no attempts have been made to test these assumptions on the causes of democratization by empirical evidence. The diffusion of democratic ideas may be an important factor, but I cannot regard it as the principal factor of democracy. If it were the principal factor, we could expect democracy to emerge as easily in any kinds of social conditions. It means that the existence of democracy should not correlate with any socio-economic or other structural variables.

Terry Lynn Karl (1990) reviewed several theories about the origins of democratic regimes in Latin America and came to the conclusion that the search 'for causes rooted in economic, social, cultural/psychological, or international factors has not yielded a general law of democratization, nor is it likely to do so in the near future despite the proliferation of new cases'. Besides, she argues that 'what the literature has considered in the past to be the preconditions of democracy may be better conceived in the future as the outcomes of democracy' (Karl 1990: 2–5). I agree that there are interactions between political and social factors, but it does not mean that we should give up our attempts to separate dependent variables from independent ones.

Zehra F. Arat (1991) tested a hypothesis on the decline of democracy by extensive empirical evidence covering 65–150 independent countries over the period 1948–82. Her main argument and hypothesis is that 'the stability of democratic systems is threatened if the elected government cannot re-inforce socio-economic rights at levels comparable to those of civil-political rights.' She formulated a complicated index of democracy and measured the lack of civil–political rights by several indicators of social and political unrest and inequality. Most of the explanatory indicators were correlated with the magnitude of annual decline in the index score of democracy as hypothesized, but correlations are weak. One interesting finding is that the shifts on the scale of democracy tend to be highest in countries located near the middle of the economic development scale. Arat concluded that she cannot 'share others' optimistic expectations about the future of democracy in developing countries'. Her gloomy assessment is: 'As long as social and economic inequalities persist, developing countries that go through a process of democratization today are doomed to return to some form of authoritarianism' (Arat 1991). Time will tell us whether she is right. I could agree with her arguments if 'inequalities' is replaced by 'the concentration of power resources'. I think that inequalities reflect the unequal distribution of various important resources.

Axel Hadenius (1992) has explored the requisites of democracy in the Third World and tested various hypotheses and assumptions by empirical evidence covering 132 developing countries in 1988. He tried to take into account all variables of any interest. His method was to use a stepwise regression to separate the chaff from the wheat. He came to the conclusion 'that no single explanatory factor strikes like an iron fist through the material' (Hadenius 1992: 146). Just as Dahl and Diamond, Linz and Lipset in their studies reviewed above, Hadenius argues that 'several attributes of different kinds stand out as important', but he also found that several variables are not as important as they were assumed to be. His empirical analysis indicated that, for example, the size of the public sector, the colonial background, the size of states, and the distribution of income and wealth are not significant explanatory factors. In the end, seven significant explanatory factors survived in the process of stepwise regression: trade with the USA, commodity concentration, percentage of Protestants, capitalism, military expenditure, literacy, and average fragmentation. Together they explained 59 per cent of the variation concerning the level of democratization (Hadenius 1992). The accumulated explanatory level is relatively high, but the problem is how to connect these very different variables with each other. He does not have any theory to link his explanatory factors. In each case, a different hypothesis or assumption is used to explain why this factor should affect the level of democracy positively or negatively. There does not seem to be any way to construct a coherent theory of democratization on the basis of these very different explanatory factors (see also Hadenius 1994).

Dirk Berg-Schlosser and Gisèle DeMeur studied conditions of democracy in interwar Europe. They tested the explanatory power of the major hypotheses and explanatory factors with a specific Boolean method in their comparison group of sixteen interwar European countries, which includes both the major 'breakthrough' cases and the major 'survivors'. They found all hypotheses and explanatory factors more or less defective but not to the same extent. Dahl's comprehensive listing of factors favourable to democracy seemed to cover better than other factors the variations observed in their cases (Berg-Schlosser and DeMeur 1994).

Donald E. Whistler has examined the mainstream democratic vision and conditions associated with modern democracy. He refers to Robert A. Dahl's and my explanations of democracy in particular and argues that the crucial condition for modern democracy is not a high level of economic development but a balance of forces between competing groups. He emphasizes the importance of the distribution of resources to democracy and says that in the modern world, 'autocracies have ceased when economic, social, and coercive resources are widely enough distributed that no subset of the population can monopolize the government' (Whistler 1993). Mancur Olson comes to a similar explanation of democracy. His question is: 'How do democracies emerge out of autocracies?' According to his theory, democracy would be most likely to emerge spontaneously when the individual or individuals or group leaders who orchestrate the overthrow of an autocracy are not capable of establishing another autocratic system. He notes that 'autocracy is prevented and democracy permitted by the accidents of history that leave a balance of power or stalemate – a dispersion of force and resources that makes it impossible for any one leader or group to overpower all of the others.' On the basis of his own theoretical argument, Olson thinks that there must be a considerable element of truth in the explanations of democracy offered by political scientists such as Robert A. Dahl and Tatu Vanhanen. He concludes: 'If the theory offered here is right, the literature that argues that the emergence of democracy is due to historical conditions and dispersions of resources that make it impossible for any one leader or group to assume power is also right' (Olson 1993).

Robert Pinkney's (1993) research question ('Why should democracy have emerged, or re-emerged, what is its significance and what are its future prospects?') is approximately the same as in this study. Therefore, it is interesting to see how he explains democratization. Pinkney discusses different explanations given for conditions conducive to democracy (economic development, political attitudes and behaviour, inter-élite relations, social structures and interactions between social groups, political institutions, sequences in development, and external influences), but he neither chooses between competing explanations nor formulates his own explanation. One interesting observation is that, according to him, 'almost all authors would agree that the forces which have established and maintained democracy in the West are different from those which have done so in the Third World' (Pinkney 1993: 1, 168). I disagree. I am trying to show in this study that the forces behind democratization have been similar in the West and in developing countries. Pinkney concludes that a desire to establish democracy is not by itself sufficient, but it is more difficult to establish what is required in addition to a desire for democracy. He thinks that 'explanations of the emergence of democracy and survival of democracy, in so far as any exist, are to be found somewhere within and between the variables of economic change, political culture, political behaviour and the functioning of political institutions, but it is impossible to prescribe any particular evolution of these variables, or interaction between them, as offering the best prospects' (Pinkney 1993: 169).

Prospects for Democracy: North, South, East, West (1993), edited by David Held, is concerned with an appraisal of alternatives to liberal democracy as well as with the assessment of liberal democracy itself. Problems of democracy are discussed from many different perspectives, but the book does not produce any clearly stated testable theory of democracy or democratization, although various assumptions on the conditions of democracy are discussed and formulated. From the perspective of this study, its part IV, in which the opportunities and potentialities for democracy in the major regions of the world are assessed, is the most interesting one.

Larry Diamond (1994) has explored the relationship of political culture to democracy. His basic assumption is that democracy requires a distinctive set of political values and orientations from its citizens: moderation, tolerance, civility, efficacy, knowledge, and participation, but he does not claim that the emergence of democracy would presuppose the existence of these values and orientations. According to him, the relationship between political culture and democracy is reciprocal. The relevant characteristics of political culture are fairly plastic. They 'can change quite dramatically in response to regime performance, historical experience, and political socialization'. Besides, it may be impossible to measure relevant characteristics of political culture. Consequently, Diamond does not formulate any clearly stated hypotheses on the relationship between political culture and democracy. His conclusion seems to be that political culture is a crucial intervening variable in the broad causal relationship between socio-economic development and democracy.

The studies discussed above illustrate contemporary approaches to study democracy and democratization (see also Gurr 1974; Gurr *et al.* 1990; Blondel 1990: 67–80; Lane and Ersson 1990: 134–43; 1994: 209–28; O'Regan 1992; Almond 1992; Etzioni-Halevy 1992; Deegan 1993; Diamond and Plattner 1993; Wekkin *et al.* 1993; Sorensen 1993; Muhlberger and Paine 1993; Edwards 1994; Shin 1994; Mbaku 1994; Poppovic and Pinheiro 1995; Moore 1995). A common theme seems to be that the emergence of democracy cannot be explained by any single factor. Many different factors and conditions can affect democratic development. Diamond, Linz and Lipset (1990) have presented and discussed the most extensive list of possible factors, but Dahl, Huntington, Hadenius, Karl, and Pinkney refer to many significant factors, too. The Lerner–Lipset hypothesis on the connection between economic development and democracy has been tested most thoroughly. Many empirical studies indicate that there is a moderate positive correlation between democracy and economic development, or between democracy and human development, as Diamond argues. It has been more difficult to test the other theories of democratization empirically. Dahl's hypothesis on different conditions of polyarchy has not been properly tested by empirical data. The same concerns the diffusion hypothesis (Gastil). Dankwart Rustow's (1970) model on the stages of democratization uses concepts that have not been operationalized. Dependency theory does not provide any testable hypothesis on the conditions of democracy or on democratization. The theoretical arguments of Whistler and Olson coincide with the theory of democratization offered in this work. In the end, the number of testable and tested theories of democratization is rather limited. The Lerner–Lipset economic development hypothesis or the wealth theory of democracy still seems to provide the best empirical point of comparison for the theory that will be used in this study.

AN EVOLUTIONARY THEORY OF DEMOCRATIZATION

I agree with those who assume that many different factors – economic development, various social structures, external factors, and the diffusion of democratic ideas – may affect the chances to establish and maintain democratic institutions in a particular country, whereas I disagree with the additional assumption according to which there is not and cannot be any single dominant explanatory factor of democratization. My argument is that there is and that there must be a common underlying factor in the process of democratization. I have derived this assumption on the existence of a common explanatory factor from the principles of the neo-Darwinian theory of evolution, which claims that all important characteristics of life have evolved in the continual struggle for existence and that they are more or less shared by all the members of the species concerned.

According to the Darwinian theory of evolution by natural selection, there must be a struggle for existence among the individuals of a population because more individuals are produced than can be supported by available resources. This inference is based on the facts that:

1 all species have great potential fertility;
2 populations normally display stability; and
3 natural resources are limited and, in a stable environment, remain relatively constant.

On the basis of these facts, Darwin concluded that a struggle for existence is inevitable, this being due to the permanent and universal scarcity of resources in nature. Only some of the individuals of a population are able to reproduce and survive. They become selected in the struggle for survival. Darwin concluded that the survival in the struggle for existence is not completely random but depends in part on the hereditary constitution of the surviving individuals. The individuals in some respects even slightly better adapted to their environment have better chances to survive than those whose characteristics are less adaptive in the same environment. This leads to evolution by natural selection (for the neo-Darwinian theory and species-specific behaviour patterns, see Dobzhansky *et al.* 1977: 96–9; Alexander 1980: 15–22; Lorenz 1982: 1–11; Mayr 1982: 479–80; 1988: 215–32; Eibl-Eibesfeldt 1984: 35–54; Brown 1991; Barkow, *et al.* 1992).

Thus the Darwinian theory explains why the struggle for existence is inevitable and incessant in nature. From this theory I got the idea that the Darwinian theory of evolution by natural selection provides a theoretical explanation for human politics and for the struggle for power. Politics can be interpreted as an expression of the universal struggle for existence in living nature. Politics is for us a species-specific way to compete for scarce resources and to distribute them among the members of a society. The permanent scarcity of some important resources and the need to distribute them by some means explain the necessity of politics. Thus the evolutionary roots of politics lie in the necessity to solve conflicts over scarce resources by some means. Because everyone seems to have an equal right to those resources, and because they are scarce, we have to compete for them. We should understand that the scarcity of resources makes this competition and struggle inevitable for us, just as in other parts of nature. It belongs to the nature of all living beings that they do their utmost to preserve their existence. Only those who are successful in this struggle are able to survive and reproduce. I got the idea that politics evolved in the struggle for scarce resources. It is still the evolutionary and constant theme of politics, and this theme connects human politics to the universal struggle for existence, which is explained by the neo-Darwinian theory of evolution by natural selection.

But what about democratization? How can we connect the variation and changes of political systems to the assumed evolutionary theme of politics? My idea is that power is used as a currency or as an intervening mechanism in the political struggle for scarce resources. People and groups struggle for power to obtain scarce resources. The more one has power, the more one can get scarce resources. Power can be understood as the ability to compel or persuade others to do something that they would not otherwise do. This ability to compel or persuade others rests on sanctions. Therefore, it is reasonable to assume that the distribution of power depends on the distribution of sanctions. If the resources used as sources of power are concentrated in the hands of one group, the same group will be the most powerful group. If the resources used as sanctions are distributed widely among several groups, it is reasonable to expect that power also becomes distributed among several groups. I assume that this relationship is regular. Those controlling most effective power resources have better chances to get power than those whose power resources are meagre or who are without any significant power resources. This argument leads me to hypothesize that: the concentration as well as the distribution of political power depends on the degree of resource distribution.

The Darwinian interpretation of politics, formulated above, provides a theoretical explanation for the necessity of this relationship. Because politics constitutes a part of the general struggle for existence, in which people tend to use all available resources, the distribution of political power must depend on the degree of resource distribution. This hypothesis presupposes a causal link between resource distribution and power distribution, but this relationship does not need to be one way from resource distribution to power distribution. To some extent, this relationship is reciprocal because power can be used to get more resources. I assume, however, that in this relationship the distribution of resources is a more independent factor than the distribution of power. Some important aspects of resource distribution are outside the scope of conscious political power, and, therefore, changes in resource distribution may take place independently from political power. When such independent changes in resource distribution have taken place and cumulated enough, they cause changes in power distribution. Political power is only one of the factors that may change the distribution of politically relevant resources among individuals and groups, whereas the distribution of power depends crucially on the distribution of suitable resources, although not always on the same kind of resources (*cf.* Vanhanen 1984a: 15–24; 1990a: 47–51; 1992b: 24–7).

The variation of political systems from the rule of the few to the rule of the many follows from the regularity discussed above. In societies where relevant power resources are concentrated in the hands of the few, political power is also concentrated in the hands of the few, and in societies where important power resources are widely distributed, political power also tends to become widely distributed. We can derive a Darwinian explanation for democracy and democratization from this regularity. Democracy is the government of the many, and autocracy is the government of the few. The concentration of power resources leads to autocracy, and the distribution of power resources leads to democracy. It can be hypothesized that: democratization takes place under conditions in which power resources have become so widely distributed that no group is any longer able to suppress its competitors or to maintain its hegemony (Vanhanen 1984a: 18; 1990a: 50).

Evolutionary argument leads me to conjecture that we can find a general and the most powerful theoretical explanation for democratization from the distribution of various resources used as sources of power. Kenneth Janda has noticed this central idea of my study. He says in a review of my earlier work: 'Vanhanen resurrects the earlier focus on distribution of wealth by proposing that democratization is explained by differences between societies in the way power resources are distributed among competing groups' (Janda 1992: 929); see also Poppovic and Pinheiro 1995). Many kinds of resources can be used as sources of power because, as Carl J. Friedrich (1950: 22–3) said, 'anything can become the basis of power. A house, a love affair, an idea, can all become instruments in the hand of one seeking power. But in order to convert them into power, the power-seeker must find human beings who value one of these things sufficiently to follow his leadership in acquiring them.' Friedrich understood the relationship between power and the sources of power.

The multiplicity of potential bases of power makes it impossible to identify and measure all the resources used as sanctions, but, on the other hand, it is plausible to assume that some types of resources tend to be used everywhere in the struggle for power. I assume that economic resources, including wealth and control over the means of production and employment; knowledge and special skills; as well as the ability to use physical force and the means of violence, are effective power resources everywhere and that they are used in all societies. I think that usually they represent the major part of the resources used in the struggle for political power. Therefore, by measuring their relative distribution, we could get a rough picture of the degree of resource distribution in a society and of the relative differences in resource distribution between societies. Of course, the necessity to restrict measurements to some general types of power resources leaves out many other possible power resources and, in particular, locally important factors, which means that the results of my measurements indicate the real degree of resource distribution only incompletely. Measurement errors may vary from country to country depending on the significance of locally specific power resources. Although this method does not make it possible to take into account all important aspects of resource distribution, I think that it is better to use few general indicators that remain the same from country to country than a different combination of explanatory variables for each country. The use of many different explanatory variables would make it impossible to test hypotheses and to generalize the results.

The evolutionary theory of democratization formulated above differs from several other theories of democracy at least in one important respect. It seeks an ultimate explanation for democratization from evolutionary principles that are assumed to remain the same from country to country, whereas the other theories discussed above seek explanations from various proximate factors whose significance varies geographically, culturally, or from one period to another. Besides, I would like to argue that my evolutionary theory of democratization may provide theoretical explanations for many of the relationships assumed in other theories. For example, a theoretical explanation for the fact that economic development correlates positively with the level of democracy can be derived from the evolutionary theory of democratization. When the level of economic development rises, various economic resources usually become more widely distributed and the number of economic interest groups increases. Thus the underlying factor behind the positive correlation between the level of economic development and democracy is in the distribution of power resources. Economic development is only a special case of the underlying causal factor (resource distribution). The same concerns the observation that democracy is more probable in the countries where the level of education is high than in the countries where it is low. When the level of education rises, intellectual power resources, knowledge and special skills, become more widely distributed among the population than in the countries where the level of education is low. The level of education represents one aspect of resource distribution, which is the underlying causal factor of democratization. Sometimes external factors affect the resource distribution in a country. Some political actors, individuals or groups, may resort to external resources in the struggle for power, or external actors themselves take part in politics. The question is again on power that is based on sanctions.

In other words, my theory and those other theories of democratization do not necessarily contradict each other because they focus on explanatory factors at different levels of explanation. My theory focuses on the ultimate underlying factor of democratization, whereas those other theories are concerned with different proximate or local factors of democratization, and many of those proximate or local factors can be regarded as special cases of the underlying common factor. I argue that a significant part of the variation in the level of democracy can be explained by the common factor of democratization given in my theory, whereas other variables can be used to explain the residual or remaining variation that is due to various local, historical, and other unique factors. Both strategies are needed in the study of democratization, but I think that they lead in some respects to different consequences. A theoretical explanation based on a common and constant factor can provide a basis for predictions and for theoretically grounded conscious strategies of democratization, which is not possible if more or less different explanations are given for each case (*cf.* Pinkney 1993). The process-oriented analyses resorting to various proximate factors cannot lead to any general theoretical explanations, although they may produce useful descriptions of democratization. In the end, I would like to empha-size that a part of variation is always due to accidental factors, which cannot be explained by any theory.

2   Research design

I think that statistical methods provide the best strategy to test the evolutionary theory of democratization outlined above. We can derive testable hypotheses from the theory and test them by empirical evidence. For this purpose, we have to define empirical variables to measure hypothetical concepts, to formulate research hypotheses on the relationships between variables, to collect empirical evidence on variables, and then to test hypotheses by statistical methods. This kind of comparative method in which the same variables are used for all countries makes the results comparable from one country to another and allows us to test hypotheses by statistical analysis techniques, although it leaves out a part of variation that is due to other factors. The results show to what extent the variation in democratization can be explained by one theoretically grounded explanatory factor – the degree of resource distribution.

In this chapter I am going to formulate the variables that will be used to measure the two hypothetical concepts: 'the level of democracy' and 'the degree of resource distribution'. I shall then introduce the units of comparison and define the period of comparison. Finally, I shall formulate research hypotheses and introduce the statistical analysis techniques by which the hypotheses will be tested.

THE LEVEL OF DEMOCRACY

It seems to have been easier for scholars to agree on the basic characteristics of democracy than on operational indicators of democracy. I have reviewed some definitions given for democracy and measures of democracy in my previous studies (see Vanhanen 1984a: 9–11, 24–8; 1990a: 6–16). In this connection, I limit my attention to some contemporary definitions of democracy and measurements of democracy. They provide points of comparison for the measures of democracy that I have used in my studies and that I will use in this study.

Definition of democracy

Let us start from S. M. Lipset's definition of democracy, which has affected my own conceptualization of democracy significantly. Lipset defined democracy in a complex society 'as a political system which supplies regular constitutional opportunities for changing the governing officials, and a social mechanism which permits the largest possible part of the population to influence major decisions by choosing among contenders for political office' (Lipset 1960: 45; see also Lipset 1959: 71; 1983: 27; Diamond and Marks 1992: 1–14). Giovanni Sartori defines democracy by explaining what it is not. Democracy is the opposite of autocracy. He says, 'Democracy is a system in which no one can choose himself, no one can invest himself with the power to rule and, therefore, no one can arrogate to himself unconditional and unlimited power' (Sartori 1987: 206; *cf.* Sartori 1995: 102). So the range of political systems extends from democracies to autocracies.

Robert A. Dahl has discussed the conceptualization of democracy in many of his studies. He says that 'a key characteristic of a democracy is the continuing responsiveness of the government to the preferences of its citizens, considered as political equals.' According to him, there are two somewhat different theoretical dimensions of democratization: public contestation and the right to participate. Dahl assumes that in the real world it is impossible for any political system to achieve the ideal of democracy, but the systems lying at the upper right corner of the space bounded by these two dimensions can be regarded as polyarchies. He uses the term polyarchy as an alternative to democracy because he thinks that 'it is important to maintain the distinction between democracy as an ideal system and the institutional arrangements that have come to be regarded as a kind of imperfect approximation of an idea' (Dahl 1971: 1–9; see also Dahl 1982: 4–11; 1989, especially 106–31). I think that these two dimensions provide a good basis to formulate measures of democratization.

J. Roland Pennock (1979: 3–15) distinguishes ideal and procedural or operational definitions of democracy and prefers a procedural definition, according to which a democracy is rule by the people where 'the people' includes all adult citizens and 'rule' means that 'public policies are determined either directly by vote of the electorate or indirectly by officials freely elected at reasonably frequent intervals and by a process in which each voter who chooses to vote counts equally ("one man, one vote") and in which a plurality is determinative'. I also prefer a procedural definition of democracy because it makes it possible to measure differences in the degree of democracy.

Larry Diamond, Juan J. Linz and S. M. Lipset use the term 'democracy' to signify a political system. They emphasize that issues of so-called 'economic and social democracy' should be separated from the question of governmental structure. Otherwise, there would be no way to analyse how variation on the political dimension is related to variation on economic and social dimensions. This is an important point of view. They define democracy to denote a system of government:

> that meets three essential conditions: meaningful and extensive *competition* among individuals and organized groups (especially political parties) for all effective positions of government power, at regular intervals and excluding the use of force; a 'highly inclusive' level of *political participation* in the selection of leaders and policies, at least through regular and fair elections, such that no major (adult) social group is excluded; and a level of *civil and political liberties* – freedom of expression, freedom of the press, freedom to form and join organizations – sufficient to ensure the integrity of political competition and participation.
>
> (Diamond, Linz and Lipset 1990: 6–7)

They added a third dimension of civil and political freedoms to Dahl's two dimensions of competition and political participation. Georg Sorensen (1993: 23–4) uses a similar definition of democracy. According to his formulation, the core of 'political democracy has three dimensions: competition, participation, and civil and political liberties'. I do not try to measure their third dimension of democracy for two reasons: (1) it does not seem possible to find any satisfactory quantitative indicators to measure the level of civil and political liberties and (2) it is reasonable to assume that the level of competition is highly correlated to the level of civil and political liberties (*cf.* Hadenius 1994: 10). Raymond Duncan Gastil argues that freedom is the most essential characteristic of democracy. Therefore, the level of democracy varies according to the extent of political rights and civil liberties (see Gastil 1990: 25–6). Kenneth A. Bollen also thinks that political rights and liberties constitute two crucial dimensions of political democracy (Bollen 1990: 10).

David Beetham means by democracy:

> a mode of decision-making about collectively binding rules and policies over which the people exercise control, and the most democratic arrangement to be that where all members of the collectivity enjoy effective equal rights to take part in such decision-making directly – one, that is to say, which realizes to the greatest conceivable degree the principles of popular control and equality in its exercise.

For Beetham the opposite of democracy is 'a system of rule where the people are totally excluded from the decision-making process and any control over it'. So there is a spectrum of political systems extending from democracies to non democracies. He thinks that this kind of conceptualization of democracy is generally accepted and incontestable (Beetham 1992: 40; see also Beetham 1993). I agree that there is a spectrum of political systems from democracies to non democracies.

Bhikhu Parekh (1992), however, argues that democracy has been defined and structured within the limits set by liberalism and that western liberal democracy cannot claim universal validity. He says that for the liberal, 'democracy therefore basically means a form of government in which people wield the ultimate political authority, which they delegate to their freely chosen representatives and which they retain the right to withdraw if the government were grossly to violate its trust'. He implies that democracy might take a different form in non western societies, but he does not specify those alternative forms of democracy nor give examples of them. Robert Pinkney discusses the nature of democracy and differentiates five 'ideal types' (radical democracy, guided democracy, liberal democracy, socialist democracy, and consociational democracy) (Pinkney 1993: 5–17). I think that it is confusing to speak of five different types of democracy. His examples of 'radical democracy', 'guided democracy', and 'socialist democracy' do not meet the criteria of democracy that will be used in this study, whereas his 'liberal democracy' and 'consociational democracy' can be regarded as variations of democracy.

Axel Hadenius formulates political democracy at the national level as follows: 'Public policy is to be governed by the freely expressed will of the people whereby all individuals are to be treated as equals.' His basic definition of democracy includes three principles of democracy: a general principle of popular sovereignty, a principle of freedom, and a principle of equality. He emphasizes that 'it only makes sense to speak of democracy as a mode of decision-making'. Then he makes an important conclusion:

> Hence, it naturally follows that political democracy must mean the same thing irrespective of the state or part of the world where it is examined. East, West, North, South – economically developed or less developed country – it makes no difference how the *concept* (and thereby our dependent variable) is to be defined.
>
> (Hadenius 1992: 9, 35)

In this point he clearly differs from Parekh, who claims that there cannot be a universalist concept of democracy, and from Pinkney, who differentiates five 'ideal types' of democracy.

Samuel P. Huntington prefers a procedural definition of democracy. He says that the most important modern formulation of this concept of democracy was presented by Joseph Schumpeter in 1942. Schumpeter paid attention to the crucial importance of competitive elections. Following in the Schumpeterian tradition, Huntington defines 'a twentieth-century political system as democratic to the extent that its most powerful collective decision makers are selected through fair, honest, and periodic elections in which candidates freely compete for votes and in which virtually all the adult population is eligible to vote' (Huntington 1991: 6–7). It is a very good procedural definition of modern democracy. For recent definitions of democracy, see also Arat 1991; Held 1992; Merkl 1993; Saward 1993; Whistler 1993; Parry and Moran 1994: 272–4.

Different words and expressions are used in the definitions of democracy reviewed above, but it seems to me that the content of those definitions is more or less the same. I agree with the principles of democracy expressed in those definitions. Consequently, I could summarize the conceptualization of democracy used in this study as follows: *Democracy is a political system in which different groups are legally entitled to compete for power and in which institutional power holders are elected by the people and are responsible to the people* (*cf.* Vanhanen 1984a: 11; 1990a: 11).

I want to remind the readers that this type of conceptualization of democracy is not accepted by all scholars, although the scholars discussed above seem to have more or less similar ideas of democracy. Parekh and Pinkney refer to different concepts of democracy. Marxist scholars, in particular, used to define democracy quite differently (see, for example, Haney 1971: 46–59; Topornin and Machulsky 1974: 39–42; Chekharin 1977: 28–31).

Indicators of democracy

It has been much more difficult to find suitable measures of democracy and to measure the variation in the level of democracy than to formulate definitions of democracy. In fact, nearly all researchers who have attempted to measure democracy have used different indicators. The situation is confusing. I have referred to some of those indicators in my previous studies (Vanhanen 1984a: 24–8; 1990a: 11–16). Because they provide comparison points for the indicators used in my own study, I again refer to some of them.

Lipset used a simple classification for democracies and dictatorships, but he used different criteria for European and non European countries. His main criteria of European democracies were the uninterrupted continuation of political democracy since the First World War and the absence over the past twenty-five years of a major political movement opposed to the democratic 'rules of the game'. For Latin America his less stringent criterion was whether a given country had had a history of more or less free elections for most of the post-First World War period. He used his own judgment to decide whether a given country fulfilled the criteria of democracy or not (Lipset 1960: 47–9). My argument is that we should use the same criteria of democracy for all countries because human nature can be assumed to be approximately the same everywhere.

Phillips Cutright improved the measurement technique by constructing an index of political development, which is a continuous variable. Each country could get from zero to sixty-three points over the twenty-one-year period of his study on the basis of the characteristics of its legislative and executive branches of government. Cutright's index takes into account such criteria of democracy as freedom of elections and the existence and size of opposition representation (30 per cent rule) in the legislature, but the weights given for various characteristics were arbitrarily determined (Cutright 1963: 253–6). A great merit of Cutright's index is that it is a continuous variable, not a dichotomous one like Lipset's, but I think that it still includes too many judgemental variables. Several other researchers have followed Cutright's example and constructed indices of democracy based on quantitative and judgemental variables (see Neubauer 1967: 1002–6; Needler 1967: 889–97; Olsen 1968: 702–3; Smith 1969: 100–5; Flanigan and Fogelman 1971; Banks 1972: 217–19; Jackman 1974: 37–8; Coulter 1975: 1–3, 156; Hewitt 1977; Bertrand and van Puijenbroek 1987; Gurr *et al.* 1990; Hadenius 1992: 36–71; and 1994).

One of the most well-founded of these measures is Kenneth A. Bollen's index of political democracy. He measures two dimensions of democracy – political sovereignty (political rights) and political liberties – by six indicators. The three measures of political sovereignty are: (1) fairness of elections, (2) effective executive selection, and (3) legislative selection. The indicators of political liberties are: (4) freedom of the press, (5) freedom of group opposition, and (6) government sanctions. His data on these indicators are more qualitative than quantitative (Bollen 1979; 1980; 1990; see also Bollen and Grandjean 1981). It is significant that Bollen excluded popular participation on the ground that 'voter turnout reflects factors that have little to do with measuring political democracy' (Bollen 1990: 8; see also Bollen 1979: 580; 1980: 374). I cannot agree with this argument, although it is true that electoral participation alone would be a poor indicator of democracy.

It would be interesting to compare the structures of all different measures of democracy, to examine what aspects of democracy have been taken into account, what kinds of variables are used to measure democracy, to what extent indicators are based on quantitative and to what extent on qualitative (judgmental) data, and how various indicators have been weighted and finally combined into indices of democracy. However, such a comparison is not necessary in this connection, because my purpose is not to introduce and assess the merits of all possible measures of democracy. The examples given are only intended to illustrate various approaches used and the confusing state of art in this field of comparative study of democracy.

Zehra F. Arat (1991) measures democracy by four components of popular sovereignty, or public control of government. She identified these as participation, inclusiveness, competitiveness, and civil liberties. The points of four variables were combined into a score of 'democraticness'. It is an interval level measure, although it is based on a set of nominal indicators. Its annual scores for the thirty-five years from 1948–1982 range from the minimum of twenty-nine to the maximum of 109 in the group of independent countries studied. This very complicated measure of democracy is based more on judgements and rough estimations than on quantitative data.

Some researchers have attempted to operationalize Robert A. Dahl's two dimensions of democratization. His associates Richard Norling and Mary

Frace Williams classified 114 countries according to eligibility to participate in elections and degree of opportunity for public contest, but they had to use complicated variables based on many weights and judgments. The result was not fully satisfactory (see Dahl 1971: 231–45). Charles S. Perry (1980) constructed another scale of contests, but it is based on judgemental data. Later Michael Coppedge and Wolfgang Reinicke constructed a scale of polyarchy composed of five variables and eighteen categories intended to measure eight 'institutional guarantees' of inclusion and public contest. However, they discarded the variable measuring the 'right to vote' because they had come to the conclusion that it was not a useful criterion for polyarchy. Consequently, their final scale of polyarchy is a unidimensional scale of contestation (Coppedge and Reinicke 1988; see also Coppedge and Reinicke 1990). My argument is that all these measures of democracy include too many judgemental elements and that they are too complicated.

Raymond D. Gastil uses a different method to measure some elements of democracy. It is based on the idea that democracy requires the existence of both political rights and civil liberties. Therefore, his Comparative Survey of Freedom uses separate scales for political rights and liberties. Each scale is divided into seven points, with one (1) the highest rating in each scale and seven (7) the lowest. On the basis of these ratings, countries are classified as free, partly free, and not free. Generally, states rated (1) and (2) are 'free'; those at (3), (4), and (5) are 'partly free', and those at (6) and (7) 'not free'. The list of democracies is made up of countries given the summary status 'free' (Gastil 1985; 1988: 3–65; 1990; McColm 1992: 47–63). The ratings are judgemental but based on a long list of empirical questions concerning the nature of a political system. The problem with this method is that it is difficult for other researchers to check the ratings because they are based more on judgements than on quantitative data.

Africa Demos (1992 vol. 2, no. 3) has formulated its own criteria to assess the quality of democracy in Africa. Their Quality of Democracy Index includes thirty different criteria that are used in assessments. The criteria cover all important aspects of democracy, but I suspect that it would be extremely difficult to collect all the necessary data from a large group of countries and to agree on judgements. However, they have applied these criteria to African political systems and classified them into five categories: (1) democratic, (2) authoritarian, (3) directed democracy, (4) contested sovereignty, and (5) regimes in transition (see *Africa Demos* 1993, vol. 3, no. 2).

David Beetham with his colleagues has formulated a unique method to measure two key aspects of democracy (popular control and political equality) by thirty-one questions of the kind 'to what extent is...?', 'how far does...?', etc. The questions imply a comparative scale of assessment, rather than a simple 'yes or no' answer. Their list of questions was developed for the UK Democratic Audit project, but they think that the questions would be relevant outside the UK and the established representative democracies in the West, too. However, they admit that it would be very labour intensive to collect the data needed to answer the questions, 'and could only with difficulty be carried out in many countries simultaneously, though in principle the questions are replicable anywhere' (Beetham 1993).

The measures of democracy reviewed above include many important and measurable aspects of democracy, but I do not regard any of them suitable for the purposes of this study. Most of those indices are too complicated, with too many indicators, which makes it extremely difficult to gather empirical data from all countries of the world and even more difficult to find objective grounds to weight the importance of different indicators. Besides, all of them require too many subjective judgements. I think that we should try to formulate intersubjectively usable and reliable measures of democracy based on available quantitative data. Just like 'metre' is scientifically a more satisfactory measure of length than subjective concepts of length varying from person to person, a quantitative measure of democracy would be more useful for scientific purposes than various measures based on subjective evaluations. Therefore, I have formulated simple quantitative measures of democracy for the purposes of my comparative study covering nearly all independent countries of the world. I think that the same criteria of democracy should be applied to all countries of the world. Indicators should be such that they require subjective judgements as little as possible and that it is possible to get necessary data on them from all countries of the world.

In this study, I am going to use the same empirical measures of democracy as in my earlier comparative studies since 1984 (see Vanhanen 1984a: 28–33; 1990a: 17–24; 1993). I try to measure two crucial dimensions of democracy (*cf.* Dahl 1971) – competition and participation – by two simple quantitative indicators. The smaller parties' share of the votes cast in parliamentary or presidential elections, or both, is used to indicate the degree of competition (Competition). It is calculated by subtracting the percentage of the votes won by the largest party from 100. The percentage of the total population who actually voted in the election concerned is used to measure the degree of electoral participation (Participation).

If both elections are taken into account, the arithmetic mean of the two percentages is used to represent the smaller parties' share and, correspondingly, the degree of electoral participation. In other words, they are weighted equally. In some cases, indicated in Appendix 1, the weight of parliamentary or executive election is 25 per cent and the weight of the other election consequently 75 per cent. This is one point where my measures of democracy require the use of judgements. It is necessary to decide for each country whether the measurements of competition and participation are based on parliamentary or presidential elections, or both, and what weights are used. For this purpose, governmental systems are classified into three categories: parliamentary dominance, executive dominance, and concurrent powers. These classifications and the weights used are indicated in Appendix 1. In this study, 'concurrent powers' category is used more frequently than in my earlier studies covering the period 1850–1988. In other words, both parliamentary and presidential elections are taken into account in cases in which both of these governmental institutions have significant political power. I hope that the more frequent use of 'concurrent powers' category will decrease errors of judgement in the classification of governmental systems.

The two indicators of democracy can be used separately, but it is plausible to assume that a combination of them would be a more realistic measure of democracy than either of them alone. The problem is how to combine the indicators of the two dimensions of democracy. They could be combined in many ways, depending on how we weight the importance of Competition and Participation. Because I do not have any theoretical grounds to consider one of them more important than the other, I have weighted them equally in the construction of an index of democratization. They are combined into an Index of Democratization (ID) by multiplying the two percentages and dividing the outcome by 100. This means that ID gets high values only if the values of both basic indicators are high. If either of them is in zero, the value of ID will also drop to zero. This method of combination is based on the assumption that both dimensions of democracy are essential for democracy. A high level of participation cannot compensate for the lack of competition, or *vice versa*. A low value of either of them indicates a low level of democracy. An alternative way to combine the two basic indicators would be to calculate their arithmetic mean, or to add them. I rejected this method for the reasons mentioned above. My argument is that both variables are important for democracy. They cannot compensate each other.

I use only two empirical indicators to measure the degree of democracy, because I think that they are the most realistic empirical indicators of the two principal dimensions of democratization: the level of competition and the extent of participation. The measurement is limited to the struggle for power in the most important governmental institutions because the use of highest political power is constitutionally concentrated in the hands of certain governmental institutions in all contemporary states. For that reason, the legal competition for power focuses on parliamentary or presidential elections, or both. Of course, the real importance of elections varies from country to country, but it is remarkable that elections are held in practically every independent country throughout the world. If only one party is entitled to take part in elections, it means that power is concentrated in the hands of this party, and other potential parties are excluded. The concentration of power in the hands of one group, no matter which this group is, represents the opposite of democracy. If power holders are not elected at all, or if no organized groups are allowed to take part in elections, the levels of competition and participation are judged to be zero.

In parliamentary elections, 'the largest party' refers to the party that received the largest single share of the votes. In the cases of party alliances it is not always clear whether the alliance or its individual member parties should be regarded as 'parties'. I have used a party's behaviour in elections as the decisive criterion. If a party belongs to a larger alliance permanently, it is not regarded as a separate party. In that case the alliance is treated as a separate 'party' because my purpose is to measure the relative strength of competing and independent political groups. If data on the distribution of votes are not available, the share of the largest party is calculated on the basis of the distribution of seats in the parliament. In presidential elections, 'the largest party' refers to the presidential candidate who won the election, or to the presidential candidate who received the highest single share of the votes in the first round. However, if there are two rounds, the calculation is usually based on the results of the second round. When the composition of a governmental institution using the highest executive or legislative power is not based on elections, the share of 'the largest party' is interpreted to be 100 per cent and the level of participation in zero. This interpretation applies to military regimes, to other autocratic governments, and to monarchies in which the ruler and/or the government responsible to the ruler dominates and exercises executive and often legislative power as well.

I think that popular participation in elections represents an essential dimension of democracy, although Kenneth A. Bollen argues that it is only marginally related to democracy (Bollen 1990: 14). If only a small minority of the adult population takes part in elections, the struggle for power is restricted to a small section of the population, and the bulk of the population is excluded from the use of power. In my study, Participation represents the percentage of the total population that actually voted. There would be alternative ways to measure the degree of electoral participation. One could calculate the percentage from the adult population (using some age limit), from the voting age population, from the adult population eligible to vote, or from the electorate. I have used the total population as the basis of calculation because more statistical data have been available on total populations than on age structures of the populations or on electorates. Besides, data on total populations are probably more reliable than data on age structures or electorates.

However, there is one serious disadvantage in this method to calculate the degree of electoral participation. 'The percentage of the total population that actually voted' does not take into account the variation in the age structures of the populations. The percentage of the adult population is significantly higher in developed countries than in poor developing countries. According to *World Development Report 1991* (Table 26), the percentage of children (0–14 years) varied from Kenya's 50.3 to Germany's 15.1 per cent in 1989. So the extreme difference was 35 percentage points. The average difference between high-income economies and developing countries was 13–16 percentage points in 1989. Therefore, it might be more justified to calculate the degree of electoral participation from the population aged fifteen years and over than from the total population, but because I have used the total population in my earlier longitudinal studies and because it is useful to keep indicators as comparable over time as possible, the degree of electoral participation is calculated from the total population in this study, too.

The indicators of democracy used in my study differ from the measures of democracy used by other researchers in two significant points: (1) I use only two simple indicators and (2) both of them are based on quantitative electoral data. Other researchers have used more numerous variables, and many of their indicators are based on more or less qualitative data. I argue that it is better to use simple quantitative indicators with certain faults than more complicated measures loaded with weights and estimations based on subjective judgements. I think that these two simple empirical indicators (Competition and Participation) are enough to measure major differences between political systems from the perspective of democracy, but I agree that they are not able to take into account all significant aspects of democracy. They may be better suited to measure rough differences between democracies and non democracies than the variation in the degree of democracy at higher levels of democracy, or the variation in the degree of autocracy among non democracies. My indicators are not able to differentiate between relatively mild autocracies and harsh military or personal dictatorships. They get the same zero value of the Index of Democratization.

Some other assumed dimensions of democracy have been left out. I do not try to measure the level of civil and political liberties and rights, which Diamond, *et al.* (1990) and several other researchers regard as the third important dimension of democracy, or as a condition of democracy. I fully agree that civil and political liberties constitute an essential aspect of democracy, but there are two reasons why I have not attempted to take them into account. First, it would be difficult to find any reliable empirical indicator for the degree of civil and political liberties. It is true that Freedom House Survey Team's ratings of political rights and civil liberties would be available, but they are based on judgements. I prefer the use of quantitative data. Second, I think that they do not represent an independent dimension of democracy. Civil and political liberties seem to be highly correlated with the possibility to compete for political power. It means that my Competition variable measures, although indirectly, the existence or lack of civil and political liberties, too. It would be difficult to imagine a political system in which the level of political competition is high but people are without effective civil and political liberties. Legal competition for political power is hardly possible without political liberties and rights. Kenneth A. Bollen does not seem to be convinced that a competitive multiparty system is necessary for democracy. He says that although in practice most nations that are politically democratic give rise to multiple parties, it is theoretically possible for a one-party system to respect political rights and political liberties' (Bollen 1990: 13). However, he does not give any example of such a one-party system. My second political variable, Participation, is not sensible to civil and political liberties. The degree of electoral participation may be high, although people are without significant civil and political liberties. The Index of Democratization, however, recognizes such anomalies. It does not give a high index value for any country in which only the degree of participation is high but the level of competition (which is highly correlated with civil and political liberties) is low.

Because other researchers have used different measures of democracy, it would be interesting to see to what extent the results of measurements differ from each other. Gastil's Comparative Survey of Freedom provides the best points of comparison because its ratings of political rights and civil liberties cover the same countries and years as my study. In an earlier study (Vanhanen 1990a: 25), I correlated the arithmetic means of Gastil's political rights and civil liberties with my two basic indicators and the Index of Democratization in the comparison group of 147 countries over the period 1980–7. Because Gastil's ratings rise when the level of democracy declines, whereas the values of my measures rise when the degree of democratization increases, we have to expect negative correlations. The results show that Competition and ID are strongly correlated with Gastil's ratings. Correlations vary from −0.782 to −0.902 in the case of Competition and from −0.772 to −0.870 in the case of ID. The explained part of the variation varies from 59 to 81 per cent. Correlations with Participation vary between −0.3 and −0.4. For this study, I added Freedom House Survey Team's ratings of political rights and civil liberties in 1991–2 and correlated the added ratings with my three measures of democratization in 1991, 1992 and 1993 (Table 2.1).

Table 2.1 The values of Competition, Participation and the Index of Democratization in 1991–3 correlated with Freedom House Survey Team's ratings of political rights (PR) and civil liberties (CL) in 1991–2

Political variables	The added ratings of political rights and civil liberties in 1991–2
Competition 1991	−0.848
Participation 1991	−0.660
ID 1991	−0.821
Competition 1992	−0.776
Participation 1992	−0.657
ID 1992	−0.784
Competition 1993	−0.767
Participation 1993	−0.646
ID 1993	−0.781

Table 2.1 shows that my measures of democratization have been approximately as strongly correlated with the ratings of political rights and civil liberties in the 1990s as in the 1980s. The Freedom House Survey Team's

ratings of political rights and civil liberties coincide with my measures of democratization in most cases. Both of them measure relative differences in the degree of democracy. However, their ratings seem to measure more the level of competition than differences in the level of electoral participation. My argument is that both of these two dimensions of democratization should be taken into account. The major difference between these two methods of measuring democratization is in the fact that the Freedom House Survey Team's ratings are based on subjective evaluations made on the grounds of various empirical data, whereas my variables are principally based on quantitative electoral data. Therefore, for other scholars it is easier to check my data than their ratings.

Kenneth A. Bollen's index of political democracy provides another interesting point of comparison. His data concern the years 1960 and 1965 (Bollen 1980: 387–9; 1990: 20–3). His index values can be correlated with the 1960–9 arithmetic means of my political variables (Appendix 5). The number of same countries is 106 for 1960 and 112 for 1965. The correlations are in the case of Competition 0.835 and 0.848 for 1960 and 1965 respectively, 0.256 and 0.335 in the case of Participation and 0.739 and 0.798 in the case of ID. These results imply that Bollen's index measures competition more than participation. The correlations between his index and my Competition and ID are relatively strong, although the unexplained part of variation (from 28 to 45 per cent) leaves room for many differences. Figure 2.1 illustrates the correlation between Bollen's index in 1965 and my ID in 1960–9.

Coppedge and Reinicke's (1988) scale of polyarchy covered the same 147 countries in 1985. Their scale of polyarchy was very strongly correlated with

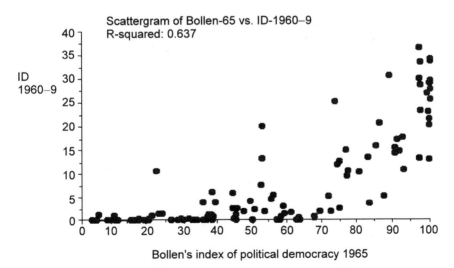

Figure 2.1 Bollen's index of political democracy, 1965, correlated with Vanhanen's Index of Democratization (ID), 1960–9

Gastil's ratings of political rights and civil liberties (0.919) in 1985, and its correlations with my Competition (−0.895) and ID (−0.820) were only slightly weaker, whereas its correlation with Participation was only −0.451. Axel Hadenius' (1992) study covers 132 Third World countries in 1988, of which 112 are the same as in my 1990 study. His index of democracy was strongly correlated with my Index of Democratization in 1988. The explained part of variation is 71 per cent (see Vanhanen 1993: 318–19). Zehra A. Arat's (1991) score of 'democraticness' also provides a point of comparison because her measure of democracy has some properties of interval scale and because her sample of countries is large. The correlation between my Index of Democratization and her score of 'democraticness' was 0.825 in the comparison group of 145 states in 1980. The explained part of variation is 68 per cent.

The fact that my measures of democracy correlate strongly with several other measures of democracy (see also Bertrand and van Puijenbroek 1987; Lane and Ersson 1990: 132–3; 1994: 100–101) indicates that different ways of measuring democracy may lead to more or less similar results. It is difficult to know which of these different measures is the most valid, but because the use of numerous and complicated variables loaded with subjective evaluations does not seem to produce better measurements of democracy than my two simple quantitative variables, it is plausible to argue in favour of my method (*cf.* Dahl 1989: 240; Vanhanen 1993). Kenneth Janda says on my ID scale: 'Although one can quibble with the ingredients of his ID scale, it has the advantage of offering an easy, objective, reasonably valid measure of democracy' (Janda 1992: 929). Mick Moore, however, argues that my method of measuring democracy is unacceptable because it is based on 'the two most controversial of the many indicators used in this business: changes in the share of votes cast for the largest party; and electoral participation' (Moore 1995: 9).

The three indicators of democracy – Competition, Participation, and the Index of Democratization – are continuous variables. Their interval level of measurement makes it possible to use all kinds of statistical methods, including correlation and regression analyses, but I am going to use a simple dichotomous classification, too, because it is necessary to separate democracies from non democracies. As Giovanni Sartori (1987: 182–5) says, it is important to distinguish two different questions concerning democracy. We can ask what is (or is not) a democracy, but we are also required to ask 'to what degree, if any, a political system is a democracy'. Sartori argues that both are equally legitimate and mutually complementary questions. Michael Saward notes that Sartori 'counsels us to incorporate thresholds into our continuums of democracy – to ask *if* a given political system is democratic before we examine the degree of to what it is democratic' (Saward 1993: 28).

In this study, the three indicators of democracy measure the degree of democracy, but any value above zero is not assumed to mean that the country is a democracy. It is necessary for a country to achieve a certain minimum level of indicators in order to be regarded as a democracy. The values of the three indicators do not tell us automatically which countries should be regarded as democracies and which ones as non democracies, but we can use their values to separate democracies from non democracies by determining the threshold value of democracy for each variable. In other words, by determining at what level of competition and participation a political system can be considered to fulfil the minimum criteria of democracy. The selection of threshold values is of necessity to some extent arbitrary, but not completely so. If the share of the smaller parties is very low, the dominance of the largest party is so overpowering that it would not be sensible to regard such a political system as a democracy. It seems to me that a reasonable minimum threshold of democracy might be around 30 per cent for Competition (*cf.* Gastil 1988: 25, who says that 'any group or leader that regularly receives 70 per cent or more of the vote indicates a weak opposition, and the probable existence of undemocratic barriers in the way of its further success'). In the case of Participation, it is reasonable to use a lower threshold value because the percentage of electoral participation is calculated from the total population, not from the adult population. In many developing countries only half or even less than half of the population are over twenty years old. Therefore I shall use 15 per cent for Participation as another minimum threshold of democracy. It is necessary for a country to cross both threshold values in order to become classified as a democracy. Besides, 5.0 index points will be used as the minimum threshold of democracy for the Index of Democratization. It is a little higher than the minimum (4.5) produced by the threshold values of Competition and Participation. The countries that have reached all three minimum thresholds of democracy are classified as democracies. If a country remains below any of the three threshold values, it is classified as a non democracy. It is clear that this dividing line between democracies and non democracies is to some extent arbitrary.

I want to emphasize that these are minimum criteria of democracy. There would be good reasons to argue that many of the countries just above the threshold of democracy are not real democracies. On the other hand, political systems only slightly below the threshold of democracy do not differ much from the countries that are only slightly above the threshold values. Therefore, it might be sensible to establish a category of semi democracies to separate democracies from non democracies. Such a category was used in my previous study (see Vanhanen 1990a: 33). The countries for which the value of Competition was at least 20 per cent but less than 30 per cent and the value of Participation at least 10 per cent but less than 15 per cent were classified as semi-democracies. However, because the category of semi democracies included only from five to seven countries, I decided to leave that transitional category out from this study in order to simplify analysis. Consequently, when the terms 'democracy' and 'non democracy' are used in my analysis later on, they are used in the operational sense defined above.

Empirical data on the two basic political variables, covering the years 1991–3, are given and documented in Appendix 1. Empirical data on these variables over the period 1850–1988 are given and documented in my earlier studies (see Vanhanen 1975; 1977a; 1977b; 1979; 1984a; 1990a). Appendix 5, however, includes decennial data on Competition, Participation, and ID over the period 1850–1980.

RESOURCE DISTRIBUTION

As indicated above, nearly anything can be used as sanctions in the struggle for power, but I limit my measurement attempts to some variables of resource distribution that can be assumed to be valid for all societies. I think that, for the purposes of this study, it is better to use a few universally-valid variables, although they do not cover all aspects of resource distribution, than a different combination of explanatory variables for each country. The use of the same variables makes the measurement results comparable, whereas the use of different variables would make it impossible to test hypotheses by statistical methods. The problem is what variables could be used to measure the relative concentration or distribution of various politically relevant power resources.

In my previous studies, I used five and later six variables to measure some aspects of the distribution of economic and intellectual power resources (Vanhanen 1975; 1977a; 1977b; 1979, 1984a, 1990a and 1992a). The same indicators, although some of them in a slightly revised form, will be used in this study:

1 The urban population as a percentage of the total population (Urban Population = UP).
2 The non agricultural population as a percentage of the total population (Non Agricultural Population=NAP).
3 The number of students in universities and equivalent degree-granting institutions per 100,000 inhabitants (Students).
4 The literate population as a percentage of the adult population (Literates).
5 The area of family farms as a percentage of the total area of holdings (Family Farms = FF).
6 The degree of decentralization of non agricultural economic resources (DD).

I had theoretical and practical grounds for selecting these variables. I assume that they measure, directly or indirectly, some aspects of the distribution of economic, intellectual, and organizational power resources. The higher the values of indicators, the higher the relative distribution of power resources. I have not yet found any satisfactory variable to measure the relative distribution of the means of violence. Therefore, I have to leave this aspect of resource distribution out of my analysis. There may be cases in which the distribution of the means of violence deviates from the distribution of economic and intellectual power resources, as well as cases in which the means of violence are more important, at least temporarily, than economic or intellectual resources. In addition to the means of violence, there may be other factors of resource distribution that have been left out of this analysis. It is clear that these six indicators only partially measure the distribution of economic and intellectual power resources, but it is reasonable to assume that these indicators are relevant in all societies. Besides, a great practical advantage of these variables is that relatively reliable empirical data are available on the first four of them. The last two variables, however, are problematic in this respect.

I have already defined and described these variables in several of my previous studies, explained how they are assumed to measure politically relevant aspects of resource distribution, and referred to their definitions and use in some other comparative studies (see Vanhanen 1979: 25–31, 44–55; 1984a: 33–7; 1990a: 51–65; 1992a: 23–6). In this connection, I shall again define briefly, each of the explanatory variables, refer to their use in other studies, and indicate in which points their definitions have changed since 1979.

Urban Population (UP)

The percentage of urban population is assumed to indicate indirectly the distribution of economic and organizational power resources. The higher the percentage of urban population, the more diversified economic activities and economic interest groups there are and, consequently, the more economic power resources are distributed among various groups. In other words, usually urbanization creates new interest groups and cleavages, which is conducive to political interest group formation.

In many other comparative studies, Urban Population has been used to indicate economic or socio-economic development (see, for example, Lerner 1958; Lipset 1959; Coleman 1960; Cutright 1963; Russett *et al.* 1964; Neubauer 1967; Olsen 1968; Smith 1969; Pride 1970; Winham 1970; Flanigan and Fogelman 1971; Marquette 1974; Coulter 1975; Banks 1981; Hadenius 1992). I agree that urbanization measures some aspects of economic development, but my point is that usually, although not always, economic development leads to the diversification of economic power resources. It means that socio-economic development itself is an indicator of resource distribution. Therefore, I think that Urban Population measures, to some extent, the relative differences between societies in the distribution of economic and organizational power resources. However, it is possible that this assumption is not as correct in the 1990s as it was earlier because the nature of urbanization has changed. Paul Kennedy notes that for thousands of years cities were centres of wealth, creativity, and cultural activities, whereas now 'Asian, Latin American, and Central American megacities of 20 million inhabitants have become increasingly centers of poverty and social collapse' (Kennedy 1993: 26).

In my 1979 and 1984 studies, the population living in cities of 20,000 or more inhabitants was used to indicate the level of urbanization. In my 1990a and 1992a studies, a slightly different definition was used. The total urban population was taken into account without any lower population limit for cities. In this study, too, 'urban population' is defined to include the population of all cities. In other words, the definition of 'urban population' is now slightly more extensive than in my earlier studies covering the period 1850–1979.

UNDP's *Human Development Report* and World Bank's *World Development Report* are the principal sources of empirical data on urban population used in this study. It has been relatively easy to get the necessary data on urban population from all countries. It is reasonable to assume that these data are fairly reliable, although they are not perfectly comparable because the definition of 'urban population' varies to some extent from country to country.

Non Agricultural Population (NAP)

The percentage of non agricultural population is assumed to indicate some aspects of the distribution of economic and human resources. The higher the percentage of non agricultural population, the more diversified the occupational structure of the population is and, consequently, the more economic and human power resources are usually distributed. The division of labour has always been a characteristic of human societies, but industrialization enormously diversified occupational structures. There are more varied economic activities and interest groups in a society in which a considerable part of the population works in non agricultural occupations than in a traditional agricultural society. My argument is the same as in the case of urban population. These two variables measure the same phenomenon from slightly different perspectives.

I have used the percentage of agricultural population to indicate the level of occupational diversification because there are more comparable empirical data from the proportion of agricultural population than from other occupational groups and because the proportion of agricultural population may be the best single indicator of occupational diversification. The percentage of non agricultural population is calculated by subtracting the share of agricultural population from 100 per cent. The percentage of agricultural population has usually been calculated from economically active population, but in some cases, and particularly in my earlier studies, data concern the total population. Otherwise the definition of 'non agricultural population' has remained the same.

In several other studies, the percentage of agricultural population has been used to indicate the level of socio-economic development on the basis of the assumption that the higher the percentage of agricultural population, the lower the level of socio-economic development (see, for example, Lipset 1959; Coleman 1960; Deutsch 1961; Cutright 1963; Russett *et al.* 1964; Neubauer 1967; Olsen 1968, Smith 1969; Pride 1970; Winham 1970; Flanigan and Fogelman 1971; Marquette 1974; Coulter 1975; Hadenius 1992). My argument is that usually the level of socio-economic development also indicates the degree of resource distribution. Therefore I use this variable to measure, indirectly, the distribution of economic and human power resources.

In this study, FAO's *Production Yearbook* is used as the principal source of data on agricultural population. Almost the same data are given in World Bank's *World Development Report* and UNDP's *Human Development Report*. It is reasonable to assume that empirical data on NAP are relatively reliable. They are based on the results of population censuses in most cases.

Students

The number of students in universities and other institutions of higher education per 100,000 inhabitants is used to indicate the distribution of intellectual resources. It is assumed that the higher the number of students per 100,000 inhabitants, the more widely intellectual resources are distributed. The use of this variable is based on the idea that knowledge is also a very important source of power, especially higher knowledge and skills needed in modern societies. If the number of educated people is small, intellectual power resources based on higher knowledge and skills are concentrated, and it would be easier to control those resources than in a society in which the number of educated people is large. Of course, it is impossible to measure the distribution of 'intellectual resources' directly and reliably, but one can assume that this variable is a good indirect indicator for that purpose.

For my earlier studies covering the period 1850–1979, I collected empirical data on the number of students from various sources, and I had to estimate the number of students in numerous cases because of the lack of statistical data. I also decided to use a time lag of one decade in the case of this variable because I assumed that some time elapses before the former students can effectively take part in politics. This means that when a statistical analysis concerned the 1930s, for example, data on the number of students were from the first year of the 1920s (see Vanhanen 1979: 46–7). In a later study (Vanhanen 1990a), covering the period 1980–8, empirical data on the number of students were from around 1980. In this study they are from around 1990. I have used Unesco's *Statistical Yearbook* as the principal source of data, but because it does not give data from all countries, some other sources have also been used. Data on the number of students per 100,000 inhabitants are biased against very small countries to some extent for the reason that it is impossible to establish and maintain all necessary institutions of higher education in small countries. In some of these cases, I have corrected data by taking into account the number of students studying abroad. Data on the number of students per 100,000 inhabitants can be regarded as relatively reliable, although the definitions of 'universities and other degree-granting institutions' vary.

In my 1979 study, the absolute number of students per 100,000 inhabitants was used in statistical analysis, whereas in my later studies absolute numbers were transformed into percentages by using 1,000 students per 100,000 inhabitants to represent the level of 100 per cent in my 1984 study and 5,000 students per 100,000 inhabitants in my 1990a and 1992a studies concerning the 1980s. In this study, too, absolute numbers have been transformed into percentages by taking 5,000 students per 100,000 inhabitants to represent 100 per cent. If the number of students is higher than 5,000 per 100,000 inhabitants, the percentage remains the same. This change in transformation rules from 1,000 to 5,000 per 100,000 inhabitants means that since 1980 five times more students have been needed to reach the same percentage as in the period 1850–1979. It should be noted, however, that I used a time lag of one decade in the period 1850–1979. Besides, the concept of higher education has not remained the same. Earlier only students of universities were taken into account in most countries, but since the 1960s the concept of higher education has become wider to include many other types of institutions. In 1990, the number of students per 100,000 inhabitants had risen higher than 1,000 in seventy-three countries, whereas it was higher than 5,000 only in Canada and the United States.

In some form, this variable has been used in several other studies to indicate the level of socio-economic development or education (see, for example, Lipset 1959; Deutsch 1961; Cutright 1963; Russett *et al.* 1964; Neubauer 1967; Olsen 1968; Smith 1969; Winham 1970; Hadenius 1992). I agree that it indicates the level of socio-economic development, but I use it to indicate the relative distribution of intellectual resources based on higher education. Modern societies need educated people with special skills and training. The same people are needed in politics. If their relative number is large, it is more difficult for the government to control them or to employ all of them, and it becomes easier for opposition groups to recruit them.

Literates

The relative number of literates is assumed to measure the distribution of intellectual power resources from a different perspective. It is assumed to measure the distribution of basic intellectual resources. The higher the percentage of literate population, the more widely basic intellectual resources are distributed. Literate persons are assumed to be more capable of taking part in modern politics than illiterates. If only a small minority of the population is able to read and write, the preconditions for democracy are much more unfavourable than in a society in which nearly all adults are literate.

The definitions of 'literates' have varied from country to country, which decreases the comparability of data, but the percentage of literates has been calculated in the same way throughout the period of comparison since the 1850s. Usually the percentage of literates has been calculated from the population ten or fifteen years of age and over.

Empirical data on literacy are based on population censuses but also on various estimations. For my earlier studies covering the period 1850–1979, data on literacy were collected from many sources (see Vanhanen 1979 and 1984a). In this study, concerning the year 1990, UNDP's *Human Development Report*, Unesco's *Statistical Yearbook*, and World Bank's *World Development Report* have been the principal sources. Data on literacy are comparable from country to country, but there may be significant variation in the quality of literacy. Besides, because original data are estimations in many cases, especially so in Africa, there are defects in the reliability of these data.

This variable, just like Students, has been used in many other studies to indicate the level of socio-economic development or of educational development (see, for example, Lerner 1958; Lipset 1959; Coleman 1960; Deutsch 1961; Cutright 1963; Russett *et al.* 1964; Neubauer 1967; Olsen 1968; Smith 1969; Winham 1970; Marquette 1974; Hadenius 1992). Axel Hadenius (1992) has emphasized its significance as a predictor of democratization. I use it to measure one aspect of the distribution of basic intellectual resources. It is reasonable to assume that the higher the level of educational development, the more widely intellectual resources are usually distributed. Therefore, my interpretation of this variable does not contradict the idea that literacy also indicates the level of socio-economic development. However, the capability of this variable to measure the variation in the distribution of basic intellectual power resources has significantly diminished over the decades as a consequence of the achievement of almost universal literacy in numerous countries. In 1990, the percentage of literacy was 95 per cent or higher in fifty-two countries.

Empirical data on Urban Population, Non Agricultural Population, Students and Literates in or around 1990 are given and documented in Appendix 2.

Family Farms (FF)

The area of family farms as a percentage of the total area of holdings is assumed to measure the relative distribution of economic power resources based on the ownership or control of agricultural land. The higher the percentage of family farms, the more widely economic power resources based on the ownership or control of agricultural land are usually distributed. The ownership or control of land is an important power resource especially in agricultural societies. It is easy to use this resource as a sanction in the struggle for power. The concentration of landownership makes a large part of the agricultural population dependent on those controlling the use of land. It is difficult for an economically and socially dependent agricultural population to take part in politics independently, to form its own economic and political interest organizations, and to participate in national politics. It is much easier for independent farmers, particularly if they are literate, to participate in national politics independently and to form their own interest organizations.

Dirk Berg-Schlosser is also convinced of the significance of this variable. He says: 'There can be no doubt that widespread small-scale farming in predominantly agrarian countries is an important factor in the emergence of democratic social and political structures' (Berg-Schlosser 1989: 142). Axel Hadenius refers to some weak correlations given in my studies of 1984 and 1987 and comes to the conclusion 'that the distribution of wealth in the agrarian sector in our time has very little significance in the context' (Hadenius 1992: 100–1). I do not agree with his conclusion. Weak correlations do not necessarily prove that the distribution of agricultural land has become insignificant from the perspective of democracy. Weak correlations may be due to the fact that a high percentage of family farms is not alone enough to support democratic politics if other types of power resources are highly concentrated. This concerns African countries in particular.

The problem is how to measure the share of family farms. In the case of the first four explanatory variables, it was relatively easy to find and define operational indicators and to apply the same definition to all countries. It is much more difficult to find a coherent indicator for family farms. This difficulty is due to the fact that the size and nature of 'family farm' may vary considerably from country to country but also within a country. Depending on the level of technology, the quality of land, and climatic conditions, the size of family farms varies greatly; from less than one hectare to thousands of hectares. It is also problematic to define the 'ownership or control' of family farms. It is clear that the farms owned by cultivator-families should be included in the category of family farms, but what about various forms of tenancy and of partially owned land under communal tenure systems?

My basic criterion has been that the category of family farms includes farms that provide employment for not more than four people, including family members. This criterion has been used to separate large farms cultivated mainly by hired workers from family-size farms. It should be noted that this criterion is not dependent on the size of farms. By 'family farms' I mean holdings that are mainly cultivated by the holder family itself. Also, the concept of 'family farms' implies that holdings are owned by the cultivator family or held in ownerlike possession. If they are leased, tenancy should not make the tenant family socially and economically dependent on the landowner (see Vanhanen 1979: 48–9, 1990a: 57–8). In this point it has been necessary to use interpretations.

The criteria of 'family farms' are such that it is impossible to apply the same hectare limit to all countries. It has been necessary to define 'family farms' separately for each country and to change these definitions over time when the level of agricultural technology has changed. Consequently, the upper hectare limit and other criteria of family farms vary from country to country and over the period of comparison. However, I have attempted to keep the concept of family farms the same over time and across countries. 'Family farms' always refer to holdings that are mainly cultivated by the holder family and that are owned by the cultivator family or held in ownerlike possession.

I have collected empirical data on the distribution of landownership from various sources, but it was not possible to find statistical data from all countries and decades. In such cases I have resorted to estimations based on other types of information (see Vanhanen 1979: 297–330; 1984a; 1990a: 240–51). For this study, FAO's reports on the 1960, 1970, and 1980 agricultural censuses have been the principal sources of data, but many other sources have also been used. The results of the 1990 agricultural censuses were not yet available. Most data are from the year 1980 or around it, but there are also data from the 1970s and 1960s. Several estimations have been made for 1990 or 1991. These differences in points of time decrease the comparability of data, but I assume that errors due to this fact are not fatal. Usually the structure of landownership remains relatively stable from decade to decade. If the structure of landownership had drastically changed, I preferred to use estimates for 1990 or 1991 rather than statistical data from earlier years or decades. This concerns particularly the former socialist countries in which the privatization of agricultural land was started in the period 1989–91.

I have used an upper hectare limit to separate family farms from larger holdings (eighty-seven countries), but it has been necessary to use also other criteria of family farms. In the case of socialist and former socialist countries, I have used the share of private farms (family farms in China and Laos) (thirty-one) to indicate the percentage of family farms. Because of the lack of statistical data, I had to estimate the percentage of private farms in nearly all these cases. This method is based on the assumption that nearly all private farms can be regarded as family farms in these countries. It has been difficult to decide how to classify communally-owned land in sub-Saharan Africa but also in some other countries. The major part of agricultural land still belongs to the category of communally-owned land in sub-Saharan Africa. The ownership and control of land is divided between individual cultivators and larger communities in these countries (see Riddell and Dickerman 1986). Dirk Berg-Schlosser (1993) emphasizes that the traditional African peasantry was structurally relatively equalitarian. I decided to include 60 per cent of the land under *de facto* indigenous tenure and of collective tribal lands (50 per cent in Equatorial Guinea and Ethiopia) into the category of family farms (thirty-seven countries in Africa). The selection of the 60 per cent limit is arbitrary, but I assume it to be reasonable. African farmers are not economically and socially as dependent from the ultimate owners or owner-community as the peasants of socialist collective farms, but they can be regarded to be economically and socially less independent than individual owner-cultivators. The same classification was applied to communally-owned land in Papua New Guinea, Solomon Islands, and Western Samoa, too. In the lack of exact data, the share of owner-operated farms or family-owned farms or holdings is used to measure the proportion of family farms in the cases of Iceland, Guyana, Qatar, United Arab Emirates, Mauritius, and Bhutan.

Family Farms in this form is a variable that has not been used by any other researcher. I have used it since 1968, although in slightly different forms, to indicate the relative distribution of economic resources based on landownership (see Vanhanen 1968 and 1971). Some other researches have, however, used different indicators to measure the distribution of agricultural land. Bruce M. Russett used three separate indicators for this purpose and found that most of the states with the more equal patterns of land distribution are stable democracies, 'whereas only three of twenty-four more unequal countries can be classified stable democracies'. The Gini index of concentration was Russett's major indicator. It is based on the Lorenz curve 'drawn by connecting the points given in a cumulative distribution, e.g. the proportion of land held by each decile of farmers', and it measures the area between the cumulated distribution and the line of equality. So it is a measure of inequality. It calculates 'over the whole population the difference between an "ideal" cumulative distribution of land (where all farms are the same size) and the actual distribution' (Russett *et al.* 1964: 237–8; 1968: 154–5). I did not adopt the Gini index of concentration because it did not seem to suit the purposes of my study. It can produce highly misleading results in many cases because it does not take into account the variation in the quality of land and in the control of land, and because the values of the Gini index may vary greatly depending on how small holdings are included in the number of holdings. Another reason why I have not attempted to use the Gini index is the fact that the necessary data on the number and size of holdings are not available from many countries. My argument is not that democracy presupposes an equal distribution of land, it is that the ownership and control of land should be so widely distributed among the agricultural population that the bulk of them would become able to take part in politics independently. For this purpose, I think, my Family Farms is more suitable than the Gini index of concentration.

Empirical data on Family Farms intended to describe the situation in or around 1990 are given and documented in Appendix 3. Unfortunately, data on most countries are from the 1980s, 1970s, or 1960s. Historical data and estimations covering the period 1850–1980 are given and documented in my earlier studies (Vanhanen 1975, 1977a, 1977b, 1979, 1990a). Decennial data on Family Farms over the period 1850–1980 are also given in Appendix 5.

The degree of decentralization of non agricultural economic resources (DD)

In my 1979 and 1984 studies covering the period 1850–1979, only the five explanatory variables defined above were used. The distribution of economic power resources was measured indirectly assuming that they are usually the more widely distributed, the higher the level of socio-economic development as indicated by Urban Population and NAP. Family Farms was intended to measure more directly the distribution of the ownership and control of the means of production, but it is limited to the ownership and control of agricultural land. In the 1980s I started to develop a method to measure or estimate the relative concentration and distribution of the means of production in non agricultural sectors of economy. It has been extremely difficult to find any satisfactory and comparable measures for this purpose. The first form of this new explanatory variable was used in my 1990 study covering the years 1980–8 (Vanhanen 1990a: 59–64, 252–74).

I started by referring to some theoretical attempts to define 'concentration' and 'decentralization' or to differentiate between economic systems on the basis of the distribution of economic power. S. R. Mohnot emphasizes that economic power is used in the struggle for survival. By 'economic power' he means the ability to control the economic life of other people. This ability is based on the ownership and/or control of productive resources and effective productive capacity. He notes that control over employment has to be distinguished from control over material resources (Mohnot 1962: 17–21; see also Vanhanen 1982: 53–6). Richard L. Carson (1973: 42) argues that the main difference between economic systems concerns the degree to which economic power is concentrated or decentralized. Robert A. Dahl also contrasts centralized and decentralized economic orders and assumes that decentralization would be favourable for democracy. He thinks that the autonomy permitted to enterprises is theoretically independent of forms of ownership, hence of capitalism and socialism. He explains, 'A capitalist order may be, but need not be, highly decentralized. A socialist order may be, but need not be, highly centralized' (Dahl 1982: 108–16). Charles E. Lindblom has differentiated between market-oriented economic systems and centrally planned systems. The crucial difference between them is that production is largely controlled by the market demands of millions of consumers in market-oriented economic systems, whereas it is directly controlled by authority, usually by the central government, in centrally planned systems. Market-oriented systems are private enterprise systems in most cases, although public enterprises play an important role in many of them, whereas most socialist systems are centrally planned (Lindblom 1977: 112–13; see also Lane and Ersson 1990: 14–31, 229–32, 242–4).

These ideas of Mohnot, Carson, Dahl and Lindblom helped me to focus on the most important aspects of economic systems that should be taken into account in attempts to measure or estimate the concentration or distribution of non agricultural economic power resources. From this perspective, the most crucial characteristic of an economic system is whether economic power resources are highly concentrated in the hands of one group, whatever that group is, or whether they are widely distributed among several relatively autonomous groups. I mean by 'economic power resources' principally the ownership and/or control over the means of production and employment. I mean by 'decentralization' that the means of production, and through them the means of livelihood, are owned or effectively controlled by several relatively independent groups, which may include individuals, corporations, public enterprises, local and regional governments, and the central government. By 'concentration' I mean that important economic resources are owned or controlled by the few, usually a more or less coherent social or political group. The controlling group may be a group of individuals, a group of big corporations (domestic or foreign-owned), a group of public enterprises, or a party controlling the state and through it the means of production owned by the state. Thus 'decentralization' and 'centralization' are inversely related to each other, which means that either of them can be used to measure the degree of resource distribution.

The problem is how to measure 'centralization' or 'decentralization'. I have not yet found any single empirical variable like Family Farms to measure the concepts 'centralization' or 'decentralization', or at least some important aspects of them. Therefore, my strategy has been to locate and take into account some definable aspects of economic systems indicating the concentration or decentralization of economic power resources and to combine them into an index.

In my study covering the years 1980–88, I tried to take into account three characteristics of economic systems indicating the degree of concentration:

1 the public sector's share of productive capacity or of employment in non agricultural sectors of economy, or in its most important sector (Public Sector);
2 the share of foreign-owned enterprises of productive capacity or of employment in non agricultural sectors of economy, or in its most important sector (Foreign Sector);
3 the share of big private enterprises (domestically owned or controlled) of productive capacity or employment in non agricultural sectors of economy, or in its most important sector (Concentrated Private Sector).

These three characteristics were combined into an index of the concentration of economic power resources by adding the percentages. The combined percentage was assumed to indicate the relative level of resource concentration. In most cases, however, data or estimates were given only for one or two of these variables that were assumed to characterize the economic system concerned. Only one variable (often together with Foreign Sector) was taken into account in the cases in which either Public Sector or Concentrated Private Sector was considered to dominate economy. The inverse percentage of the combined percentage of resource concentration was assumed to indicate the degree of decentralization of non agricultural economic resources (DDN). Its value can vary from zero to 100, although, according to my estimations, no country reached 100 percent. The data and estimations concerned the situation in or around 1980 (see Vanhanen 1990a: 62–4).

In this study, concerning the situation in the beginning of the 1990s, I have attempted to simplify this index and to make it conceptually more coherent than the original index. Economic systems are classified into four categories from the perspective of resource distribution. The categories are:

1 centrally planned economy with a high degree of public ownership (CPE);
2 public sector dominated economy with a significant private sector and/or with significant foreign ownership (PSD);
3 market oriented economy with a concentrated private sector and/or with a large public sector and/or with significant foreign ownership (CPS);
4 market oriented economy with diversified ownership (MOE).

It is assumed that the degree of resource concentration (DC) is the highest in the first and the lowest in the fourth category, but, from this perspective, categories are not mutually exclusive. They are, to some extent, overlapping. The degree of concentration can vary from 0 to 40 in MOE, from 40 to 80 in CPS, from 60 to 80 in PSD, and from 80 to 100 in CPE. Each country is classified into one of these four categories on the basis of its economic system. After that, the degree of concentration (DC) is determined within the category ranges given above. The inverse percentage of DC represents the degree of decentralization (DD), which will be used in statistical analysis.

I think that this new index of decentralization is conceptually more coherent than the one used in my previous study. It takes into account both the nature of economic systems in the continuum from centrally planned economies (command economies) to market-oriented economic systems and the variation in the degree of resource concentration within each of the four major categories.

Jan-Erik Lane and Svante Ersson (1990: 230–44), following Gastil's framework, classify politico-economic regimes into four categories: (1) capitalist, (2) capitalist-state, (3) mixed capitalist, and (4) socialist. The degree of state intervention differentiates between the three 'capitalist' categories.

One might ask why I link democratization to the decentralization of economic power resources and not to capitalist economic development.

John A. Hall, for example, argues that because every contemporary democratic society is capitalist, capitalism 'is a base condition for democracy' (1993: 287–8). David Potter concludes, referring to evidence from Asia, 'that capitalist development (and its internal contradictions) is a necessary condition for democratization' (Potter 1993: 371; see also Arat 1994). I do not use the concept of 'capitalism' in this study because economic power resources may be highly concentrated or distributed in economic systems called 'capitalist'. In fact, Lane and Ersson divide 'capitalist' politico-economic systems into three categories. According to a Marxist definition of capitalism, given by Paul Cammack (1994: 178), 'capitalism is a mode of production in which a minority who own the means of production confront a majority who do not'. According to my interpretation, his definition applies even better to socialist systems in which the means of production are controlled and *de facto* owned by the leaders of the ruling communist party. Consequently, I have estimated the degree of concentration (DC) to be the highest in centrally planned economic systems (command economies), but it may be high in many 'capitalist' systems, too. On the other hand, there are 'capitalist' systems in which the degree of concentration is regarded to be the lowest. Therefore, capitalism or 'capitalist economic development' cannot be used as the explanatory factor of democratization. It does not always indicate a high degree of resource distribution, which is linked with democratization in this study. Capitalist economic development is conducive to democratization only in cases in which it furthers the distribution of economic power resources among competing groups.

From the perspective of democratization, socialism and capitalism are not the opposing poles; the theoretically relevant continuum is between the concentration and decentralization of economic power resources. Centrally planned economies (command economies) and market-oriented economies reflect this contrast, although not perfectly. In a later study, Lane and Ersson come to a similar conclusion. They say: 'What matters is the introduction of economic institutions that decrease the concentration of economic power. Decentralized capitalism and mixed capitalism tend to enhance democracy, whereas a planned economy and a state-capitalist system is detrimental' (Lane and Ersson 1994: 228).

Percentages given in Appendix 4 on the degree of concentration of non agricultural economic power resources (DC) are my estimations, but they are based on various information of the nature of economic systems. I have used *The Europa World Year Book* (1991–4); A. S. Banks *et al.*, *Economic Handbook of the World* (1981); G. T. Kurian, *Encyclopedia of the Third World* (1987 and 1992); D. Nohlen and F. Nuscheler (eds), *Handbuch der Dritten Welt* (1982–3), and several other handbooks and many monographs and special studies documented in Appendix 4. Several estimations are based on relatively reliable statistical information of some key sectors of non agricultural economy, but many other estimations are based on more general information of the nature of economic systems. My intention has been to measure relative differences between countries in the degree of resource concentration. The margin of error may not be more than 10 percentage points in many cases, but in some cases it may be 20 percentage points or even more.

Empirical data on the estimated degree of concentration of non agricultural economic resources are given and documented in Appendix 4.

Indices of resource distribution

The six explanatory variables defined above can be used separately in statistical analysis, but because they are intended to measure the same ultimate explanatory factor – resource distribution – from different perspectives, it is better to combine them into a coherent index of power resources. Then we can use this index to explain the variation in the Index of Democratization (ID). But how to combine the six explanatory variables? That is the problem. In fact, there are many ways to combine the six variables depending on how we weight each of them.

Index of power resources (IPR)

One simple way would be to weight explanatory variables equally and to calculate their arithmetic mean. I have preferred, however, a different method to combine them. It seems to me that the six basic variables indicate three different dimensions of resource distribution. Urban Population and NAP indicate the degree of occupational diversification and the level of socio-economic development. I assume that both of them measure the decentralization of economic and organizational power resources indirectly. The higher the level of socio-economic development and occupational diversification as indicated by Urban Population and NAP, the more widely important economic resources and organizational capabilities are usually distributed. Because they indicate the same dimension of resource distribution from slightly different perspectives, I combined them into an Index of Occupational Diversification (IOD) by calculating their arithmetic mean. This index may be a more reliable indicator of resource decentralization than either of them alone.

Students and Literates indicate the distribution of knowledge and intellectual power resources from two different perspectives. The relative number of students measures differences between societies in the distribution of higher knowledge and special skills needed in modern societies. The percentage of literate population indicates the distribution of basic intellectual resources needed to take part in national politics. These two educational variables are combined into an Index of Knowledge Distribution (IKD) by calculating their arithmetic mean. It is assumed that the higher the value of IKD, the more widely intellectual power resources are distributed in a society. I think that intellectual power resources may be as important in the struggle for power as economic resources. Knowledge is also power.

Family Farms (FF) and the degree of decentralization of non agricultural economic power resources (DD) respectively indicate the degree of resource distribution in agricultural and non agricultural sectors of economy. They are assumed to measure more directly the distribution of economic power resources than Urban Population and NAP. Both of them are intended to measure the concentration and distribution of the ownership and control of the means of production. They are combined into an Index of the Distribution of Economic Power Resources (DER), but not simply by calculating their arithmetic mean. Because the relative significance of agricultural and non agricultural sectors of the economy varies greatly from country to country, it is reasonable to weight the values of FF and DD by their relative importance. I decided to use the percentages of agricultural and non agricultural populations to weight the relative importance of these two sectors. Consequently the two indicators are combined by multiplying the value of FF by the percentage of agricultural population (AP) and the value of DD by the percentage of non agricultural population (NAP), after which the weighted values of FF and DD are simply added up. In other words, DER = (FF x AP) + (DD x NAP). It is assumed that the higher the value of DER, the more widely economic power resources based on the ownership and/or control of the means of production are distributed in a society.

In this way I have combined the six original explanatory variables into three sectional indices (IOD, IKD and DER). Each of them is assumed to measure a different but equally important dimension of resource distribution. Together they are intended to indicate relative differences between societies in the distribution of economic and intellectual power resources. Because I have no method to estimate what differences there might be between IOD, IKD and DER in their relative significance, I decided to give them equal weight in statistical analysis. I also assume that the concentration of power resources in any of these dimensions may be enough to block democratization. In other words, it may be that even high levels of resource distribution in two dimensions cannot compensate for the lack of resource distribution in one dimension. Therefore, I decided to combine these three sectional indices into an Index of Power Resources (IPR) not by calculating their arithmetic mean but by multiplying them and by dividing the outcome by 10,000. It is assumed that the higher the value of IPR, the more widely politically relevant power resources are usually distributed among various sections of the population and the more favourable social conditions are for democratization. Thus this index (IPR) will be my principal explanatory variable and operational substitute for the hypothetical concept of 'resource distribution'. Iain McLeon says about this index that although 'Vanhanen's choice and use of such an index are statistically naïve, the thinking behind it seems sensible. The idea is that the more evenly

resources of power are distributed, the more likely is democratization'
(McLeon 1994: 37; *cf.* Blondel 1995: 82–3).

Index of power resources and structural imbalance (IPRI)

The sudden and unexpected collapse of socialist systems and democratization in Eastern Europe in 1989–91 exposed one serious shortcoming of IPR:
it is unable to differentiate between countries in which all three sectional
indices indicate the concentration of power resources and countries in which
only one sectional index is at or near zero. According to IOD and IKD,
power resources were nearly as widely distributed in Eastern Europe as in
Western Europe in 1980, but DER indicated an extreme concentration of
power resources because agricultural and non agricultural means of production were concentrated in the hands of the government and the hegemonic party. Consequently, IPR values for East European countries (except
Poland and Yugoslavia where the bulk of agricultural land had remained
in private ownership) were at or near zero in 1980. The concentration
of political power (lack of democracy) and the concentration of power
resources seemed to be in balance. Therefore, I was unable to predict
democratization in Eastern Europe. I noticed the structural imbalance in
East European socialist countries but I was unable to take it into account
in my predictions. I referred to the example of socialist countries and
concluded in 1984:

> The example of these countries shows that a high concentration of any
> one crucial power resource is enough to prevent the emergence of
> democracy, even though other environmental conditions (IOD and
> IKD) may be ripe for democracy. Because their IPR values cannot be
> much increased as long as land ownership and other major means of
> production continue to be concentrated, I predict that these countries
> will probably remain below the threshold of democracy. On the other
> hand, the pressure for democratization will probably be enhanced, and
> the consequences of this pressure are incalculable. The social basis of
> hegemonic governmental structures is rather narrow in socialist countries
> because they are upheld only by the concentration of the means of
> coercion and of economic power resources. Other social conditions,
> particularly a high level of education, are conducive to the emergence
> of democracy. It is difficult to estimate the relative importance of the
> different power resources. The gradual evolution of more democratic
> political institutions is always possible.
>
> (Vanhanen 1984a: 132)

This failure to predict democratization in Eastern Europe challenged me
to reconsider the way how I should combine my six explanatory variables.
I returned to the idea of 'unbalanced components of IPR', which I had
used to explain breakdowns of democracy in some cases. I had noted in

connection with new democracies for which the value of one component of IPR was exceptionally low:

It is interesting that in most of these countries with unbalanced components of IPR democracy was later to break down.... The above observations according to which democracy is more likely to break down in countries with unbalanced components of IPR than in countries with well balanced components of IPR support the assumption that the concentration of any one crucial power resource may be enough to block the emergence of democracy.

(Vanhanen 1984a: 127)

Now I came to a complementary assumption that 'unbalanced components of IPR' make not only democracies but autocracies, too, vulnerable. I argued (see Vanhanen 1991a; Vanhanen and Kimber 1994) that it might be possible to find a systematic explanation for the collapse of hegemonic political systems and the emergence of democracy in Eastern Europe from discrepancies in explanatory factors. The first four explanatory variables had predicted democratization in those countries for decades, and only the concentration of economic power resources, as indicated by the last two explanatory variables, had been in harmony with the concentration of political power.

I formulated an Index of Structural Imbalance (ISI) to measure the extent of discrepancy between various explanatory variables. It is based on the mean deviation of the three sectional indices (IOD, IKD and DER). The mean deviation is the arithmetic mean of the absolute differences of each score from the mean. For example, when the values of IOD, IKD and DER are 78.0, 67.5 and 11.2 respectively (Bulgaria), their arithmetic mean is 52.2. In this case the absolute differences from the mean are 25.8, 15.3 and 41.0 respectively and the mean deviation (the arithmetic mean of the absolute differences from the mean) 27.4. The higher the ISI values are, the more single dimensions of resource distribution differ from each other. I assume that political systems are exceptionally insecure in countries with high ISI values because some structural factors are conducive to democracy and others conducive to autocracy. High values of ISI indicate the existence of serious structural imbalance and imply that drastic changes in political structures are possible.

In 1980, the arithmetic mean of ISI values was 12.0 and the standard deviation 7.1 in my comparison group of 147 states (Vanhanen 1991a). ISI was higher than 19.2 (one standard deviation from the mean 12.0) for twenty-one countries and less than 4.9 (one standard deviation from the mean) for twenty-one countries. The first group with the highest ISI values included six East European countries (Bulgaria, Czechoslovakia, DDR, Hungary, Romania and the Soviet Union). Structural imbalance characterized the countries of the first group. One or two sectional indices had high values, and the values of one or two other sectional indices were low or at zero. The IPR values were low for nearly all countries of the first group because a low value for any sectional index is sufficient to drop the IPR to near zero. Nineteen of the twenty-one countries of the first group were non democracies as predicted by their low IPR values.

The problem was that low IPR values explained the lack of democracy in Eastern Europe in the period of 1980–8, but they did not predict the democratization that took place in 1989–90. How to solve this problem? I came to the conclusion that low IPR values do not always indicate the concentration of power resources and a low potentially for democratization equally reliably because IPR may conceal structural factors conducive to democracy. High ISI values indicate that some structural factors are highly favourable for democratization, although some others are highly unfavourable. Consequently, chances of democracy may be better in a country with a high ISI value than in a country with a low ISI value, although their IPR values were the same. Therefore, we should take high ISI values into account in predicting the prospects for democracy on the basis of IPR. If I had used ISI values in addition to IPR values in predicting the prospects of democratization in the 1980s, my predictions for Eastern Europe would have been more accurate because their high ISI values implied the fragility of hegemonic political systems.

The values of ISI can be used separately from IPR, but it is also possible to combine them into a new Index of Power Resources and Structural Imbalance (IPRI). There are many ways of combining them, depending on how the significance of ISI value is weighted. I decided to combine them by adding a quarter of the value of ISI to the value of IPR. Thus the new IPRI is calculated by the following formula: IPRI = IPR + 1/4 of ISI (see Vanhanen 1991a; 1992a: 24–6; Vanhanen and Kimber 1994).

Summary of explanatory variables

The following list includes all the explanatory variables and indices of this study. It should be noted that some of them cover the whole period of comparison since the 1850s, whereas some others are limited to the period 1980–93.

Basic explanatory variables

1 Urban Population (in 1850–1970, the percentage of the population living in cities of 20,000 or more inhabitants; in 1980–90, urban population as a percentage of the total population).
2 Non agricultural population (NAP).
3 Students (in 1850–1970, 1,000 students per 100,000 inhabitants is used to represent the level of 100 per cent; in 1980–90, 5,000 students per 100,000 inhabitants is used to represent the level of 100 per cent).
4 Literates (the percentage of literates from the adult population).

5 Family Farms (FF).

Empirical data on these five variables cover the whole period of comparison since the 1850s.

6 The degree of concentration of non agricultural economic resources (DC) and its opposite, the degree of decentralization of non agricultural economic resources (DD). This variable covers only the period 1980–93.

Sectional indices of explanatory variables

7 Index of Occupational Diversification (IOD). The arithmetic mean of Urban Population and NAP.

8 Index of Knowledge Distribution (IKD). The arithmetic mean of Students (percentage) and Literates.

These two sectional indices cover the whole period of comparison since the 1850s.

9 Index of the Distribution of Economic Power Resources (DER). FF and DD are combined by weighting the values of FF and DD by the percentage of agricultural population (AP) and non agricultural population (NAP) respectively. DER = (FF × AP) + (DD × NAP). This index covers only the period 1980–93.

Combined indices of explanatory variables

10 Index of Power Resources (IPR). A combination of IOD, IKD, and DER. IPR = (IOD × IKD × DER)/10,000. In the period 1850–1970, FF is used in place of DER.

11 IPRI. IPR is weighted by the value of ISI. IPRI = IPR + 1/4 of ISI.

These two combined indices cover the whole period of comparison since the 1850s.

PERIOD AND UNITS OF COMPARISON

The principal period of empirical analysis includes the years 1991–3 in this study. Most new data on explanatory variables are from 1990 or around 1990, and I use the same value for all three years over the period 1991–3. Data on political variables are separately from each year over the period 1991–3.

However, I shall also use data of my previous comparative studies in correlation and regression analyses. A previous longitudinal study (Vanhanen 1984a) covers the period 1850–1979. Data on explanatory variables are from the beginning of each decade in that study, and data on political variables are ten-year (decennial) arithmetical means. Another cross-national study (Vanhanen 1990a) covers the period 1980–8. Most data on explanatory variables are from 1980 or around 1980 in that study, and data on political variables are separately from each year over the period 1980–8. In this study, the political data of the year 1980 will be used to represent the 1980s in correlation and regression analyses.

In principle, this study is intended to include all independent contemporary states, but, in practice, it was necessary to make some restrictions. The major restriction is that the study includes only the independent states whose population in 1990 was over 100,000 inhabitants. One reason for the exclusion of small states is that it is more difficult to get reliable data on very small states than from bigger states, but my main argument is that many of the very small states are crucially dependent on some foreign powers that provide financial, administrative, and military support, for example, Antigua and Barbuda, Dominica, Grenada, Kiribati, the Federated States of Micronesia (whose population in 1990 was 100,000), St Kitts and Nevis, Tonga, and Tuvalu (see Banks 1990). Therefore, the nature of their political institutions may depend more on foreign support than on domestic factors. Second, only the states that were independent in 1991 are included. This criterion excluded from the study some of the states that were independent in the 1980s. The German Democratic Republic united with the Federal Republic of Germany in 1990. Consequently, Germany replaced them. The former Yemen Arab Republic and People's Democratic Republic of Yemen merged in 1990 and established a united Yemen. The Soviet Union disintegrated and ceased to exist in 1991. Its former republics became independent states. The Federation of Russia can be regarded as the principal successor state of the former Soviet Union. The other successor states are Armenia, Belarus, Estonia, Georgia, Latvia, Lithuania, Moldova, Ukraine, Azerbaijan, Kazakhstan, Kyrgyzstan, Tajikistan, Turkmenistan and Uzbekistan. Yugoslavia disintegrated in 1990–1 when Croatia, Slovenia, Macedonia, and Bosnia-Hertzegovina seceded from the federation and became independent states. Consequently, Yugoslavia for the period 1991–3 includes only Serbia and Montenegro. Of these new states, I left Bosnia-Hertzegovina out of this study because of its ethnic civil war. There was no effective government controlling the whole area of Bosnia-Hertzegovina in the period 1991–3. The former Czechoslovakia was divided into the Czech Republic and Slovakia from the beginning of 1993. In this study Czechoslovakia continued until 1992, after which the Czech Republic is regarded as the successor state of Czechoslovakia in 1993. Slovakia was left out of this analysis because it did not exist as an independent state in 1991. Taiwan (ROC) is included in this study over the period 1991–3, although its status as an independent state is not clear. Both the governments of China and Taiwan (ROC) are committed to the idea of the united China including Taiwan.

The number of observation units in this study is twenty-five higher than in the previous study covering the period 1980–8. The emergence of new independent states in the 1980s and the lowering of the minimum population to 100,000 increased the number of observation units by nine (Belize, Brunei, Maldives, Namibia, St Lucia, St Vincent and the Grenadines, São Tomé and Príncipe, Vanuatu, and Western Samoa). The unifications of Germany and Yemen decreased the number of states by two, and the disintegrations of the Soviet Union and Yugoslavia increased the number of states by seventeen. Finally, the inclusion of Taiwan (ROC) increased the number of observation units by one.

My previous study of the period 1980–8 (Vanhanen 1990a) covers 147 states that were independent in 1980 and whose population in 1980 was more than 200,000. In my 1984 longitudinal study (Vanhanen 1984a), the number of decennial comparison units varied from thirty-seven in 1850–9 to 119 in 1970–9. The study covers the states that were independent in the 1970s and their predecessors and whose population in 1970 was at least 500,000 inhabitants and area not less than 10,000 sq km. The total number of decennial comparison units is 820 in that study. These differences in the selection of comparison units mean that the relative number of very small states has increased significantly in the studies covering the period 1980–93. The empirical data of my earlier studies that will be used in statistical analyses of this study are given in Appendix 5.

METHODS OF ANALYSIS

Mattei Dogan says that the 'chariot of science is trailed by three horses: theory, data and method. If the three horses do not run at the same speed the chariot may lose its equilibrium'. According to his observations, there 'is today in the field of comparative politics a serious gap between substance and method, particularly in the arena of quantitative research' (Dogan 1994: 35). I have tried to keep the three horses in balance. I use a deductive theory, from which I have deduced testable hypotheses. I have operationalized the central theoretical concepts into empirical indicators and gathered quantitative data on these indicators. The quantification of dependent and independent variables makes it possible to use various statistical methods of analysis. Research techniques are related to the nature of data (*cf.* Manheim and Rich 1986, particularly pp. 15–30, 43–67).

Because all data on empirical indicators are at the level of interval measurement, I can test hypotheses on democratization by the techniques of correlation and regression analysis, but I shall use some other techniques of comparison, too. The principal idea is to evaluate the prospects of democracy on the basis of past relationships between political and explanatory variables. If they were strongly correlated in the past, it is reasonable to assume that they will also be strongly correlated in the future. Therefore, we have to measure the strength of relationship between political and explanatory variables and to explore how well single countries have been adapted to the general pattern of relationship. The stronger the relationship, the more we can trust to the predictions based on the present values of explanatory variables. The major research hypotheses are the same as in my previous study (Vanhanen 1990a: 66–7):

1 The political variables of this study, the Index of Democratization in particular, are positively correlated with the explanatory variables, the Index of Power Resources in particular.
2 All countries tend to cross the threshold of democracy at about the same level of the Index of Power Resources.

I try to use Popper's method of trial and the elimination of error. The hypotheses are tested by empirical evidence to see to what extent they are able to explain democratization. The hypotheses are predictions derived from the evolutionary theory of democratization formulated in the previous chapter. They are falsifiable statements, and my intention is to see to what extent empirical evidence contradicts them. In other words, to what extent they agree with the facts (*cf.* Miller 1983: 101–80; Popper 1992: 3–51). It is possible to falsify these research hypotheses by empirical evidence given in Appendices 1–5. The first hypothesis can be regarded as falsified if correlations between explanatory and political variables are not clearly positive. Negative correlations and correlations near zero would falsify the hypothesis, which presupposes the existence of positive correlation between political and explanatory variables. The stronger the correlations are, the more confidently we can assume that the distribution of power resources is causally related to the variation of democratization. If the explained part of variation is more than 50 per cent, it would support my theoretical assumption that the distribution of power resources is the fundamental factor behind democratization.

The second hypothesis can be regarded as falsified if the results of regression analysis show that all countries have not tended to cross the threshold of democracy at about the same level of IPR. For this purpose, we have to define what is meant by 'at about the same level of IPR'. If ID and IPR were exactly in the same scale, we could hypothesize that countries tend to cross the threshold of democracy as soon as their IPR rises to 5.0 index points because 5.0 ID index points was defined as a minimum threshold of democracy and because, according to my theory, the level of democracy depends directly on the level of resource distribution. This means that the hypothetical regression equation would be ID est. $= 0 + 1 \times$ IPR. In fact, IPR and ID are almost in the same scale. Therefore we can accept the hypothetical regression equation and assume that 5.0 IPR index points represents the average transition level of IPR. However, we have to accept some variation around the average transition level because our operational indicators are not perfect substitutes for hypothetical concepts 'the level of democratization' and 'the degree of resource distribution' and because correlations between ID and IPR are not complete. We should define the transition level of IPR in such a way that it includes the major part of variation due to measurement errors and accidental factors but excludes significant deviations. This will be done in the next chapter in connection with regression analysis.

When the transition level of IPR is defined, we can hypothesize that all countries above the upper limit of the IPR level of transition tend to be democracies and all countries below the lower limit of transition tend to be non democracies. It should be noted that this hypothesis does not predict the nature of political systems for the countries within the transition level of IPR. They can be democracies or non democracies. The comparison of the IPR values with the values of the three political variables indicates in which countries the level of democratization is in harmony with the second hypothesis and which countries contradict the hypothesis. The results of regression analysis disclose the size of deviations and the most deviating cases. Deviating cases weaken the hypothesis, but if the number of deviations remains relatively small, they are not enough to falsify the hypothesis. The hypothesis should be regarded as falsified if a significant number of the countries above the upper limit of the IPR level of transition are non democracies and a significant number of the countries below the lower IPR limit of transition are democracies. Large positive residuals indicate that the level of democratization is higher than expected, and large negative residuals indicate that the level of democratization is lower than expected. In this way the results of regression analysis help us to make predictions on the prospects of democracy in particular countries.

Iain McLeon (1994) thinks that it would have been better to use multiple regressions instead of simple regressions. He says on my regression study (Vanhanen 1990a) that it 'as a whole is impaired by a wrong-headed decision to rely on simple regressions of democratization on a (dubiously composed) index of "power resources" rather than letting multiple regression take the place of arbitrary index construction' (McLeon 1994: 28). My grounds for the use of an index of power resources are theoretical. I am not primarily interested in the explanatory power of any particular social variable. I am interested in the explanatory power of my theoretical explanatory factor, the degree of resource distribution. Socioeconomic variables are intended to measure, mostly indirectly, relative differences between countries in the degree of resource distribution. Therefore I have combined different explanatory variables into an index. I assume that each of the three dimensions of power resources (indicated by IOD, IKD and DER) is equally important and that they cannot replace each other. Therefore they are combined into an index by multiplying their values. A combined index makes it possible to use simple regression. Besides, I have assumed on theoretical grounds that the combined index (IPR) is able to explain more of the variation in the degree of democratization than any of the sectional indices or original indicators alone.

The research hypotheses will be tested by correlation and regression analyses in world groups including all the units of comparison. The largest group of comparison includes 820 decennial units of comparison from the period 1850–1979, 147 countries from the year 1980, and 172 countries from the years 1991–3. Correlation and regression analyses will be carried out separately in this combined longitudinal group of 1,139 observation units and in the cross-sectional group of 1991–3. The results of statistical analyses will disclose to what extent the relationship has remained the same over time.

A more detailed analysis will be restricted to the comparison group of 172 contemporary states of the period 1991–3. For the purposes of this analysis, the countries are divided into seven regional groups on the basis of geographical and cultural differences (see Table 2.2).

Table 2.2 Seven regional groups

Regional group	N
1 Europe and North America	40
2 Latin America and the Caribbean	29
3 North Africa, the Middle East and Central Asia	29
4 Sub-Saharan Africa	44
5 South Asia	7
6 East Asia and Southeast Asia	16
7 Oceania	7
Total	172

The classification of countries into regional groups is to some extent arbitrary, for there is no stable and universally accepted way to divide countries into continental, cultural, or other regional groups (*cf.*, for example, Deasy *et al.* 1958; Nohlen and Nuscheler 1983; Wesson 1988). Europe and North America cover all geographically connected countries of European peoples from the United States to Russia, although many of these countries include racial and other ethnic minorities and although a part of Russia extends to Asia. Turkey and Cyprus are politically closely connected with European countries, and they are sometimes included in the group of European countries, but I decided to include them in the group of the Middle East countries because of historical, cultural, and geographical reasons (*cf.* Held 1994: 7–9). Latin America and the Caribbean constitute a geographically clearly defined area, although there are cultural and ethnic differences between Latin American and the Caribbean countries.

North Africa, the Middle East and Central Asia constitute a heterogeneous group of countries, but they are geographically connected with each other and they are culturally united by Islam (except Israel and partly Cyprus, Kazakhstan, Lebanon, and Sudan). Azerbaijan and the five Central Asian countries of the former Soviet Union (Kazakhstan, Kyrgyzstan, Tajikistan, Turkmenistan and Uzbekistan), in which Muslims form the majority of the population, are included in this regional group. The southern border of this region in Africa is problematic. I decided to include

Sudan and Mauritania in this regional group for geographical reasons and because of their hegemonic Arab populations, although black Africans constitute a significant part of the population in both countries. Ilter Turan is right in his comment that North Africa, the Middle East and Central Asia are separate regions of the world that are rarely grouped together. I combined these three regions because North Africa and Central Asia have strong links to the Middle East. North African countries are not only Muslim countries but also Arab countries, and the Central Asian countries have significant ethnic links to Turkey and Iran (*cf.* Held 1994: 7–9).

Sub-Saharan Africa includes all the other countries of Africa except the seven North African Arab countries (Morocco, Algeria, Tunisia, Libya, Egypt, Sudan and Mauritania). The regional group of South Asia includes India, Pakistan, Bangladesh, and Sri Lanka, which belonged to British India, as well as the Republic of Maldives, which is a former British protectorate, and Nepal and Bhután, which retained their *de jure* independence throughout the colonial period. The regional group of East Asia and Southeast Asia covers the rest of Asian countries, including Burma (Myanmar), which belonged to British India. Oceania (see Henderson's commentary) includes Australia and New Zealand dominated by European populations and five smaller Pacific states, which are mainly populated by Melanesian and Polynesian stocks.

It will be interesting to compare the state of democratization and the conditions of democracy in different regional groups because my theory of democratization is intended to apply to all countries across cultural, racial, and geographical differences. This study differs from several other studies in which it is assumed that the same factors cannot be used to explain democracy and democratization in all parts of the world. Robert Pinkney, for example, says about democracy in the Third World that where 'democracy exists, it does not appear to have sprung from the same roots as in the West, although some of the roots have an affinity with their Western counterparts' (Pinkney 1993: 38). My argument is that because human nature is approximately similar in all parts of the world, it is reasonable to expect that approximately similar factors have been related to the emergence and failures of democracy everywhere in the world. Empirical evidence can be used to test this assumption.

3 Empirical analysis of democratization: 1850–1993

My intention is to test the two research hypotheses formulated in chapter 2 by empirical evidence. The results of empirical analysis provide a basis to estimate and predict prospects of democracy in single countries. The stronger the hypothesized relationship between political and explanatory variables is, the more accurate predictions on the prospects of democracy can be made.

Because my theory presupposes that the relationship between political and explanatory variables remains the same over time, I have to assume that their relationship is approximately the same in the 1990s as it has been since the 1850s. It means that the degree of democracy depends principally on the degree of resource distribution. If the relationship has remained stable over time, we have good reasons to expect that the same will continue in the 1990s and even after that. The stability of the relationship between political and explanatory variables can be checked by correlation and regression analyses. They can be carried out separately in the longitudinal comparison group, which includes all the units of comparison of my previous comparative studies for the period since the 1850s, and in the cross-sectional comparison group including only the 172 countries of the period 1991–3. My predictions on the prospects of democracy will be principally based on the results of longitudinal regression analyses.

LONGITUDINAL CORRELATIONS

Let us first measure the strength of relationship between political and explanatory variables in the longitudinal group of 1,139 units of comparison. According to the first research hypothesis, the political indicators of this study are assumed to correlate positively with the explanatory variables. Correlations should be relatively strong, especially between the Index of Democratization (ID) and the Index of Power Resources (IPR). As stated above, this longitudinal comparison group includes 820 decennial observation units for the period 1850–1979, 147 countries for the period 1980–8, and 172 countries for the period 1991–3. In the cases for the periods 1980–8 and 1991–3, the longitudinal comparison group includes political data only from the years 1980 and 1993 respectively. It would be possible to use political data for the years 1991, 1992 and 1993 in turn in the longitudinal comparison group, but because the results of correlation analysis would be nearly the same, only the year 1993 is taken into account.

Longitudinal correlation analysis concerns the three political indicators, the three sectional indices (IOD, IKD and DER), the Index of Power Resources (IPR), and the Index of Power Resources and Structural Imbalance (IPRI). It should be noted that FF is used in the place of DER over the period 1850–1979 because data on the second component of DER (the degree of decentralization of non agricultural economic resources = DD) are available only from two points of time (1980 and 1990–1). The intercorrelations of the five explanatory variables are given in Table 3.1 and the correlations between political and explanatory variables in Table 3.2.

Table 3.1 Intercorrelations of the five explanatory variables in the comparison group of 1,139 decennial observation units, 1850–1993

Variable	1	2	3	4	5
1 IOD	1.000	0.835	0.369	0.740	0.781
2 IKD		1.000	0.493	0.752	0.789
3 DER(FF, 1850–1979)			1.000	0.703	0.703
4 IPR				1.000	0.991
5 IPRI					1.000

Table 3.1 indicates that IOD (Index of Occupational Diversification) and IKD (Index of Knowledge Distribution) are strongly intercorrelated (0.835), whereas DER(FF) has only weak correlations with IOD (0.369) and IKD (0.493). This means that DER(FF) indicates a dimension of resource distribution that is nearly independent from the two other dimensions. IPR and IPRI are correlated strongly with their three components (IOD, IKD and DER). It is significant that DER(FF) correlates with the two combined indices nearly as strongly as IOD and IKD. The intercorrelation of IPR and IPRI is extremely strong (0.991). IPRI seems to differ from IPR only slightly.

Table 3.2 Correlations between the three political and five explanatory variables in the longitudinal comparison group of 1,139 decennial observation units, 1850–1993

Explanatory variable	Competition	Participation	ID
IOD	0.561	0.586	0.663
IKD	0.616	0.673	0.659
DER(FF)	0.514	0.433	0.601
IPR	0.621	0.602	0.813
IPRI	0.614	0.628	0.809

The two basic political indicators (Competition and Participation) are correlated positively, but their correlation 0.459 is weak. The explained part of variation is only 21 per cent. It means that the two dimensions of democratization measured by them are relatively independent from each other. Therefore it is useful to take both of them into account. Their combination, the Index of Democratization (ID), can be assumed to be a more realistic indicator of the level of democratization than either of them alone.

Correlations between the three political variables and the five explanatory indices test the first research hypothesis. Table 3.2 shows that all correlations are positive as hypothesized. IOD, IKD and DER(FF) are moderately correlated with the three political indicators. IOD and IKD are slightly more strongly correlated with the political variables than DER(FF). The explained part of variation in political indicators varies from 19 to 44 per cent.

The most interesting correlations are between the two combined indices and the three political indicators. There is not much difference between the two combined indices. The highest correlations are, as hypothesized, between the two combined indices and ID. These correlations are significantly higher than the correlations with Competition and Participation. The explained part of variation (66 and 65 per cent respectively) is more than 20 percentage points higher than for Competition and Participation. It implies that the Index of Democratization measures better the level of democratization than its two components alone. When IOD, IKD and DER(FF) were used together in multiple regression to explain the variation in the Index of Democratization, the explained part of variation was 59 per cent, or 7 percentage points less than what IPR explains.

Empirical data failed to falsify the first research hypothesis. All correlations between political and explanatory variables are positive as hypothesized, and the relationship between IPR and ID is so strong that only 34 per cent of the variation remained unexplained in 1850–1993. The relationship between political and explanatory variables seems to have remained relatively stable since the 1850s. So the results support my assumption that there is a common underlying factor of democratization which applies to all countries and which has remained approximately the same at least since the 1850s. It would be unrealistic to expect complete correlations because my indicators are only imperfect substitutes for the theoretical concepts, because there are measurement errors in my data, and because there may be many other factors affecting the level of democratization, including institutional variation, historical factors, various local factors, external actors, and the role of political leaders. Besides, politics is never fully deterministic. Random factors have always a role in politics.

According to my interpretation, correlations have remained stable over time because human nature is the same today as it was in the 1850s. People tend to use all available resources in the struggle for power and scarce resources. Therefore the values of ID and IPR remain strongly correlated, although their correlations are not perfect. The basic pattern, however, seems to have remained the same over time: the concentration of important power resources leads to the concentration of political power and to autocratic or hegemonic institutions, whereas the distribution of the same resources among many groups leads to the distribution of political power and to democratic institutions.

CROSS-SECTIONAL CORRELATIONS

Let us next examine how political and explanatory variables were correlated in the comparison group of 172 countries in 1991–3. Data on explanatory variables are from one point of time in or around 1990–1, whereas data on political variables are from three years 1991–3. The political variables are the same as in the longitudinal analysis, but the number of explanatory variables is higher in this analysis than in the longitudinal analysis. In addition to the three sectional indices (IOD, IKD and DER) and the two combined indices (IPR and IPRI), this analysis also includes the six basic explanatory variables (Urban Population, NAP, Students, Literates, Family Farms and the degree of decentralization of non agricultural economic resources = DD).

The two basic political variables were more highly correlated with each other in 1991–3 than in the longitudinal comparison group (0.624 in 1991, 0.635 in 1992 and 0.616 in 1993), but they are still relatively independent from each other. The intercorrelations of the six basic explanatory variables and five indices are given in Table 3.3.

Table 3.3 Intercorrelations of the six basic explanatory variables and the five sectional and combined indices in the comparison group of 172 countries, 1991–3

Explanatory variable	2	3	4	5	6
Basic explanatory variables					
1 Urban Population	0.848	0.718	0.616	0.038	0.419
2 Non Agricultural Population		0.719	0.748	−0.027	0.398
3 Students			0.662	0.120	0.533
4 Literates				−0.082	0.396
5 Family Farms					0.524
6 DD					

Sectional indices and combined indices	8	9	10	11
7 IOD	0.800	0.014	0.692	0.746
8 IKD		0.140	0.759	0.795
9 DER			0.650	0.590
10 IPR				0.992
11 IPRI				

Of the six single explanatory variables, Urban Population and Non Agricultural Population (NAP) are most highly intercorrelated (0.848). Students and Literates are moderately correlated with each other and with Urban Population and NAP, whereas the correlations of Family Farms with the first four single variables are near zero. This is mainly due to the fact that the values of Family Farms are relatively high in sub-Saharan Africa, whereas the values of the other basic variables are low. Family Farms is moderately correlated with DD, which is only weakly or moderately correlated with the other single explanatory variables. Because several explanatory variables, FF and DD in particular, are relatively independent from each other, we can expect that a combination of explanatory variables measures the degree of resource distribution more realistically than any of the single explanatory variables alone.

Following the pattern of the six single explanatory variables, IOD and IKD are strongly correlated with each other (0.800), whereas DER is completely independent from them (correlations 0.014 and 0.140 respectively). Because the three sectional indices, DER in particular, are relatively independent from each other, it is reasonable to expect that a combination of them is a better indicator of resource distribution than any of the sectional indices alone. In the longitudinal comparison group, the correlation between IOD and IKD is nearly the same (0.835), whereas FF(DER) is more strongly correlated with the two other sectional indices than in this cross-sectional comparison group (see Table 3.1).

The intercorrelation of the two alternative combinations of IOD, IKD and DER is the most interesting one. The purpose of alternative combinations is to explore to what extent their explanatory power depends on the structure of combination and to what extent the results of regression analyses vary depending on the nature of a combined index. The lower their intercorrelation is, the more their explanatory power may vary and the more the results of regression analyses would differ from country to country. Table 3.3 shows, however, that the intercorrelation of the two combined indices is extremely high (0.992). The explained part of variation is 99 per cent. It means that the results of regression analyses for single countries will be approximately the same in nearly all cases. Because the new alternative combined index (IPRI) differs only slightly from the original simple IPR, I can still use the original IPR as the principal explanatory variable. In single cases, however, IPRI may produce significantly different results.

The correlations between the three political and eleven explanatory variables are given in Table 3.4. They test the first research hypothesis. All correlations should be positive, and IPR and IPRI are assumed to be more highly correlated with political variables than single explanatory variables.

As expected, all explanatory variables, except Family Farms, have clear positive correlations with the three political variables. Thus the results support the first research hypothesis, although correlations are a little weaker than in the longitudinal group of 1,139 observation units. It is

Table 3.4 Correlations between the three political and the eleven explanatory variables in the cross-sectional comparison group of 172 countries, 1991–3

Explanatory variable	C-91	P-91	ID-91	C-92	P-92	ID-92	C-93	P-93	ID-93
Single explanatory variables									
1 UP	0.492	0.442	0.576	0.455	0.455	0.568	0.446	0.449	0.562
2 NAP	0.472	0.503	0.553	0.431	0.524	0.559	0.386	0.529	0.539
3 Students	0.578	0.517	0.640	0.545	0.545	0.636	0.519	0.559	0.627
4 Literates	0.513	0.576	0.579	0.516	0.640	0.608	0.465	0.662	0.591
5 FF	0.178	0.020	0.256	0.222	0.059	0.269	0.214	0.041	0.264
6 DD	0.689	0.450	0.745	0.652	0.468	0.704	0.620	0.445	0.684
Sectional indices									
7 IOD	0.500	0.493	0.586	0.459	0.511	0.585	0.430	0.511	0.571
8 IKD	0.596	0.602	0.666	0.580	0.654	0.681	0.538	0.673	0.666
9 DER	0.440	0.223	0.510	0.443	0.240	0.479	0.436	0.215	0.471
Combined indices									
10 IPR	0.671	0.568	0.808	0.630	0.595	0.781	0.606	0.591	0.768
11 IPRI	0.668	0.587	0.809	0.624	0.612	0.783	0.602	0.611	0.772

interesting to note that there is a clear difference in the strength of correlations between the three subgroups of explanatory variables. On average, correlations are weakest between the single explanatory variables and the three political variables. Correlations are somewhat stronger between the three sectional indices and the three political variables, and the highest correlations are between the combined indices and the three political variables. Why are the combined indices more highly correlated with political variables than single explanatory variables? My explanation is that combined indices are better measures of resource distribution than single variables. Because the degree of democracy is assumed to depend on the degree of resource distribution, correlations between combined indices and political variables should be higher than those between single explanatory variables and political variables. There is also a systematic difference in the strength of correlations between the two basic political variables and the Index of Democratization (ID). On average, the two basic political variables are not as strongly correlated with explanatory variables than ID. The arithmetic mean of eleven correlations for Competition was 0.478 in 1993, for Participation 0.481 and for ID 0.592. My explanation for this clear difference is that the combination of the two basic political variables is a better indicator of democratization than either of the two basic political variables alone. Competition alone is not enough to measure the degree of democratization. It is better to also take into account the variation in the degree of electoral participation.

Let us next examine the strength of relationships between single explanatory variables and the three political variables. The correlations of Urban Population, NAP, Students and Literates with the three political variables are nearly the same. In most cases, however, ID is more strongly correlated with explanatory variables than either of the two basic political variables. Contrary to the first research hypothesis, the correlations of FF with the three political variables are very weak. How to interpret such results? Do they falsify the first research hypothesis? Should we regard Family Farms as a useless explanatory variable? I am not ready to do so. In the longitudinal comparison group, its correlations with the three political variables are nearly as high as those of IOD and IKD. Its low correlations in this comparison group are probably due to structural imbalances in African countries in particular. The values of Family Farms are so high for most African countries that they presuppose democracy, whereas the values of other explanatory variables are low. According to my interpretation, Family Farms is favourable for democracy in Africa, too, but it alone is not enough to produce democracy or to maintain it. The situation is the opposite in several East European countries where the values of Family Farms are still low, although the values of the four first explanatory variables are highly favourable for democracy. Because of these structural imbalances, the correlations of FF with the three political indicators are near zero, but it does not mean that the distribution of agricultural land would have lost its significance as a factor of democratization.

DD is more highly correlated with Competition and ID than any of the other single explanatory variables (see Table 3.4). How to interpret its exceptionally high correlations? Are they due to the fact that data on the degree of decentralization of non agricultural economic resources (DD) are more often based on my estimations than on hard empirical data? Have my estimations been biased? It is difficult to know whether my estimations have been biased to support the hypothesis or not because we cannot check them by objective empirical data. I can only say that I tried to make estimations as objectively as possible on the basis of available information. I also want to point out that DD is only one of the six explanatory variables and that data on DD are not used in the combined indices of resource distribution directly. DD is combined with FF into an Index of the Distribution of Economic Power Resources (DER), and this sectional index is used in the combined indices.

The six explanatory variables were combined into three sectional indices of resource distribution (IOD, IKD and DER) in order to decrease possible errors and biases in single variables. I assumed that the arithmetic mean of two variables measuring the same dimension of resource distribution may be a better indicator of resource distribution than either of the two variables alone. The correlations of IOD and IKD with the three political variables are clearly higher than those of the third sectional index DER. The relatively low correlations of DER are the results of very weak correlations of FF and relatively strong correlations of DD. The three sectional indices are intended to measure the distribution of politically relevant power resources from three different perspectives. The explained part of variation in ID varied from 22 per cent (DER) to 44 per cent (IKD) in 1993.

The three sectional indices were combined into the Index of Power Resources (IPR) and the Index of Power Resources and Structural Imbalance (IPRI) in order to increase the explained part of variation. The results of correlation analysis support this assumption as indicated above. Let us now examine whether there are any significant differences in the explanatory power of the two combined indices of power resources. In the cases of Competition and Participation, there does not seem to be any significant difference in the explanatory power of IPR and IPRI. According to the first research hypothesis, the highest correlations should appear between the combined indices of resource distribution and ID. The results of correlation analysis support this assumption. The correlations between the two combined indices and ID are higher than any other correlations between explanatory and political variables. The explained part of variation in ID varies from 59 to 65 per cent. Thus the results of empirical analysis support the assumption based on theoretical arguments, according to which the multiplication of the three sectional indices would produce a more powerful explanatory variable. Because the correlations between ID and the two variations of IPR were nearly the same in 1991–3, it was not possible to increase the explained part of variation in ID by combining IPR and ISI (IPRI). Therefore, I can still use the original simple IPR as the principal explanatory variable.

When the six basic explanatory variables are used together in multiple regression to explain the variation in ID, the explained part of variation is 68 per cent for 1991, 65 per cent for 1992, and 62 per cent for 1993. These percentages are slightly higher than in the cases of IPR and IPRI. The three sectional indices explain together in multiple regression 65 per cent of the variation in ID in 1991, 62 per cent in 1992, and 59 per cent in 1993, or approximately as much as IPR and IPRI. These results indicate that the use of multiple regression does not increase the explained part of variation in the degree of democratization.

In this cross-sectional comparison group, the explained part of variation in ID in 1991 was approximately as high as in the longitudinal comparison group of 1850–1991, but the strength of correlations decreased in 1992 and 1993. The correlation between ID and IPR decreased from 0.808 in 1991 to 0.768 in 1993. The difference in the explained part of variation is 6 percentage points. Should we conclude that the dependence of the degree of democracy on the degree of resource distribution is decreasing in the 1990s? I would not like to make such a conclusion. It is more probable that the weakening of this relationship in 1992 and 1993 is only a temporary phase produced by the sudden breakthrough of democracy in Eastern Europe in 1989–92 and in several countries of sub-Saharan Africa in 1991–3. The great economic reforms that have already started in Eastern Europe may help to re-establish a better balance between the level of democracy and the degree of resource distribution in a few years. It is more difficult to say what is going to happen in many new democracies in sub-Saharan Africa. We shall return to this problem in the next chapter. However, I do not exclude the possibility that the validity of some of my political and explanatory variables has decreased. For example, the percentage of literates ceases to measure differences in the distribution of intellectual power resources when it approaches 100 per cent in most countries.

The testing of the first research hypothesis by empirical evidence did not falsify the hypothesis. On the contrary, moderate and strong correlations between political and explanatory variables support the hypothesis on the positive relationship between the degree of democracy and the degree of resource distribution. Correlations between the combined indices of explanatory variables and ID are so strong that they provide a relatively reliable basis to make predictions on the chances of democracy in single countries and regions of the world. Regression analysis will disclose how single countries and decennial observation units are related to the average pattern of relationship between IPR and ID. Because of strong correlation between IPR and ID, we can expect that most of the observation units will be near the regression line, although there will also be deviating cases. It will be interesting to see what countries deviate most from the regression line and what countries clearly contradict the second research hypothesis.

GNP PER CAPITA AND HUMAN DEVELOPMENT INDEX (HDI)

The examination of alternative theoretical approaches to explain democratization (chapter 2) led me to the conclusion that the Lerner–Lipset economic development hypothesis or the wealth theory of democratization provides the best empirical point of comparison for my Darwinian theory of democratization. Now my intention is to test the explanatory power of Lerner–Lipset hypothesis by correlating my three political variables in 1991, 1992 and 1993 with GNP per capita in 1991 or around 1991 (see Table 3.5). GNP per capita was selected to indicate the variation in economic development or wealth because it has been used as the principal explanatory indicator in studies testing the Lerner–Lipset hypothesis (see, for example, Diamond 1992). Nearly all of my data on GNP per capita are from *World Development Report 1993* (year 1991) and *Human Development Report* (year 1990). In the cases of Albania, Croatia, Slovenia, Cuba, Afghanistan, Iraq, Kuwait, Lebanon, Angola, Djibouti, Liberia, Myanmar, Brunei, North Korea, Mongolia, Taiwan (ROC), and Vietnam, data are from *Third World Guide 93/94* and for Libya from *World Development Report 1991*. In the lack of empirical data, I had to estimate GNP per capita for Macedonia (1,600) and Yugoslavia (1,600). It should be noted that statistical data on GNP per capita are only very rough estimations in most cases and that GNP per capita measures more the commercial value of goods and services produced than the wealth or welfare of nations (see Dogan 1994: 43–6).

The correlations between GNP per capita in 1991 and my political variables in 1991–3 given in Table 3.5 confirm the Lerner–Lipset hypothesis on

Table 3.5 Competition, Participation and ID in 1991, 1992 and 1993 correlated with GNP per capita in 1991 and Human Development Index 1990 in the comparison group of 172 countries

Political variable/Year	GNP per capita 1991	Human Development Index 1990
Competition		
1991	0.449	0.580
1992	0.399	0.556
1993	0.387	0.512
Participation		
1991	0.403	0.595
1992	0.410	0.644
1993	0.397	0.653
Index of Democratization		
1991	0.617	0.669
1992	0.583	0.679
1993	0.571	0.664

the positive relationship between democracy and the level of economic development or wealth, but these correlations are much weaker than the corresponding correlations in Table 3.4. The explained part of variation in ID varies from 33 per cent in 1993 to 38 per cent in 1991. It is more than 20 percentage points less than in the correlations between IPR and ID in 1991, 1992 and 1993 in the same comparison group of 172 countries (see Table 3.4). In other words, the explanatory power of GNP per capita is much weaker than the explanatory power of my Index of Power Resources. Correlations between GNP per capita and Competition and Participation are also significantly weaker than corresponding correlations in Table 3.4. Besides, I would like to argue that the observed positive relationship does not contradict my theory on the causal relationship between democracy and resource distribution because GNP per capita can be regarded as an indirect indicator of resource distribution, too. It is reasonable to assume that the higher the GNP per capita is, the more widely economic power resources are usually, although not always and not systematically, distributed among the population.

Figure 3.1 gives the results of regression analysis of ID-93 on GNP per capita in 1991 for single countries in the comparison group of 172 countries. It shows that the relationship between ID and GNP per capita is not strong and that it is not possible to determine any level of GNP per capita under which democracy is impossible. In fact, about half of the contemporary democracies seem to be poor countries. I think that it is difficult to argue on the basis of Figure 3.1 that democracy is possible only in relatively wealthy countries, although it is true that democracy definitely has better chances in wealthy than in poor countries. *The Economist* (27 August 1994), however, concludes that the correlation between political freedom and prosperity is a close one. Mick Moore (1995) also argues for the prosperity theory of democracy.

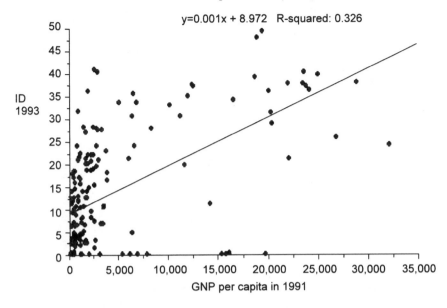

Figure 3.1 The results of regression analysis of ID-93 on GNP per capita in 1991 for single countries in the comparison group of 172 countries

Multiple regression can be used to disclose to what extent GNP per capita could explain the variation in ID independently from IPR. This can be done by using IPR and GNP per capita together as independent variables and ID-93 as the dependent variable. Together IPR and GNP per capita explained 59.5 per cent of the variation in ID in 1993 in the cross-sectional comparison group of 172 countries, whereas IPR alone explained 59 per cent of the variation in ID-93. This means that by using GNP per capita as an independent variable in addition to IPR we are able to increase the explained part of variation in ID only marginally (0.5 percentage points). Therefore, it seems to me that it is not necessary to take GNP per capita into account separately because its explanatory power is already included in IPR. GNP-91 is moderately correlated with my explanatory variables. Correlations vary from 0.435 (FF) to 0.621 (IOD). The correlation between GNP-91 and IPR is 0.798, which means that their covariation is 64 per cent.

Larry Diamond argues that the Human Development Index (HDI), formulated by the United Nations Development Program (UNDP) (1991), would be a better development indicator than GNP per capita. According to his analysis, the HDI shows a substantially higher correlation (0.71) with the combined index of political freedom than does per capita GNP (0.51) (Diamond 1992: 100–2). He comes to the conclusion that 'the contribution of economic development to democracy is substantially mediated through improvements in the physical quality of life' (Diamond 1992: 107). Jan-Erik Lane and Svante Ersson present similar arguments on the relationship between democracy and the human development index, although they also stress the significance of affluence and the structure of the economic system. (Lane and Ersson 1994: 214–18). It is interesting to see whether the explanatory power of HDI is as high or higher than that of IPR and to what extent HDI can increase the explained part of variation in ID when it is used as an independent variable together with IPR. The data on the Human Development Index (1990) used in this analysis are from *Human Development Report 1993*. It gives data on 167 countries of this comparison group. Because it did not give data on five countries, I had to make estimations: Croatia (800), Macedonia (700), Slovenia (800), Yugoslavia (700), and Taiwan (ROC) (800).

Let us first see to what extent HDI is correlated with my explanatory variables and how much it can statistically explain of the variation in ID. HDI-90 is strongly correlated with my first four explanatory variables (Urban Population 0.762, NAP 0.876, Students 0.746 and Literates 0.904) in the cross-sectional comparison group of 172 countries, whereas it is completely independent from Family Farms (0.019) and only moderately correlated with DD (0.498). Following the same pattern, its correlations with IOD (0.856) and IKD (0.910) are strong, whereas it is nearly independent from DER (0.099). Its correlation with IPR is 0.702, which means that their covariation is not more than 49 per cent. Table 3.5 shows that HDI-90 is more strongly correlated with my political indicators than GNP per capita. The explained part of variation in ID varies from 44 to 46 per cent, which is approximately 10 percentage points more than in the case of GNP per capita. In this point the results of this analysis and those of Diamond's (1992) are nearly the same, although he used a different indicator to measure the degree of democracy (Freedom House data on political rights and civil liberties in 1990) and although his comparison group was smaller (142 countries). However, the explained part of variation in ID-93 is still 15 percentage points less than in the case of IPR. I think that its clearly weaker explanatory power is mainly due to the fact that HDI does not take into account differences in resource distribution as directly as my Family Farms and DD variables do.

Figure 3.2 illustrates the results of regression analysis of ID-93 on HDI-90 in this comparison group of 172 countries. The regression line of ID-93 on HDI crosses the ID threshold of democracy (5.0) approximately at the HDI level of 300 index points. It means that, on the average, when a country reached the HDI level of 300 index points, it was assumed to cross the ID threshold of democracy, too. We can see from Figure 3.2 that many of the countries below the HDI level of 300 index points are also below the ID level of 5.0 index points as hypothesized and that many of the countries above the HDI level of 300 index points are also above the ID level of 5.0 index points. There are, however, numerous deviating cases. It is true that, as Diamond argues, we can predict the nature of a country's political system more accurately on the basis of HDI than on the basis of GNP per capita, but the number of deviating cases still remains high.

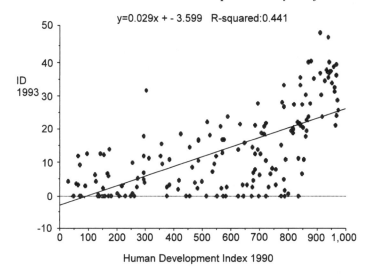

Figure 3.2 The results of regression analysis of ID-93 on HDI-90 for single countries in the comparison group of 172 countries

Because HDI and IPR differ from each other, it is reasonable to expect that together they could explain more of the variation in ID than either one alone. Multiple regression can be used to test this assumption. When HDI and IPR are used together as the independent variables, the explained part of variation in ID-93 increases from 59 to 62 per cent. It means that when HDI is added to IPR, the explained part of variation in ID increases approximately 3 percentage points. IPR includes the major part of its explanatory power just as in the case of GNP per capita. An increase of 3 percentage points is not insignificant, but I have to leave HDI out of my statistical analysis because I am not sure how it is related to my theoretical explanation of democratization. Larry Diamond argues that the more well-to-do the people of a country, on average, the more likely they will favour, achieve, and maintain a democratic system for their country (Diamond 1992: 109). I would like to argue that well-to-do people are more likely to 'favor, achieve, and maintain a democratic system for their country' than less well-to-do people because they have more resources to take part in politics and defend their interests. Attitudes become adapted to social circumstances. When most people and their groups have resources to defend their interests, it becomes necessary to make compromises in the struggle for power. Democracy emerges from the necessity of compromises.

REGRESSION ANALYSIS

The second research hypothesis, according to which all countries tend to cross the threshold of democracy at about the same level of IPR, can be tested by regression analysis. The Index of Democratization (ID) will be used as the dependent variable. Its value of 5.0 index points was defined as a minimum threshold of democracy. The other threshold values are 30 per cent for Competition and 15 per cent for Participation. Usually a country that has crossed 5.0 ID index points has also crossed the two other minimum thresholds of democracy, but there are several cases in which such a country is still below the minimum threshold of Competition or Participation. Therefore it is necessary to check whether a country above the threshold of 5.0 ID index points is also above the thresholds of Competition and Participation.

The Index of Power Resources (IPR) will be used as the principal explanatory variable, but the results produced by it will be compared with those produced by the Index of Power Resources and Structural Imbalance (IPRI). The problem is how to define 'at about the same level of IPR'. According to the hypothetical regression equation (ID est. $= 0 + 1.0 \times$ IPR) given in the previous chapter, 5.0 IPR index points represents the average transition level of IPR. Because ID and IPR are nearly at the same scale (the arithmetical mean of ID is 6.911 and that of IPR 7.289 in the comparison group of 1850–1993), observation units should cross, on the average, the threshold of democracy approximately at the IPR level of 5.0 index points. However, because the correlation between ID and IPR is not complete, it is reasonable to accept some variation around the average IPR level of transition. The actual regression equation of ID on IPR can help us to define the range of the transition level of IPR. The standard error of estimate of Y on X can be used to guide the definition of the transition level of IPR, although, ultimately, I have to define the range of the transition level arbitrarily.

I shall focus on the regression equations of ID on IPR and of ID on IPRI in the longitudinal comparison group of 1,139 observation units, although the corresponding regression equations have been calculated in the cross-sectional comparison group of 172 countries (1993), too. Because IPR and IPRI are very highly intercorrelated (see Tables 3.1 and 3.3), the results of regression analyses for single countries will be approximately the same irrespective of the combined index used as the independent variable. In some cases, however, results may differ significantly. Therefore it is useful to compare the results of the two regression analyses. These regression equations and standard errors of estimate are given in Table 3.6.

In this chapter, I introduce the results of regression analyses and test the second research hypothesis by them. We shall see to what extent the 1,139 observation units of the period 1850–1995 were above or below the transition level of IPR and IPRI as hypothesized and which countries contradicted the hypothesis. The results of regression analyses are given for all the observation units since the 1850s, but I focus on the contemporary 172 countries of the period 1991–3. In the next chapter, the results will be used to evaluate the chances of democracy and democratization in single contemporary countries.

Table 3.6 Regression equations of Y on X and standard errors of estimate in the two comparison groups of 1850–1993 (N = 1,139) and 1993 (N = 172)

Regression equation	Standard error of estimate
Comparison group of 1850–1993 (N = 1,139)	
ID est. = 1.482 + 0.745 × IPR	6.107
ID est. = −0.145 + 0.734 × IPRI	6.177
Comparison group of 1993 (N = 172)	
ID est. = 4.607 + 0.662 × IPR	8.138
ID est. = 2.295 + 0.681× IPRI	8.077

Because my evolutionary theory of democratization presupposes that democratization has taken place in similar conditions since the 1850s at least, it is theoretically more reasonable to test the research hypothesis by empirical evidence covering all observation units since the 1850s than by cross-sectional evidence from only one point of time. Therefore I shall formulate research hypotheses on the conditions of democratization on the basis of the longitudinal empirical evidence.

In the longitudinal comparison group of 1850–1993, the regression line of ID on IPR crosses the ID level of 5.0 index points at the IPR level of 4.8, which differs only slightly from the hypothetical IPR level of 5.0 index points. The standard error of estimate of ID on IPR is 6.1. Let us select arbitrarily 1/2 of one standard error of estimate to define the range of the transition level of IPR. It means that the transition level of IPR will extend 1.5 IPR index points around the average 4.8. Thus 'at about the same level of IPR' means IPR values from 3.3 to 6.3 IPR index points. Countries are expected to cross the threshold of democracy at this level of resource distribution. Now the second research hypothesis given in chapter 2 (see p. 63) can be restated in a more exact form. It is hypothesized that:

2.1 All countries above the upper limit of the IPR level of transition (6.3) tend to be democracies, and all countries below the lower limit of transition (3.3) tend to be non democracies.

Figure 3.3 illustrates the results of regression analysis calculated in the longitudinal comparison group of 1,139 observation units. In this figure, the transition level of IPR from 3.3 to 6.3 index points is indicated by vertical lines and the ID threshold of democracy (5.0 ID index points) by a horizontal line. According to the research hypothesis 2.1, all countries above the transition level of IPR (6.3 index points) should be democracies and all countries below the transition level of IPR (3.3 index points) should be non democracies. We can see from Figure 2.1 that most observation units were democracies or non democracies as expected in the period 1850–1993, but there were also numerous deviating cases. The countries below the ID threshold of democracy and above the upper limit of the transition level of IPR (6.3) can be regarded as deviating non democracies. They were

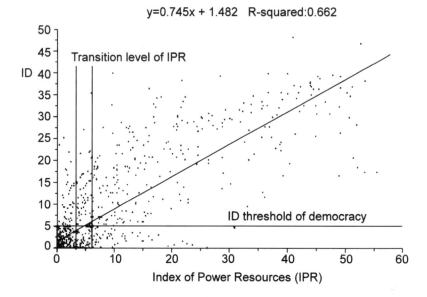

Figure 3.3 The results of regression analysis of ID on IPR for single countries in the longitudinal comparison group of 1,139 observation units, 1850–1993

expected to be democracies because of their relatively high IPR values, but they had failed to cross the threshold of democracy. The countries above the ID threshold of democracy (5.0 index points) and below the lower limit of the transition level of IPR (3.3) can be regarded as deviating democracies. Contrary to the research hypothesis, they had crossed the threshold of democracy in spite of their relatively low IPR value. The problem is how to explain the emergence of so many deviating democracies and non democracies.

When IPRI is used as the independent variable, the regression line of ID on IPRI in the longitudinal comparison group of 1,139 observation units crosses the ID level of 5.0 index points at the IPRI level of 7.0. It is a higher level than in the case of IPR because IPRI is a combination of IPR and 1/4 of ISI. The arithmetic mean of IPRI is 9.6 in the comparison group of 1850–1993. The standard error of estimate of ID on IPRI (6.177) is nearly the same as in the case of IPR. Consequently, the transition level of IPRI can be defined to extend 1.5 IPRI index points around the average 7.0, or from 5.5 to 8.5 index points, and the second research hypothesis given in chapter 2 (see p. 63) gets the following form:

2.2 All countries above the upper limit of the IPRI level of transition (8.5) tend to be democracies, and all countries below the lower limit of transition (5.5) tend to be non democracies.

Figure 3.4 illustrates the results of regression analysis of ID on IPRI in this comparison group. Just as in Figure 3.3, vertical lines approximately

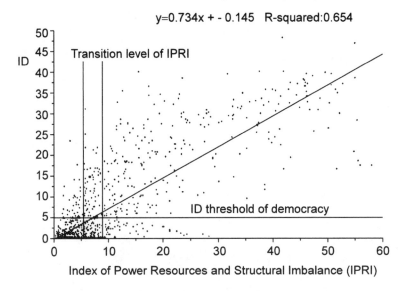

y=0.734x + - 0.145   R-squared:0.654

Index of Power Resources and Structural Imbalance (IPRI)

Figure 3.4 The results of regression analysis of ID on IPRI for single countries in the comparison group of 1,139 decennial observation units, 1850–1993

indicate the transition level of IPRI from 5.5 to 8.5 index points and a horizontal line the ID threshold of democracy. Figure 3.4 shows that most countries were democracies or non democracies as expected, but there were many deviating non democracies (below ID threshold of democracy and above the transition level of IPRI) and deviating democracies (above the ID threshold of democracy and below the transition level of IPRI), too. Deviating non democracies and democracies contradict the research hypothesis 2.2, but the number of correctly predicted democracies and non democracies is many times higher than the number of deviating cases. Empirical evidence supports the second research hypothesis, although not without exceptions.

The patterns of regression line are different in the cross-sectional comparison group of 172 countries in 1993. In the 1990s, several countries crossed the threshold of democracy at a considerably lower level of IPR and IPRI than earlier. The arithmetic mean of ID was 13.57 in 1993 and the arithmetic means of IPR and IPRI were 13.54 and 16.56 respectively. Consequently, it has become impossible to establish any lower limit of IPR below which countries should be non democracies. The regression line of ID-93 on IPR crosses the ID threshold of democracy (5.0 index points) at the IPR level of 0.7 index points. Because the standard error of estimate of ID-93 on IPR is 8.1, we could define the transition level of IPR to extend 2.0 IPR index points around the the average 0.7, or from −1.3 to 2.7 IPR index points. It means that there cannot be any cases below the lower limit of the transition. This transition level differs greatly from the hypothetical one and from the transition level based on the regression equation in the longitudinal comparison group. I assume that the regression equation of ID on IPR in the longitudinal comparison group indicates better the true relationship between the level of democracy and the degree of resource distribution and provides a theoretically more reliable ground for predictions than relationships in a cross-sectional comparison group of 1991–3. Therefore, I shall use the results of longitudinal regression analyses. The results of the regression analysis in the cross-sectional comparison group for single countries in 1993 are given in Figure 3.5, but the transition level of IPR indicated in this Figure is the same as in Figure 3.3.

When IPRI is used as the independent variable in the cross-sectional comparison group of 172 countries, the regression line of ID-93 on IPRI crosses the level of 5.0 ID index points approximately at the IPRI level of 4.0. One standard error of estimate of ID-93 on IPRI is 8.1. Consequently, we could define the transition level of IPRI to extend 2.0 index points around the average 4.0, or from 2.0 to 6.0 IPRI index points. The results of regression analysis of ID-93 on IPRI are given in Figure 3.6. We can see from this Figure that if we were to use 2.0 IPRI index points as the lower limit of transition, only two countries would be below that limit. It means that the transition level of IPRI would be unable to differentiate the countries in which the degree of resource distribution is too low to establish democracy. Many countries crossed the threshold of democracy at a very low level of IPR and IPRI in the beginning of the 1990s, but I assume that it has been exceptional and that the transition level of IPR and IPRI will rise

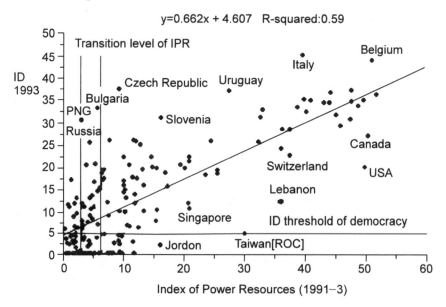

Figure 3.5 The results of regression analysis of ID-93 on IPR for single countries in the cross-sectional comparison group of 172 countries in 1993

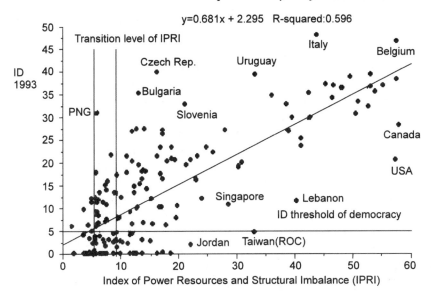

Figure 3.6 The results of regression analysis of ID-93 on IPRI in the cross-sectional comparison group of 172 countries in 1993

later on. I trust more to the results of the longitudinal regression analyses. Therefore I use in Figure 3.6 the same transition level of IPRI as in the Figure 3.4. Most of the countries deviating clearly from the regression line seem to be the same as in Figure 3.5.

It seems justified to conclude on the basis of these four figures that empirical evidence supports the two research hypotheses given above. Countries have tended to cross the threshold of democracy at about the same level of explanatory variables throughout the period 1850–1993. Everywhere the distribution of important power resources has tended to increase the pressure for democratization. It means that it would have been possible to make relatively accurate predictions on the chances of democracy in particular countries on the basis of their IPR or IPRI values. Numerous deviating cases of the past indicate, however, that such predictions would not have been correct in all cases. Because correlations between ID and the principal explanatory variables are not complete, there is room for random variation and for variation caused by other relevant factors, which are not taken into account by my explanatory variables. We should explore data on each country in greater detail and particularly data on deviating countries.

Figures 3.3–3.6 include complete data on the results of four regression analyses, but it is difficult to recognize single observation units from these figures. Therefore, the exact results of the regression analyses for the contemporary 172 countries are given in Table 3.7. Besides, the results of the regression analysis of ID on IPR in the longitudinal comparison group are

Table 3.7 The results of regression analysis of ID on IPR and of ID on IPRI in the longitudinal comparison group of 1,139 observation units of the period 1850–1993 for the sub-group of 172 countries in 1993

Country/Region	C-93	P-93	ID-93	IPR	Residual: ID	Predicted: ID	IPRI	Residual: ID	Predicted: ID
Europe and North America									
1 Albania	32	24	7.7	4.2	3.1	4.6	7.2	2.6	5.1
2 Armenia	41	45	18.4	7.0	11.7	6.7	13.7	8.5	8.9
3 Austria	59	60	35.4	40.1	4.0	31.4	40.8	5.6	29.8
4 Belarus	19	34	6.5	2.0	3.5	3.0	11.6	−1.9	8.4
5 Belgium	76	62	47.1	52.8	6.3	40.8	55.4	6.6	40.5
6 Bulgaria	60	59	35.4	5.9	29.5	5.9	12.7	26.2	9.2
7 Canada	59	48	28.3	52.1	−12.1	40.3	55.8	−12.5	40.8
8 Croatia	49	54	26.5	13.1	15.3	11.2	16.6	14.5	12.0
9 Czechoslovakia	66	61	40.3	9.7	31.6	8.7	15.6	29.0	11.3
10 Denmark	63	63	39.7	49.3	1.5	38.2	51.1	2.4	37.3
11 Estonia	59	30	17.7	10.4	8.5	9.2	16.2	6.0	11.7
12 Finland	63	58	36.5	45.5	1.1	35.4	46.5	2.5	34.0
13 France	63	49	30.9	47.4	−5.9	36.8	48.7	−4.7	35.6
14 Georgia	43	46	19.8	6.6	13.4	6.4	12.6	10.7	9.1
15 Germany	63	59	37.2	42.4	4.1	33.1	45.0	4.3	32.9
16 Greece	53	66	35.0	34.1	8.1	26.9	34.7	9.7	25.3
17 Hungary	57	48	27.4	12.4	16.7	10.7	16.5	15.4	12.0
18 Iceland	61	61	37.2	51.3	−2.5	39.7	53.2	−1.7	38.9
19 Ireland	61	49	30.0	37.6	0.5	29.5	38.1	2.2	27.8
20 Italy	70	69	48.3	41.0	16.3	32.0	42.1	17.6	30.7
21 Latvia	51	21	10.5	10.5	1.2	9.3	16.4	−1.4	11.9
22 Lithuania	47	50	23.5	10.4	14.3	9.2	16.2	11.8	11.7
23 Luxembourg	68	55	37.4	41.2	5.2	32.2	43.7	5.5	31.9
24 Macedonia	49	25	12.2	12.3	1.6	10.6	14.7	1.6	10.6
25 Malta	48	69	33.1	33.9	6.4	26.7	37.2	6.0	27.1
26 Moldova	16	50	8.0	3.4	4.0	4.0	9.3	1.3	6.7
27 Netherlands	64	60	38.4	53.5	−2.9	41.3	55.3	−2.0	40.4
28 Norway	63	57	35.9	50.4	−3.1	39.0	51.8	−2.0	37.9
29 Poland	53	37	19.6	17.5	5.1	14.5	20.5	4.7	14.9
30 Portugal	39	53	20.7	20.8	3.7	17.0	21.2	5.3	15.4
31 Romania	55	50	27.5	8.0	20.1	7.4	12.3	18.6	8.9
32 Russia	60	45	27.0	4.6	22.1	4.9	11.5	18.7	8.3
33 Slovenia	56	59	33.0	16.7	19.1	13.9	20.2	18.3	14.7
34 Spain	61	60	36.6	44.5	2.0	34.6	46.2	2.9	33.7
35 Sweden	62	63	39.1	45.7	3.6	35.5	47.8	4.2	34.9
36 Switzerland	79	30	23.7	38.8	−6.7	30.4	39.6	−5.2	28.9
37 Ukraine	38	57	21.7	4.0	17.2	4.5	10.6	14.1	7.6
38 UK	58	58	33.6	46.6	−2.6	36.2	49.1	−2.3	35.9
39 USA	53	39	20.7	51.5	−19.1	39.8	55.2	−19.6	40.3
40 Yugoslavia	46	45	20.7	16.0	7.3	13.4	18.6	7.2	13.5
Latin America and the Caribbean									
41 Argentina	44	49	27.0	33.4	0.6	26.4	37.5	−0.4	27.4
42 Bahamas	45	43	19.3	26.4	−1.8	21.1	29.2	−2.0	21.3
43 Barbados	50	47	23.5	21.6	5.9	17.6	23.8	6.2	17.3
44 Belize	45	32	14.4	12.3	3.8	10.6	13.9	4.3	10.1
45 Bolivia	50	21	10.5	9.6	1.9	8.6	12.5	1.5	9.0
46 Brazil	62	33	20.5	13.6	8.9	11.6	17.2	8.0	12.5
47 Chile	42	48	20.2	26.4	−0.9	21.1	29.7	−1.4	21.6
48 Colombia	49	16	7.8	15.8	−5.4	13.2	18.8	−5.8	13.6
49 Costa Rica	49	44	21.6	20.0	5.2	16.4	22.3	5.4	16.2
50 Cuba	0	33	0	4.4	−4.8	4.8	11.7	−8.4	8.4
51 Dom. Rep.	64	26	16.6	13.8	4.8	11.8	16.6	4.6	12.0

Country/Region	C-93	P-93	ID-93	IPR	Residual: ID	Predicted: ID	IPRI	Residual: ID	Predicted: ID
52 Ecuador	57	37	21.1	15.3	8.2	12.9	18.0	8.0	13.1
53 El Salvador	51	20	10.2	10.6	0.8	9.4	12.2	1.4	8.8
54 Guatemala	41	9	3.7	3.8	−0.6	4.3	5.4	−0.1	3.8
55 Guyana	47	38	17.9	6.8	11.4	6.5	10.5	10.3	7.6
56 Haiti	0	0	0	4.2	−4.6	4.6	6.2	−4.4	4.4
57 Honduras	47	30	14.1	5.0	8.9	5.2	7.2	9.0	5.1
58 Jamaica	40	26	10.4	13.8	−1.4	11.8	15.9	−1.1	11.5
59 Mexico	44	24	10.6	15.9	−2.7	13.3	19.0	−3.2	13.8
60 Nicaragua	45	37	16.6	10.4	7.4	9.2	13.2	7.1	9.5
61 Panama	48	45	21.6	11.4	11.6	10.0	15.6	10.3	11.3
62 Paraguay	57	24	13.7	4.7	8.7	5.0	8.5	7.6	6.1
63 Peru	53	31	16.4	17.9	1.6	14.8	22.1	0.3	16.1
64 St Lucia	43	43	18.5	11.8	8.2	10.3	13.3	8.9	9.6
65 St Vincent	34	40	13.6	10.8	4.1	9.5	11.9	5.0	8.6
66 Suriname	31	21	6.5	11.4	−3.5	10.0	14.9	−4.3	10.8
67 Trinidad & T.	55	41	22.5	21.6	4.9	17.6	24.8	4.5	18.0
68 Uruguay	62	64	39.7	28.5	17.0	22.7	32.0	16.4	23.3
69 Venezuela	71	27	19.2	24.3	−0.4	19.6	29.2	−2.1	21.3

North Africa, the Middle East and Central Asia

70 Afghanistan	0	0	0	2.5	−3.3	3.3	5.3	−3.7	3.7
71 Algeria	0	0		8.0	−7.4	7.4	11.2	−8.1	8.1
72 Azerbaijan	6	52	3.1	2.1	0.1	3.0	8.8	−3.2	6.3
73 Bahrain	0	0	0	12.1	−10.5	10.5	17.8	−12.9	12.9
74 Cyprus	57	48	27.4	25.3	7.1	20.3	26.9	7.8	19.6
75 Egypt	12	20	2.4	8.7	−5.6	8.0	9.9	−4.7	7.1
76 Iran	31	30	9.3	7.8	2.0	7.3	11.1	1.3	8.0
77 Iraq	0	0	0	8.6	−7.9	7.9	13.1	−9.5	9.5
78 Israel	65	53	34.4	41.7	1.9	32.5	44.7	1.8	32.6
79 Jordan	22	9	2.0	16.5	−11.8	13.8	21.1	−13.3	15.3
80 Kazakhstan	3	50	1.5	2.2	−1.6	3.1	9.0	−5.0	6.5
81 Kuwait	19	2	0.4	9.7	−8.3	8.7	16.6	−11.6	12.0
82 Kyrgyzstan	5	48	2.4	1.8	−0.4	2.8	8.3	−3.5	5.9
83 Lebanon	73	16	11.7	36.3	−16.8	28.5	38.8	−16.6	28.3
84 Libya	0	0	0	8.3	−7.7	7.7	13.2	−9.5	9.5
85 Mauritania	26	23	6.0	3.3	2.1	3.9	5.6	2.0	4.0
86 Morocco	39	11	4.3	9.4	−4.2	8.5	11.5	−4.0	8.3
87 Oman	0	0	0	3.1	−3.8	3.8	4.8	−3.4	3.4
88 Qatar	0	0	0	10.0	−8.9	8.9	15.6	−11.3	11.3
89 Saudi Arabia	0	0	0	8.2	−7.6	7.6	12.0	−8.7	8.7
90 Sudan	0	0	0	1.7	−2.7	2.7	3.6	−2.5	2.5
91 Syria	17	40	6.8	11.0	−2.9	9.7	13.3	−2.8	9.6
92 Tajikistan	6	50	3.0	1.7	0.3	2.7	7.7	−2.5	5.5
93 Tunisia	10	26	2.6	11.9	−7.7	10.3	14.4	−7.8	10.4
94 Turkey	58	21	12.2	21.4	−5.2	17.4	23.1	−4.6	16.8
95 Turkmenistan	5	50	2.5	0.8	0.4	2.1	6.8	−2.3	4.8
96 UAR	0	0	0	6.1	−6.0	6.0	12.2	−8.8	8.8
97 Uzbekistan	9	50	4.5	1.9	1.6	2.9	8.3	−1.4	5.9
98 Yemen	29	10	2.9	4.4	−1.9	4.8	6.6	−1.8	4.7

Sub-Saharan Africa

99 Angola	23	18	4.1	2.2	1.0	3.1	3.3	1.8	2.3
100 Benin	56	22	12.3	2.1	9.3	3.0	4.9	8.9	3.4
101 Botswana	35	20	7.0	5.9	−1.1	5.9	7.0	2.0	5.0
102 Burkina Faso	33	11	3.6	0.6	1.7	1.9	5.3	−0.1	3.7
103 Burundi	13	17	2.2	1.1	−0.1	2.3	5.5	−1.7	3.9
104 Cameroon	55	21	11.5	5.3	6.1	5.4	6.6	6.8	4.7
105 Cape Verde	29	29	8.4	5.1	3.1	5.3	6.0	4.1	4.3

Table 3.7 (contd.)

Country/Region	C-93	P-93	ID-93	IPR	Residual: ID	Predicted: ID	IPRI	Residual: ID	Predicted: ID
104 Central A.R.	53	23	12.2	3.3	8.3	3.9	5.6	8.2	4.0
107 Chad	0	0	0	2.1	−3.0	3.0	5.3	−3.7	3.7
108 Comoros	39	25	9.7	2.5	6.4	3.3	3.6	7.2	2.5
109 Congo	44	35	15.4	6.0	9.4	6.0	7.0	10.4	5.0
110 Côte d'Ivoire	12	19	2.3	4.7	−2.7	5.0	5.0	−1.9	4.2
111 Djibouti	19	15	2.8	2.3	−0.4	3.2	9.5	−4.0	6.8
112 Eq. Guinea	1	20	0	2.8	−3.6	3.6	3.8	−2.6	2.6
113 Ethiopia	0	0	0	2.3	−3.2	3.2	5.1	−3.6	3.6
114 Gabon	49	33	16.2	6.3	10.0	6.2	7.5	10.8	5.4
115 Gambia	36	25	9.0	1.8	6.2	2.8	5.8	4.9	4.1
116 Ghana	24	19	4.6	7.0	−2.1	6.7	8.9	−1.8	6.4
117 Guinea	24	17	4.1	1.3	1.6	2.5	3.5	1.7	2.4
118 Guinea-Biss.	0	0	0	2.0	−3.0	3.0	5.5	−3.9	3.9
119 Kenya	55	21	11.5	3.8	7.2	4.3	5.7	7.5	4.0
120 Lesotho	12	14	1.7	4.2	−2.9	4.6	7.1	−3.4	5.1
121 Liberia	0	0	0	1.9	−2.9	2.9	3.7	−2.6	2.6
122 Madagascar	38	29	11.0	4.8	5.9	5.1	7.2	5.9	5.1
123 Malawi	0	0	0	1.7	−2.7	2.7	3.9	−2.7	2.7
124 Mali	33	9	3.0	1.6	0.3	2.7	5.3	−0.7	3.7
125 Mauritius	52	53	27.6	12.0	17.2	10.4	13.5	17.8	9.8
126 Mozambique	0	0	0	1.0	−2.2	2.2	1.9	−1.2	1.2
127 Namibia	21	24	5.0	2.2	1.9	3.1	4.9	1.6	3.4
128 Niger	43	27	11.6	1.2	9.2	2.4	4.9	8.2	3.4
129 Nigeria	0	0	0	4.9	−5.1	5.1	6.9	−4.9	4.9
130 Rwanda	0	40	0	1.1	−2.3	2.3	5.5	−3.9	3.9
131 São Tomé	32	29	9.3	4.7	4.3	5.0	5.7	5.3	4.0
132 Senegal	42	15	6.3	2.6	2.9	3.4	4.3	3.3	3.0
133 Sierra Leone	0	0	0	1.9	−2.9	2.9	5.1	−3.6	3.6
134 Somalia	0	0	0	1.9	−2.9	2.9	4.4	−3.1	3.1
135 South Africa	52	6	3.1	9.5	−5.5	8.6	13.1	−6.4	9.5
136 Swaziland	0	0	0	3.8	−4.3	4.3	4.8	−3.4	3.4
137 Tanzania	2	21	0.4	2.4	−2.9	3.3	4.5	−2.8	3.2
138 Togo	2	28	0.6	3.0	−3.1	3.7	5.2	−3.1	3.7
139 Uganda	0	0	0	1.9	−2.9	2.9	5.5	−3.9	3.9
140 Zaire	0	0	0	5.4	−5.5	5.5	6.5	−4.6	4.6
141 Zambia	25	15	3.7	5.7	−2.0	5.7	6.1	−0.6	4.3
142 Zimbabwe	12	27	3.2	3.5	−0.9	4.1	4.4	0.1	3.1
South Asia									
143 Bangladesh	49	28	13.7	2.5	10.4	3.3	6.2	9.3	4.4
144 Bhután	0	0	0	0.6	−1.9	1.9	3.5	−2.4	2.4
145 India	55	32	17.6	5.4	12.1	5.5	9.0	11.1	6.5
146 Maldives	8	28	2.2	9.7	−6.5	8.7	10.8	−5.6	7.8
147 Nepal	46	26	12.0	0.9	9.8	2.2	5.9	7.8	4.2
148 Pakistan	52	13	6.8	3.5	2.7	4.1	5.9	2.6	4.2
149 Sri Lanka	49	32	15.7	10.5	6.4	9.3	12.8	6.5	9.2
East Asia and Southeast Asia									
150 Brunei	0	0	0	3.9	−4.4	4.4	9.5	−6.8	6.8
151 Cambodia	27	22	5.9	0.4	4.1	1.8	1.5	4.9	1.0
152 China	0	0	0	3.5	−4.1	4.1	4.4	−6.8	6.8
153 Indonesia	16	25	4.0	10.1	−5.0	9.0	11.1	−4.0	8.0
154 Japan	67	38	25.5	37.4	−3.8	29.3	39.5	−3.3	28.8
155 Korea, North	0	25	0	1.1	−2.3	2.3	7.2	−5.1	5.1
156 Korea, South	60	50	30.0	38.8	−0.4	30.4	41.0	0.1	29.9
157 Laos	0	45	0	2.6	−3.4	3.4	4.2	−2.9	2.9
158 Malaysia	48	31	14.9	10.4	5.7	9.2	11.8	6.4	8.5

Country/Region	C-93	P-93	ID-93	IPR	Residual: ID	Predicted: ID	IPRI	Residual: ID	Predicted: ID
159 Mongolia	42	49	20.6	7.0	13.9	6.7	11.6	12.2	8.4
160 Myanmar	0	0	0	7.7	−7.2	7.2	8.3	−5.9	5.9
161 Philippines	67	35	23.4	15.1	10.7	12.7	18.1	10.3	13.1
162 Singapore	39	28	10.9	21.6	−6.7	17.6	27.4	−9.0	19.9
163 Taiwan	20	23	4.6	31.1	−20.0	24.6	31.8	−18.6	23.2
164 Thailand	39	16	6.2	12.9	−4.9	11.1	17.0	−6.1	12.3
165 Vietnam	0	53	0	2.7	−3.5	3.5	5.0	−3.5	3.5
Oceania									
166 Australia	55	59	32.4	49.0	−5.6	38.0	50.8	−4.7	37.1
167 Fiji	57	32	18.2	12.6	7.3	10.9	13.1	8.7	9.5
168 New Zealand	65	57	37.0	49.3	−1.2	38.2	51.1	−0.3	37.3
169 Papua N.G.	80	39	31.2	3.3	27.3	3.9	5.8	27.1	4.1
170 Solomon Is.	55	33	18.1	1.4	15.6	2.5	5.6	14.1	4.0
171 Vanuatu	59	37	21.8	5.6	16.1	5.7	7.9	16.1	5.7
172 W. Samoa	45	28	12.6	7.6	5.5	7.1	9.6	5.7	6.9

given for the 967 decennial observation units of the period 1850–1980 in Appendix 5, whereas the complete results of the regression analysis of ID on IPRI are given only in Figure 3.4. It should be noticed that the results given in Table 3.7 are based on the longitudinal regression equations of the period 1850–1993, not on the cross-sectional regression equations of the year 1993. It means that the relationship between political and explanatory variables is expected to follow the same pattern in the 1990s as in earlier decades since the 1850s. I assume that it is possible to evaluate and predict the chances of democracy in particular countries on the basis of the relationship between the level of democracy and the degree of resource distribution observed in the period 1850–1993. When important power resources are distributed among the many, we can expect the emergence of democracy, and when they are concentrated in the hands of the few, we can expect the emergence of autocratic political systems. This basic relationship seems to have remained relatively stable throughout the period of comparison since the 1850s.

The data given in Table 3.7 disclose how accurately the degree of democratization in 1993 followed the average pattern of relationship between ID and IPR and between ID and IPRI over the period 1850–1993 in single countries. First, the actual values of the three political variables (Competition, Participation and the Index of Democratization) in 1993 are given for each country in Table 3.7. The next three columns include the results of the regression analysis of ID on IPR. The actual value of IPR is given for each country and after that the residual and predicted value of ID produced by the regression equation of ID on IPR. A predicted value of ID indicates what the level of ID should be according to the regression equation of ID on IPR. The regression line of ID on IPR indicates the predicted values of ID (see Figure 3.3). A residual is the difference between the actual value of ID and the predicted value of ID. It indicates the vertical distance between an actual value of ID and the regression line. Positive residuals indicate that the level of democracy in 1993 was higher than expected. Negative residuals indicate that the level of democracy was lower than expected. The smaller the residual of a single country is, the more accurately it was possible to predict its degree of democratization on the basis of the regression equation of ID on IPR. The last three colums include the corresponding results of the regression analysis of ID on IPRI.

Countries contradicting the second research hypothesis

The results of the two regression analyses test the research hypotheses 2.1 and 2.2, according to which all countries are expected to cross the threshold of democracy at about the same level of resource distribution as expressed by IPR and IPRI. We can see directly from the data given in Table 3.7 which countries were democracies or non democracies as hypothesized in 1993 and which countries contradicted the research hypotheses. Table 3.8 summarizes the results of regression analyses from the perspective of the two research hypotheses. Democracies and non democracies are cross-tabulated by the three levels of IPR and IPRI given in research hypotheses. The transition levels of IPR and IPRI respectively are used to divide the continuum into three levels. According to the second research hypothesis, countries above the upper limit of the transition level tend to be democracies, and countries below the lower limit of transition tend to be non democracies. We can see from Table 3.8 to what extent empirical evidence confirmed or contradicted the research hypotheses 2.1 and 2.2. It should be noticed that all three threshold values, not only the ID threshold of 5.0 index points, have been taken into account in the classification of countries into democracies and non democracies. It means that some countries with ID values 5.0 or higher (Belarus, Moldova, Mauritania, Syria, Cape Verde, Namibia, Pakistan, and Cambodia) are regarded as non democracies because

Table 3.8 Democracies and non democracies cross-tabulated by the transition level of IPR and IPRI respectively in the sub-group of 172 countries in 1993

Political system	IPR above 6.3		IPR 3.3–6.3		IPR below 3.3		Total
	N	%	N	%	N	%	N
Democracies	76	80.8	17	50.0	8	18.2	101
Non democracies	18	19.2	17	50.0	36	81.8	71
Total	94	100.0	34	100.0	44	100.0	172
	IPRI above 8.5		IPRI 5.5–8.5		IPRI below 5.5		
	N	%	N	%	N	%	
Democracies	80	76.2	17	47.2	4	12.9	101
Non democracies	25	23.8	19	52.8	27	87.1	71
Total	105	100.0	36	100.0	31	100.0	172

their value of Competition or Participation was below the threshold value of democracy (30 per cent for Competition and 15 per cent for Participation).

Table 3.8 shows to what extent the countries above the upper transition limit of IPR or IPRI were democracies and those below the lower limit of transition non democracies in 1993. According to IPR, our principal explanatory variable, 80.8 per cent of the countries above the IPR upper limit of transition (6.3) were democracies as hypothesized and 81.8 per cent of the countries below the IPR lower limit of transition (3.3) were non democracies as hypothesized. These results support the second hypothesis, although numerous deviating cases contradict it. Table 3.8 shows that 19.2 per cent of the countries above the IPR level of transition were, contrary to the hypothesis 2.1, non democracies and 18.2 per cent of the countries below the IPR lower limit of transition were, contrary to the hypothesis 2.1, democracies. It was not possible to predict the nature of political systems at the transition level of IPR. In fact, 50 per cent of them were democracies and 50 per cent non democracies in 1993. The number of deviations is significant, but not high enough to falsify the second research hypothesis. Because the relationship between IPR and ID is not complete, some deviating cases are inevitable.

According to IPRI, 76.2 per cent of the countries above the upper IPRI limit of transition level (8.5) were democracies as expected and 87.1 per cent of the countries below the lower limit of transition level (5.5) were non democracies as expected. The percentage of deviating non democracies was 23.8 and of deviating democracies 12.9. These results differ in some points from those based on IPR. The number of deviating non democracies (25) is significantly higher than in the case of IPR (18), whereas the number of deviating democracies is much smaller (4). In most points, the results support the hypothesis 2.2. As expected, most countries were democracies or non democracies.

From the perspective of my theory, it would be interesting to know whether the deviating cases are permanent or only temporary. The cross-sectional data of 1993 do not answer this question, but we can find an answer from the longitudinal data given in Appendix 5. My previous longitudinal study (Vanhanen 1984a) indicated that usually deviations lasted not more than one or two decades. Therefore, it is reasonable to assume that the deviating cases of 1993 are also temporary. We can expect that deviating democracies drop below the ID threshold of democracy, or they cease to be deviations, when their IPR values rise. In the case of non democracies, we can expect that they rise above the threshold of democracy, or they cease to be deviations, if their IPR values decrease. However, it is not self-evident in which way a particular deviating country will achieve a better balance between the degree of resource distribution and the degree of democratization.

In this chapter, I focus on deviating non democracies and democracies. Prospects for democracy in all countries will be discussed in greater detail in the next chapter. Let us now see what were the deviating democracies and non democracies in 1993 and how seriously they contradicted the research hypotheses. It is reasonable to assume that the countries deviating both on the basis of IPR and IPRI are more seriously deviating cases than countries that deviate only on the basis of IPR or IPRI. We should also take into account the size of residuals. If the residuals of a deviating country are small, let us say less than one standard error of estimate (6.1 in both cases), it can be regarded as a less seriously deviating case than a country whose residuals are larger because its actual value of ID differs only relatively little from the regression line. Consequently, the deviating democracies and non democracies indicated in Table 3.8 are classified into two main categories in Table 3.9: (1) complete deviations and (2) partial deviations. Complete deviations include the countries that contradict the second research hypothesis both on the basis of IPR and IPRI and whose both residuals are, in addition to this, larger than one standard error of estimate. Partial deviations include the countries that contradict the second research hypothesis both on the basis of IPR and IPRI but whose residuals are smaller than one standard error of estimate, as well as the countries that contradict the second research hypothesis only on the basis of IPR or IPRI.

Table 3.9 shows that the number of complete deviations was relatively small in 1993. Only three African countries (Benin, Comoros, and Niger) were deviating democracies according to all three criteria defined above, and all of them are quite recent deviations. It is interesting to see whether democratic institutions become stabilized in these countries. My explanatory variables predict the failure of democracy in these countries. Ten other countries (Algeria, Bahrain, Iraq, Jordan, Kuwait, Libya, Qatar, Saudi Arabia, Taiwan and Tunisia) were deviating non democracies according to all three criteria given above. It is remarkable that all of them, except Taiwan (ROC), are Muslim countries of the Middle East and North Africa. It is difficult to avoid an assumption that Muslim culture is in some way related to the delaying of democratization in these countries. Of course, it is also possible that my explanatory indicators have not been able to take into account some important aspects of power resources in these Muslim countries. It is remarkable that nearly all these Muslim countries are oil producing countries. It may be that as a consequence of the control of oil resources important economic and coercive power resources are more highly concentrated in the hands of the governments than I have estimated (see Appendix 4). However, on the basis of the explanatory indicators used in this study, I have to predict democratization in these Muslim countries. The process of democratization has already started in some of them, in Algeria, Jordan, Kuwait, and Tunisia, in particular. Taiwan (ROC) is a different case. Democratization was delayed in Taiwan because of its special political situation and continual conflict with mainland China.

The number of partial deviations is higher. Senegal is a deviating democracy because its IPR and IPRI values are below the lower limits of the transition levels of IPR and IPRI, but because its residuals are very small

Table 3.9 Deviating democracies and non democracies divided into the two main categories of complete and partial deviations in 1993

1 Complete deviations

A. *Deviating democracies* (IPR below 3.3, IPRI below 5.5, and both residuals larger than 6.1)	B. *Deviating non democracies* (IPR above 6.3, IPRI above 8.5, and both residuals larger than 6.1)
Benin Comoros Niger	Algeria Bahrain Iraq Jordan Kuwait Libya Qatar Saudi Arabia Tunisia Taiwan (ROC)

2 Partial deviations

IPR below 3.3 and IPRI below 5.5, but one or both residuals smaller than 6.1	IPR above 6.3 and IPRI above 8.5, but one or both residuals smaller than 6.1
Senegal	Egypt Morocco Syria Ghana South Africa Maldives Indonesia

Only IPR below 3.3	Only IPR above 6.3
Gambia Bangladesh Nepal Solomon Islands	Myanmar (Burma)

Only IPRI below 5.5	Only IPRI above 8.5
	Belarus Moldova Cuba Azerbaijan Kazakhstan United Arab Emirates Djibouti Brunei

(2.9 and 3.3 respectively), it cannot be regarded as a seriously deviating case. In fact, its actual level of democracy differs only slightly from the predicted one. The same concerns deviating non democracies Egypt,

Morocco, Syria, Ghana, South Africa, Maldives, and Indonesia, which remained below the threshold of democracy, although they should have been democracies on the basis of their IPR and IPRI values. Residuals were relatively small for all of them in 1993, which means that the actual level of democracy did not differ much from the predicted one. Five of these seven countries are Muslim countries. So we come again to the question of the possible role of Muslim culture. I have to predict democratization in all these countries. Some democratic institutions already exist in all of them. In Ghana the struggle for democracy continues and may lead to the crossing of the threshold of democracy very soon. South Africa crossed the threshold of democracy in the 1994 parliamentary elections.

Gambia, Bangladesh, Nepal, and the Solomon Islands were highly deviating democracies on the basis of IPR but not on the basis of IPRI in 1993. In these poor countries, the distribution of agricultural land seems to be the only structural factor supporting democracy clearly. It is questionable whether it alone is enough to maintain democratic institutions. The failure of democracy is possible in all these countries, although it does not need to be inevitable. A military coup ended one-party dominated democracy in Gambia in 1994. Myanmar (Burma) is a deviating non democracy on the basis of its IPR value (7.0) but not on the basis of its IPRI value. The pressure for democratization is strong in Myanmar, but its military governments have, until now, been able to suppress democratic movements. I have to predict democratization in Myanmar because of its IPR value and because its neighbouring countries India, Bangladesh, and Thailand have been able to cross the threshold of democracy.

Eight other countries (Belarus, Moldova, Cuba, Azerbaijan, Kazakhstan, the United Arab Emirates, Djibouti and Brunei) are deviating non democracies only on the basis of their relatively high IPRI values. Moldova crossed the threshold of democracy in the 1994 parliamentary elections (see IPU 1993–4), and Belarus approached the threshold in the 1994 presidential and the 1995 parliamentary elections (see Keesing's 1994: 40109; 1995: 405678). It is reasonable to expect democratization in Cuba on the basis of its IPRI value. The other five deviating non democracies are again Muslim countries. According to their IPR values, power resources are still so highly concentrated that democratization is not inevitable, whereas their IPRI values indicate that some power resources are distributed sufficiently widely to support democratization. The concentration of economic power resources constitutes the major obstacle for democratization.

According to my interpretation, empirical evidence has not falsified the research hypotheses 2.1 and 2.2 because approximately 80 per cent of the countries were democracies or non democracies in 1993 as hypothesized. It means that most countries have tended to cross the threshold of democracy at about the same level of resource distribution across all cultural and regional differences. On the one hand, deviating cases indicate that my explanatory variables have not been able to explain the existence or lack of democracy in all single cases. On the other hand, they provide a basis to predict democratization or failures of democracy. The major purpose of this study is to explore to what extent the variation of the degree of democracy can be explained by the few universal explanatory variables selected on the basis of the evolutionary theory of democratization. The strong regularity in the relationship between the degree of democracy and the degree of resource distribution provides an empirical ground for predictions.

Countries with extremely large residuals

The actual values of nearly all countries deviate more or less from the regression lines of ID on IPR and ID on IPRI. Because the relationship between ID and the explanatory variables is not complete, some deviations are inevitable. Residuals measure the size of deviations. We do not need to pay attention to relatively small residuals around the regression line. One standard error of estimate separates relatively small deviations from large ones. Usually about 68 per cent of all the cases fall in the interval between one standard deviation above the mean and one standard deviation below it. In the longitudinal comparison group, one standard error of estimate is 6.1 in the regression equation of ID on IPR and 6.2 in the regression equation of ID on IPRI (see Table 3.6). This means that the level of democracy in countries with residuals less than 6.1 and 6.2 respectively was approximately in balance with the degree of resource distribution. We should pay attention to countries with residuals larger than one standard error of estimate. However, because the number of such countries is relatively large (about 30 per cent) and because some of the large deviations may be due to measurement errors and various accidental factors, it is better to focus on the most extreme residuals in this connection.

Two standard errors of estimate (12.2 and 12.4 respectively) separate the most extreme residuals from other large ones. Normally about 95 per cent of the cases fall between two standard errors of estimate above and below the regression line. It should be noticed that all countries with extremely large residuals do not need to contradict the research hypotheses 2.1 and 2.2. A country, for example, may have a very large positive or negative residual but still remain a democracy as hypothesized. A country with a large positive residual contradicts the second research hypothesis only if its IPR is below the lower transition level of IPR (3.3) or its IPRI below the lower transition level of IPRI (5.5). A country with a very large negative residual contradicts the second research hypothesis only if its IPR is above 6.3 or IPRI above 8.5 and if its ID is below 5.0 index points. Therefore, we have to separate countries with extremely large deviations from the regression line from the countries that contradict the second research hypothesis. They may be, but do not need to be, the same countries. The countries with residuals larger than two standard errors of estimate are given in Table 3.10.

Table 3.10 The countries deviating from the regression lines of ID on IPR and ID on IPRI more than two standard errors of estimate on the basis of the longitudinal regression equations (1850–1993) in 1993

ID on IPR *Residuals larger than 12.2*	ID on IPRI *Residuals larger than 12.4*
Extremely large positive residuals	
Bulgaria	Bulgaria
Croatia	Croatia
Czech Republic	Czech Republic
Georgia	–
Hungary	Hungary
Italy	Italy
Lithuania	–
Romania	Romania
Russia	Russia
Slovenia	Slovenia
Ukraine	Ukraine
Uruguay	Uruguay
Mauritius	Mauritius
Mongolia	–
Papua New Guinea	Papua New Guinea
Solomon Islands	Solomon Islands
Vanuatu	Vanuatu
Extremely large negative residuals	
–	Canada
United States	United States
–	Bahrain
–	Jordan
Lebanon	Lebanon
Taiwan (ROC)	Taiwan (ROC)

We can see from Table 3.10 that only four (the Solomon Islands, Bahrain, Jordan, and Taiwan) of the twenty-three countries with extremely large residuals are the same as listed in Table 3.9. The Solomon Islands is an extremely deviating democracy and Bahrain, Jordan, and Taiwan highly deviating non democracies. The other nineteen countries of Table 3.10 are democracies as expected, but they deviate greatly from the regression lines. The level of democracy as measured by the Index of Democratization is much lower than expected in Canada, the United States, and Lebanon, whereas it is much higher than expected in the other sixteen countries. The problem is why they deviate so much from the regression line.

It may be that the high negative residuals of Canada and the United States are in some way connected with their electoral systems that have reduced the level of electoral participation and the number of relevant parties. The values of IPR and IPRI are extremely high for both countries. In Lebanon, the heritage of the civil war since 1975 and the country's complicated electoral system may explain the very low degree of electoral participation in the 1992 parliamentary elections.

The other sixteen democracies with extremely large positive residuals constitute a heterogeneous group of countries, but it is remarkable that eleven of them are former socialist countries (Bulgaria, Croatia, the Czech Republic, Georgia, Hungary, Lithuania, Romania, Russia, Slovenia, Ukraine, and Mongolia). The adoption of democratic institutions took place abruptly in these countries, not evolving through gradual changes. Structural changes in their economic systems were started at the same time with political democratization, but it is not possible to change economic structures as quickly as political institutions. Economic power resources were still highly concentrated in 1991 (see Appendices 3 and 4). Consequently, the values of IPR and IPRI remained relatively low for these countries, although the values of the four first explanatory variables were high. This structural imbalance explains the extremely large positive residuals of these countries. I do not expect the decrease of democratization in any of these countries. A better balance will be achieved through economic reforms that distribute the ownership and control of agricultural and non agricultural economic power resources more widely in these societies. The values of FF and DD are now (1995) significantly higher than in 1991 in most of these countries.

The remaining five democracies with extremely large positive residuals (Italy, Uruguay, Mauritius, Papua New Guinea, and Vanuatu) do not have much in common. Italy's large positive residuals may be due to its extremely proportional electoral system and to a civic duty to vote, which have increased the values of Competition and Participation. Uruguay's high positive residuals are due to its exceptionally high level of electoral participation. The system of compulsory voting explains, at least partly, the fact that the level of electoral participation is higher than in any other country of Latin America and that it is one of the highest in the world. Because of these exceptional institutional factors, I do not predict the decrease of democracy in Italy and Uruguay. Mauritius is a more complicated case. Its level of democracy is not exceptionally high. It is approximately the same as in Cyprus, for instance, but because the level of resource distribution is much lower than in Cyprus, positive residuals become high. Mauritius has been the most stabilized democracy in sub-Saharan Africa. The success of democracy in this small island state seems to be connected to the adaptation of its political institutions to the country's ethnically heterogeneous population (see Cziffra 1995). The discrepancy between relatively high values of political variables and low values of explanatory variables is more serious in the cases of Papua New Guinea and Vanuatu than in the previous cases. Although their values of IPR and IPRI are at the transition levels, a partial failure of democratic institutions would not be surprising in these countries. It may be that foreign economic and administrative support has helped to maintain democratic institutions in these countries.

The results of regression analyses given and discussed in this chapter provide detailed information of the relationship between the level of democracy and resource distribution in single countries in 1993. I shall use this information in my attempts to predict the prospects of democracy in single countries in the next chapter.

4 Predictions for single countries by regions

In the previous chapter, two research hypotheses on the conditions of democracy were tested by empirical data covering most independent states of the period 1850–1993. It was found that the major explanatory factor of this study, the distribution of power resources, explained about 66 per cent of the variation in the degree of democracy in the total comparison group of 1,139 decennial observation units. The hypothesized relationship between the level of democracy and the distribution of economic, intellectual and other power resources seems to be very strong and persistent, although it is not complete and leaves room for other factors. I have attempted to explore to what extent the variation in the level of democracy can be explained by one explanatory factor indicating the degree of resource distribution because the finding of a constant relationship could provide a solid basis for predictions.

There are other researchers who assume that causes of democratization vary from place to place, or that they vary over time, which would make it impossible to explain democratization by any single factor (see Diamond, Linz and Lipset 1990; Huntington 1991; Hadenius 1992; Sorensen 1993). They are right to a certain degree because every case has its unique characteristics, but my point is that universal regularities are more important than unique variations. Because I assume that all human populations share the same human nature and evolved behavioural predispositions, it is reasonable to conjecture that there are and must be regularities in political behaviour and also in the formation of political institutions. The Darwinian interpretation of politics, introduced in chapter 1, led me to formulate a theory on the emergence of democracy. It is based on the idea that politics is a part of the general struggle for existence. Therefore the struggle for scarce resources has always been the central theme in politics, although the nature of scarce resources varies greatly. Various resources are used as sanctions in the struggle for power. Power is always based on the control of some effective sanctions. Consequently, the concentration of resources leads to autocratic power structures and the dispersion of effective resources leads to the dispersion of power among several competing groups; it means, ultimately, to democratic power structures. I deduced research hypotheses on democratization from this theoretical argumentation and tested them by empirical evidence. Because empirical evidence since the 1850s has supported my theoretical assumptions on the causal factors of democratization, I dare to conjecture that the same factors will affect the prospect for democracy in the 1990s and even beyond 2000 more than any other factors. Therefore, I shall evaluate the prospects of democracy in single countries on the basis of the assumption that everywhere the concentration of power resources leads to hegemonic political structures and obstructs the establishment of democratic structures, whereas the distribution of important power resources undermines hegemonic political structures and creates favourable conditions for the establishment of democratic power structures.

REGIONAL COMPARISONS

In this chapter, I shall discuss the prospects for democracy in single countries by regional groups. There are significant differences in the assumed conditions of democracy among our seven regional groups. In addition, some regional differences in culture, history, and local factors may affect the chances of democracy. Therefore, it is appropriate to start by comparing regional arithmetic means of political and explanatory variables in 1990–3. They indicate to what extent the average level of democracy and the conditions of democracy varied by region in 1990–3. We can also compare the regional means of residuals produced by regression analyses. They indicate how accurately the average relationship between ID and explanatory variables applied to different regional groups and whether there were any significant differences among regions in the predicted and actual levels of democracy as indicated by ID. Significant differences in the regional arithmetic means of residuals would imply that some regional factors, which are not taken into account by my indicators, affect the relationship between political and explanatory variables. In such cases we should try to find out what those factors might be and whether they are compatible with my theory or contradict it. If there is not much difference in the arithmetic means and directions of residuals, it would imply that cultural, historical, local, and other possible factors do not disturb the relationship between the indicators measuring the levels of democracy and resource distribution. The comparison of regional groups is limited to cross-sectional data in 1990–3. Let us first examine the arithmetic means of variables given in Table 4.1.

Table 4.1 shows that there are considerable regional differences both in the level of democracy and in the conditions of democracy. The average level of democracy (ID) is much above the arithmetic mean of 172 countries in the regions of Europe and North America and of Oceania, whereas it is much below the average in the regions of North Africa, the Middle East and Central Asia and of sub-Saharan Africa. The three other regions are near the arithmetic mean. The same regional differences appear in the conditions of democracy with some variations. The average degree of

Table 4.1 The regional arithmetic means of ID-93 and some explanatory variables in the cross-sectional comparison group, 1990–3

Regional group	N	C-93	P-93	ID-93	IOD	IKD	DER	IPR	IPRI
Europe and North America	40	54.8	58.8	28.4	78.4	69.4	46.4	27.7	31.1
Latin America etc.	29	46.1	32.7	15.8	65.0	58.5	36.5	14.7	17.7
North Africa etc.	29	17.0	21.0	4.8	64.9	46.2	32.3	9.9	13.8
Sub-Saharan Africa	44	22.0	16.5	5.1	31.5	26.6	42.3	3.6	5.8
South Asia	7	37.0	22.7	9.7	27.9	29.1	51.5	4.7	7.7
East Asia and Southeast Asia	16	26.6	27.5	9.1	52.8	53.2	37.8	12.9	15.6
Oceania	7	59.4	40.7	24.5	35.9	49.8	56.9	18.4	20.6
Total	172	35.3	30.2	13.6	56.0	48.7	41.1	13.5	16.6
Period 1850–1980	967	22.3	17.4	5.7	32.5	30.8	31.7	6.2	8.4
Period 1850–1993	1139	24.3	19.3	6.9	36.0	33.5	33.1	7.3	9.6

resource distribution (IPR) is much above the average in Europe and North America and significantly below the average in sub-Saharan Africa and South Asia.

The regional means of IPR and ID correspond quite closely to each other in the regions of Europe and North America, Latin America and the Caribbean, East Asia and Southeast Asia, and Oceania, whereas they are in discrepancy in North Africa, the Middle East and Central Asia. In South Asia and sub-Saharan Africa the average level of democracy is clearly higher (9.7 and 5.1 respectively) than what we could expect on the basis of IPR (4.7 and 3.5 respectively), whereas in North Africa, the Middle East and Central Asia it is much lower (4.8) than what we could expect on the basis of IPR (9.9). How to explain these regional deviations? I think that the three components of IPR provide a partial answer to this problem. The arithmetic mean of DER is very high for South Asia and it is the lowest for the region of North Africa, the Middle East and Central Asia. It may be that the relatively high degree of the distribution of economic power resources (DER) maintains a higher level of democracy in South Asia than what could be expected on the basis of relatively low values of IPR. Correspondingly, the concentration of economic power resources, especially of non agricultural resources, may have supported the survival of hegemonic power structures in many countries of North Africa, the Middle East and Central Asia, as well as in some countries of East Asia and Southeast Asia. However, it is possible that some regional factors not taken into account in my explanatory variables provide better explanations for regional discrepancies than the differences in DER values.

The comparison of the arithmetic means of the period 1990–3 (N = 172) and of the period 1850–1980 (N = 967) discloses the trend of change in the contemporary world. The arithmetic means of ID and IPR were in 1990–3 more than two times higher than in the period 1850–1980. This fact leads to the conclusion that, on the average, social conditions of democracy are now much better than they were in earlier decades. Therefore, it is natural that the number of democracies has also increased. This is my theoretical explanation for the significant increase in the number of democracies since the 1970s. If the same upward trend continues in social conditions of democracy, we can predict that the number of democracies and the level of democracy will also increase in the future (*cf.* Gurr *et al.* 1990).

It is also interesting to compare whether there are significant regional differences in the accuracy of predictions and in the direction of residuals. A residual produced by regression equation of Y on X indicates how much the actual value of Y variable (ID) differs from the predicted value (regression line). A positive residual indicates that the actual value of Y (in this case the level of democracy) is higher than expected on the basis of X variable (in this case the degree of resource distribution). Negative residuals indicate that the level of democracy is lower than expected on the basis of regression equation. Because the regression line represents the average relationship between Y and X variables, the sum of positive and negative residuals is zero. The regional arithmetic means of residuals of the regression equations of ID on IPR and ID on IPRI are given in Table 4.2.

Table 4.2 The regional arithmetic means of residuals of the longitudinal (1850–1993) regression equations of ID on IPR and ID on IPRI for the cross-sectional sub-group of 172 countries in 1993

Regional group	N	ID on IPR residuals	ID on IPRI residuals
Europe and North America	40	6.7	6.2
Latin America and the Caribbean	29	2.4	2.0
North Africa, the Middle East, and Central Asia	29	−3.1	−4.4
Sub-Saharan Africa	44	0.8	0.7
South Asia	7	2.8	2.4
East Asia and Southeast Asia	16	−1.1	−1.4
Australasia and Pacific	7	9.3	9.5
Total	172	2.0	1.6

Table 4.2 indicates the existence of significant regional differences both in the size of arithmetic means and in the direction of residuals. Positive arithmetic means show that the actual level of democracy is, on the average, higher than expected. Correspondingly, negative arithmetic means of residuals indicate that the actual level of democracy is lower than expected. In the total cross-sectional group of 172 countries, the arithmetic means of residuals were positive in 1993. In other words, the level of democracy was higher than expected on the basis of the average pattern of relationship over the period 1850–1993. The average level of democratization was approximately at the expected level in the regional group of sub-Saharan Africa, whereas it was much higher than expected in Europe and North America and in Oceania. It was clearly higher than expected in Latin America and

South Asia and clearly lower than expected in North Africa, the Middle East and Central Asia as well as in East Asia and Southeast Asia.

How to explain regional differences in the arithmetic means of residuals? They may reflect real regional discrepancies that predict, in the case of positive residuals, a decrease in the level of democratization if the values of explanatory variables do not rise, and, in the case of negative residuals, a rise in the level of democratization if the values of explanatory variables do not decrease. Of course, it is also possible that, in the case of positive residuals, my indicators of democratization have exaggerated the real level of democracy or that my indicators of resource distribution have under-estimated the real degree of resource distribution. In the case of negative arithmetic means of residuals, we could make opposite assumptions. How-ever, it is more probable that a major part of regional differences is due to some temporal or regional factors not taken into account in my explanatory variables. For example, large positive residuals of Europe were produced by the sudden emergence of democracy in former socialist countries. It is plausible to expect that these discrepancies will decrease when the values of explanatory variables rise as a consequence of economic reforms started in those countries. In Oceania, large positive residuals are due to discre-pancies in the Pacific island states. I think that explanations based on temporal and regional factors are more reasonable than the assumption that my indicators have systematically exaggerated or underestimated the degree of democracy or resource distribution in certain regional groups. Significant regional differences in arithmetic means of residuals imply that there are regional factors that affect the relationship between the indicators of democratization and resource distribution. Regional factors may be compatible with my theory, or they may be factors that cannot be connected with the theory. The fact that it was not possible to explain 34 per cent of the variation in ID in 1850–1993 by IPR leaves room for regional explanatory factors, too. For example, could we explain the much lower than expected level of democratization in the region of North Africa, the Middle East and Central Asia by some characteristics of Muslim culture?

From the perspective of predictions, significant negative residuals imply that there is potential pressure for democratization, whereas large positive residuals show that the level of democratization is already higher than expected. On the basis of the regional arithmetic means of residuals exam-ined above it is not possible to evaluate the chances of democracy in particular countries, although it is reasonable to assume that the Muslim region of North Africa, the Middle East and Central Asia, as well as East Asia and Southeast Asia, in particular are regions where we can expect the emergence of new democracies in the 1990s and beyond 2000. In the following, I will discuss the chances of democracy in particular countries by regional groups and make several predictions based on the values of explanatory factors and the results of regression analyses.

EUROPE AND NORTH AMERICA

The region of Europe and North America extends from Alaska in North America through Europe to Siberia in Russia. This vast area is presently almost completely populated by Europeans and by peoples who originated from Europe, and it is dominated by Christianity, except Albania and some regions of Russia and the former Yugoslavia. This region has been very heterogeneous politically and economically, but the collapse of socialist systems in Eastern Europe and in the Soviet Union in 1989–91 opened a road toward a greater cultural, political and economic integration and homogeneity. Therefore I thought it sensible to combine these forty countries of the north into the same regional group.

Table 3.7 (chapter 3) indicates that thirty-eight of the forty countries were democracies in 1993, but the level of democracy varies greatly and the conditions of democracy even more. The IPR and IPRI values are much lower for the former socialist countries of Eastern Europe and for the new states established in the area of the former Soviet Union than for the other countries of this region. Table 4.1 shows that the regional arithmetic means of IPR and IPRI are higher for this region than for any other regional group. It means that, on the average, the prospects for democracy are better for the countries of this regional group than in any other part of the world.

Although Europe and North America constitute the core area of democracy in the world, prospects for democracy are not equally favourable in all the countries of the region. The values of some explanatory variables vary considerably from country to country. My predictions on the prospects of democracy for single countries will be principally based on the values of explanatory variables and the results of regression analyses, but in some cases I also take into account other relevant information. Table 3.7 includes data on the three political variables in 1993 and on IPR and IPRI in 1990–1.

Table 4.3 complements this information of political and explanatory variables. It includes data on the six single explanatory variables, the three sectional indices (IOD, IKD and DER) and ISI. Data on single explanatory variables are from Appendices 2–4. In Table 4.3, the forty countries of Europe and North America are divided into two categories by the transition level of IPR (see chapter 3). The categories are: (1) IPR above 6.3 and (2) IPR from 3.3 to 6.3. In both categories, countries are listed in alphabetical order. According to the second research hypothesis, the countries of the first category should be democracies, whereas the countries at the transition level of resource distribution (the second category) can be either democracies or non democracies. This hypothesis and the two IPR categories, together with data on single explanatory variables and IPRI and ISI, provide the general basis for my predictions on the prospects of democracy in particular countries.

Table 4.3 shows that thirty-four of the forty countries are in the category IPR above 6.3, which means that they should already be democracies. In fact,

Table 4.3 Values of explanatory (1990–1) variables in 40 countries of Europe and North America

Country	UP	NAP	Stu	Lit	FF	DD	IOD	IKD	DER	ISI
1 IPR above 6.3										
Armenia	68	89	41	93	40	10	78.5	67.0	13.3	26.7
Austria	58	94	53	99	62	70	76.0	76.0	69.5	2.9
Belgium	97	97	55	99	95	70	97.0	77.0	70.7	10.3
Canada	77	97	100	99	66	60	87.0	99.5	60.2	14.7
Croatia	56	78	29	93	75	20	67.0	61.0	32.1	14.2
Czechoslovakia	77	91	24	97	10	20	84.0	60.5	19.1	23.6
Denmark	85	95	56	99	85	70	90.0	77.5	70.7	7.1
Estonia	71	91	33	96	20	20	81.0	64.5	20.0	23.4
Finland	60	92	67	99	98	70	76.0	83.0	72.2	4.0
France	74	95	60	99	83	70	84.5	79.5	70.6	5.1
Georgia	56	86	38	93	40	10	71.0	65.5	14.2	24.0
Germany	85	96	56	99	70	60	90.5	77.5	60.4	10.5
Greece	62	76	39	93	91	70	69.0	66.0	75.0	2.5
Hungary	61	88	19	97	20	30	74.5	58.0	28.8	16.6
Iceland	91	93	41	99	74	80	92.0	70.0	79.6	7.6
Ireland	57	86	52	99	68	70	71.5	75.5	69.7	2.2
Italy	69	93	50	97	55	70	81.0	73.5	68.9	4.4
Latvia	71	91	34	96	20	20	81.0	65.0	20.0	23.6
Lithuania	69	90	35	96	20	20	79.5	65.5	20.0	23.3
Luxembourg	84	96	30	99	96	70	90.0	64.5	71.0	9.9
Macedonia	50	70	22	90	75	20	60.0	56.0	36.5	9.6
Malta	87	96	18	87	83	70	91.5	52.5	70.5	13.3
Netherlands	89	96	64	99	94	70	92.5	81.5	71.0	7.2
Norway	75	95	67	99	98	70	85.0	83.0	71.4	5.6
Poland	62	79	29	96	76	30	70.5	62.5	39.7	11.7
Portugal	34	84	38	85	44	60	59.0	61.5	57.4	1.5
Romania	53	80	14	95	30	20	66.5	54.5	22.0	17.1
Slovenia	56	86	37	93	75	30	71.0	65.0	36.3	14.1
Spain	78	89	63	97	39	70	83.5	80.0	66.6	6.7
Sweden	84	96	45	99	86	70	90.0	72.0	70.6	8.3
Switzerland	60	96	41	99	94	70	78.0	70.0	71.0	3.3
United Kingdom	89	98	44	99	56	70	93.5	71.5	69.7	10.2
United States	75	98	100	99	54	60	86.5	99.5	59.9	14.7
Yugoslavia	56	78	27	93	75	30	67.0	60.0	39.9	10.4
2 IPR from 3.3 to 6.3										
Albania	35	52	14	85	30	10	43.5	49.5	19.6	12.0
Belarus	67	81	34	95	1	5	74.0	64.5	4.2	28.8
Bulgaria	68	88	42	93	20	10	78.0	67.5	11.2	27.4
Moldova	48	79	25	95	5	10	63.5	60.0	8.9	23.5
Russia	74	80	38	94	5	10	77.0	66.0	9.0	27.8
Ukraine	68	75	34	95	5	10	71.5	64.5	8.7	26.4

all of them were above all the three thresholds of democracy in 1993. My general prediction for the countries of this category is that they have good chances to maintain democratic structures, although the social precondi- tions of democracy vary significantly. The other six European countries are at the transition level of IPR. Four of them are democracies, whereas Belarus and Moldova were below the Competition threshold of democracy in 1993. My general prediction for these countries is that democratic systems have good chances to become stabilized because economic and social reforms are diversifying the control of economic and intellectual power resources and the Index of Power Resources will probably cross the upper limit of the transition level of IPR very soon. We can examine the prospects of democracy in single countries in greater detail by regional sub-groups: (1) North America, (2) Western Europe, (3) former socialist countries of Eastern Europe, and (4) new states in the area of the former Soviet Union.

North America

In the two countries of North America (Canada and the United States), social conditions are extremely favourable for democracy. Their IPR values are among the highest in the world. The only problem is that the level of democracy is, according to my indicators, considerably lower than expected. Table 3.7 shows that negative residuals are very large for the United States in particular. They are mainly due to its relatively low level of electoral participation. I have argued that a major part of the exceptionally low level of electoral participation in the United States can be explained by its plurality system in elections, which excludes many minority groups from electoral politics (see Vanhanen 1991b: 135–59).

Of course, one could argue that some other democratic characteristics of its political system compensate for a low level of electoral participation and that, consequently, my indicators of democratization underrate the real level of democracy in the United States. Robert W. Jackman and Ross A. Miller (1995) assume that the high frequency of elections in Switzerland and the United States could explain their exceptionally low turnout. It may be a partial explanation, but I still think that a very low level of electoral participation implies a serious fault in the American democracy.

Western Europe

The sub-group of Western Europe includes nineteen countries. Social conditions are very favourable for democracy in all these countries. It is sensible to predict that democracy will survive in these countries because of their high level of resource distribution. They are not problematic countries from the perspective of democracy, although Greece, Portugal and Spain have been democracies only about twenty years. Residuals are small for most West European countries, which indicates that the level of democracy is in balance with the degree of resource distribution. Only Italy had large positive residuals in 1993.

Although the level of democracy seems to be in balance with the degree of resource distribution in Western Europe, it does not exclude the possibility of significant changes in the nature of democratic rule. I want to pay attention to three new dimensions of democratization in Western Europe.

1   The use of referendums has become more frequent. Governments have allowed voters to make important political decisions through referendums, which represent a new dimension of democratization. My indicators of electoral competition and participation are not able to measure this dimension of democracy. In Switzerland referendums have played a significant role in democratic politics since the last century. Therefore I would like to argue that the level of democracy in Switzerland is considerably higher than my variables indicate. Because of the extensive use of referendums in Switzerland, it certainly is one of the most democratic countries in the world. It is an example for other countries of Western Europe. It may be that referendums provide a major outlet for the pressure of democratization in the future.

2   The striving of women to share political power with men on terms of equality constitutes an important new dimension of democratization especially in Western Europe but also in other parts of the world. It is true that women have already acquired universal franchise in nearly all countries of the world on equal terms with men, but they are still greatly underrepresented in parliaments and other institutions using political and economic power (see Vanhanen 1984b; Haavio-Mannila *et al.* 1985; Lovenduski 1986). It might be possible and reasonable to complement the Index of Democratization (ID) by using the percentage of elected women in parliaments as the third basic dimension of democracy.

3   Another new dimension of democratization is connected with the need to democratize the governmental structures of the European Union. The political integration of Western Europe within the framework of the European Union makes it necessary to share power between national governments and the institutions of the European Union. The problem is how to establish an acceptable balance between the powers of national governments and the EUs institutions and how to make the institutions of the EU more directly responsible to European voters (see Arter 1993).

Former socialist countries of Eastern Europe

The collapse of socialist systems in Eastern Europe in 1989–91 was not predicted by my major explanatory variable IPR. Its values of 1980 indicated that the concentration of political power was in good balance with the concentration of power resources as indicated by IPR (see Vanhanen 1990a) in most of those countries. Poland and Yugoslavia were exceptions. The bulk of agricultural land had remained in private ownership throughout the socialist period in these two countries. This failure to anticipate the collapse of hegemonic political systems in Eastern Europe and in the Soviet Union was partly due to my decision to use only one combination of explanatory indicators. If I had used alternative combinations of explanatory variables

(Mean and IPRI), it would have been possible for me to indicate more clearly the fragile nature of socialist systems at the beginning of the 1980s, if not to predict their collapse and democratization (*cf.* Vanhanen 1984a and 1991a).

In this study, IPRI is used as an alternative combination of explanatory variables to check the predictions based on IPR. I still believe that my explanatory variables provide a fairly reliable basis to make predictions on the chances of democratization, but they leave room for different inter-pretations and for different lines of political action. We should also remem-ber that the establishment and survival of socialist systems depended more on the power resources of the Soviet Union than on the domestic distribu-tion of economic and intellectual power resources in Eastern Europe. When the Soviet Union lost its desire to maintain socialist systems in Eastern Europe, their governments were not any longer able to resist or suppress domestic demands of democratization (*cf.* Waller 1994). According to Thomas Niklasson, the changes in the Soviet Union made the explosion in Eastern Europe come earlier, but an explosion would have come even without Gorbachev because 'there was an internal dynamic in all of the six Eastern and Central European states which led to a situation ripe for radical change' (Niklasson 1994: 217; see also Hyde-Price 1994). The col-lapse of socialist systems led immediately not only to the establishment of democratic political systems but also to various structural changes intended to disperse the control of economic and other power resources. According to my estimations, the values of Family Farms rose to 10–30 per cent in Albania, Bulgaria, Czechoslovakia, Hungary, and Romania, and the values of DD (the degree of decentralization of non agricultural economic resources) from zero or near zero to 10–30 per cent, too. These changes increased the degree of resource distribution and thus improved social conditions of democracy, but extremely high ISI values indicate that struc-tural imbalances continue in Eastern Europe. Structural changes in econ-omy did not precede political system changes in Eastern Europe, but they followed very soon, which indicates a close relationship between the dis-tribution of political power and the distribution of important power resources. Originally the forces behind the pressure for political change resorted more to intellectual power resources and mass power than to the control of economic or coercive power resources.

In 1991, Albania and Bulgaria were still at the transition level of IPR, but both of them were above the threshold of democracy in 1993. According to my estimations, the value of Family Farms had risen to 30 per cent in Albania and 20 per cent in Bulgaria in 1991, and the value of DD to 10 per cent in both countries. These changes in economic power structures are in harmony with democratization. Because economic reforms are continuing in both countries, social conditions are becoming more favourable for democracy. Therefore, I predict the survival of democratic systems in both countries.

For the other eight East European countries, IPR was above 6.3 in 1991, and all of these countries are democracies as hypothesized. Residuals were highly positive for the Czech Republic, Croatia, Hungary, Romania and Slovenia in 1993. A better balance had been achieved in Macedonia, Poland and Yugoslavia. However, considerable differences in residuals may be due to accidental and temporary factors in these countries. New multiparty systems have not yet become stabilized in Eastern Europe, and significant fluctuations are possible in the share of the largest party. Therefore we should not pay too much attention to temporary differences in political indicators. It is enough to observe that multiparty systems have emerged throughout Eastern Europe and that free elections have been organized (for the first free elections, see Kuusela 1994). The transition to market economy and privatization will increase the degree of resource distribution and improve social conditions of democracy. It seems to me that the survival of democracy is secure in the Czech Republic, Hungary, Poland, Romania and Slovenia. The situation may be more problematic in Yugoslavia as well as in Croatia and Macedonia (*cf.* Lewis 1993, who argues that prospects for democracy are better in Czechoslovakia, Hungary and Poland than in the Balkans and in most areas of the former Soviet Union).

In Yugoslavia social conditions have been conducive to democracy since the 1950s (see Appendix 5), but its native communist party (the League of Communists of Yugoslavia) was strong enough to maintain its hegemony acquired through a civil war in the 1940s until the breakdown of communist rule in the other parts of Eastern Europe in 1989–90. In Spain General Franco's Falangist Movement was similarly capable of defending its hegemony obtained through a civil war in the 1930s until the 1970s. The process of democratization started in Yugoslavia from its republics and led to the emergence of independence movements in all republics outside Serbia. Slovenia, Croatia, Macedonia and Bosnia–Herzegovina declared their independence in 1991 despite the resistance of Yugoslavia's federal government and Serbia. Armed conflicts with Yugoslavia's federal army and civil wars between ethnic groups followed independence in all republics, except in Macedonia. Bosnia–Herzegovina is excluded from this study because it disintegrated completely in ethnic wars and in wars with Yugoslavia (Serbia) and Croatia. In Croatia, Macedonia and Slovenia free elections were held already in 1990, whereas free parliamentary elections were not organized at the federal level before the dissolution of the federal state. The first competitive parliamentary elections were held in Yugoslavia (including Serbia and Montenegro) in 1992. The values of most explanatory variables for Croatia, Macedonia and Slovenia are the same as for the former united Yugoslavia because I did not find separate data on those new states. According to my variables, the degree of resource distribution is high enough to support competitive political structures. My prediction is that all these states are capable of maintaining democratic political systems despite serious ethnic conflicts.

New states of the former Soviet Union

Just as in Yugoslavia, the process of democratization in the Soviet Union led to the dissolution of the former federal state. Since the October Revolution in 1917 and the civil war in 1918–22, the communist party had ruled the ethnically heterogeneous state and held it together by force. When the communist hegemony started to break down in the latter half of the 1980s, ethnically-based opposition movements and parties emerged in all republics. After the failed coup in August 1991, the Communist Party of the Soviet Union was dissolved, and all fifteen union republics became independent. The Soviet Union ceased to exist. Of the new independent states, Armenia, Belarus, Estonia, Georgia, Latvia, Lithuania, Moldova, Russia and Ukraine are included in the regional group of Europe, whereas Azerbaijan, Kazakhstan, Kyrgyzstan, Tajikistan, Turkmenistan and Uzbekistan are included in the regional group of Central Asia. After the collapse of the Soviet Union, the Commonwealth of Independent States was established on 21 December 1991, but CIS is not a state and not even a confederacy.

In five of these countries (Armenia, Estonia, Georgia, Latvia and Lithuania), IPR was above 6.3 in 1991, and all of them are democracies as hypothesized. Four other countries (Belarus, Moldova, Russia and Ukraine) were at the transition level of IPR in 1991. Belarus and Moldova remained below the Competition threshold of democracy in 1993; the other two countries were above all the minimum thresholds of democracy in 1993. My general prediction for the countries of this regional sub-group is that democratic institutions will survive, although multiparty systems have not yet become stabilized.

The three Baltic states – Estonia, Latvia and Lithuania – regained their independence in 1991. The process of democratization, which was connected with their struggle for independence in 1987–91, had already started before independence as a consequence of relatively free parliamentary elections in 1990. The level of democratization was relatively well balanced with the level of resource distribution in 1993, and residuals were positive. Social conditions are favourable for democracy, and they will become even more favourable in the future as a consequence of the transition to market economy and of the process of privatization in agriculture and in non agricultural industries. According to my explanatory variables, democracy is in harmony with social conditions in the three Baltic states. They have good chances to remain democracies.

In Armenia the 1990 parliamentary election was highly competitive. The Armenian Pan-National Movement defeated the hitherto ruling Armenian Communist Party. In 1991 the same party was victorious in the first presidential election. Residuals are large and positive, but a better balance may be achieved in a few years when the value of IPR rises as a consequence of privatization programmes in agriculture and in other industries. Because its

IPR is already 7.0, I predict that a democratic system will become stabilized in Armenia.

In Belarus communists retained power in the 1990 parliamentary election, and a president was elected from the same group in 1991. The presidential and legislative elections in 1994 and 1995 were much more competitive. The privatization process has been very slow in Belarus, but it is dispersing economic resources and thus creating a better environment for competitive politics. My prediction is that democratic institutions will also become stabilized in Belarus.

Politics in Georgia have been violent since independence, but parliamentary and presidential elections in October 1992 seem to have stabilized the situation, although positive residuals were large in 1993. Its IPR is rising as a consequence of privatization programmes, but ethnic civil wars constitute an unpredictable factor. I have to predict the survival of democratic institutions because its IPR value (6.6) is high enough.

Ethnic conflicts between Moldovians and Russians (and Ukrainians) have characterized politics in Moldova since 1990. They led to a separatist movement of Russians and Ukrainians, who established the Transdnestr Moldavian Soviet Socialist Republic in 1991. The nationalist Popular Front of Moldova was victorious in the 1990 parliamentary elections, although 80 per cent of the elected candidates were members of the communist party. Because of a low level of Competition (11.0), Moldova remained below the threshold of democracy in 1993. Its IPR is still at the transition level (3.4), but if privatization continues in agriculture and in non agricultural industries, its IPR will soon cross the upper limit of transition. Therefore I can predict the success of democratization in Moldova despite its serious ethnic conflicts.

The struggle for democracy still continues in Russia. Communists retained a large majority in the 1990 election, which was only partially free, whereas Boris Yeltsin won over his communist opponents in the presidential election in 1991. After that Yeltsin and the 1990 elected parliament, dominated by communists, struggled for power until October 1993. The values of the first four explanatory variables were not much higher in 1991 than in 1980, but, according to my estimations, the value of Family Farms had risen from zero to 5 per cent and the value of DD from zero to 10. These changes helped IPR to rise from zero to 4.6 index points. The trend of change is toward a market economy and privatization both in agriculture and in other industries. Economic power resources are becoming more widely dispersed among many groups, which is favourable to competitive politics. Russia crossed the threshold of democracy in the parliamentary elections of December 1993. My prediction is that a democratic system will survive in Russia.

Ukraine crossed the threshold of democracy in the 1990 parliamentary and in the 1991 presidential elections. Members of the former communist 'nomenclature' remained in power, but they are challenged by nationalist and other opposition parties. Economic reforms dispersing economic power resources have progressed slowly, but Ukraine is moving toward a market economy. It means that the estimated values of FF (5.0) and DD (10.0) will rise. Therefore I can predict that Ukraine will remain as a democracy.

LATIN AMERICA AND THE CARIBBEAN

The region of Latin America and the Caribbean is geographically compact but culturally and ethnically heterogeneous. Latin America comprises continental countries and some Caribbean islands that earlier belonged to the colonial empires of Spain and Portugal, whereas most of the small Caribbean island states as well as Belize and Guyana are former British colonies. Suriname was a colony of the Netherlands. The original Indian population is still important in several Latin American countries, although most Latin Americans are of mixed racial origins. The descendants of Spanish and Portuguese conquistadors and later European immigrants constitute the politically and economically dominant section of the population in most Latin American countries. In the Caribbean, the majority of the population are descendants of former African slaves or of labourers imported from India. The cultural and ethnic heterogeneity of the population has affected the political and economic systems of this region in many ways. I assume that the sharing of economic resources and political power is more difficult in ethnically heterogeneous societies than in ethnically more homogeneous countries. This factor may have delayed the dispersion of economic and intellectual resources and the process of democratization in Latin America.

The surprising victory of democracy in Latin America in the 1980s was not unexpected from the perspective of resource distribution, for IPR values were high enough to support democracy in nearly all countries (*cf.* Vanhanen 1990a: 123–5). In fact, I predicted democratization in Latin American countries in my studies published in 1975 and 1979. My predictions for single countries were based on the results of regression analyses. The later political history of these countries shows that nearly all predictions were correct (see Vanhanen 1975 and 1979). Table 4.2 discloses that the level of democracy was approximately in balance with the degree of resource distribution in 1993. The regional arithmetic means of residuals were only slightly positive. Therefore I would like to argue that my explanatory theory and variables provide a satisfactory explanation for democracy in Latin America, although Paul Cammack claims, referring to the universal move to democracy in Latin America, that there 'is as little support here as ever for devotees of robust correlations and universal laws' (Cammack 1994: 175–6). Compared to Europe, the arithmetic mean of ID was 12.6 index points lower in this regional group in 1993, but the arithmetic mean of IPR was also 13 index points lower than in Europe. Social conditions are favourable to democracy, although not as favourable as in Europe and North America. There are significant differences between countries both

Table 4.4 Values of explanatory (1990–1) variables in 29 countries of Latin America
and the Caribbean

Country	UP	NAP	Stu	Lit	FF	DD	IOD	IKD	DER	ISI
1 IPR above 6.3										
Argentina	86	90	66	95	22	50	88.0	80.5	47.2	16.4
Bahamas	64	94	39	99	24	50	79.0	69.0	48.4	11.4
Barbados	45	93	33	99	15	50	69.0	66.0	47.5	8.9
Belize	50	63	12	95	25	50	56.5	53.5	40.7	6.4
Bolivia	51	58	39	77	31	30	54.5	58.0	30.4	11.5
Brazil	75	76	21	81	20	40	75.5	51.0	35.2	14.4
Chile	85	87	39	93	23	50	86.0	66.0	46.5	13.2
Colombia	70	73	30	87	32	40	71.5	58.5	37.8	12.1
Costa Rica	47	76	49	93	33	50	61.5	71.0	45.9	9.0
Dominican Rep.	60	64	39	83	30	40	62.0	61.0	36.4	11.2
Ecuador	56	70	39	86	36	40	63.0	62.5	38.8	10.6
El Salvador	44	63	30	73	36	40	53.5	51.5	38.5	6.2
Guyana	35	78	12	96	30	20	56.5	54.0	22.2	14.7
Jamaica	52	73	13	98	39	40	62.5	55.5	39.7	8.6
Mexico	73	70	31	87	32	40	71.5	59.0	37.6	12.3
Nicaragua	60	63	17	81	25	40	61.5	49.0	34.4	11.4
Panama	53	75	44	88	18	30	64.0	66.0	27.0	16.9
Peru	70	65	69	85	24	40	67.5	77.0	34.4	16.8
St Lucia	47	70	6	93	42	40	58.5	49.5	40.6	6.0
St Vincent	27	74	6	98	44	40	50.5	52.0	41.0	4.6
Suriname	47	84	20	95	32	30	65.5	57.5	30.3	13.9
Trinidad and Tobago	69	92	12	96	46	50	80.5	54.0	49.7	12.7
Uruguay	86	86	46	96	27	50	86.0	71.0	46.8	14.1
Venezuela	91	89	57	88	15	40	90.0	72.5	37.2	19.6
2 IPR from 3.3 to 6.3										
Cuba	75	81	46	94	21	5	78.0	70.0	8.0	29.3
Guatemala	39	49	15	55	29	20	44.0	35.0	24.6	6.6
Haiti	28	36	2	53	52	40	32.0	27.5	47.7	8.0
Honduras	44	45	17	73	13	40	44.5	45.0	25.2	8.7
Paraguay	48	54	15	90	15	20	51.0	52.5	17.7	15.1

in the level of democracy and in the social conditions of democracy. Table
4.4, including the same variables as Table 4.3, complements information of
political and explanatory variables given in Table 3.7 and in other parts of
this study. My predictions on the prospects for democracy in single countries are based on the values of explanatory variables and on the residuals of
regression analyses, although I also try to take into account probable
changes in social conditions. The twenty-nine countries of Latin America
and the Caribbean are divided into the same categories by the transition
level of IPR as in Table 4.3.

Latin America and the Caribbean: IPR above 6.3

We can see from Table 4.4 that twenty-four of the twenty-nine countries
were in the category IPR above 6.3 in 1990. All of them were democracies in

1993 as hypothesized. My general prediction is that these countries have good chances of maintaining democratic institutions, although we should note that several of them have been democracies only since the 1980s. Of the Latin American countries, Colombia, the Dominican Republic and Venezuela have been above the threshold of democracy since the 1960s and Costa Rica since the 1920s. The Caribbean states: Bahamas, Barbados, Belize, Jamaica, Trinidad and Tobago, St Lucia, and St Vincent have been democracies since independence (*cf.* Griffin 1993). Democratic institutions have been under serious stress in Colombia (see Hartlyn 1989) and Venezuela (see Levine 1989) in particular, but they have survived. It seems reasonable to predict that democratic institutions will survive in all these countries because their IPR values are sufficiently high.

In the other thirteen countries of this category, democratic institutions were established or re-established at the end of the 1970s or in the 1980s. Social conditions seem to be very favourable for democracy in Argentina, Chile and Uruguay, which means that new, successful, military coups have become improbable in these countries. Social conditions are not as favourable for democracy in Ecuador, Mexico, Panama and Peru, and democratic systems seem to be more fragile in these four countries. Mexico has been above the threshold of democracy only since the 1988 elections (*cf.* Levy 1989), and its status as a democracy is still questionable because of the dominance of the old hegemonic party. Peru experienced a presidential coup in 1992 (see Costa 1993). Despite the fragility of democratic institutions in some of these countries, I have to predict that democracy will survive in all of them because of their relatively high IPR values.

Bolivia, Brazil, El Salvador, Nicaragua, and Suriname have experienced military or other coups and periods of authoritarian rule. Bolivia is a country of innumerable coups and many failed attempts to establish democracy. Therefore it may be hard to believe that democracy has now become stabilized. However, because the level of resource distribution is sufficiently high (IPR 9.6), I have to predict the survival of democracy in Bolivia. In Brazil, social conditions of democracy are only slightly better (IPR 13.6) than in Bolivia, but because both combinations of explanatory variables are clearly above the transition level of democracy (see Table 3.7), I can predict the survival of democracy in Brazil without reservations. In El Salvador and Nicaragua, democracy emerged from prolonged and bitter civil wars. These two countries illustrate my theoretical arguments on the conditions of democracy. When it was impossible for either side to suppress its opponents by force, they ultimately found it more advantageous to compromise and to share power through elections. Democratic compromises emerged from the balance of opponents to resist each other by violent means (*cf.* Prevost 1994). Although democratic institutions have just started to function in these two countries, I predict that democracy will survive because both combinations of explanatory variables are clearly above the transition level of democracy.

In Guyana and Suriname, significant ethnic cleavages have complicated the struggle for democracy. In 1991 Guyana was still below the Competition threshold of democracy, but it crossed it in the 1992 parliamentary election. Its IPR (6.8) is slightly above the upper limit of transition. This means that social conditions are not yet so favourable for democracy that I could predict the survival of democracy without any reservations. In Suriname social conditions seem to be somewhat better (IPR 11.0) for democracy. The country crossed the threshold of democracy in the 1991 parliamentary election. On the grounds of its explanatory variables, I have to predict the survival of democracy.

Latin America and the Caribbean: IPR from 3.5 to 6.5

Five Latin American countries – Cuba, Guatemala, Haiti, Honduras and Paraguay – are still at the transition level of IPR. In 1993, Honduras and Paraguay were above the threshold of democracy, whereas Cuba, Guatemala and Haiti remained non democracies.

In Honduras a low level of education and the concentration of landownership have obstructed democratization. Formal institutions of democracy have been established, but they are not secure in Honduras where the military has often been involved in politics. In Paraguay the concentration of economic power resources (FF 15 and DD 20) is unfavourable for democracy. Social conditions are not yet safe for democracy, and breakdowns of democratic institutions are still possible although not inevitable. Social conditions may be slightly better for democracy than in Guatemala, but I have to emphasize that the level of resource distribution is not yet high enough to make democracy inevitable or secure.

Cuba has remained a socialist non democracy since the 1960s. The social basis of its hegemonic political system has become more and more fragile. The concentration of economic power resources (FF 21 and DD 5) is in harmony with the concentration of political power, but the other explanatory variables are highly favourable for democracy (IOD 78 and IKD 70). Consequently the value of the Index of Structural Imbalance (ISI) is higher for Cuba (29.3) than for any other country. Structural imbalance is as great in Cuba as it was in the Soviet Union and Eastern Europe before the collapse of socialist systems. Its low IPR value (4.4) does not presuppose a democratic political system, whereas IPRI (11.7) is high enough for democracy. Besides, the collapse of communist systems in Europe deprived foreign support from the Cuban communist regime. In this case, it may be more reasonable to evaluate the prospects for democracy on the basis of its IPRI value than on the basis of its much lower IPR value. We can expect democratization in Cuba, although it is not possible to predict when and in what way it is going to happen. The examples of Spain and Yugoslavia show that sometimes authoritarian systems were able to survive much longer than expected on the basis of resource distribution. In Spain and

Yugoslavia IPR values predicted democratization several decades before it actually happened. Cuba's IPR value is still at the transition level of IPR.

In Guatemala social conditions are not secure for democracy. Economic power resources are highly concentrated, and ethnic splits obstruct the dispersion of economic and intellectual power resources. It has been extremely difficult to establish and stabilize democratic institutions in Guatemala. My prediction is that the struggle for democracy will continue in Guatemala, but the stabilization of democratic institutions is not yet sure. The ethnic civil war strengthens the position of the military.

Haiti has traditionally been among the least developed Latin American countries. Its IOD and IKD values are the lowest in this regional group, whereas its DER value (47.7) is one of the highest in Latin America, probably too high. The ownership and control of agricultural land seems to be widely dispersed, which is conducive to democracy, but this factor alone has not been enough to provide a solid social basis for democratic politics. Besides, land holdings are very small, and most cultivators are poor. It may be that the control of land is more concentrated than my indicators show. According to my interpretation, many attempts to establish democratic institutions have failed in Haiti because the level of resource distribution is still too low. I cannot predict the survival of democracy in Haiti, although the level of several explanatory variables makes democracy possible. President Aristide, elected in the December 1990 presidential election, returned from the United States in October 1994 with the help of the US-led multinational force (see Keesing's 1994: 40222–3). It is not yet clear whether democratic institutions survive in Haiti without foreign military support.

The concentration of agricultural and non agricultural economic power resources in the hands of the ruling sections of the population has been the greatest obstacle to democracy in Latin America since the beginning (*cf.* Seligson 1987b: 184–5). The concentration of economic power resources is related to the history of ethnic structures in Latin America. Deep ethnic divisions have made it difficult to reduce economic and educational inequalities. However, the spread of literacy and education has been the most important structural factor undermining the social basis of autocratic political systems. It is reasonable to expect that dispersion of economic power resources will continue in Latin America as a consequence of the rise of educational level and of the policies of democratically elected governments. Such developments would strengthen the social basis of competitive politics. For these reasons I predict the survival of democracy in Latin America and the Caribbean.

All other scholars are not as optimistic. Glaucio A. D. Soares was careful in his assessments some years ago. He said that 'the recent turns of Argentina, Brazil and Uruguay, among others, in a democratic direction should not be considered as a definite trends towards institutionalized, *stable* democracy: both democracy and dictatorship are unstable in Latin America' (Soares 1988). James S. Malloy argued in 1987 that, in Latin America, there is no unilinear tendency toward democracy or toward authoritarian rule. Rather, the predominant pattern is cyclical, with alternating democratic and authoritarian 'moments'. Further, he thinks that 'the wide diversity from case to case precludes the development at this point of broad general models or theories of the shifts between authoritarian and democratic modes of governance in Latin America' (Malloy 1987: 236–7). Mitchell. A. Seligson also supported the cyclical hypothesis. According to him, 'there are strong grounds for predicting that the present cycle of democracy in Latin America will be ephemeral', but, referring to broad socio-economic trends, particularly to the rising trends of GNP per capita and literacy, he argued that 'the present cycle of democracy is likely to be different in nature, potentially more robust in character, and probably more durable, than the ones that preceded it' (Seligson 1987a: 4–9; see also Seligson 1988). In the case of Central America, Seligson came to the conclusion 'that the economic and socio-cultural conditions that have been prerequisites for democratic growth elsewhere in the world have been emerging over the past ten to fifteen years throughout Central America' (Seligson 1987b: 175). Laurence Whitehead (1993) is optimistic with certain reservations. He assumes that 'most Latin American democracies are likely to remain provisional, incomplete and unconsolidated, at least for the next few years' (Whitehead 1993: 325; see also Karl 1995). I think that the pattern of regime change in Latin America ceased to be cyclical in the 1980s. According to my theoretical interpretation, most Latin American countries entered the category of democracies more or less permanently because their IPR values have increased significantly.

NORTH AFRICA, THE MIDDLE EAST AND CENTRAL ASIA

This regional group extends from Morocco in the west to Kyrgyzstan in Central Asia and includes the core area of Muslim and Arab countries. Muslims constitute the majority of the population in twenty-seven of the twenty-nine countries, although their majority is slight in Lebanon and Kazakhstan. Israel and Cyprus (the Greek section of Cyprus) are religiously the most deviating countries in this region of Muslim culture. The religious divide between Sunni and Shia Muslims is important in some countries, particularly in Iraq. There are also other significant ethnic divisions in several countries. An interesting question is whether some characteristics of Muslim culture make democratization more difficult in Islamic countries than in the countries of other cultural areas.

We can see from Table 4.2 that the regional arithmetic means of residuals based on regression equations of ID on IPR and ID on IPRI are clearly negative for this regional group. It means that, on the average, the level of democratization has been much lower than expected. Because Muslim culture unites the countries of this regional group and separates them from most countries of the other regional groups, one could argue that some features of Muslim culture strengthen the concentration of political power. It may be that power-holders can increase their control of intellectual power resources by identifying themselves with Islam just like former Christian rulers in Europe were allied with the Church (*cf.* Kazancigil 1991). Giacomo Luciani, however, argues that the role of oil rent as a factor perpetuating authoritarian government may be more important than the cultural and social peculiarities of Arab societies (Luciani 1994). It is a noteworthy hypothesis. It connects the persistence of authoritarian governments to the concentration of economic power resources.

I would like to hypothesize that because Islam allows polygyny, reproductive resources are less equally distributed in Muslim countries than in other countries. Males controlling women and excluding other men from women tend to concentrate·other resources in their hands, too, in order to defend their reproductive privileges. Laura L. Betzig's study (1986) indicates that despotism has historically been correlated with polygyny all over the world. According to her conclusion, 'Despotism, defined as an exercised right to murder arbitrarily and with impunity, virtually invariably coincides with the greatest degree of polygyny, and presumably, with a correspondingly high degree of differential reproduction'. From this perspective, one could assume that it is easier to establish and maintain democracy in such Islamic countries in which monogamy has become a general practice than in more polygynous Islamic countries. However, the significance of this factor is decreasing in the Arab world. According to Philippe Fargues (1994: 170), 'Polygamy, which seems never to have been very common in the Arab world, is decreasing everywhere: it happens only in between 2 and 10 per cent of marriages (it is prohibited in Tunisia).'

Scholars have long discussed the possibility of democracy in Islamic countries. Most of them have been pessimistic about the chances of democracy in the Middle East (*cf.* Kazancigil 1991; Deegan 1993). Larry Diamond *et al.* excluded the Arab world in particular from their comparative analysis of democracy in developing countries. According to their argument, 'the Islamic countries of the Middle East and North Africa generally lack much previous democratic experience, and appear to have little prospects of transition even to semidemocracy' (Diamond et al. 1989, Vol. 3: XX; see also Deegan 1993: 4–9; Bromley 1993: 404). Samuel P. Huntington's view is nearly as pessimistic. He notes that, with one exception (Turkey), 'no Islamic country has sustained a fully democratic political system for any length of time'. Islamic doctrine contains elements that may be both congenial and uncongenial to democracy, although 'Islamic concepts of politics differ from and contradict the premises of democratic politics' (Huntington 1991: 307). Heather Deegan does not regard democratization to be completely impossible in the Middle East. One fundamental and encouraging sign is 'the fact that a debate about democratization has begun' (Deegan 1993: 135). Ilter Turan notes that western researchers have tended to exaggerate the political role of Islam. According to Turan, 'religious resurgence is a product of specific variables or circumstances which have occurred in different societies with different religions' (Turan 1991). Nazib Ayubi (1991: 6, 230) emphasizes that the Quran did not stipulate a specific form for the state or the government.

Raghild El-Solh (1993) refers to a survey of attitudes towards representative democracy among Arab intellectuals during the period 1985–90. The results show that Islamists appear to be divided into three groups in their attitudes towards democracy. The first group includes those who reject democracy outright, the second distinctive group includes those who believe that true Islam is inherently democratic, and the third group of Islamists comprises those who put more emphasis on democracy in its representative forms. Bearing these differences in mind, he concludes that 'those who tend to highlight certain Islamist anti-democratic theories and/or practices, and to equate them with the attitudes of Islamists in general, are committing an error of judgement' (El-Solh 1993: 64; see also Bahgat 1994). Reinoud Leenders argues against Professor Mustapha Kamel Al Sayyed's pessimistic view, according to which 'democracy in the Arab world has to wait another 30 years or so'. Leenders refers to several factors undermining the position of authoritarian regimes and emphasizes the significance of liberalization in particular. According to him, the process of liberalization is self-fulfilling: 'ultimately it will break the strength of authoritarian regimes, inaugurating a democratic era'. On the other hand, he agrees that the upsurge of fundamentalism gives reason for some pessimism on the future of democracy in the Arab world (Leenders 1993; see also Norton 1995). So it seems to be. Zealous Islamists, who consider democracy to be illegitimate, may constitute the most serious obstacle for democratization in the Muslim world (*cf.* Kazancigil 1991; Ayubi 1993). However, Nazib Ayubi assumes that the Islamists will not succeed in taking power in any of the Arab countries in the foreseeable future, with Egypt being a possible exception (Ayubi 1991; 235).

Polygyny, religious extremism, or some other features of Muslim culture may delay democratization because of their tendency to concentrate power resources, but I am not willing to argue that Muslim culture makes the emergence of democracy impossible. Democracy will emerge when the level of resource distribution rises sufficiently. The fact that democratic systems have functioned in some Islamic countries, particularly in Turkey, Malaysia, Pakistan and Bangladesh, indicates that Muslim culture does not provide an insurmountable obstacle for democratization (*cf.* Waterbury 1994). Data on explanatory variables are given in Table 4.5, in which the twenty-nine countries of this regional group are divided into three categories by the transition level of IPR.

We can see from Table 3.7 (chapter 3) that the number of deviating cases is higher in this regional group than in any other. According to IPR, there are twelve deviating non democracies and, according to IPRI, the number of

Table 4.5 Values of explanatory (1990–1) variables in 29 countries of North Africa, the Middle East and Central Asia

Country	UP	NAP	Stu	Lit	FF	DD	IOD	IKD	DER	ISI
1 IPR above 6.3										
Algeria	52	76	23	57	35	30	64.0	40.0	31.2	12.6
Bahrain	83	98	27	77	62	25	90.5	52.0	25.7	23.0
Cyprus	53	79	21	87	75	70	66.0	54.0	71.0	6.4
Egypt	44	59	34	48	57	30	51.5	41.0	41.1	4.6
Iran	57	72	17	54	44	30	64.5	35.5	33.9	13.2
Iraq	71	79	25	60	35	25	75.0	42.5	27.0	17.9
Israel	92	96	56	95	28	60	94.0	75.5	58.7	12.0
Jordan	68	94	50	80	52	30	81.0	65.0	31.3	18.5
Kuwait	96	98	25	73	45	20	97.0	49.0	20.5	27.7
Lebanon	84	91	61	80	48	60	87.5	70.5	58.9	10.1
Libya	70	86	23	64	53	20	78.0	43.5	24.6	19.5
Morocco	48	63	19	49	66	40	55.5	34.0	49.6	7.4
Qatar	79	97	30	79	50	20	88.0	54.5	20.9	22.3
Saudi Arabia	77	61	21	62	42	20	69.0	41.5	28.6	15.1
Syria	50	76	35	64	68	25	63.0	49.5	35.3	9.3
Tunisia	54	76	17	65	60	40	65.0	41.0	44.8	9.8
Turkey	61	52	27	81	92	50	56.5	54.0	70.2	6.6
2 IPR from 3.3 to 6.3										
Mauritania	47	36	6	34	54	15	41.5	20.0	40.0	9.2
United Arab Em.	78	97	13	55	40	20	87.5	34.0	20.6	24.6
Yemen	29	44	9	39	66	30	36.5	24.0	50.2	8.9
3 IPR below 3.3										
Afghanistan	18	45	3	29	65	30	31.5	16.0	49.2	11.3
Azerbaijan	53	85	29	93	5	5	69.0	61.0	5.0	26.7
Kazakhstan	58	80	34	93	5	5	69.0	63.5	5.0	27.2
Kyrgyzstan	38	84	27	93	5	5	61.0	60.0	5.0	26.2
Oman	11	60	8	35	71	20	35.5	21.5	40.4	7.0
Sudan	22	40	5	27	45	20	31.0	16.0	35.0	7.6
Tajikistan	31	86	26	93	5	5	58.5	59.5	5.0	24.0
Turkmenistan	45	64	23	93	5	1	54.5	58.0	2.4	23.9
Uzbekistan	40	83	33	93	5	5	61.5	63.0	5.0	25.4

deviating non democracies is fifteen. The level of democratization and the degree of resource distribution are not in harmony with each other in most of these countries. Detailed data on explanatory variables given in Table 4.5 clarify the nature of discrepancies.

North Africa, the Middle East and Central Asia: IPR above 6.3

According to the second research hypothesis, all the seventeen countries above the IPR level of 6.3 index points should be democracies, but only five of them (Cyprus, Iran, Israel, Lebanon and Turkey) were in 1993. It is interesting to note that these five democracies constitute a geographically compact area in the northern part of the Middle East. They border on

European countries, and their contacts with Europe have a long history. I am inclined to argue that economic, educational, and social structures conducive to democratization spread from Europe to these neighbouring countries and helped them to establish democratic institutions. Cyprus, Lebanon and Israel have been democracies since their independence. In Turkey, the democratic transition took place in 1950. Since then Turkey has experienced three authoritarian interludes, but democratic institutions have always re-emerged (see Kazancigil 1991). We can assume that the next countries crossing the threshold of democracy in the Middle East will most probably be neighbours of these earlier democracies. The nature of democracy in Iran is still highly questionable because the country has been dominated by the fundamentalist clergy since the Islamic revolution in 1979 and because there are no officially recognized political parties (*cf.* Waterbury 1994: 44). Presidential and parliamentary elections have, however, been competitive within the limits allowed by the ruling clergy. Jean-Francois Bayart (1994: 295–8) emphasizes that Iranian political society is now too diversified and complex for anyone to be able to impose as clear a hegemony as that of the Shah in the 1970s, although it is not yet 'democratic'. Because most social variables are favourable for democracy in Iran, I have to predict that the country will remain above the minimum threshold of democracy.

The other twelve countries of this category were deviating non democracies in 1993. The problem is how to explain so many cases contradicting the second research hypothesis. Let us start from the values of the three components of IPR (IOD, IKD and DER) because there are significant structural imbalances in several countries. Structural imbalances as indicated by high ISI values may provide a partial explanation in Bahrain, Kuwait, Libya, and Qatar. Economic power resources based on the control of oil industries are concentrated in the hands of the government in these four countries, although some other resources seem to be widely distributed. The IOD values (Index of Occupational Diversification) are exceptionally high for these countries. Economic power resources are highly concentrated in some other countries of this region, too, as indicated by relatively low DER values. However, I do not have any special explanations for these countries. They constitute the most numerous regional concentration of deviating non democracies in the world. Seven of them are Middle East countries and four others are North African countries. It is remarkable that all of them are Arab countries. They contradict my second research hypothesis, but it should be noted that they are quite recent deviations. In 1980 their IPR values were still below the upper limit of the IPR level of transition (see Vanhanen 1990a: 149). They have been deviating cases only since the 1980s when their IPR values crossed the upper limit of transition level. It may be that the control of economic power resources is even more highly concentrated in these countries than I have estimated (*cf.* Luciani 1994). Let us examine each of them.

Algeria is a country in which the struggle for power between secular and fundamentalist political forces is very intense. As a consequence of popular pressure for democratization, a multiparty system was legalized in 1989, and competitive parliamentary elections were held in December 1992. However, when the Islamic Salvation Front (FIS) seemed to be the clear winner in the first round of voting, a military coup stopped the process of democratization in order to prevent the fundamentalist FIS obtaining power (*cf.* Brumberg 1992; Norton 1995). Thus the struggle for power continues in Algeria. The concentration of coercive and non agricultural economic resources supports the survival of an authoritarian regime. Besides, the victory of a fundamentalist party would not necessarily lead to the establishment of democratic institutions. Secular and fundamentalist forces should find a compromise. Algeria's IPR value predicts democratization, but it may take a long time for competing groups to agree on a compromise (*cf.* Luciani 1994: 144–9).

Bahrain is a highly urbanized oil state ruled by its traditional chiefs. The concentration of economic resources in the hands of the emir and the other members of the royal family supports the traditional absolute monarchy, but the spread of education undermines the traditional order. I assume that the pressure for democratization will increase. Its high IPR value (12.1) is mainly due to a very high degree of urbanization. According to IPR and IPRI, conditions are already ripe for democratization, but past experience indicates that in some cases traditional political orders have been able to resist the pressure for democratization even by two or three decades.

Egypt differs from Bahrain in many respects, although its IPR is nearly as high (8.7). Economic power resources are significantly more widely distributed than in Bahrain, and the three components of IPR are almost at the same level, which provides a more favourable environment for democratization than structural imbalances. The process of democratization has already started in Egypt, particularly through partially competitive parliamentary elections (*cf.* Ayubi 1993; Bahgat 1994: 53–5; Owen 1994). My prediction is that democratization will continue in Egypt. It should cross the threshold of democracy very soon. However, the growth of population may become a serious obstacle to democratization because it maintains poverty and makes it difficult to disperse educational and economic resources to the growing number of people.

Iraq is more urbanized (IOD 75.0) than Egypt and Iran, but economic power resources may be more highly concentrated in the hands of the government (DD 25). The country has been ruled by military governments since the overthrow of the monarchy in 1958. The Kurdish insurgency and the deep antagonism between Sunni and Shi'ite Muslims have strengthened the position of the military and delayed democratization. Despite these disturbing local factors, I have to predict that the process of democratization will start in Iraq, too (*cf.* Ayubi 1993: 13–15). A military regime has often been the last form of authoritarian rule before democratization.

Jordan has been a deviating case since the 1980s (see Vanhanen 1984a and 1990a) because of its high IPR value. The three components of IPR are relatively well balanced. A problem is why Jordan has not crossed the threshold of democracy. Its high values of IPR and IPRI predict democratization. In 1992 a major step toward democracy was taken when the National Assembly approved legislation that lifted a thirty-five-year ban on political parties (*cf.* Ayubi 1993: 12–13; Bahgat 1994: 56–8). I expect that Jordan will cross the threshold of democracy very soon.

Kuwait is another oil state ruled by traditional sheiks and their families. It is extremely urbanized (IOD 97.0), whereas economic resources are still concentrated (DER 20.5) in the hands of the ruling families. I would like to point out that the level of education has risen steeply. The distribution of intellectual power resources has undermined the legitimacy of the traditional authoritarian rule and led to popular demands of democratization. There are not yet legal political parties. Parliamentary elections in 1992 were partly competitive, although they were held on a non party basis. They indicated the existence of potential opposition (see Luciani 1994: 144). My indicators predict democratization in Kuwait, but its high degree of structural imbalance (ISI 27.3) makes democratization uncertain. The concentration of economic and coercive power resources may be enough to suppress the demands of democracy. In addition, the structure of Kuwait's population complicates the process of democratization. The large number of non citizens makes it difficult to cross the minimum threshold of electoral participation.

For Libya, the values of the three components of IPR are nearly the same as in Kuwait, but the level of education seems to be lower. Libya is also a country whose economy is based on oil and whose oil resources are controlled by the government. Libya has been ruled by military-based governments since the overthrow of the monarchy in 1969. Political parties are not allowed to function. Libya's authoritarian system is closely associated with its dominant leader, Colonel Moamer al Kadhafi. I should predict democratization in Libya in the near future on the basis of IPR and IPRI, but because economic and coercive power resources are still highly concentrated, I hesitate to make such a prediction. However, I can predict that popular pressure for democracy will increase in Libya, too.

In Morocco the process of democratization started long ago, but it has been a slow process because of the dominant position of the king. There is a multiparty system, and parliamentary elections have been competitive. Morocco's example shows that competitive party systems are possible in Muslim countries. From the perspective of democratization, the dominance of the king is a major problem. The government should be responsible to the elected parliament. Social conditions are favourable for democratization (IPR 9.4), although the level of literacy is still relatively low (49 per cent). It should be noted that Morocco's political system is nearly in balance with the degree of resource distribution. Negative residuals are small (see Table 3.7). Morocco's political system has gradually adapted to the increased level of resource distribution and democratized. It is only slightly below the Participation threshold of democracy. I assume that Morocco will cross the threshold of democracy soon.

In Qatar and Saudi Arabia the concentration of oil resources in the hands of the government and ruling families supports the survival of absolute monarchies, whereas occupational structure (IOD) and, increasingly, knowledge distribution (IKD) are favourable to democratization. I assume that the spread of literacy and modern education will gradually undermine the concentration of other types of power resources and thus improve the chances of democratization. Because both combinations of explanatory variables are sufficiently high, I have to predict democratization in Qatar and Saudi Arabia, although the process of democratization has not yet started. The concentration of crucial economic and coercive resources may be higher than my indicators show. Therefore, it is possible that democratization will be delayed by two or three decades.

In Syria the process of democratization has already started, and the country was only slightly below the Competition threshold of democracy in 1993. However, Nazih N. Ayubi (1993: 10–12) points out that Syria's parliament is still a consultative, quasi-corporatist body (*cf.* Perthes 1994). Syria is a Muslim and Arab country where a multiparty system is slowly emerging. The values of the three components of IPR are better balanced in Syria than in most other Arab countries, which is conducive to democratization. I think that Syria will be among the first Arab countries to democratize. It is interesting to note that Syria, Jordan, and Egypt, which are the most likely Arab countries to democratize in the Middle East in the near future, are geographically neighbours of existing democracies (Israel, Lebanon, and Turkey).

In Tunisia social conditions are approximately as favourable for democratization than in Syria, but the level of education seems to be somewhat lower. The process of democratization has started, and parliamentary elections have been competitive. I have to predict democratization in Tunisia because the level of explanatory variables is sufficiently high. In Tunisia, as well as in several other countries of this region, the main dividing line is between secular and fundamentalist political forces. It is difficult for them to compromise and to share power with each other (see Krämer 1994). Nazih N. Ayubi (1993: 101) refers to the possibility that Islamist 'fundamentalist' groups might eventually form the basis for a post-absolutist political order in the Middle East countries.

North Africa, the Middle East and Central Asia: IPR from 3.3 to 6.3

Mauritania, the United Arab Emirates and Yemen are the three countries at the transition level of IPR. According to my hypothesis, democratization has become possible at that level of resource distribution, although it is not yet inevitable.

In Mauritania a new constitution approved in 1991 made competitive elections possible. They were held in 1992, but the country still remained below the Competition threshold of democracy. The main opposition parties claimed, according to W. Tordoff, that 'President (Colonel) Ould Taya was unfairly re-elected in the country's first multiparty elections in January 1992 and therefore boycotted the subsequent legislative elections' (Tordoff 1994: 106). The very serious ethnic conflict and civil war between the ruling Moors and African tribal groups makes the function of democratic institutions difficult. In addition, the level of education is very low. Democratization does not seem to be probable in the near future.

The United Arab Emirates is similar to Kuwait, Qatar and Saudi Arabia. The concentration of economic power resources in the hands of the ruling families supports the survival of an authoritarian political system. The level of education is still relatively low, but the spread of education forms the most important structural change undermining the social basis of autocratic rule. Democratization is not yet probable in the UAE, but popular pressure for democracy will increase as a consequence of the spread of education.

In Yemen economic power resources are more widely distributed than in the UAE, whereas the level of education is much lower. Democratization started with the unification of the two Yemens in 1990. Because economic power resources are not as highly concentrated as in the other countries of the Arab peninsula, democratization may be easier in Yemen despite its low level of knowledge distribution. Yemen approached the threshold of democracy in the 1993 parliamentary elections, but the starting of the civil war between the northern and southern parts of the country in 1994 stopped the process of democratization (see Keesing's 1994). It seems to me that we do not see the consolidation of democracy in Yemen in the near future.

North Africa, the Middle East and Central Asia: IPR below 3.3

IPR values were below the transition level in nine countries in 1991. Therefore my general prediction for these countries is that democratization is not yet probable, but it is necessary to specify this general prediction by taking into account particular local conditions. It is remarkable that six of these nine states are former Central Asian republics of the disintegrated Soviet Union.

In the case of Afghanistan, the values of the three components of IPR are nearly the same as in Yemen, but a great difference between these two countries concerns their ethnic structures. The population of Afghanistan is divided into many ethnic groups, which have provided social bases for the formation of competing military groups. Its endemic civil war can be regarded as a process of democratization. A military balance of power has been achieved but not yet a compromise on the sharing of power by establishing democratic institutions. An impasse in the civil war may lead to the establishment of a democratic compromise, but it is impossible to predict when it might happen. Therefore, my prediction is that Afghanistan remains as a non democracy in the near future.

In Azerbaijan IOD and IKD values are high enough for democratization, whereas the concentration of economic power resources (DER 5.0) supports an authoritarian political system. The situation is basically the same in the other Central Asian states (Kazakhstan, Kyrgyzstan, Tajikistan, Turkmenistan and Uzbekistan) that seceded from the Soviet Union in 1991. The ISI values indicating structural imbalances are extremely high for all these countries. The concentration of economic and coercive power resources forms the major obstacle for the emergence of democracy, whereas occupational diversification and a relatively high level of education predict democratization. If privatization and transition to a market economy continue in these states, the social preconditions of democracy improve. However, it is not certain that privatization will continue in these countries (see Roy 1994). Because of structural imbalances, the values of IPRI are already high enough for democratization in Azerbaijan and Kazakhstan, whereas Kyrgyzstan, Tajikistan, Turkmenistan and Uzbekistan are at the transition level of IPRI. Consequently, the establishment of democratic institutions is more probable in these Central Asian states than in Afghanistan. The process of democratization has started from the establishment of opposition parties and at least partially competitive elections (see Olcott 1993; Pryde 1994). However, these countries were not able to cross the threshold of democracy in the presidential and parliamentary elections organized in 1994 and 1995.

In Azerbaijan politics has remained violent (see Keesing's 1994–5). In the other five Central Asian states power is concentrated in the hands of the presidents and former communist parties, but elections have been at least partially competitive. Kazakhstan is the largest of the new independent states in the former Soviet Central Asia. In 1993, all political institutions were still controlled by the former Communist Party, but a new multiparty system emerged in the 1994 parliamentary election (see Keesing's 1994: 39913). President Nazarbayev, however, dissolved the parliament in March 1995 and organized a referendum in April 1995, in which 95 per cent of the voters agreed to postpone elections and to extend President Nazarbayev's term in office until the year 2000 (Donelly 1995; Keesing's 1995: 40453–4)). Party politics is becoming canalized along ethnic lines in Kazakhstan where ethnic Kazakhs constitute only 42 per cent of the population. The serious ethnic conflict between Kazakhs and Russians (and other ethnic minorities) forms an unpredictable factor in the process of democratization (*cf.* Bremmer and Welt 1995).

In Kyrgyzstan, legislative elections were competitive in February 1995 (Keesing's 1995: 40407), but power is in the hands of President Akayev. In Tajikistan the opposition boycotted the presidential election in November 1994 and the legislative elections in February 1995, but elections were competitive (see Keesing's 1994: 40279; 1995: 40407). In Turkmenistan, all candidates were returned unopposed in the legislative elections in December 1994. Most of them belong to the ruling Turkmen Democratic Party (formerly the Communist Party) (Keesing's 1995: 40322). In Uzbekistan, the ruling party won more than 70 per cent of the seats in the legislative elections in December 1994 (Keesing's 1994: 40362). In a referendum in March 1995, 99.6 per cent of the voters backed the extension of President Islam Karimov's term by three years (Keesing's 1995: 40453). It seems that until now the low IPR values have correctly predicted the failures to establish fully democratic political systems in these states.

Oman is the least developed country in the Arab peninsula. The values of all explanatory variables, particularly of IKD, are still low. Therefore, my prediction is that Oman will remain below the threshold of democracy until social conditions become more favourable for democratization.

Several attempts at democratization have failed in Sudan since the 1950s. The country was ruled by a military government in 1990–93. A civil war between dominant Arabs and African tribes continued. Because of the concentration of power resources and of the persistent civil war, democratization is not yet probable in Sudan.

According to my variables, more democratizations are to be expected in the region of North Africa, the Middle East and Central Asia than in any other region of the world. It will be interesting to see to what extent these predictions come true. The problems and obstacles of democracy vary within this region significantly. In the six states of the former Soviet Union, the concentration of economic resources is an inheritance from the Soviet period. Transition to market economy and privatization are the main strategies to improve social conditions of democracy in those countries. The concentration of economic power resources, especially the control of oil resources, constitutes the most formidable obstacle of democratization in several Arab countries (Algeria, Bahrain, Iraq, Kuwait, Libya, Qatar, Saudi Arabia, and the United Arab Emirates). Giacomo Luciani (1994: 152) says that he 'would be surprised if any of the rentier states were to democratize'. Besides, the concentration of reproductive resources may still form an additional dimension of resource concentration in some of these countries.

The best chances of democratization seem to be in the countries in which socio-economic development has been balanced (the three components of IPR approximately at the same level). This sub-group includes Egypt, Jordan, Morocco, Syria, and Tunisia. The prospects for democracy are especially poor in countries where intellectual power resources are highly concentrated because of a low level of education. This sub-group of countries includes Afghanistan, Oman, Mauritania, Sudan and Yemen in particular.

SUB-SAHARAN AFRICA

Sub-Saharan Africa includes all the African countries south of the Arab North Africa as well as the island states of Cape Verde, Comoros, Equatorial

Guinea, Madagascar, Mauritius, and São Tomé and Príncipe. Nearly all of the forty-four states of this regional group are populated by Africans, who are divided into numerous tribes and other ethnic groups and who speak many tribal languages. Tribal and linguistic territories do not always coincide with state boundaries, which has caused numerous interstate and even more intrastate conflicts. In addition, some countries are populated by different racial groups, which has caused very serious ethnic-interest conflicts. In the north, Chad as well as Mauritania and Sudan are divided into Arab and African populations. Competing racial groups have had violent conflicts and civil wars. In the south, the Republic of South Africa was dominated by its white minority until the first parliamentary elections based on universal franchise in 1994. Mauritius is populated by various racial groups and mixed populations, including Africans, Hindus and Muslims from India, and Europeans. It is remarkable that everywhere deep ethnic divisions have been used to organize people in politics. Religiously sub-Saharan Africa is very heterogeneous. The population is divided into Muslims, Christians and animists (traditional African beliefs). Sometimes religious differences overlap tribal or racial splits, but in many cases they cross each other. Ethnic pluralism is a factor which affects politics in nearly all African countries, but it is not among the explanatory factors of this study (see Morrison *et al.* 1989).

Table 4.1 indicates that social conditions are less conducive to democracy in sub-Saharan Africa than in any other region and that the actual level of democracy was in 1993, together with the region of North Africa, the Middle East and Central Asia, the lowest in the world. Small regional arithmetic means of residuals (see Table 4.2) mean that a low level of democratization has been in harmony with the concentration of power resources. In fact, low IPR values in sub-Saharan Africa predicted the lack of democracy quite well until the 1980s (see Vanhanen 1984a and 1990a), but the situation changed dramatically in the period 1989–93 when the wave of democratization also reached sub-Saharan Africa. It was triggered by the collapse of socialist systems in Eastern Europe, but there were also many domestic reasons for the struggle to change regimes. Democratization in sub-Saharan Africa in 1989–93 implies that Gastil's (1985) diffusion theory of democratization is relevant in some cases. Samuel Decalo refers to Eastern Europe, but adds that the continent 'was already more than *ripe* for upheaval, and there were additional, internal and external factors that played a crucial role in leading the democratic pressures to successful fruition'. He stresses the significance of an international donor community that started to demand 'better governance' (Decalo 1992).

Dirk Berg-Schlosser emphasizes that the present wave of democratization in Africa, 'even though benefiting from the changes in the international environment, has to a large extent been brought about by the dismal failure of most civil-authoritarian or military regimes in the economic field and the ensuing discontent in large parts of the population' (Berg-Schlosser 1993).

Similarly, Christopher Clapham (1993) points out that the failure of state-centred 'development' had created a favourable internal climate for a system change in Africa. He is very sceptical on the chances of democracy in Africa. His general conclusion is that 'the prospects for continued democracy in Africa remain extremely uncertain' (Clapham 1993: 11; see also Callaghy 1994). Berg-Schlosser is clearly more optimistic. According to his assessment, 'there seems to be no insurmountable impediment that some form of a more open and accountable but also more effective government cannot be brought about' (Berg-Schlosser 1993). According to Geoffrey Hawthorn (1993), hope for a minimal democracy in sub-Saharan Africa is 'in those associations which the successive architects of "the modern state" in Africa, pre-colonial, colonial and post-colonial, have all dismissed as primordial, parochial and divisive'. It is an important insight. I also think that tribal and other primordial structures should be used as the building blocks of democracy in sub-Saharan Africa. Steven Muhlberger and Phil Paine point out that the precolonial Africa was not as authoritatively ruled as often portrayed. Its 'precolonial kings were no more than oligarchs and war chiefs of limited power. Precolonial Africa was a latticework of decentralized farming villages and autonomous towns only occasionally subjected to genuine monarchical states' (Muhlberger and Paine 1993: 32–4). General Olusegun Obasanjo stresses the same point, a strong and rich democratic tradition that has its roots at the village level (Obasanjo 1993; *cf.* Abedeji 1994: 126).

The arithmetic means of residuals are still small in sub-Saharan Africa, but this harmony between the level of democracy and the degree of resource distribution is limited to regional averages. Many single countries are highly deviating cases. Sub-Saharan Africa provides now the greatest challenge to my theory of democratization. The pressure for democratization is strong and mounting all over the continent, but, according to my explanatory variables, chances to establish democratic institutions are still poor in most countries of this region. Therefore, my theory on the conditions of democratization will be tested in many countries of Africa in the 1990s and in the beginning of the next century. William Tordoff's conclusion is that 'Africa's objective circumstances do not exclude political democracy; yet democracy in Africa is a tender plant which may prove difficult to maintain in the longer term' (Tordoff 1994: 113; see also Tadesse 1991; Woodward 1994: 129–30; Ndue 1994; Hadenius 1994).

Table 3.7 (chapter 3) indicates that sixteen of the forty-four countries were above the ID threshold of democracy in 1993, but Cape Verde and Namibia were still below the Competition threshold of democracy. This leaves us fourteen countries that were above all minimum thresholds of democracy, of which only Mauritius was expected to be a democracy on the basis of IPR and IPRI, and eight other democracies were at the transition level of IPR. The five democracies below the transition level of IPR (Benin, Comoros, Gambia, Niger, and Senegal) contradicted the

Table 4.6 Values of explanatory (1990–1) variables in 44 countries of sub-Saharan Africa

Country	UP	NAP	Stu	Lit	FF	DD	IOD	IKD	DER	ISI
1 IPR above 6.3										
Ghana	33	50	3	60	67	40	41.5	31.5	53.5	7.6
Mauritius	41	77	4	80	43	50	59.0	42.0	48.4	6.1
South Africa	50	86	23	80	9	30	68.0	51.5	27.1	14.5
2 IPR from 3.3 to 6.3										
Botswana	28	37	6	74	55	30	32.5	40.0	45.7	4.6
Cameroon	41	39	6	54	60	20	40.0	30.0	44.4	5.4
Cape Verde	29	57	4	66	39	30	43.0	35.0	33.9	3.8
Central African R.	47	37	2	38	50	20	42.0	20.0	38.9	9.1
Congo	41	40	10	57	60	20	40.5	33.5	44.0	3.9
Côte d'Ivoire	40	44	4	54	53	20	42.0	29.0	38.5	5.0
Gabon	46	32	7	61	60	20	39.0	34.0	47.2	4.8
Kenya	24	23	4	69	46	40	23.5	36.5	44.6	7.6
Lesotho	20	20	2	78	60	20	20.0	40.0	52.0	11.6
Madagascar	24	23	6	80	56	20	23.5	43.0	47.7	9.7
Nigeria	35	35	6	51	60	30	35.0	28.5	49.5	7.9
São Tomé and Prín.	26	44	4	60	20	20	35.0	32.0	42.4	4.0
Swaziland	28	34	9	71	36	20	31.0	40.0	30.6	4.1
Zaire	29	34	4	72	58	20	31.5	38.0	45.1	4.6
Zambia	42	31	4	73	50	20	36.5	38.5	40.7	1.4
Zimbabwe	28	32	10	67	30	30	30.0	38.5	30.0	3.8
3 IPR below 3.3										
Angola	27	30	1	42	42	20	28.5	21.5	35.4	4.6
Benin	38	39	5	23	52	20	38.5	14.0	39.5	11.1
Burkina Faso	9	16	1	18	60	20	12.5	9.5	53.6	18.9
Burundi	6	9	1	50	60	15	7.5	25.5	55.9	17.5
Chad	30	25	1	30	60	20	27.5	15.5	50.0	12.7
Comoros	28	21	2	55	38	30	24.5	28.5	36.3	4.4
Djibouti	81	85	2	19	60	20	83.0	10.5	26.0	28.8
Equatorial Guinea	29	44	1	50	30	30	36.5	25.5	30.0	3.9
Ethiopia	13	25	1	50	60	10	19.0	25.5	47.5	11.2
Gambia	23	19	4	27	60	30	21.0	15.5	54.3	16.0
Guinea	26	26	2	24	48	15	26.0	13.0	39.4	8.8
Guinea-Bissau	20	21	2	36	60	20	20.5	19.0	51.6	14.2
Liberia	46	30	4	39	26	15	38.0	21.5	22.7	7.1
Malawi	12	25	1	45	51	10	18.5	23.0	40.7	8.9
Mali	19	19	1	32	60	15	19.0	16.5	51.4	15.0
Mozambique	27	18	0	33	29	15	22.5	16.5	26.5	3.6
Namibia	28	65	6	40	22	20	46.5	23.0	20.7	11.0
Niger	20	13	1	28	53	20	16.5	14.5	48.7	14.8
Rwanda	6	9	1	50	60	20	7.5	25.5	56.4	17.7
Senegal	38	22	5	38	44	30	30.0	21.5	40.9	6.7
Sierra Leone	32	38	2	21	56	30	35.0	11.5	46.1	12.9
Somalia	36	30	4	24	49	20	33.0	14.0	40.3	10.1
Tanzania	22	19	0	55	48	20	20.5	27.5	42.7	8.3
Togo	26	30	4	43	57	20	28.0	23.5	45.9	9.0
Uganda	10	19	2	48	60	20	14.5	25.0	52.4	14.8

second research hypothesis. They are 'too early' democracies. They constituted the most numerous concentration of deviating democracies in 1993.

These preliminary observations indicate that in most African countries the concentration of political power in the hands of authoritarian governments is in harmony with the concentration of various power resources, but the number of deviating cases has become large and it may be growing. Several countries have crossed the threshold of democracy at a lower level of explanatory variables than expected. Table 4.6, in which the forty-four countries of sub-Saharan Africa are divided into three categories by the transition level of IPR, offers additional information that can be used in evaluating the prospects of democracy in particular sub-Saharan countries.

Sub-Saharan Africa: IPR above 6.3

The three countries of this category (Ghana, Mauritius and South Africa) are dispersed around Africa. Mauritius was a democracy in 1993 as hypothesized, whereas Ghana was slightly below the Competition threshold of democracy and South Africa clearly below the Participation threshold.

In Ghana the level of resource distribution (IPR 7.0) seems to be high enough for democracy, and popular pressure for democratization has been continual. Ghana approached the threshold of democracy in the 1992 presidential and parliamentary elections (*cf.* Tordoff 1994: 107–8, according to whom the opposition parties boycotted the parliamentary elections in December 1992 because of electoral malpractices). Ghana is a deviating non democracy, but, from the perspective of regression analyses, it is not a problematic case. Its negative residuals are very small (see Table 3.7). I think that it has a good chance of crossing the threshold of democracy in the near future.

In Mauritius social conditions are more favourable for democracy than in any other sub-Saharan African country, and Mauritius has maintained democratic institutions since its independence in 1968. The three components of IPR are in balance. I predict that Mauritius will remain a democracy.

In South Africa its dominating white minority has enjoyed democracy since the establishment of the Union of South Africa in 1910, but because the country's black majority was without political rights and freedoms, South Africa was unable to cross the Participation threshold of democracy. The black majority demanded political equality and supported its demands by various forms of pressure. A compromise on constitutional reforms was achieved in 1993, and the first non racial democratic parliamentary elections were held in April 1994 (see Keesing's 1994: 39942–3, 39990–2). South Africa crossed the threshold of democracy and ceased to be a deviating non democracy. According to my explanatory variables, power resources are sufficiently distributed to support democracy in South Africa, but the country's extremely deep racial cleavages make the function of democracy difficult. Its success may crucially depend on the suitability of political institutions that will be established by the freely elected new parliament (*cf*. Horowitz 1991; Cloete 1992).

Sub-Saharan Africa: IPR from 3.3 to 6.3

Sixteen sub-Saharan African countries were at the transition level of IPR in 1990. According to my hypothesis, authoritarian systems are expected to democratize at this level of resource distribution, though it is still possible to maintain authoritarian and hegemonic political structures. Political systems can be expected to be most unstable at the transition level of resource distribution. Power resources are sufficiently distributed to make a continual struggle for power among competing groups possible. Of the sixteen countries at the transition level of IPR, Botswana, Cameroon, Central African Republic, Congo, Gabon, Kenya, Madagascar, and São Tomé and Príncipe were above all minimum thresholds of democracy in 1993. Cape Verde and Namibia were slightly below the Competition threshold of democracy. The other eight countries were approaching the threshold of democracy or were still ruled by military or other authoritarian governments. There is pressure for democracy in all these countries. Let us discuss them separately.

In Botswana the three dimensions of resource distribution (IOD, IKD and DER) seem to be in balance, which is favourable for political stability. Democratic institutions have survived since independence in 1966. The fact that the Tswana tribal groups constitute 90 per cent of the population and that the ruling Botswana Democratic Party has represented this section of the population has probably furthered the stability of the party system. The ruling party has not been in serious danger of losing its power, although elections have been free. I expect Botswana to remain a democracy.

Cameroon crossed the threshold of democracy in competitive parliamentary and presidential elections in 1992, but it should be noted that most opposition parties boycotted the elections, 'because they contended that the electoral code unduly favored the ruling party' (IFES 1992, No. 1: 10). The opposition parties alleged that the official results of the presidential election in October 1992 had been 'doctored' (Tordoff 1994: 106; see also John W. Forje's commentary). The level of resource distribution seems to be sufficient to support democratic politics, but it is not high enough to make democracy secure.

The world-wide crisis of socialism led to the introduction of multiparty elections in Cape Verde in 1991. An opposition movement, the Movement for Democracy, was victorious both in parliamentary and presidential elections, and the country approached the threshold of democracy. On the basis of IPR (5.1), democratic institutions have as good chances in Cape Verde as in Botswana and Cameroon.

Central African Republic crossed the threshold of democracy in the elections of 1993, which ended General Kolingba's authoritarian rule.

High positive residuals imply, however, that the level of democratization is higher than the degree of resource distribution can support. The social basis of democratic politics is not yet secure.

In Congo a one-party Marxist regime was rejected in 1991, and the country crossed the threshold of democracy in competitive parliamentary and presidential elections in 1992. However, parliamentary elections in June 1993 were followed by sporadic, but increasing, outbursts of violence (see Tordoff 1994: 106). The level of democratization (ID) is much higher than expected on the basis of IPR and IPRI.

Côte d'Ivoire is still dominated by one party, although other legal parties were allowed to participate in the 1990 elections. The struggle for democratization continues in Côte d'Ivoire. According to regression analyses, the level of democracy is approximately in balance with the degree of resource distribution (see Table 3.7).

Gabon crossed the threshold of democracy in the 1990 elections. Power resources seem to be sufficiently distributed to support democratic politics, but large positive residuals imply that, on the basis of resource distribution, the level of democratization should be considerably lower.

In Kenya the struggle between opposition forces demanding democracy and the ruling Kenya African National Union (KANU) led to multiparty elections and democratization in 1993, although KANU was able to retain its control (*cf.* Barkan 1993; Kasfir 1993). The present level of democratization is clearly higher than expected on the basis of IPR and IPRI (see Table 3.7). Therefore, it is quite possible that some kind of hegemonic system will continue. In fact, according to the Kenyan opposition, the country's political system is not democratic (see Matiba 1995).

In Lesotho, after a long period of military governments, competitive parliamentary elections were held in 1993. The former opposition party (Basutho Congress Party) was victorious (75 per cent). Its present hegemonic system seems to be approximately in balance with the relatively low degree of resource distribution.

In Madagascar a strenuous struggle for democracy has continued for several years. The opposition groups achieved a crucial victory in the presidential and parliamentary elections of 1993, and Madagascar crossed the threshold of democracy (*cf.* Martin and O'Reilley 1993). The dominant position of the ruling coalition is in harmony with the country's relatively low IPR value. Positive residuals are moderate (see Table 3.7).

In Nigeria the military government and various opposition forces have struggled for power and democracy for many years. General Babangida's military government started a controlled transition to restricted democracy by allowing two political parties to compete in parliamentary elections in 1992 and presidential elections in 1993, but the experiment failed and ended in a new military coup in 1993. Nigeria's negative residuals predict an emergence of some kind of democratic system. The ethnic diversity of its population has obstructed the stabilization of democratic rule, although, on the other hand, large ethnic clusters could provide a natural basis for a pluralistic party system.

São Tomé and Príncipe crossed the threshold of democracy in the 1991 parliamentary elections, but it is too early to say whether its multiparty system becomes stabilized or not. The level of democratization in 1993 was clearly higher than expected on the basis of explanatory variables. Therefore, I cannot be sure on the survival of democratic institutions in São Tomé and Príncipe. We can expect an emergence of a system dominated by one party (for later developments, see Keesing's 1994: 40090, 40217).

Swaziland is a rare African country in which a traditional royal family has been able to maintain its power. The popular pressure for democratization has been relatively slight, although not insignificant. Small negative residuals imply that the direction of change would be toward democratization.

In Zaire the struggle for power has been fierce since 1990, but it has not yet led to the emergence of democracy through competitive elections (see Africa Demos 1993, vol. 3, no. 1: 5–6). Its moderate negative residuals (see Table 3.7) imply that some kind of competitive political system would better suit its social conditions than an autocratic system dominated by a president.

In Zambia the United National Independence Party agreed to end its monopoly of power in 1990. In the competitive parliamentary and presidential elections in 1991, the Movement for Multiparty Democracy won, but its victory was so overwhelming that Zambia still remained under the Competition threshold of democracy (*cf.* Tordoff 1994: 108–10). However, Zambia's very small negative residuals indicate that a system dominated by one party is approximately in balance with the degree of resource distribution (see Table 3.7).

In Zimbabwe, President Mugabe attempted to establish a one-party system. His Zimbabwe African National Union–Patriotic Front won 97 per cent of the seats in the 1990 parliamentary election, and Zimbabwe sank deeper below the threshold of democracy than earlier. Some opposition parties continued to function, and it is reasonable to expect that they will increase their support in the next elections. Its zero residuals imply that a hegemonic system is in harmony with the country's relatively low level of resource distribution (see Table 3.7).

This brief review of sixteen countries at the transition level of IPR indicates that there has been pressure for democratization in all of them and that eight of them were above all the minimum thresholds of democracy in 1993. On the other hand, the examination of residuals given in Table 3.7 discloses that some kind of hegemonic system would still be better in harmony with the relatively low degree of resource distribution in many of them than a more pluralistic democratic system. Because it is very difficult to establish and stabilize an intermediate form between democracy and non democracy, the political systems at the transition level of IPR are fragile, and the level of democratization tends to fluctuate. Empirical evidence supports this assumption.

Sub-Saharan Africa: IPR below 3.3

The value of IPR was below 3.3 in twenty-five sub-Saharan African countries in 1990. Because power resources are highly concentrated in these countries, my general prediction is that democracy will not emerge in these countries, or attempts to establish democratic institutions will fail much more easily than in the countries with higher IPR values. Concentration of power resources leads to the appearance of different types of authoritarian regimes. Most of these countries suffer from widespread poverty, which implies that power resources may be even more concentrated than my IPR values indicate. However, contrary to the second hypothesis, five of these countries (Benin, Comoros, Gambia, Niger, and Senegal) had crossed the threshold of democracy in 1993. The number of deviating democracies is higher in sub-Saharan Africa than in any other regional group. How to explain these deviations, or are there any systematic explanations for them? Let us see how political systems were responding to the demands of democratization in these countries at the beginning of the 1990s.

Angola's attempt to end the civil war and to establish democratic institutions in 1991–2 only partially succeeded because Jonas Savimbi's UNITA refused to acknowledge its electoral defeat in the 1992 elections and to join a coalition government with MPLA-PT. Savimbi's UNITA decided to continue its civil war against the government party, which had abandoned Marxism–Leninism in December 1990 in favour of 'democratic socialism'. Angola remained below the threshold of democracy in 1992 and 1993. On the basis of its low IPR and IPRI values, I have to predict that attempts at democratization will more probably fail than succeed.

Benin was more successful in its transition to democracy in 1991. President Kerekou's government abandoned Marxism–Leninism in December 1989 and opened a way to multiparty democracy (for the period of military rule, see Decalo 1990). Benin crossed the threshold of democracy in the parliamentary and presidential elections of 1991. Large positive residuals (Table 3.7) show that its present level of democratization is much higher than expected. A hegemonic system would be in better balance with the low degree of resource distribution. We can see from Table 4.6 that the values of all explanatory variables, except Family Farms, are very low indeed. Therefore my explanatory variables are unable to explain the emergence and survival of democracy in a country like Benin.

Burkina Faso approached the threshold of democracy in the parliamentary election of 1992 (*cf.* Tordoff 1994: 106–7). According to my explanatory variables, the distribution of agricultural land is the only structural factor favourable for democratization in Burkina Faso. The values of all other explanatory variables are extremely low (see Table 4.6). Its residuals are near zero, which indicates that a hegemonic system is in harmony with Burkina Faso's social conditions.

Burundi was ruled by a military government in 1991, but a new constitution presupposing democratic institutions was accepted by referendum in 1992, and the country crossed the threshold of democracy in the 1993 elections (see Tucker and Smith 1993). The struggle for power between the former ruling Tutsi minority and the Hutu majority made it difficult to share power democratically. The Hutu president elected in 1993 was murdered in an attempted coup soon after his election. The next president elected by the National Assembly in January 1994 was killed when his aircraft crashed on 6 April 1994. The formal institutions of the established democratic system survived these accidents and renewed ethnic violences but the country dropped below the threshold of democracy as a consequence of the murder of the president in 1993 and of indirect presidential elections in 1994 (see Reyntjens 1995). Burundi's low level of resource distribution (IPR 1.1) does not yet presuppose a democratic system. Besides, the ethnic animosity between Hutus and Tutsis makes the function of any governmental system extremely difficult.

Chad remained under military governments in 1990–3, and a civil war continued between northerners and southerners. Because its residuals are only slightly negative (see Table 3.7), the establishment and stabilization of a democratic system is not probable. A hegemonic system seems to be better suited to its social conditions.

Comoros started the process of democratization in 1990 when a competitive presidential election was held. The country crossed the threshold of democracy in the parliamentary election of 1992 and remained above the threshold in the next elections. Politics in Comoros has been marred by violence. Its very high positive residuals (Table 3.7) indicate that the level of democratization is much higher than expected on the basis of resource distribution and that we should expect a significant decrease in the level of democratization.

Djibouti approached the threshold of democracy in the parliamentary election of 1992, but remained as a non democracy. Tension and violent conflicts between the Afar and Issa ethnic groups have characterized politics in Djibouti. It has been difficult for them to agree on the sharing of power. Because of the rebellion of the Front for the Restoration of Unity and Democracy (FRUD), the established democratic institutions cannot function properly (see Keesing's 1994: 39899). A hegemonic system seems to be better suited to its social conditions than a democracy, but, on the other hand, democratic sharing of power would better suit its ethnic situation than hegemonic concentration of power in the hands of one ethnic group.

Equatorial Guinea was ruled by a civil–military government in 1990–3, although the new constitution adopted by referendum in 1991 presupposes a multiparty system. Its low level of resource distribution does not predict the establishment of a democratic system.

In Ethiopia Colonel Mengistu's Marxist government was overthrown in 1991, after which various rebel forces, representing different regional and tribal groupings, formed the government. The country remained under the threshold of democracy (*cf.* Taylor 1993). According to my explanatory variables, we cannot yet expect a democratic system in Ethiopia. A hegemonic system based on limited competition and participation would be better suited to its social conditions. In the elections for the Constituent Assembly in July 1994, the ruling Ethiopian People's Revolutionary Democratic Front won 484 out of the 547 seats (Keesing's 1994: 40091). It may be able to establish a hegemonic system capable of securing law and order.

Gambia was the most persistent deviating democracy in Africa since the country's independence in 1965. The People's Progressive Party (PPP) representing the country's largest ethnic group (Mandingo) remained in power. It may be that, just like in Botswana, the country's ethnic structure was conducive to a multiparty system dominated by the party representing the largest tribal group (*cf.* Clapham 1993: 6, who notes that the ruling party 'has never been seriously challenged'). Gambia contradicted the second research hypothesis, although its positive residuals remained moderate because of the dominant position of the ruling party. It ceased to be a deviating democracy as a consequence of a military coup in 1994 (see Keesing's 1994).

Guinea approached the threshold of democracy in the competitive presidential election of 1993, but because voting took place amid violence and confusion and because legislative elections were postponed, the country remained below the threshold of democracy. The elected President Lansana Conte has been in office since the 1984 coup (Keesing's 1994: 39767). The low values of explanatory variables (see Table 4.6) do not predict democratization.

Guinea-Bissau's ruling party, the African Party for the Independence of Guinea-Bissau and Cape Verde, approved the introduction of multiparty democracy in 1991. The low level of resource distribution in Guinea-Bissau does not presuppose a democratic political system, but, contrary to the second research hypothesis, Guinea-Bissau seemed to have crossed the threshold of democracy in the parliamentary and presidential elections in 1994. It became a new highly deviating democracy (see Keesing's 1994: 40130).

In Liberia, after the collapse of the Doe regime in 1990, tribal rebel forces have continued the violent struggle for power. A hegemonic system would suit the social conditions of Liberia, but the ethnic heterogeneity of its population has made the stabilization of any governmental system difficult.

Malawi was under the authoritarian rule of President Banda and his Malawi Congress Party since the country's independence in 1966 until 1994, when the first multiparty elections were held. On the basis of IPR and other explanatory indices, some kind of hegemonic political system is more probable under Malawi's social conditions than a full democracy, but the country crossed the threshold of democracy in the 1994 elections (see Keesing's 1994: 39993–4) and, at least temporarily, became a highly deviating democracy.

In Mali, General Moussa Traoré's authoritarian government was overthrown by a military coup in 1991, after which Mali approached the threshold of democracy in the 1992 parliamentary and presidential elections (*cf.* Tordoff 1994: 107). Its low level of democratization in 1993 was in balance with the low values of IPR and IPRI as indicated by residuals that were near zero.

In Mozambique the ruling party (Frelimo) abandoned Marxism–Leninism in 1989 and promised democratic reforms. The sixteen-year civil war between the government and Renamo rebel forces was ended by a peace agreement in October 1992. The intention was to organize multiparty legislative and presidential elections in 1993, but they were postponed to October 1994 (see Keesing's 1994: 39948). Its very low degree of resource distribution (IPR 1.0) does not predict democratization, but Mozambique, just like Guinea-Bissau, crossed the threshold of democracy in parliamentary and presidential elections of 1994 and became a highly deviating democracy (Keesing's 1994: 40262–3). Unfortunately my explanatory variables do not predict the survival of democracy in Mozambique.

In Namibia economic power resources are still concentrated in the hands of the country's small white minority, but some other explanatory variables indicate a higher level of resource distribution. The first parliamentary elections of 1989 were competitive, but the country remained below the Competition threshold of democracy because of the unanimous and indirect presidential election of 1990 (*cf.* Shelton 1993). Its present low level of democratization seems to be in balance with the degree of resource distribution (see Table 3.7). In the 1994 parliamentary and presidential elections SWAPO won over 70 per cent of the votes cast (Keesing's 1994: 40310–1), and Namibia still remained below the threshold of democracy.

Niger crossed the threshold of democracy in the 1993 parliamentary and presidential elections (for the period of military rule, see Decalo 1990). Its large positive residuals imply that the level of democratization is too high compared to the degree of resource distribution. I have to predict a significant decrease in the level of democratization.

Rwanda remained as a one-party state through the period 1990–3. Politics has been violent because of the continual struggle between the Hutu majority and the Tutsi minority. The death of President Habyarima, together with President Ntaryamira of Burundi, on 6 April 1994, unleashed ethnic violence on a horrific scale. Rwanda's low level of resource distribution does not presuppose democracy. However, because of the very deep ethnic split between Hutus and Tutsis, some kind of power sharing would be needed.

Senegal was one of the first one-party states to start the process of democratization, but despite competitive elections, the country remained slightly below the threshold of democracy in 1990–2. It crossed the threshold in the 1993 parliamentary and presidential elections, but the Senegalese Socialist Party remained the dominant party. This kind of dominant party system seems to suit the country's social conditions. Positive residuals were small in 1993 (*cf.* Kanté 1994). Senegal provides a rare example of a sub-Saharan country in which democratization has evolved through gradual changes.

In Sierra Leone an attempt to introduce a multiparty system led to a new military coup in April 1992. Its negative residuals were small in 1993 (see Table 3.7). Some kind of hegemonic system would be in balance with its low degree of resource distribution.

In Somalia a bloody civil war raged through the period 1990–3. Prospects for democracy are not good. The degree of resource distribution seems to be too low to support a democratic political system. Its civil war, however, indicates that coercive power resources are widely distributed among the clans and that it is difficult for any single group to establish its hegemony (for the clan system and the civil war, see Samatar 1991).

Tanzania remained a one-party dominated state in 1990–3, although legal avenues were opened for a multiparty system in 1992 (see Mushi 1992). Its small negative residuals indicate that the level of resource distribution does not presuppose a much higher level of democratization. A competitive party system with a dominant party might be best suited to its social conditions.

Togo remained below the threshold of democracy throughout the period 1990–3. General Eyadema, who has ruled the country since 1967 (see Decalo 1990: 217–40), won the 1993 presidential election, which was boycotted by the main opposition parties. In the parliamentary elections in February 1994, opposition parties achieved a majority, and the country seemed to cross the threshold of democracy (see Keesing's 1994: 39848, 39897, 39946). Because of Togo's low level of resource distribution and ethnic animosities, the position of democratic institutions is fragile.

Uganda was ruled by General Museveni throughout the period 1990–3. The first step toward democratization was taken through the non party elections to the Constituent Assembly in March 1994. A hegemonic political system would be in harmony with the concentration of power resources in Uganda, but it has been extremely difficult to establish and stabilize such a system because of deep ethnic divisions (*cf.* Dicklich 1994).

The above review of twenty-five sub-Saharan countries below the transition level of IPR indicates that the concentration of power resources is approximately in balance with a low level of democratization or the lack of democracy in most of these countries. The five countries that were above the minimum thresholds of democracy in 1993 and that thereby contradicted the second research hypothesis are problematic. The number of deviating democracies has increased since 1993, although Gambia dropped below the threshold of democracy as a consequence of a military coup in 1994. The group of new deviating democracies include Guinea-Bissau,

Malawi, Mozambique, and Togo. The successful establishment of democratic institutions in these countries is a great achievement, which shows that democracy is also possible in very poor countries. It also implies that it is difficult to establish any absolute lower level of resource distribution below which democratization is impossible. However, I have to predict serious difficulties and possible breakdowns for these deviating democracies because my theory claims that the concentration of power resources leads to the concentration of political power. I let these deviating democracies test my theory. In fact, the nature of democracy is questionable in several of these deviating democracies because of civil wars or serious ethnic conflicts and violence in elections. It is very interesting to see what happens in these new democracies.

The low degree of resource distribution in sub-Saharan Africa is more due to low values of IOD and IKD than to DER whose values are relatively high because of the prevalence of a family farm system. The distribution of agricultural land among the peasant population is favourable for democratization, but poor and illiterate farmers do not provide a strong and active basis for competitive politics. Non agricultural economic resources are concentrated in the hands of the government, local businessmen and entrepreneurs, and foreign companies, although it is difficult to estimate the degree of concentration. The privatization of public sector companies and the emergence of domestic entrepreneurs would diversify the control of economic power resources and improve the social environment of democratic politics. According to W. Tordoff (1994: 112), forty African states were officially committed to privatize public sector companies in 1990. The percentages of urban population and non agricultural population are relatively low, which means that economic and occupational interest conflicts do not yet provide a solid basis for party politics. The low levels of literacy and higher education constitute the most unfavourable structural factors in most sub-Saharan African countries. The number of people capable of taking part in modern politics is small, and those people are concentrated in the cities. It is difficult for poorly educated farmers and workers to organize themselves politically and to defend their interests by political means. Small élite groups, mostly urban élites, dominate politics. John Mukum Mbaku argues that 'rent seeking represents an important constraint to the implementation of appropriate democratization strategies in Africa'. Dominant groups use state powers to enrich themselves and their supporters (Mbaku 1994).

It seems to me that the best strategy to strengthen the social basis of democratic politics in Africa would be to further the spread of literacy and education. When intellectual resources become more widely distributed, competing interest groups and parties have better chances to recruit leaders from their own ranks capable of taking part in national politics. Extreme poverty, however, makes it difficult for large sections of the population to acquire education and intellectual resources. Extreme poverty in many of these countries is a factor that decreases the chances of democracy because it implies that economic power resources are even more highly concentrated than my variables indicate. The percentage of people in absolute poverty is more than 40 per cent in nearly all of the countries below the threshold of democracy and even more than 60 per cent in most of them (see Human Development Report 1994, Table 18). It is extremely difficult to maintain democratic institutions in such conditions.

Poverty, overpopulation and hunger are factors that may undermine attempts to establish and maintain democratic institutions in many African countries. According to statistical data given in Human Development Report 1994, the percentage of people in absolute poverty is higher in sub-Saharan Africa than in any other regional group. Widespread poverty implies that large sections of the population are unable to participate in politics and that power resources become concentrated in the hands of relatively small sections of the population. The continuing growth of population increases poverty and hunger.

Samuel Decalo pays attention to the poverty of African countries and assumes that only some countries – the more important ones – are likely, with continued neo-colonial bandages and external aid, to surmount the obstacles of democracy and develop relatively stable multiparty systems. Many other African countries, he continues, 'will be seen as a bad bet and let loose to drift their own way, backsliding into political strife, social chaos, single-party and military rule' (Decalo 1992: 35). My statistical analysis, unfortunately, has led to relatively pessimistic predictions on the prospects of democracy in Africa, too. I want to emphasize, however, that in 1990 three sub-Saharan African countries were above the transition level of IPR and sixteen other countries had entered the transition level of IPR. This means that democratization has become possible in many sub-Saharan countries, although social conditions are still, according to my explanatory variables, unfavourable for democracy in most of them.

SOUTH ASIA

The seven countries of South Asia constitute geographically a compact region around the Indian subcontinent south of the Himalayas. During the colonial period, nearly all of them belonged to the British Indian Empire. Nepal and Bhután, however, remained *de jure* independent, although they were under some kind of British suzerainty (*cf.* Muni 1991). The islands of the Maldives were under British protection. The common historical background has increased the cultural homogeneity of the Indian subcontinent, but I want to point out that there are great racial, religious, linguistic and other ethnic divisions between and within the countries that may affect the nature of political systems.

Table 4.2 shows that the arithmetic means of residuals were clearly positive in this regional group in 1993, which means that the degree of democracy was, on the average, higher than expected on the basis of explanatory variables. Table 3.7 (chapter 3) discloses that four of the seven countries were democracies in 1993. Bangladesh and Nepal were deviating democracies on the grounds of IPR, although not on the grounds of IPRI. The Maldives was a deviating non democracy because of its relatively high IPR value. Thus three of the seven countries contradicted the second research hypothesis in 1993. The IPR values predicted poorly the level of democratization for most of these countries. It is quite possible that my explanatory variables do not take into account some significant local factors affecting the degree of resource distribution in South Asian countries.

Data on explanatory variables are give in Table 4.7. The seven countries of South Asia are classified into three categories by the transition level of IPR.

Table 4.7 Values of explanatory (1990–1) variables in 7 countries of South Asia

Country	UP	NAP	Stu	Lit	FF	DD	IOD	IKD	DER	ISI
1 IPR above 6.3										
Maldives	30	75	0	92	40	40	52.5	46.0	40.0	4.2
Sri Lanka	21	48	10	88	73	50	34.5	49.0	62.0	9.3
2 IPR from 3.3 to 6.3										
India	26	33	11	48	68	50	29.5	29.5	62.1	14.5
Pakistan	32	50	5	35	46	40	41.0	20.0	43.0	9.8
3 IPR below 3.3										
Bangladesh	16	31	8	35	68	25	21.5	21.0	54.6	14.9
Bhután	5	9	3	38	40	40	7.0	20.5	40.0	11.7
Nepal	10	8	10	26	61	30	9.0	18.0	58.5	20.0

South Asia: IPR above 6.3

Of the two countries of this category, Sri Lanka is a democracy as hypothesized. The Maldives is a non democracy contradicting the second research hypothesis. The Maldives was below the threshold of democracy in 1993, and its residuals were clearly negative (see Table 3.7). Because of President Gayoom's dominant position, I classified its political system as presidential. A problem is how to estimate the significance of the Majlis (parliament). The Majlis chooses by secret ballot a single nominee for president. The nomination is confirmed or rejected in a nationwide referendum. Gayoom has had no serious competitor in elections. It is unique for the Maldives that people live in small atolls, which are far away from each other. Each atoll community can elect two members to the Majlis, but no political parties are allowed to take part in elections. The ban of political parties prevents opposition groups organizing themselves. The geographical dispersion of the population into small atolls may also be a factor that obstructs the establishment of political organizations. The degree of resource distribution (IPR 9.7) seems to be high enough to support a competitive political system, but it may be that it is lower than my indicators show. According to Clarence Maloney, there 'are a few families who control most assets such as the shipping company, tourist hotels, and real estate in Male. These families tend to control the government' (Maloney 1995). Therefore, I am not sure whether the Maldives is really a deviating case.

Sri Lanka is a democracy as expected on the basis of IPR (10.5) and IPRI. It is remarkable that it has been able to maintain democratic institutions despite the long ethnic war between the Tamil minority and the Sinhalese majority. In this respect it has been similar to Israel. My prediction is that democratic institutions will survive in Sri Lanka. A satisfactory compromise with the Tamil rebels would strengthen the social environment of democratic politics in Sri Lanka.

South Asia: IPR from 3.3 to 6.3

India and Pakistan are at the transition level of IPR and IPRI. India has been a democracy since the first direct parliamentary elections in 1951–2. I expect it to remain a democracy, although its level of democracy is much higher than expected on the basis of explanatory variables. Positive residuals are large. India is not a deviating case in my study because the level of resource distribution is high enough to support competitive politics. Large and persistent positive residuals indicate, however, that the level of democracy is not in balance with the much lower degree of resource distribution. In this case I assume that there are local factors, not taken into account in my explanatory variables, that increase the degree of resource distribution significantly. These local factors are connected with the extreme ethnic diversity of India's population and also with geographical distances that make the concentration of power into one centre difficult. Language divides the population and politicians into many separate groups. Religious groups, caste groups, and tribal groups have the same function. All these factors distinguish the population and divide power resources among separate groups (see Vanhanen 1982 and 1991b). In other words, though the level of democratization in India is much higher than expected on the basis of my explanatory variables, it does not necessarily contradict my theory on the causal relationship between democratization and the degree of resource distribution. In India, numerous ethnic splits seem to divide power resources effectively among many competing groups (*cf.* Shukla 1994).

Pakistan was slightly below the Participation threshold of democracy in 1993 because its politically important president is elected indirectly. Ethnic divisions have supported multiparty politics in Pakistan, too, but it has been difficult to stabilize democratic institutions in Pakistan. The position of the military is much stronger than in India. Pakistan is an example of an Islamic country in which a multiparty system functions. Its small positive residuals indicate that the level of democratization was approximately in balance with the degree of resource distribution in 1993.

South Asia: IPR below 3.3

Bangladesh, Bhután and Nepal should be non democracies because of their low IPR values, but Bangladesh and Nepal crossed the threshold of democracy in 1991 and have remained democracies. They contradict the second research hypothesis clearly.

Bangladesh's low value of IPR (2.5) is mainly due to very low values of IOD and IKD (see Table 4.7). Family Farms is the only explanatory variable clearly favourable for democracy. Because the ownership of agricultural land is widely distributed, the value of DER is relatively high (54.6), and the value of IPRI rises to the transition level. This means that Bangladesh is a deviating democracy only on the basis of IPR. However, its very large positive residuals indicate that the level of democracy is much higher than expected and that it is a highly deviating case. I do not have any additional explanation for the success of democracy in Bangladesh. It cannot be explained by a high degree of ethnic pluralism as in India. I should predict the failure of democracy in Bangladesh on the basis of its low IPR value, but because IPRI indicates a higher degree of resource distribution, I hesitate to make any definite prediction. The example of Bangladesh indicates that democratic institutions may function even in a very poor Islamic country. Poverty may constitute the greatest danger for democracy in Bangladesh.

Bhután is a non democracy as expected on the basis of its extremely low IPR value (0.6). All types of power resources are still highly concentrated in the hands of the country's traditionally ruling groups. My prediction is that it will remain as a non democracy in the near future, although ethnic minorities have already demanded democratization (*cf.* Muni 1991).

According to my variables, social conditions in Nepal are even more unfavourable for democracy than in Bangladesh. The difference with Bangladesh is due to Nepal's very low value of IOD (urban population and non agricultural population). Because economic power resources seem to be relatively widely distributed, the value of IPRI is clearly higher than the value of IPR. After a long struggle for democracy, Nepal crossed the threshold of democracy in the parliamentary election of 1991 (see Baral 1994). Positive residuals are large, which indicates a serious imbalance between the level of democratization and the degree of resource distribution. Nepal is a clearly deviating democracy. I should predict a breakdown of its democratic system on the basis of the low IPR value, but not necessarily on the basis of somewhat higher IPRI value (see Table 3.7). However, it is possible that power resources are more widely distributed in Nepal than my variables indicate. A high degree of ethnic pluralism may be a factor supporting competitive politics in Nepal. S. D. Muni (1991) notes that India's 'security concerns in relation to Nepal and Bhután have influenced democratic political processes there'. It is possible that India's influence supports the survival of democracy in Nepal, although it has not been enough to establish a democratic order in Bhután.

I have attempted to explore the reasons for many deviations in South Asia. The Maldives remains a problematic non democracy. In the case of India, I assume that politically relevant power resources are distributed significantly more widely than my variables indicate because of its high degree of ethnic pluralism, which could explain India's persistently high positive residuals. According to the IPRI combination of explanatory variables, Bangladesh and Nepal are not deviating democracies, but their low IPR values and very large positive residuals make them deviations. I do not have any special explanation for Bangladesh. In the case of Nepal, a high degree of ethnic pluralism may represent an additional dimension of resource distribution, which supports competitive politics, as well as the influence of India. In the cases of Bhután, Pakistan, and Sri Lanka, the level of democratization (ID) was approximately in balance with the degree of resource distribution (IPR) in 1993.

The emergence and survival of democracy in most South Asian countries proves that democracy also is possible in poor countries when some important power resources are sufficiently distributed among competing sections of the population. However, extreme poverty makes the future of democratic rule in Bangladesh and Nepal uncertain. It is difficult to estimate how the persistence of poverty, which is causally related to the continual growth of the population, will affect democratic institutions in these and other South Asian countries.

EAST ASIA AND SOUTHEAST ASIA

The sixteen countries of this regional group constitute a relatively racially homogeneous area that is dominated by northern and southern Mongoloid peoples, whereas it is a heterogeneous area historically and culturally. China, Japan, and Thailand remained more or less independent throughout the colonial period, whereas the other parts of the region experienced the colonial rule of Japan (Korea and Taiwan), the United Kingdom (Brunei, Malaysia and Singapore), France (Cambodia, Laos and Vietnam), the Netherlands (Indonesia) and the United States (the Philippines). Mongolia was earlier dominated by China and then by the Soviet Union. Different religions compete with each other in many countries, although the majority of the population may belong to one religious group. Buddhism (Cambodia, Korea, Laos, Myanmar, Mongolia, Thailand and Vietnam), Christianity (the Philippines and South Korea), Confucianism (China, Korea, Singapore and Taiwan), Islam (Brunei, Malaysia and Indonesia), and Shintoism (Japan) are the main religions.

Table 4.2 indicates that the arithmetic means of residuals were slightly negative in 1993, which means that the degree of democracy deviated, on

Table 4.8 Values of explanatory (1990–1) variables in 16 countries of East Asia and Southeast Asia

Country	UP	NAP	Stu	Lit	FF	DD	IOD	IKD	DER	ISI
1 IPR above 6.3										
Indonesia	31	51	17	82	60	40	41.0	49.5	49.8	3.8
Japan	77	94	44	99	79	60	85.5	71.5	61.1	8.5
Korea, South	72	75	78	96	93	50	73.5	87.0	60.7	8.8
Malaysia	43	68	14	78	42	40	55.5	46.0	40.6	5.4
Mongolia	52	70	28	93	40	10	61.0	60.5	19.0	18.6
Myanmar (Burma)	25	53	9	81	60	30	39.0	45.0	44.1	2.5
Philippines	43	53	55	90	47	40	48.0	72.5	43.3	11.9
Singapore	100	99	19	88	92	40	99.5	53.5	40.5	23.3
Taiwan (ROC)	51	87	53	89	86	60	69.0	71.0	63.4	2.9
Thailand	23	36	35	93	84	40	29.5	64.0	68.2	16.3
2 IPR from 3.3 to 6.3										
Brunei	58	95	5	86	30	10	76.5	45.5	11.0	22.9
China	28	33	4	73	30	30	30.5	38.5	30.0	3.7
3 IPR below 3.3										
Cambodia	12	30	2	35	10	10	21.0	18.5	10.0	4.3
Korea, North	60	66	13	95	—	5	63.0	54.0	3.3	24.5
Laos	19	28	2	54	50	15	23.5	28.0	40.2	6.4
Vietnam	20	39	3	88	30	5	29.5	45.5	20.2	9.2

the average, only little from the expected level. In Table 4.8 these sixteen countries are classified into three categories by the transition level of IPR.

East Asia and Southeast Asia: IPR above 6.3

Seven of the ten countries of this category were democracies as hypothesized in 1993, whereas the other three countries (Indonesia, Myanmar and Taiwan) were still below the threshold of democracy.

Indonesia is a kind of semi-democracy, in which parliamentary elections are partially free, but executive power has remained in the hands of General Suharto since the 1966 bloody coup. Suharto has been elected as president by indirect elections. The three components of IPR are approximately at the same level, and IPR is so high (10.1) that Indonesia should be a democracy. Therefore, I have to predict that Indonesia will cross the threshold of democracy in the 1990s or in the first years of the next century. It should be noted, however, that Indonesia's negative residuals (see Table 3.7) are relatively small. Democratization was delayed in Spain until the death of General Franco. We can expect that General Suharto's death or resignation will start the transition to full democracy in Indonesia.

Japan has been above the threshold of democracy since the Second World War, and its degree of democracy as indicated by ID has been in good balance with its IPR values. Japan will remain a democracy. South Korea remained as a highly deviating non democracy since the 1960s until the 1987 presidential election when it crossed the threshold of democracy. A long popular pressure for democratization preceded the breakthrough of democracy in 1987. Now its degree of democracy is in balance with its high degree of resource distribution. My prediction is that South Korea will survive as a democracy.

Malaysia has been above the threshold of democracy since the 1960s, and it has good chances to continue as a democracy. The three components of IPR are in balance, and important power resources are distributed widely enough (IPR 10.5) to maintain a democratic political system. The National Alliance, the country's dominating party, has become adapted to the multi-racial nature of Malaysia.

Mongolia crossed the threshold of democracy in the parliamentary elections of 1990 and 1992. However, the nature of its democracy is still problematic for the reason that the ruling People's Revolutionary Party of Mongolia (Communist) won 92 per cent of the seats in the parliament in 1992, although its share of the votes was not more than 57 per cent. The values of IOD and IKD are relatively high (see Table 4.8), but economic power resources are still concentrated in the hands of the government. There may be errors in my data on Family Farms and DD. My prediction is that Mongolia will remain above the threshold of democracy, although its positive residuals are really high. Economic reforms intended to establish a market economy and to increase the share of private ownership of the means of production will strengthen the social basis of competitive politics.

Myanmar (Burma) is another deviating non democracy. Its IPR value is high enough (7.7) to support democratic politics, but the country has been ruled by military governments since 1962. There has been strong popular pressure for democratization in Burma. Mass protests led to the change of government in 1988 and to the legalization of political parties. Legislative elections in 1991 were competed by ninety-three parties, but the military government ignored the results of elections. An explanation for the failure of Myanmar to cross the threshold of democracy can be found from the exceptionally strong position of the armed forces, which have struggled against ethnic guerrilla groups since the 1950s. The war against guerrilla groups strengthened the position of the military and made it capable of using its coercive power resources in the struggle for political power. My prediction is that the struggle for democracy will continue in Myanmar and that attempts will be made to cross the threshold of democracy in the near future.

The Philippines crossed the threshold of democracy in the 1986 presidential election, and it has remained a democracy ever since. The three components of IPR are relatively well balanced, and IPR is high enough (14.1) to support democratic competition for political power. I predict that the Philippines will continue as a democracy. Its high positive residuals indicate, however, that the level of democratization is significantly higher than expected.

According to my variables, Singapore is a democracy, but its status as a democracy is still questionable for the reason that the ruling People's

Action Party has got nearly all the seats in parliament. Its share of the seats is 95 per cent, although it received only 61 per cent of the votes in 1991. The situation is the same as in Mongolia. Of the three components of IPR, the value of IOD (99) is extremely high because Singapore is a city state. Consequently, ISI (23.3) indicates a very high degree of structural imbalance. The degree of resource distribution is so high (IPR 21.6) that I have to predict the survival of democracy without any qualifications. I expect that the share of the opposition parties will increase in the parliament.

Taiwan (ROC) is socio-economically a highly developed country in which power resources are widely distributed (IPR 31.1). It should be a democracy, but in 1993 it was still below the threshold of democracy, and negative residuals were extremely high, although the process of democratization had started in the 1980s. Historical factors connected with the establishment of the Kuomintang Party's rule in Taiwan may explain the delay in democratization. Because the Republic of China's government, after its transition to Taiwan in 1949, regarded itself as the government of the whole of China, it was not willing to make itself responsible only to the inhabitants of Taiwan. Therefore delegates elected in 1947 to governmental institutions were frozen in office until the beginning of the 1990s. In addition, because of the war with mainland China and of the continual military tension, Taiwan was under martial law for thirty-eight years until 1987. After the lifting of martial law, the process of democratization became possible. In 1990 the Council of Grand Justices ruled that all senior parliamentarians must retire by 31 December 1991 (see Republic of China Yearbook 1991–92: 75–107). Taiwan (ROC) started its transition to full democracy in the parliamentary elections to the National Assembly in 1991 and to the Legislative Branch in 1992. In 1994 the National Assembly accepted a package of constitutional reforms including provisions for the direct election of the president in 1996 (see Keesing's 1994: 40101). My prediction is that Taiwan will cross the threshold of democracy in the 1990s.

Thailand's political system has been very fragile since the 1930s. Democratic experiments have alternated with military governments and authoritarian regimes. The level of resource distribution is high enough (IPR 12.9) to support democracy, but nevertheless the military has been continually able to usurp power. A period of democratic rule ended in a military coup in February 1991. Thailand dropped below the threshold of democracy and became a deviating non democracy. It crossed the threshold of democracy again in the 1992 parliamentary elections and ceased to be a deviating case. On the basis of explanatory variables, I have to predict that democracy will survive in Thailand.

East Asia and Southeast Asia: IPR from 3.3 to 6.3

Brunei and China are the two countries at the transition level of IPR. Brunei is a Muslim oil state like Kuwait. It is an absolute monarchy. The

concentration of economic power resources (DER 11.0) supports the concentration of political power in the hands of the sultan, but the values of
IOD and IKD presuppose democracy. This structural imbalance (ISI 22.9)
indicates that the present political system is not in harmony with social
conditions. In fact, there has been popular pressure for democratization.
The sultan has ruled by decree, and a state of emergency has been in force
since a large-scale revolt in December 1962 (see Keesing's Record of World
Events 1993, Volume 39 Reference Supplement: R62). Britain has provided
a Gurkha battalion, which is stationed in Brunei (Kurian 1987: 276). It can
be regarded as an external power resource at the disposal of the sultan. My
prediction is that pressure for democratization will increase in Brunei, but it
is difficult to estimate how long the sultan will be able to resist democratization. Because some important power resources are already widely distributed, Brunei's political system will ultimately democratize.

China is a very interesting case from the perspective of democratization.
Until now it has remained as a non democracy, but the process of modernization started in 1978 is changing and has already changed social preconditions of democracy. Socialist economic structures have been gradually
dismantled, although the system has not collapsed as in Eastern Europe,
and economic power resources have become more widely distributed both
in agriculture and in non agricultural industries (*cf.* Baogang He 1994).
Empirical data on the extent of structural changes are unfortunately scarce.
I assume that privatization and the adoption of mechanisms of market
economy will disperse economic power resources and create a favourable
social environment for the emergence of competitive politics. The three
components of IPR are approximately in balance, which provides a solid
basis for democratization. I predict that democratization will not take place
immediately, but because economic power resources are becoming more
and more widely distributed, popular pressure for democratization will also
increase. Negative residuals are still relatively small, which means that the
discrepancy between the level of democratization and the degree of resource
distribution is not yet fatal for the country's authoritarian system. Baogang
He (1994: 24) notes that 'there are enormous institutional tensions between
limited economic pluralism and a monolith political structure'. He assumes
that 'the authoritarian solution can not last very long'. I would like to
emphasize that the authoritarian system still has chances of survival because
important economic resources and the means of violence have remained in
the control of the government.

East Asia and Southeast Asia: IPR below 3.3

The four countries of this category are present or former socialist countries.
It is common for them that economic power resources were concentrated in
the hands of the government in 1990, but the values of IOD and IKD were
also relatively low, except in North Korea. In this respect they differ from

the former socialist countries of Eastern Europe and the Soviet Union where the values of IOD and IKD were high. This difference explains, according to my interpretation, the delay and failures of democratization in these Asian socialist countries. Because of the lower level of education and the distribution of intellectual power resources, popular pressure for democratization has been much weaker in Asian socialist countries than it was in Eastern Europe and in the former Soviet Union.

In Cambodia, the values of all explanatory variables are extremely low (IPR 0.4), and the country was a non democracy as expected in 1993, although only slightly below the Competition threshold. The signing of a peace agreement in October 1991 started a process of democratization and transition to a market economy. It has been difficult to end the civil war that started in the 1970s and to agree on the sharing of power. The first free elections were held in 1993 under the protection of the United Nations. Because of the low values of IPR and IPRI, I have to predict that Cambodia is not yet able to maintain a democratic system. Also, its high level of poverty decreases the chances of democratization. The civil war between the government and the Khmer Rouge continues.

In North Korea the first four explanatory variables are more favourable for democracy than in China, whereas the value of DER is extremely low (3.3). The state still almost completely controls the means of production both in agriculture and in non agricultural industries. Political power has been held as tightly in the hands of the Communist party (Korean Workers' Party) and its leaders. Education and all organizations are also controlled by the state, but the fact that IOD and IKD values are relatively high implies the existence of structural imbalance (ISI 24.5), which may become dangerous for the country's autocratic political system. As a consequence of this structural imbalance, the value of IPRI has already entered the transition level. I have to predict, on the basis of IPR, that we cannot yet expect democratization in North Korea, but the value of IPRI indicates that it has become possible. The situation is similar to that in Cuba.

Laos is a non democracy as expected on the grounds of its IPR value. The country has been ruled by the Lao People's Revolutionary Party (Communist) since 1975, after a long civil war. Because of a high estimated share of family farms, the value of DER (40.2) is much higher than the values of IOD and IKD. In this respect it differs from the other socialist countries in Asia and resembles many sub-Saharan African countries. My prediction is that Laos will remain below the threshold of democracy in the near future.

In Vietnam, the concentration of economic power resources in the hands of the government supports the hegemony of the Vietnamese Communist Party, whereas a significantly higher value of IKD implies that intellectual resources are more widely distributed. Vietnam has not yet started extensive economic reforms intended to replace its socialist command economy with a market economy, although partial privatizations are taking place. I have to predict that Vietnam will continue as a non democracy in the near future. However, a hegemonic party system would be better in harmony with its social conditions than a one-party rule.

Social conditions and political systems vary greatly in the countries of East Asia and Southeast Asia. It is remarkable that the degree of resource distribution (IPR) predicted the nature of political systems quite well in most cases in 1993. Taiwan (ROC) is the most deviating case, but some local factors may explain the delay of democratization in Taiwan. The other two deviating non democracies deviate less from the regression line.

The five socialist or former socialist countries below the threshold of democracy constitute a geographically coherent bastion of socialism in Asia, but because significant economic reforms taking place in its core area in China are undermining socialist structures, it is questionable how long these socialist systems can resist the lure of privatization and market economies and the increasing popular pressure for democratization. The socialist systems of Asia may withstand these pressures longer than the former socialist countries of Eastern Europe were able to do because the percentage of urban population and the level of education are much lower than in Eastern Europe. It means that it is not as easy to organize mass movements to demand democratic reforms as in Eastern Europe, or to recruit leaders from the ranks of intellectuals.

OCEANIA

This regional group includes Australia and New Zealand, which are populated mainly by white Europeans, and Fiji, Papua New Guinea, Solomon Islands, Vanuatu, and Western Samoa, which are populated by original Melanesians and Polynesians of the Pacific. In Fiji, however, nearly half of the inhabitants are descendants from bonded workers brought from India, which has caused serious ethnic conflicts between indigenous Fijians and Indians. In New Zealand indigenous Polynesian Maori constitute 12 per cent of the population.

Table 4.2 shows that the arithmetic means of residuals are positive and larger than for any other regional group, which means that the level of democracy was considerably higher than expected in 1993. The problem is how to explain the success of democracy in the relatively poor countries of Oceania. Table 4.9, in which these countries are divided into three categories by the transition level of IPR, complements data on political and explanatory variables.

Oceania: IPR above 6.3

The four countries of this category were democracies as hypothesized in 1993. Australia and New Zealand have been democracies since the

Table 4.9 Values of explanatory (1990–1) variables in 7 countries of Oceania

Country	UP	NAP	Stu	Lit	FF	DD	IOD	IKD	DER	ISI
1 IPR above 6.3										
Australia	85	95	57	99	67	70	90.0	78.0	69.8	7.2
Fiji	37	61	10	87	58	50	49.0	48.5	53.1	1.9
New Zealand	84	91	66	99	51	70	87.5	82.5	68.3	7.4
Western Samoa	27	36	7	92	48	50	31.5	49.5	48.7	7.8
2 IPR from 3.3 to 6.3										
Papua New Guinea	16	33	3	52	58	30	24.5	27.5	48.8	10.1
Vanuatu	27	32	6	65	50	60	29.5	35.5	53.2	9.2
3 IPR below 3.3										
Solomon Islands	9	10	3	51	57	50	9.5	27.0	56.3	16.9

establishment of these states. The level of democracy as indicated by ID is in balance with the degree of resource distribution (IPR) in both countries. Residuals have remained relatively small. The very high values of IPR and IPRI predict the survival of democracy in these countries.

Fiji is an exceptional country in this regional group because of its ethnic structure. Political parties were established along ethnic lines, and the country's electoral system was adapted to ethnic divisions. Democratic institutions functioned as long as the parties of indigenous Fijians were capable of retaining a majority, but when the party of the Indian community won in the 1987 parliamentary elections, the military usurped power and cancelled the constitution. Fiji dropped below the threshold of democracy and became a deviating non democracy. A new constitution, promulgated in 1990, guaranteed the Melanesian control of the legislature by reserving thirty-seven of its seventy seats for indigenous Fijians. Fiji crossed the threshold of democracy again in the 1992 parliamentary elections and ceased to be a deviating non democracy. Because social conditions are favourable for democracy (IPR 12.6), my prediction is that democracy will survive in Fiji, although ethnic interest conflicts will continue.

Western Samoa is a democracy as expected on the basis of IPR (7.6) and IPRI. Its moderate positive residuals show that the country's level of democracy is approximately in balance with the degree of resource distribution. Democracy will survive in Western Samoa.

Oceania: IPR from 3.3 to 6.3

Papua New Guinea has been a deviating democracy since its independence in 1975, but its IPR achieved the lower limit of the transition level of IPR in 1990. The three components of IPR are not in balance (see Table 4.9). The values of IOD and IKD are low, whereas the value of DER is relatively high (48.8) because agricultural land seems to be widely distributed. The country's ethnic structure is a local factor that has supported the survival of democratic institutions. The fact that over 700 dialects are spoken in the country has made the formation of ethnic alliances and consensus necessary. There is no single numerically dominant ethnic group. Another factor that should be taken into account is an external one. Australia has provided a lot of administrative and financial assistance, which has supported the maintenance of governmental services and administration. The poverty of the population and a low level of higher education are unfavourable structural factors. Papua New Guinea's high level of democratization (ID 31.2) and low level of resource distribution (IPR 3.3) show a discrepancy that cannot be explained away. Extremely large positive residuals predict a dramatic decrease in the level of democratization, but because some local factors (affecting resource distribution) unknown to me may support competitive politics, I hesitate to make any definitive prediction.

Vanuatu has been a democracy since its independence in 1980, but its very large positive residuals indicate that the level of democracy is considerably higher than expected on the basis of IPR and IPRI. It is possible that there are local factors, not taken into account by my explanatory variables, that increase the degree of resource distribution. However, because of its very high positive residuals, I have to predict that the level of democratization will decrease.

Oceania: IPR below 3.3

The Solomon Islands is the only country in this category of IPR. It has been a deviating democracy since its independence in 1978. The values of the first three explanatory variables are extremely low, whereas the values of the three other explanatory variables are moderately high. Consequently, the value of IPR is very low (1.4), whereas the value of IPRI is just above the lower limit of transition level. The ethnic structure of the Solomon Islands is as dispersed as in Papua New Guinea, although Melanesians constitute 93 per cent of the population. Over sixty Melanesian languages and dialects are spoken. It makes it impossible to establish political parties on the basis of any single ethnic group. A local factor that may have supported the survival of civilian governments is the fact that the Solomon Islands is without its own army. It is under the protection of the UK military guarantees. Its low IPR value predicts the breakdown of democratic institutions, but some local factors discussed above may be more favourable for democracy. Therefore, it is difficult to make any definitive prediction, although I have to expect a significant decrease in the level of democracy.

It is common to the Solomon Islands, Vanuatu and Western Samoa that they are small island states. One could argue, as Dag Anckar does, that their smallness and remoteness are in some way connected with the success of democracy (Anckar 1994; see also Blondel 1995: 84). The success of democracy in Pacific island states populated by Melanesians and Polynesians indicates that democracy is not racially or geographically limited to the countries of white Europeans. It also implies that my present explanatory variables may not be able to take into account all the important aspects of resource distribution. However, I would like to point out that the success of democracy in these island states is in harmony with the wide distribution of economic power resources. The fact that the bulk of the population is not economically or socially dependent on any large landowners, on corporations, or on the rulers of the state has certainly been favourable for competitive politics. In addition, external factors and resources may have been more important in the establishment of democratic institutions in these island states than is usual. John Henderson, in his comments, comes to the conclusion that he is not as optimistic on the survival of democracy in Pasific islands as I am. He refers to the possibility of military coups and particularly to the re-assertion of traditional political systems. It is a very interesting assumption.

5 Conclusions: Regularities since the 1850s

The results of this comparative study indicate that it is possible to trace the emergence of democracy to one regular and dominant causal factor, the relative distribution of power resources, although many other factors may also affect the process of democratization. It was hypothesized, on the basis of evolutionary argumentation, that democratization would take place under conditions in which power resources become so widely distributed that no group is any longer able to suppress its competitors or to maintain its hegemony. Six social variables were formulated to measure the variation of resource distribution from different perspectives, and they were combined into an Index of Power Resources (IPR). Two political variables – Competition and Participation – were formulated to measure two crucial dimensions of democratization. They were combined into an Index of Democratization (ID). The results of statistical analysis show that it was possible to explain 66 per cent of the variation in the degree of democracy (ID) by the variation of resource distribution (IPR) in the longitudinal comparison group of 1,139 observation units of 1850–1993 and 59–65 per cent in the cross-sectional comparison group of 172 countries in 1991–3. The results of correlation analyses support the basic hypothesis very strongly. In addition, the results of regression analysis indicate that most countries tended to cross the threshold of democracy at approximately the same level of resource distribution as hypothesized. These strong regularities have continued at least since the 1850s.

I have argued that the Darwinian or evolutionary theory of democratization, from which the research hypotheses were derived, provides a theoretical explanation for these regularities. The emergence and survival of democracy must be causally related to the degree of resource distribution because politics constitutes a part of the struggle for existence in which people tend to use all available resources. Consequently, if politically relevant economic, intellectual, and other power resources are widely distributed among competing groups, circumstances are favourable for the emergence of democratic power sharing. If power resources are concentrated in the hands of one group, conditions are favourable for the survival of autocratic political structures and for the failures of democracy. This regularity seems to be very strong because all human populations share the same human nature.

There are other theoretical explanations for democracy and democratization. I referred to some of them, particularly to the Lerner–Lipset economic development hypothesis and to Diamond's physical quality of life hypothesis, and attempted to compare the explanatory power of different explanatory variables. The results show that my IPR explains significantly more of the variation in the degree of democracy than GNP per capita (Lerner–Lipset) or Human Development Index (Diamond). Also, when GNP per capita and HDI were used together with IPR as explanatory variables, the explained part of variation in the Index of Democratization increased only marginally. In other words, the explanatory powers of GNP per capita and HDI are already included in IPR.

On the grounds of these comparisons, I concluded that my theory seems to provide a more powerful explanation for democratization than hypotheses based on economic development or physical quality of life. I assumed that a theoretical explanation for the observed positive relationship between the level of economic development and democracy and between the Human Development Index and democracy is that economic development and HDI also reflect differences in the relative distribution of power resources. Usually power resources are more widely distributed, the higher the level of economic development and the higher the physical quality of life. However, there are important exceptions that differentiate between the explanatory power of IPR and that of GNP per capita and HDI. There are several relatively wealthy countries in which power resources are highly concentrated and which consequently have been non democracies and several poor countries that were able to cross the threshold of democracy because some crucial power resources are distributed widely enough. Correspondingly, there are several countries in which the physical quality of life seems to deviate significantly from the relative distribution of power resources. According to my evolutionary theory of democratization, the chances of democracy are not limited only to relatively wealthy countries because power resources may also be sufficiently widely distributed in some poor countries. This is a crucial and politically significant difference between my theory and the Lerner–Lipset economic development theory. As Malak Poppovic and Paulo Sérgio Pinheiro (1995: 78) note: 'Contrary to the widespread view that a fairly high level of national wealth is necessary to foster democracy, Vanhanen's ideas offer a degree of hope for poor nations' (see also Mbaku 1994). Approximately half of the contemporary democracies are relatively poor countries.

The strong observed relationship between the degree of resource distribution (IPR) and the level of democracy (ID) provided a basis on which to make rough predictions on the chances of democracy in particular countries (chapter 4). High IPR values predict democratization and the survival of democratic structures, whereas low IPR values predict that attempts at democratization would fail and that autocratic political structures would survive. In addition, various strategies of democratization could be derived from this strong relationship between IPR and ID. It would be reasonable to argue that social reforms intended to further the distribution of economic, intellectual, and other power resources among various social groups would strengthen the social basis of democracy or create favourable conditions for democratization.

UNEXPLAINED VARIATION

The idea of this study was to explore to what extent the variation in democratization (ID) could be explained by one theoretically grounded explanatory variable, the variation in resource distribution (IPR). I assumed that, for various reasons, the hypothesized relationship between IPR and ID would not and could not be perfect. Considering the fact that so many other factors, including inevitable random factors, may affect the nature of political systems, the explained part of variation in ID can be regarded as extremely high. However, 34 per cent of the variation in ID remained unexplained. Why? I do not know what factors might be behind the unexplained part of variation in ID, although I have referred to various possible explanations in particular cases, and my purpose has not been to find explanations for all variations in the degree of democracy.

An interesting question is, however, to what extent the unexplained part of variation might be due to the fact that the empirical substitutes for the hypothetical concepts 'the degree of democracy' and 'the degree of resource distribution' used in this study are not perfect and to what extent it might be due to other causal factors and various random factors. There may be at least three types of faults in the empirical variables used in this study:

1 they are not complete substitutes for the hypothetical concepts;
2 they include measurement errors; and
3 they do not cover all types of relevant power resources, particularly not local and external resources.

Other causal factors may include historical, institutional, ethnic, and cultural factors that are independent from resource distribution. Finally, random factors have always a role in politics. Let us examine how these factors might affect the relationship between IPR and ID.

Imperfect indicators

It is clear that my two political variables and six social variables are only imperfect substitutes for the hypothetical concepts 'the degree of democracy' and 'the degree of resource distribution'. My simple electoral indicators, Competition and Participation, are assumed to measure two crucial dimensions of democratization – competition and participation – and their combination (the Index of Democratization) the combined level of democracy, but they cannot take into account all important aspects of democracy. As I emphasized, they may be better suited to measure rough differences between democracies and non democracies than the variation in the degree of democracy at higher levels of democracy, or the variation in the degree of autocracy among non democracies. The results of measurements disclose that they are indeed only approximate measures of democracy. Measurements have produced several anomalies. Robert H. Dix remarks that:

> Vanhanen's strict reliance on numbers and thresholds for competition, participation, and democracy sometimes leads patent misassessments. To take but one example. El Salvador easily meets Vanhanen's criteria for democracy during the decade of the 1970s. Yet elections, which were indeed held and were formally competitive, were essentially fraudulent because the military perpetuated its control behind a civil facade.
>
> (Dix 1994: 102)

I agree that the strict application of the same formal criteria to all countries produces anomalies. My measures of democracy are not able to take into account all differences in the quality of democracy and in the quality of autocracy. Let us take up some other anomalies. The ID values of the United States and Switzerland in 1993 were relatively low (20.7 and 23.7) compared, for example, to the ID values of Bulgaria (35.4), the Czech Republic (40.3), Panama (21.6), Mongolia (20.6), and Papua New Guinea (31.2). However, I have not attempted to correct these and other anomalies because it would lead to the use of subjective and *ad hoc* criteria, which would decrease the intersubjective usefulness of my indicators. The correction of obvious anomalies might produce more realistic assessments of the relative level of democracy and might also increase the explained part of variation, but I regarded it methodologically better to apply the same formal criteria to all countries in spite of some inevitable anomalies.

Perhaps it is possible for somebody to invent additional empirical indicators that account for differences in the quality of democracy, including differences in the actual extent of political freedoms. I deliberately left out of direct measurement the level of civil and political liberties and rights for two reasons: (1) there are no quantitative measures for civil and political liberties and rights and (2) my Competition variable is an indirect indicator of the level of civil and political liberties and rights, too, for usually electoral competition between political parties presupposes the existence of civil and political liberties and rights. The fact that my Competition variable is highly correlated with Gastils's and Bollen's ratings of political liberties and rights supports this assumption (see chapter 2). It is obvious that a part of the unexplained variation in ID is due to the imperfect nature of my political indicators. However, until now I have not been able to invent more perfect indicators that could be applied equally to all countries.

The six social variables intended to measure three dimensions of resource distribution may be even more imperfect than the two political indicators, but they have done their job in this study satisfactorily. I wanted to find some empirical indicators of resource distribution that would be relevant to all countries and whose significance would remain more or less the same from country to country. I think that the six social variables (Urban Population, NAP, Students, Literates, Family Farms, and DD) are suited to this purpose. They are assumed to measure the relative distribution of power resources, directly or indirectly, from different perspectives. Because the relative distribution of power resources represents the theoretically grounded causal factor, I have been more interested in their combined explanatory power than in their separate explanatory powers. The six variables were combined into an Index of Power Resources (IPR) that was used as the principal explanatory variable. The Index of Power Resources and Structural Imbalance (IPRI) is a slightly different version of IPR. In IPRI, the value of IPR is weighted by the value of the Index of Structural Imbalance (ISI) in order to differentiate countries for which the values of all three sectional indices (IOD, IKD, and DER) are near zero from countries for which the values of one or two sectional indices are relatively high. The weight of ISI (1/4) in this combination is arbitrarily, although not randomly, selected. There would have been many other ways to weight the relative significance of ISI, but I thought that this combination might produce most realistic results. It seems to me that, in most cases, the results of measurements reflect realistically the relative differences of resource distribution between countries, but there may also be some anomalies in these measurement results. It is difficult to estimate the validity of these measurements because there are no reliable points of comparison.

Certainly the IPR and IPRI values given in this study represent only approximations, but they are the only available estimations of the relative degree of resource distribution in different countries of the world. I assume that if it had been possible to measure differences in resource distribution more validly, the explained part of variation in ID would be somewhat higher than the results of this study show. It is a challenge for other researchers to invent more valid indicators for the distribution of power resources.

Measurement errors

Another source of unexplained variation may be in various measurement errors. It was possible to find relatively reliable empirical data on the two political variables from nearly all countries, but the classification of governmental systems into the three categories (parliamentary dominance, executive dominance and concurrent powers) includes possibilities of mis-assessments. For example, it is not self-evident how we should weight the executive branch of government in traditional monarchies like Jordan, Morocco, Kuwait, Swaziland, Lesotho, Nepal, and Thailand, or the relative significance of executive and parliamentary branches of government in the Czech Republic, Hungary, Bangladesh, Maldives, Pakistan, and Singapore. The classification of a country into any of the three categories does not make much difference if both legislative and presidential elections are direct, but it matters if presidential elections are indirect, or if executive power is regarded to be in the hands of the king or other traditional rulers. I think that most of the classifications of governmental systems used in this study are not problematic, but there are some cases in which different interpretations might have been possible.

Empirical data on the first four explanatory variables are relatively reliable, although not in all single cases. Data on Family Farms are much more problematic. The category of Family Farms is intended to include farms that provide employment for not more than four people, including family members, but because there are great differences in agricultural technologies and circumstances from country to country, I had to define the criteria of family farms separately for each country and because of the lack of suitable statistical data it was necessary to estimate the share of family farms in many cases. This concerns particularly sub-Saharan African countries. I assume that my data provide a fairly correct picture of the relative significance of family farms in different countries, but it is probable that there are many measurement errors in these data. Measurement errors are most probable in the data given on the degree of decentralization of non agricultural economic resources (DD). The same criteria were applied to all countries, but because there are no ready statistical data on this variable, I had to estimate the values of DD for all countries (see Appendix 4), just as Gastil and later on the Freedom House Survey Team have estimated the ratings of political rights and civil liberties on the basis of various empirical data.

Local and external power resources

It should be noted that I have used the same explanatory variables to all countries, and only them, to measure the relative distribution of politically relevant power resources. It is quite possible that the significance of these variables varies locally and that there are various types of locally significant power resources that my general explanatory variables are not able to take into account. Let us think, for example, of the significance of ethnic divisions in many countries. They may strengthen, at least in some cases, the distribution of power resources among competing groups. There may be other locally significant factors that increase the concentration of power resources. My point is that if it were possible to take into account various local factors affecting the distribution of power resources, the relationship between ID and IPR would become stronger.

I have not attempted to measure or estimate the significance of external power resources used in domestic politics because I have not found any reliable empirical indicator for that purpose. I assume that in some cases, particularly in the case of very small states, external power resources may be significant. They may improve or decrease the chances of democracy. On the one hand, the former socialist countries of Eastern Europe provide good examples of countries where the use of external power resources caused the downfall of democratic structures and prevented democratization for several decades. On the other hand, there are numerous former colonial countries in which external power resources were used to establish democratic institutions much earlier than might otherwise have happened. In many of those countries, democratic institutions collapsed after independence because domestic power resources were not sufficiently distributed to support democratic competition for power. It may be that external power resources have crucially supported the survival of democratic institutions in some small countries.

It is reasonable to assume that the exclusion of local and external power resources has decreased the explanatory power of IPR. They may account for a part of the unexplained variation in ID. The theory of democratization used in this study refers to all types of relevant power resources, including local and external resources, but operationally defined indicators of resource distribution were not able to take all of them into account.

Other causal factors

Some part of the unexplained variation in ID is probably due to factors that are not connected to the degree of resource distribution. These other factors may include historical legacies, differences in colonial background, geographical factors, ethnic structures, institutional factors, leadership qualities, and diffusion of ideas. Many researchers have focused on some of these factors in their attempts to explain democratization (see Dahl 1971; Diamond, *et al.* 1990; Huntington 1991; Arat 1991; Hadenius 1992). Jean Blondel says, referring to the results of my earlier study: 'Since a substantial proportion of the variation remains to be explained, however, we need to turn to the examination of the exceptional part played by some groupings in plural societies and to the role of the "national culture" ' (Blondel 1990: 69–71; *cf.* Blondel 1995: 82–5). It is quite possible that differences in 'national culture' explain a part of the unexplained variation in ID.

My point is that although many other factors affect the process of democratization, their role has usually been marginal compared to the significance of resource distribution. They hardly provide any systematic explanations that could be applied to all countries. Of course, any systematic explanation is not needed if it is assumed that democratization is always connected with particular historical and other circumstances and that, therefore, we cannot expect any regularities in democratizations. I have attempted to show by this comparative study that there are strong regularities in the process of democratization and that these regularities are more important than particular factors causing deviations, but I do not try to deny the significance of historical, cultural, ethnic, and other factors in particular cases. The study of such other factors is needed to complement the explanation of democratization.

Random factors

A part of unexplained variation in ID is probably due to various random factors that have a role in politics as in other biological phenomena. Random factors in politics are like mutations. There are no means to anticipate their forms and appearance. Random factors include, for instance, exceptional personalities (Lenin, Hitler and Mao, for example) who are capable of changing the course of politics, of initiating new political or social structures, of plunging a country into war or revolution, or inventing new ideologies and myths. In some cases, historical and external factors could also be regarded as random factors.

The Darwinian or evolutionary theory of democratization used in this study may be capable of explaining somewhat more of the variation in the degree of democratization than the correlation between IPR and ID indicates (66 per cent) because my empirical variables cannot take into account all relevant aspects of democracy and resource distribution. However, it is not possible to determine how much more of the variation in the degree of democracy could be explained if we had more complete variables. The unexplained part of variation in ID caused by the faults of my empirical variables and measurement errors may rise to 10 percentage points. The rest of the unexplained variation in ID is probably due to various random factors and other possible causal factors discussed above.

THE PERSISTENCE OF DEVIATING CASES

Because the empirical relationship between ID and IPR (and IPRI) is and has always been incomplete, some small and large deviations are inevitable. An interesting question concerns the persistence of deviations. Have some countries always contradicted the research hypotheses, or have deviating cases varied over time? This is a theoretically important question. If empirical evidence shows that particular countries deviated or have deviated from the hypothesized relationship during long periods, it would weaken the second research hypothesis on the tendency of all countries to cross the threshold of democracy under approximately similar conditions more than short-term deviations lasting only one or two decades. The historical data given in Appendix 5 help to clarify this problem. The contemporary deviating cases in 1993 were indicated and discussed in chapter 3. The historical deviating democracies and non democracies of the period 1850–1980 are

Table 5.1 Deviating democracies and non democracies by regional groups over the period 1850–1980

Deviating democracies	Deviating non democracies
Europe and North America	
Finland 1917–19	Austria 1930–37
	Canada 1870–89
	Czechoslovakia 1940–49
	Denmark 1890–1919*
	German Democratic Republic 1950–59
	Germany 1880–1919, 1930–49*
	Greece 1940–49
	Hungary 1920–39, 1950–59
	Netherlands 1900–09
	Norway 1870–1909*
	Poland 1930–80*
	Romania 1950–59
	Spain 1960–69
	Sweden 1910–19
	Switzerland 1860–1919*
	United Kingdom 1910–1919
	United States 1850–69
	Yugoslavia 1960–80*
Latin America and the Caribbean	
Brazil 1950–59	Argentina 1970–80
Costa Rica 1930–39	Chile 1970–80
Cuba 1940–49	Mexico 1970–80
Guyana 1966–69	Uruguay 1920–29, 1970–80
Panama 1950–59	Brazil 1980
Venezuela 1960–69	Panama 1980
North Africa, the Middle East, and Central Asia	
Turkey 1950–59	Egypt 1970–79
	Jordan 1980–93
	Lebanon 1970–79
	Turkey 1980
Sub-Saharan Africa	
Lesotho 1965–69	
Sierra Leone 1961–69	
Somalia 1960–69	
Gambia 1980–93	
Nigeria 1980	
Uganda 1980	
Zimbabwe 1980	
South Asia	
India 1950–69	Sri Lanka 1980
East Asia and Southeast Asia	
Malaysia 1960–69	Philippines 1970–80
	Singapore 1980
Oceania	
Papua New Guinea 1980	
Solomon Islands 1980–93	

listed in Table 5.1. The deviations that lasted continuously for three or more decades are marked by an asterisk. It should be noted that the values of political variables are decennial arithmetic means during the period 1850–1979, whereas the data of the 1980s concern only one year (1980). Therefore, the decades of deviations given in Table 5.1 do not usually correspond exactly with the actual years of deviations.

In Table 5.1, the criteria of deviating democracies and non democracies are the same as defined in chapter 3. A country below any of the three threshold values of political variables (Competition 30 per cent, Participation 15 per cent, and ID 5.0 index points) is a non democracy and a country above all of them is a democracy. A democracy for which the value of IPR is below 3.3 index points is a deviating democracy, and a non democracy for which the value of IPR is above 6.3 is regarded as a deviating non democracy.

We can see from Table 5.1 that deviating cases were distributed around the world in the period 1850–1980, but they were most numerous in Europe and Latin America. In the regional group of Europe and North America, nearly all deviating countries were non democracies. Finland 1917–19 was the only short-term deviating democracy. For many emerging democracies in this regional group, it was difficult to cross the minimum threshold of Participation (15 per cent), although the value of IPR had already crossed the upper limit of transition (6.3), and a country should have become a democracy. This concerned Canada 1870–89, Denmark 1890–1919, Germany 1880–1919, Netherlands 1900–9, Norway 1870–1909, Poland 1930–9, Sweden 1910–19, Switzerland 1860–1919, United Kingdom 1910–19, and the United States 1850–69. When the degree of electoral participation increased, these countries crossed the last threshold of democracy, except Poland where the communist usurpation of power in the 1940s interrupted the process of democratization for forty years. It was characteristic for democratization in most countries of this regional group that a high level of competition preceded an increase in electoral participation.

The other deviating non democracies were different. In Austria and Germany, the democratic institutions established in the 1920s collapsed in the 1930s as a consequence of the rise of Nazism. Their high values of IPR, however, predicted a return of democracy. Hungary was a deviating non democracy on the basis of all political variables in 1920–39, Greece in 1940–9, and Spain in 1960–9. Czechoslovakia, the German Democratic Republic, Hungary, Poland, Romania, and Yugoslavia, where communist parties usurped power after the Second World War, became deviating non democracies in the 1940s or 1950s for some years. When the IPR values dropped as a consequence of nationalizations carried out in these countries, they ceased to be deviations, except Poland and Yugoslavia where most of agricultural land remained in the hands of peasant farmers.

The only historical deviations lasting three or more decades occurred in Europe. Because of a too low degree of electoral participation, Switzerland was a deviating non democracy for six decades, Germany and Norway for four decades, and Denmark for three decades. Because of their socialist systems, Poland remained a deviating non democracy for four decades and Yugoslavia for three decades. So we have six European countries that contradicted the second research hypothesis continuously for three or more decades, but all of them were not serious deviations. The residuals of Denmark, Germany 1880–99, and Switzerland were smaller than one standard error of estimate (6.1), and of Norway only a little higher. The negative residuals were highest for Poland and Yugoslavia in the period 1960–80.

In all the other regional groups, continuous deviations lasted only one or two decades, which implies that the degree of democracy and the degree of resource distribution tend to achieve a better balance relatively soon. Only three countries (Gambia, Jordan, and the Solomon Islands) that were deviations in 1980 also remained deviating cases in 1993. All the other deviating democracies and non democracies of 1993 (see Table 3.9) are more recent deviations. The fact that there are not any serious long-term deviating cases among the countries of this comparison group supports the second research hypothesis of the tendency of all countries to democratize approximately at the same level of resource distribution.

In Latin America, nearly all deviations lasted only one decade. Deviating democracies ceased to be deviations when the value of IPR rose (Costa Rica, Guyana, Panama, and Venezuela) or when the values of political variables decreased (Brazil and Cuba). Deviating non democracies, except Mexico and Uruguay 1920–9, were due to military coups, and they ceased to be deviations when the establishment of democratic institutions increased the values of political variables.

In the Islamic countries of North Africa, the Middle East, and Central Asia the number of deviations was quite small in the period 1850–1980, whereas most contemporary deviating non democracies belong to this regional group. It is a remarkable change.

In sub-Saharan Africa, all deviations were deviating democracies in the period 1960–93. Lesotho, Sierra Leone, Somalia, Gambia, and Zimbabwe inherited from the colonial period democratic institutions that survived some years after the achievement of independence. The re-establishment of democratic institutions made Nigeria and Uganda deviating democracies in 1980, but democracy collapsed in both countries later in the 1980s.

In South Asia, India was a deviating democracy in 1950–69, but it ceased to be a deviation when its IPR entered the transition level. Sri Lanka was a deviating non democracy only temporarily in 1980 because of its exceptional indirect presidential election in 1978.

In Southeast Asia, Malaysia became a short-term deviating democracy in the 1960s. A presidential autocracy dropped the Philippines into the category of deviating non democracies in the 1970s, when its IPR already presupposed a democratic system. One-party dominated Singapore was a clearly deviating non democracy in 1980, but it succeeded in crossing the threshold of democracy later in the 1980s.

Two Pacific island states, Papua New Guinea and the Solomon Islands have been highly deviating democracies, although Papua New Guinea ceased to contradict the research hypothesis 2.2 when its IPR achieved the lower limit of the transition level (3.3) in the 1990s. However, its positive residual (27.3) is still one of the highest.

The examination of deviating democracies and non democracies over the period 1850–1993 shows that nearly all deviations contradicting the research hypothesis 2.2 were relatively short-term. There were some deviations of longer duration, but they were not very serious because of relatively small residuals or because of external factors (Poland). Most countries crossed the threshold of democracy at the transition level of IPR as hypothesized. They were democracies or non democracies depending on the degree of resource distribution as indicated by IPR. According to my interpretation, the struggle for power in which participants resort to all available power resources maintains a balance between the level of power sharing and the degree of resource distribution. It makes it difficult to stabilize a situation in which the level of power sharing and the degree of resource distribution differ greatly from each other. If power resources are widely distributed, it becomes difficult to maintain autocratic power structures, and if resources are concentrated, it becomes difficult to establish and maintain democratic political systems. Therefore deviating non democracies and democracies have historically been of short duration. Because this regularity has been strong in the past until now, it is plausible to assume that the same will be repeated in the future. So this regularity makes it possible to make rough predictions on the chances of democracy in particular countries on the basis of their IPR and IPRI values.

PROSPECTS OF DEMOCRACY BY REGIONAL GROUPS

One idea of this study was to explore whether it might be possible to make reasonably accurate predictions on the prospects of democracy in particular countries on the basis of the theoretical explanation of democratization given in this study. The results of empirical analysis show that the regular relationship between ID and IPR would have made it possible to present approximately correct predictions on the chances of democracy in most countries on the basis of IPR (or IPRI) values. Jean Blondel notes that the method suggested by Vanhanen 'thus helps to predict which countries are likely to be liberal democracies (and *vice versa*); it also identifies exceptions and accounts for a high proportion of them' (Blondel 1995: 85).

In chapter 4, chances of democracy in particular countries were evaluated on the basis of their IPR and IPRI values in 1991 and of the regression analysis of ID on IPR in the longitudinal comparison group of 1,139 observation units in the period 1850–1993. The criteria of predictions were formulated in the research hypothesis 2.1 and 2.2 given in chapter 3. My predictions are principally based on the values of IPR and IPRI, although I found it necessary to take additional local factors into account in some cases. They are domestic or external factors that can be assumed to affect the distribution of politically relevant power resources in the countries concerned. However, I tried to avoid *ad hoc* explanations and predictions because the purpose is to explore to what extent it is possible to explain and predict democracy on the basis of one theoretically selected explanatory factor — the degree of politically relevant resource distribution. The future will test my predictions. It will be interesting to see how correct or incorrect they are in particular cases.

Now I summarize the results of this study and the predictions on the prospects of democracy by a regional regression analysis of ID-93 on IPR-91 in the cross-sectional comparison group of 172 contemporary countries (see Figure 5.1). The regional arithmetic means of ID-93 and IPR (Table 4.1) are used as observation units in this analysis. So we have only seven regional observation units. The regional arithmetic means of ID-93 and IPR-91 are much more strongly correlated (0.898) than the 172 single countries in 1993 (0.768). The explained part of variation in ID rises to 80 per cent in this regional comparison group. Figure 5.1 illustrates regional differences in the relationship between the Index of Democratization and the Index of Power Resources.

The regional groups of Europe and North America, Latin America and the Caribbean, as well as sub-Saharan Africa are on the regression line, or nearly on the regression line, whereas the average level of democratization is

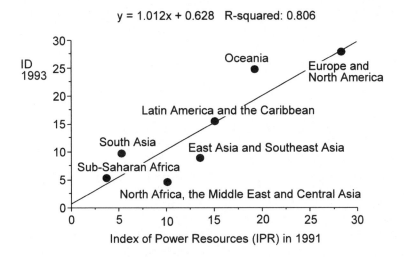

Figure 5.1 The results of regression analysis in which the regional arithmetic mean of ID-93 is used as the dependent variable and the regional arithmetic mean of IPR-91 as the independent variable in the comparison group of seven regions in 1993

clearly higher than expected in the regional groups of Oceania and South Asia and clearly lower than expected in East Asia and Southeast Asia as well as in North Africa, the Middle East and Central Asia. Positive residuals predict a decline in the level of democratization, and negative residuals predict the emergence of new democracies. According to my theoretical argument, the chances of democracy are better, the higher the degree of resource distribution (IPR and IPRI). This means that environmental conditions are most favourable for democracy in the regions of Europe and Oceania and least favourable in the regions of sub-Saharan Africa and South Asia. The results of regional regression analysis disclose that the actual level of democratization has followed this expected pattern quite well. Latin America is between these four extreme regional groups on the regression line. Two other regional groups, East Asia and Southeast Asia and North Africa, the Middle East and Central Asia are problematic because they contradict the hypothesis to some extent. The average level of democratization in North Africa, the Middle East and Central Asia is lower than in sub-Saharan Africa and South Asia, although it should be higher. This is the most remarkable regional deviation from the hypothesized relationship. Consequently, I have to predict a significant rise of the level of democracy in the Islamic world of the Middle East.

My major predictions on the prospects of democratization can be summarized as follows:

1 democratic systems will survive and become stabilized in Eastern Europe;
2 democracy survives in Latin America, although it is still difficult to stabilize democratic institutions;
3 new democracies will emerge in the Muslim countries of North Africa, the Middle East and Central Asia;
4 it is still difficult to establish and stabilize democratic systems in sub-Saharan Africa, and some of the new democracies will probably collapse in violent struggles for power;
5 democratic systems will survive in South Asia, although they are still in danger in Bangladesh and Nepal in particular because of extreme poverty, and a new democracy may emerge in the Maldives;
6 in East Asia and Southeast Asia, Taiwan (ROC) will cross the threshold of democracy, and the pressure for democratization will increase in China and Indonesia in particular; and
7 external support may help the survival of democracy in small and poor Oceanian island states.

Let us see what happens in the future.

Predictions for single countries can be seen from Table 3.7. In general, positive residuals imply that the level of democracy is higher than expected and negative residuals that it is lower than expected. I emphasized that small residuals do not provide a reliable basis on which to predict changes because they may be due to measurement errors or to various other factors affecting the relationship between IPR and ID. Large residuals provide a more reliable basis on which to predict changes, but it should be noted that a better balance between IPR and ID can be achieved not only by changes in ID but also by changes in IPR. Therefore, high positive residuals do not need to lead to a decrease of the level of democracy if the degree of resource distribution rises, and high negative residuals do not need to lead to democratization or to the rise of the level of democracy if the degree of resource distribution decreases. My prediction is that a better balance between IPR and ID will be achieved in the future, but it can be achieved either by changes in IPR or in ID. Usually, however, social structures affecting the degree of resource distribution change slowly. Therefore, it is reasonable to assume that a better balance between IPR and ID will be achieved through changes in ID. My predictions on the chances of democracy in particular countries are usually based on this assumption but, in some cases, particularly in the cases of former socialist countries, probable significant changes in IPR values were taken into account.

STRATEGIES OF DEMOCRATIZATION

The results of this study imply that the emergence of democracy may have been, in most cases, an unintended consequence of structural changes in social conditions, but, in principle, it has always been possible to further or obstruct democratization by conscious strategies of democratization. Certain social structures and conditions are more conducive to democratic politics than some others, and some political institutions may be more suited to organize democratic politics than some others. Therefore, the strategies of democratization and the visions of political leadership matter, and there is always room for variation in strategies. Usually, the less favourable structural conditions are for democracy, the more the success or failure of democratization depends on the skills of political leadership and on the strategies chosen by them, although beyond a certain point no strategies may be enough to overcome the obstacles of unfavourable social conditions. When power resources are highly concentrated, an authoritarian system is more natural than a democratic system.

The nature of political strategies varies from universally valid strategies to particular local strategies. Two major types of conscious political strategies of democratization can be differentiated: (1) by transforming social structures affecting the distribution of economic and intellectual power resources and (2) by establishing political institutions that make it possible to share power democratically between competing groups. The results of this study support the assumption that social reforms increasing the distribution of power resources among competing groups are universally valid strategies to further democratization. It is more problematic to know what types of political institutions might be best suited to maintain democratic politics (see also Vanhanen 1992a: 157–8). In the following, I try to summarize some arguments on the possibilities of affecting the process of democratization by conscious political strategies of democratization. My attention is focused on strategies to improve the chances of democracy by means of social engineering and to facilitate the emergence and stabilization of democratic structures by selecting appropriate institutions.

Strategies of social engineering

Empirical evidence since the 1850s shows that increases in resource distribution have regularly supported popular efforts to democratize political systems. Therefore it is plausible to argue that strategies of democratization should begin with attempts to distribute economic, intellectual and other relevant power resources more widely among various groups of the population. A problem is how to do this in countries where existing social conditions are highly unfavourable for democracy. It is not easy to carry out social and economic reforms in such countries because the existing concentration of power resources serves the interests of the most powerful groups. Why should they change social conditions to make them more unfavourable for themselves? In fact, they have rarely done so. Nevertheless, social conditions have changed significantly. It is reasonable to assume that changes in resource distribution have usually been more or less unintended consequences of technological changes, modernization, and industrialization. Power holders have not been able to anticipate various social consequences of technological changes and of social reforms carried out by themselves, or they have not been able to control the consequences.

However, there are also many examples of conscious attempts to change the distribution of economic and intellectual power resources by means of social reforms. The best contemporary examples of the conscious use of this strategy are from Eastern Europe and the Soviet Union. After the establishment of socialist systems, economic structures were changed through collectivization in order to adapt the distribution of economic resources to the socialist concentration of political power. The control of education also became highly concentrated. When socialist systems started to collapse at the end of the 1980s, structural changes were initiated to decentralize economic power resources and the control of education because it was understood that political pluralism presupposes the decentralization of economic and intellectual power resources. In Eastern Europe and the Soviet Union, political democratization preceded, in most cases, the decentralization of economic power resources through privatization, whereas in China the decentralization of economic power resources has preceded political democratization that has not yet started. In many European and Latin American countries, as well as in India, Japan, South Korea, Taiwan, and in some other Asian countries, land reforms and educational reforms preceded democratization or were started with democratization in order to consolidate new democratic structures. It should be noted that social engineering can be used to further democratization by decentralizing economic and other power resources, or to prevent democratization and to consolidate autocratic power structures by concentrating economic and other power resources.

An interesting question is to what extent chances to decentralize economic, intellectual, and other power resources are constrained by the level of economic development or by the level of national wealth. In other words, is a real decentralization of economic and other power resources possible only in relatively wealthy societies, or is it independent from the level of national wealth and economic development? Empirical evidence indicates that there is a moderate positive correlation between the level of economic development as indicated by GNP per capita and the degree of resource distribution, but this association also leaves room for decentralized economic and social systems among poor countries. There are poor countries in which some important power resources are widely distributed (India, for example), and it does not need to be impossible to further resource distribution by political programmes in such countries. In most African countries, for example, economic power resources based on the control of agricultural land and various other resources may be relatively widely distributed. The weak national governments are not able to control local communities and their populations effectively. The same concerns relatively weak private corporations and economic enterprises. Fred W. Riggs (1995) speaks succinctly about anarchy combined with weak authoritarianism. Because most people are not economically and socially controlled by the state or private power holders in such conditions, democratic competition for power becomes possible, although people are poor and the level of socio-economic development is low.

Malak Poppovic and Paulo Sérgio Pinheiro refer to this aspect of my theory of democratization. They say, 'If we accept the proposition that resource distribution is the real causal factor, this helps to explain the non linearity between economic development and democracy/respect for human rights'. Consequently, they recommend the redistribution of power resources to consolidate democracy (Poppovic and Pinheiro 1995; see also Mbaku 1994). Important power resources tend to be highly concentrated in many poor countries, but it is not inevitable. If there is political will, it may be possible to widen the distribution of at least some economic and intellectual resources in poor countries, too.

In Latin America, the best way to strengthen the social basis of democracy would be to carry out land reforms that create viable family farms and transform agricultural workers and tenants into independent farmers. In sub-Saharan Africa and in many countries of Asia, the systems of basic education should be improved in order that peasants and workers can take part in politics independently (*cf.* Samatar 1991, who recommends a plan of mass education for Somalia). In the former socialist countries, the establishment of market economies and the privatization of collective farms and public enterprises will certainly strengthen the social basis of democratic politics.

Strategies of political engineering

The chances of achieving and maintaining democracy in a country depend not only on the existence of favourable social conditions, discussed above, but also on the appropriateness of its political institutions. The selection of political institutions is usually conscious and based on rational calculations, although it can be argued that the consequences of that selection have not always been properly understood. The problem of political architecture concerns the construction of political institutions that in particular circumstances provide channels for meaningful political participation and facilitate democratic sharing of power among competing groups.

Arthur W. Lewis has argued strongly against the use of the Anglo-American electoral system of first-past-the-post in plural societies. He recommends, to African plural societies in particular, proportional representation: 'The plural society goes back to the primary meaning of democracy, according to which all those who are affected by a decision should have a chance to participate in making a decision. This leads to proportional representation, with all parties offered seats in all decision making bodies, including the cabinet itself' (Lewis 1965: 64–74). Arend Lijphart has recommended his model of consociational democracy for plural societies. Its basic idea is that all sections of the population should participate in political decision-making in plural societies. The model of consociational democracy is characterized by four features:

1 government by a grand coalition;
2 the mutual veto, which serves as an additional protection of vital minority interests;
3 proportionality as the principal standard of political representation; and
4 a high degree of autonomy for each segment.

(Lijphart 1980: 25)

Juan J. Linz has argued for parliamentarism and against presidentialism. His conclusion is that parliamentary democracy would suit the conditions of developing countries better than presidential democracy because it is more flexible (see Linz 1990a, 1990b, 1990c). Fred W. Riggs' research project on 'Ethnonational Conflict and Viable Constitutionalism' is based on the idea that some forms of democratic constitutional government are more likely to prevent ethnonational conflicts and to consolidate democracy than others (see Riggs 1994; 1995).

It is reasonable to assume that democracy presupposes institutional arrangements that more or less satisfy all, or nearly all, participants. They should feel that they have an equal opportunity to participate in politics and get their fair share of power. If institutional arrangements favour some groups of participants unfairly or discriminate against some others, or if they create unfair obstacles to the participation and representation of some groups, it is plausible to expect dissatisfaction and troubles. Human nature is such that we prefer equality and reciprocity to discrimination and inequality. If human populations were homogeneous, any institutions might succeed relatively well, but in fact all human populations are heterogeneous in many ways. This makes it difficult to construct institutions that are sufficiently fair to all. It is particularly hard to invent and establish fair institutions in ethnically divided societies.

What kinds of political institutions might satisfy the demands of equality and reciprocity in the best possible way? I think that it is possible to make some recommendations. First, federalism is better suited than a unitary form of state to (1) all geographically large countries and (2) ethnically divided countries where the major ethnic cleavages are territorial by nature. Second, proportional representation could serve the needs of fair representation of all significant groups better than the plurality/majority system, which easily leads to over-representation of the dominant group and under-representation or complete exclusion of smaller groups. Third, parliamentarism combined with proportional representation could provide better chances for equal participation in decision-making than a presidential system, which concentrates the use of political power in the hands of a single group. I emphasize that this assumption concerns primarily parliamentarism combined with a proportional electoral system. A parliamentary system combined with a plurality/majority system does not necessarily differ very much from presidential systems (see Vanhanen 1990b, 1990c, 1991c). Empirical evidence supports these assumptions, although relationships are not strong. A comparative study covering 147 states in 1988 disclosed that federal institutions and proportional electoral systems are more frequently connected with democracies than unitary state institutions and plurality/ majority systems respectively. Parliamentary systems are more frequent among democracies than presidential systems (see Vanhanen 1991c).

Chances to consolidate democracy by institutional reforms are limited, but in some cases such reforms might be helpful. In Latin America, for example, change-overs from presidential systems to parliamentary systems might stabilize political parties and democratic institutions (*cf.* Linz *et al.* 1990). John Mukum Mbaku, referring to my studies, recommends for Africa federalism, proportional representation, and parliamentarism. He says that in ethnically plural societies of Africa, 'federalism must be combined with proportional representation in order to provide adequate and effective protection to all important groups'. Further, he argues that 'a parliamentary system combined with a proportional electoral system should provide an effective system for equal participation in political decision-making by all relevant groups in the African countries' (Mbaku 1994; see also Reynolds 1995). I would also like to pay attention to the significance of traditional African political structures. It might be advantageous to utilize traditional hierarchical structures in the establishment of democratic institutions. Said S. Samatar, for example, has suggested that traditional leading elders and senior notables of the clan should be empowered in Somalia by creating a house of clan elders (Samatar 1991: 30). I think that it is a reasonable suggestion. Gradualism in democratization would be wise, but it is extremely difficult in practice.

This study has not focused on the strategies of democratization, although, in particular cases, I have referred to social and institutional reforms that might improve social and institutional frameworks of democratic politics and although I have strongly emphasized the basic message, according to which democracy presupposes a sufficient distribution of crucial power resources among competing and conflicting groups. It is for political activists and groups in each country to invent suitable strategies of democratization. I just hope that the regularities in the process of democratization disclosed in this study can help them to make rational structural and institutional selections.

INCALCULABLE FACTORS

The same explanatory variables have explained a major part of the variation in the degree of democracy since the 1850s. There have been strong and predictable regularities in the pattern of democratization. The predictions on the prospects of democracy in particular countries presented in the previous chapter are based on the assumption that the same regularities will continue in the future. It is plausible to assume that the hypothesized causal relationship between the degree of resource distribution and the chances of democracy will continue in the future because the characteristics of human nature have remained more or less the same. Consequently, if the rise of IPR values continues in the world as it has continued since the 1850s, it is reasonable to expect that the degree of democracy will also rise and that more and more countries will cross the threshold of democracy. There is no natural upper limit for the percentage of democracies. However, the future is always open and to some extent unpredictable. We cannot be sure that social conditions will become more and more favourable for democracy. There are incalculable factors that may affect the distribution of economic, intellectual, and other relevant power resources and change social conditions less favourable for democracy in some countries or regions of the world. Because they are incalculable factors, we cannot know in advance what they might be and how they might affect the chances of democracy. Population growth and poverty may be such incalculable factors.

If the striking growth of population continues in most developing countries and causes the doubling of population in two or three decades (see UNDP, Human Development Report 1994, Table 23), social conditions might worsen dramatically in many countries. Poverty, hunger, and other forms of misery might increase significantly and people might resort to violence in the struggle for territories and other scarce resources more frequently than earlier. As a consequence, the degree of resource distribution might decrease, social structures collapse, and social conditions become more unfavourable for democracy than earlier. However, it is difficult to anticipate how the increase of misery, hunger, and poverty would modify social structures and affect the distribution of power resources within societies (*cf.* Fargues 1994). The available scarce statistical data and estimates on the percentage of population in absolute poverty do not make it clear whether poverty is increasing or decreasing in the world, but the fact is that the gap between rich and poor countries has grown dramatically since the Second World War (see Seligson and Passé-Smith 1993). In many developing countries, more than half of the population is estimated to be in absolute poverty (see UNDP, Human Development Report 1990, Table 16; 1994, Table 18; The World Bank, Social Indicators of Development 1988 and 1991–92; Karl 1995:78). It means that the number of people who have minimum resources needed to take part in politics is relatively small in such countries. It is reasonable to assume that if the proportion of people in absolute poverty rises, the relative number of people capable of taking part in politics will decrease. It would make it easier for the few to control the many and to establish autocratic political structures. From this perspective, many extremely poor countries of sub-Saharan Africa are particularly interesting.

In addition to the growth of population and poverty, there may be other incalculable factors that affect the distribution of power resources in industrial countries as well as in developing countries in the future. Therefore, my predictions on the prospects of democracy in particular countries and on the trends of democratization in the world in general are to some extent uncertain because they are based on the assumption that the past trends will continue in the future. I am sure that people and social groups will struggle for power in the future as intensively as in the past and that the distribution of relevant power resources among the many will lead to the establishment of democratic political institutions and support the survival of democracy, but I cannot be sure that power resources will become more and more widely distributed in the future, as assumed in most of my predictions. Therefore, there is an element of incalculable uncertainty in these predictions. It will be exciting for those who live to see what happens in the next decades. The future will test my predictions and theory of democratization.

Appendices

Appendix 1

This appendix contains statistical data on the percentage of the largest party and the number of voters as a percentage of the total number of voters in the parliamentary and/or presidential (executive) elections in 172 countries by regional groups in 1991–3.

SYMBOLS:

N/A data not available
( ) data in brackets are the writer's estimates

NOTES BY COUNTRIES

Complete bibliographic data appear in the Bibliography. Data on total populations given in Unesco's *Statistical Yearbook 1994* (Table 1:1) and *FAO Production Yearbook 1990* were used in the calculations concerning the degree of electoral participation (per cent of total population).

State/Election year/Largest party or elected presidential candidate	Votes for the largest party % of total votes	Total votes Number	% of total population
Europe and North America			
1 Albania			
Concurrent powers			
Parliamentary elections:			
1991 Party of Labour of Albania (PLA)	56	1,963,568	59
1992 Democratic Party (DP)	62	1,600,000	48
Presidential elections:			
1991 Ramiz Alia (PLA)	71	243	0
1992 Sali Berish (DP)	74	133	0

Sources: 1991–Inter-Parliamentary Union (=IPU) 1990–1; Keesing's Record of World Events (=Keesing's) 1991: 38160; 1992 – IPU 1991–2; Keesing's 1992: 38829, 38878.

2 Armenia			
Concurrent powers			
Parliamentary elections:			
1990 Armenian Pan-National Movement	35	N/A	(50)

State/Election year/Largest party or elected presidential candidate	Votes for the largest party % of total votes	Total votes Number	% of total population

Presidential elections:
1991 Levon Ter Petrosyan (APN)   83   N/A   (40)

Sources: 1990 – Eastern Europe and the Commonwealth of Independent States (=Eastern Europe) 1992. Distribution of seats. 1991 – Keesing's 1991: 38538. Turnout was 70–90 per cent.

3 Austria
Parliamentary dominance
1990 Socialist party   41   4,704,894   60

Source: *1990*: IPU 1990–1.

4 Belarus
Concurrent powers
Parliamentary elections:
1990 Communist party   92   7,000,000   68

Presidential elections:
1991 Stanislaw Shushkevich   69   312   0

Sources: 1990 – BBC Summary of World Broadcasting (=SWB) Part 1. USSR. Third Series SU/0708, 9 March 1990. More than 6 million people voted. Turnout was 87 per cent. See also Slider 1990; Eastern Europe 1992. 1991 – Keesing's 1991: 38416. President was elected by the Supreme Soviet.

5 Belgium
Parliamentary dominance
1991 CVP/PSC   24   6,162,160   62

Sources: 1991 – IPU 1991–2; Keesing's 1991: 38589.

6 Bulgaria
Concurrent powers
Parliamentary elections:
1991 Union of Democratic Forces (UDF) 34   5,540,837   62

Presidential elections:
1990 Zhelyu Zhelev (UDF)   73   389   0
1992 Zhelyu Zhelev   45   5,091,109   57

Sources: Keesing's 1990: 37619. 1991 – IPU 1991–2; Keesing's 1991: 38539. 1992 – The Europa World Year Book (=Europa) 1993: 611.

7 Canada
Parliamentary dominance
1988 Progressive Conservative Party   43   13,173,499   51
1993 Liberal Party   41   13,388,500   48

Sources: 1988 – IPU 1988–9. 1993 – IPU 1993–4.

8 Croatia
Concurrent powers
Parliamentary elections:
1990 Croatian Democratic Union (HDZ) 59   N/A   (54)
1992 Croatian Democratic Union (HDZ) 44   2,565,240   54

State/Election year/Largest party or elected presidential candidate	Votes for the largest party % of total votes	Total votes Number	% of total population
Presidential elections:			
1990 Franjo Tudjiman (HDZ)	(100)	N/A	0
1992 Franjo Tudjiman (HDZ)	58	2,627,061	55

Sources: 1990 – Keesing's 1990, 37381; Eastern Europe 1992. Distribution of seats. The Croatian Assembly elected Tudjiman. 1992 – IPU 1992–3; Europa 1993; Keesing's 1992: 39064; IFES Elections Today. News from the International Foundation for Electoral Systems (=IFES) 1992: No. 2.

9 Czechoslovakia (Czech Republic 1993)
Parliamentary dominance

1990 Civic Forum and Public Against Violence	47	10,638,493	68
1992 Civic Democratic Party/Christian Democratic Party	34	9,583,436	61

Sources: 1990 – IPU 1989–90; Keesing's 1990: 37619. 1992 – IPU 1991–2; Keesing's 1992: 38944–5.

10 Denmark
Parliamentary dominance

1990 Social Democratic Party	37	3,239,662	63

1990: IPU 1990–1.

11 Estonia
Concurrent powers
Parliamentary elections:

1990 Popular Front	32	910,000	58
1992 Fatherland	22	462,000	30

Presidential elections:

1990 Arnold Rüütel	100	N/A	0
1992 Lennart Meri	59	463,528	30

Sources: 1990 – Taagepera 1990. *Cf.* Keesing's 1990: 37322. 1992 – IPU 1992–3; Keesing's 1992: 39110–11; Europa 1993; Fitzmaurice 1993; Viro vuosikirja 1993. Because no single candidate had won an absolute majority of the popular vote (463,528) in the presidential election, the Parliament elected Lennart Meri as president by 59 per cent of the votes.

12 Finland
Concurrent powers
Parliamentary elections:

1991 Finland's Centre	25	2,723,019	54

Presidential election:

1988 Mauno Koivisto (SDP)	48	3,094,449	62

Sources: 1988 – Central Statistical Office of Finland, Presidential election 1988. 1991 – IPU 1990–1.

13 France
Concurrent powers
Parliamentary elections:

1988 Socialist party	35	24,432,095	44
1993 Rally for the Republic (RPR)	20	25,442,403	44

State/Election year/Largest party or elected presidential candidate	Votes for the largest party % of total votes	Total votes Number	% of total population
Presidential election:			
1988 Francois Mitterand	54	30,923,349	55

Sources: 1988 – IPU 1987–8. The results of the first ballot (National Assembly); Keesing's 1988: 35979–81. The second round of the presidential election. 1993 – IPU 1992–3; Keesing's 1993: 39381–2. First round (National Assembly).

14 Georgia
Concurrent powers
Parliamentary elections:

1990 Round Table/Free Georgia	54	N/A	(45)
1992 Peace bloc	19	2,592,117	47

Presidential elections:

1991 Zviad Gamsakhurdia	87	N/A	(45)
1992 Eduard Shevardnadze	95	N/A	(45)

Sources: 1990 – Europa 1993; Keesing's 1990: 37788, 37863–4; Fuller 1990. 1991 – Keesing's 1991: 38206; Fuller 1991. 1992 – IPU 1992–3; Keesing's 1992: 38731, 39156; Allison *et al.* 1993; Electoral Studies 1993: 12, 2: 199. Distribution of seats.

15 Germany
Parliamentary dominance

1990 Christian Democratic Union	37	46,455,772	61

Source: 1990 – IPU 1991–2.

16 Greece
Parliamentary dominance

1990 New Democracy	47	6,585,197	65
1993 PASOK	47	6,900,616	66

Sources: 1990 – IPU 1989–90. 1993 – IPU 1993–4.

17 Hungary
Parliamentary dominance

1990 Hungarian Democratic Forum	43	4,958,580	48

Sources: 1990 – IPU 1989–90; Keesing's 1990: 37667. Distribution of seats.

18 Iceland
Parliamentary dominance

1991 Independence Party	39	157,746	61

Source: 1991 – IPU 1990–1.

19 Ireland
Parliamentary dominance

1989 Fianna Fail	44	1,656,813	47
1992 Fianna Fail	39	1,724,853	49

Sources: 1989 – IPU 1989–90. 1992 – IPU 1992–3.

20 Italy
Parliamentary dominance

1987 Christian Democratic Party	34	38,473,000	67
1992 Christian Democratic Party	30	39,243,506	69

Sources: 1987 – IPU 1986–7; Keesing's 1987: 35586–8; Hine 1987. 1992 – IPU 1991–2.

State/Election year/Largest party or elected presidential candidate	Votes for the largest party % of total votes	Total votes Number	% of total population
21 Latvia Concurrent powers Parliamentary elections:			
1990 Popular Front of Latvia	65	1,880,000	70
1993 Latvian Way	32	1,119,432	42
Presidential elections:			
1990 Anatolijs Gorbunov	78	126	0
1993 Guntis Ulmanis	67	79	0

Sources: 1990 – Taagepera 1990; Eastern Europe 1992. Distribution of seats; Keesing's 1990: 37461. The Latvian Supreme Soviet elected Gorbunov. 1993 – IPU 1992–3; IFES 1993: No. 1; Keesing's 1993: 39524, 39570. The new parliament of Latvia elected Ulmanis.

22 Lithuania Concurrent powers Parliamentary elections:			
1990 Sajudis	49	1,883,000	51
1992 Democratic Labour Party	45	1,812,798	48
Presidential elections:			
1990 Vytautas Landsbergis	68	133	0
1993 Algirdas Brazauskas (DLP)	60	2,011,795	53

Sources: 1990 – Taagepera 1990; Girnius 1991. *Cf.* Keesing's 1990, 37299–300. The Supreme Council elected Landsbergis. 1992 – IPU 1992–3; IFES 1993: No. 3. 1993 – Keesing's 1993: 39334.

23 Luxembourg Parliamentary dominance			
1989 Christian Social Party	32	191,332	55

Source: 1989 – IPU 1988–9.

24 Macedonia Concurrent powers Parliamentary elections:			
1990 Internal Macedonian Revolutionary Organization/Democratic Party of Macedonian National Unity	31	N/A	(50)
Presidential elections:			
1991 Kiro Gligorov (LCM-PDR)	(70)	N/A	0

Sources: 1990 – Eastern Europe 1992; Keesing's 1990: 37923. Distribution of seats. 1991 – Keesing's 1991: 37974. The Assembly elected Gligorov by two-thirds majority.

25 Malta Parliamentary dominance			
1987 Nationalist Party	51	235,168	68
1992 Nationalist Party	52	247,139	69

Sources: 1987 – IPU 1986–7; Hove 1987. 1992 – IPU 1991–2; Keesing's 1992: 38784.

26 Moldova Concurrent powers Parliamentary elections:			
1990 Supporters of the Popular Front of Moldavia	70	2,407,000	55

State/Election year/Largest party or elected presidential candidate	*Votes for the largest party* *% of total votes*	*Total votes* *Number*	*% of total population*
Presidential elections:			
1991 Mircea Snegur	98	N/A	(45)

Sources: 1990 – Europa 1993; Keesing's 1990: 37322; Socor 1991 (distribution of seats). 1991 – Keesing's 1991: 38657; Europa 1993. The presidential election was partially boycotted in the predominantly Russian area of the Dnestr region.

27 Netherlands
Parliamentary dominance

1989 Christian Democratic Appeal (CDA)	36	8,891,508	60

Source: 1989 – IPU 1989–90.

28 Norway
Parliamentary dominance

1989 Labour Party	34	2,647,604	62
1993 Labour Party	37	2,461,949	57

Sources: 1989 – IPU 1989–90. 1993 – IPU 1993–4.

29 Poland
Concurrent powers
Parliamentary elections:

1991 Democratic Union	12	11,218,602	29
1993 Democratic Left Alliance (SLD)	20	13,796,227	36
Presidential elections:			
1990 Lech Walesa	74	14,305,794	38

Sources: 1990 – Keesing's 1990: 37921; Europa 1991. The second round of the presidential election. 1991 – IPU 1991–2; Kuusela 1994; Keesing's 1991: 38536. 1993 – IPU 1993–4; Smolar 1994.

30 Portugal
Concurrent powers
Parliamentary elections:

1991 Social Democratic Party (PSD)	51	5,624,757	57
Presidential elections:			
1991 Mario Soares (PS)	70	4,917,854	50

Sources: 1991 – IPU 1993–4; Europa 1993; Keesing's 1991: 37968, 38545–8.

31 Romania
Concurrent powers
Parliamentary elections:

1990 National Salvation Front	66	13,707,159	59
1992 Democratic National Salvation Front	28	10,905,539	48
Presidential elections:			
1990 Ion Iliescu	85	14,146,195	61
1992 Ion Iliescu	61	11,989,855	53

Sources: 1990 – IPU 1989–90; Europa 1991; Keesing's 1990, 37441–2. 1992 – IPU 1992–3; Keesing's 1992: 39104, 39150. The second round of the presidential election (61 per cent). Votes are from the first round of presidential voting.

State/Election year/Largest party or elected presidential candidate	Votes for the largest party % of total votes	Total votes Number	% of total population
32 Russia			
Concurrent powers			
Parliamentary elections:			
1990 Communists	86	79,872,000	54
1993 Liberal Democratic Party of Russia	23	53,966,818	36
Presidential elections			
1991 Boris Yeltsin	57	79,498,240	54

Sources: 1990 – SWB Part 1: USSR, SU/0722, 26 March 1990; Komarov 1992: 63–5; Mann 1990. 1991 – Keesing's 1991 38273; Eastern Europe 1992. 1993 – IFES 1994, April: 35–6. *Cf.* IPU 1993–4; Tolz 1994; Keesing's 1993: 39782–3.

33 Slovenia			
Concurrent powers			
Parliamentary elections:			
1990 Democratic Opposition of Slovenia			
(DEMOS)	55	1,200,000	61
1992 Liberal Democratic Party	23	1,191,017	61
Presidential elections:			
1990 Milan Kucan	58	N/A	(61)
1992 Milan Kucan	64	(1,140,000)	58

Sources: 1990 – Keesing's 1990: 37381; Eastern Europe 1992. 1992 – IPU 1992–3; Keesing's 1992: 39240–1; Europa 1993; IFES 1993: No. 3.

34 Spain			
Parliamentary dominance			
1989 Socialist Workers' Party (PSOE)	40	20,313,469	52
1993 Socialist Workers' Party (PSOE)	39	23,590,801	60

Sources: 1989 – IPU 1989–90. 1993 – IPU 1992–3; Keesing's 1993: 39528; IFES 1993: No. 1.

35 Sweden			
Parliamentary dominance			
1991 Social Democratic Party	38	5,470,882	63

Sources: 1991 – IPU 1991–2; Keesing's 1991: 38444.

36 Switzerland			
Parliamentary dominance			
1991 FDP/PRD	21	2,044,109	30

Sources: 1991 – IPU 1991–2; Keesing's 1991: 38542–3.

37 Ukraine			
Concurrent powers			
Parliamentary elections:			
1990 Communists	62	N/A	(55)
Presidential elections:			
1991 Leonid Kravchuk	62	30,563,954	59

Sources: 1990 – SWB Part 1: USSR, SU/0722, 26 March 1990; Eastern Europe 1992; Europa 1993. Turnout was 80 per cent. 1991 – Keesing's 1991: 38656; Eastern Europe 1992.

State/Election year/Largest party or elected presidential candidate	Votes for the largest party % of total votes	Total votes Number	% of total population
38 United Kingdom			
Parliamentary dominance			
1987 Conservative party	42	32,536,205	58
1992 Conservative party	42	33,609,431	58

Sources: 1987 – IPU 1986–7. 1992 – IPU 1991–2; Keesing's 1992: 38869–70.

39 United States			
Concurrent powers			
Parliamentary elections:			
1990 Democratic Party	51	61,352,951	25
1992 Democratic Party	51	96,037,285	38
Presidential elections:			
1988 George Bush	54	88,962,851	36
1992 Bill Clinton	43	104,420,887	41

Sources: 1988 – IPU 1988–9; Congressional Quarterly Weekly Report, Vol. 46, No. 46, Nov.12, 1988. 1990 – IPU 1990–1. 1992 – IPU 1992–3; Europa 1993; Keesing's 1992: 39174.

40 Yugoslavia			
Parliamentary dominance			
1986 Socialist Alliance	100	N/A	0
1992 Socialist Party of Serbia	54	4,709,992	45

Sources: 1986 – IPU 1985–6. The members of the Assembly of the Socialist Federal Republic of Yugoslavia were elected by indirect elections. 1992 – IPU 1992–3; Europa 1993; Keesing's 1992: 38970, 39240. Distribution of seats. The Federal Republic of Yugoslavia included only Serbia and Montenegro in 1992–3.

Latin America and the Caribbean			
41 Argentina			
Concurrent powers			
Parliamentary elections:			
1991 Justicialist Party	37	17,172,067	52
1993 Justicialist Party	42	15,910,884	47
Presidential elections:			
1989 Carlos Saul Menem	48	16,600,437	52

Sources: 1989 – Europa 1991. 1991 – IPU 1991–2; Keesing's 1991: 38527. 1993 – IPU 1993–4.

42 Bahamas			
Parliamentary dominance			
1987 Progressive Liberal Party	54	99,874	42
1992 Free National Movement (FNM)	55	112,057	43

Sources: 1987 – IPU 1986–7. 1992 – IPU 1992–3.

43 Barbados			
Parliamentary dominance			
1991 Democratic Labour Party	50	120,258	47

Source: 1991 – IPU 1990–1.

State/Election year/Largest party or elected presidential candidate	*Votes for the largest party % of total votes*	*Total votes Number*	*% of total population*

44 Belize
Parliamentary dominance
1989 People's United Party   50   58,951   32
1993 United Democratic Party (UDP)   55   N/A   (32)

Sources: 1989 – IPU 1989–90. 1993 – IPU 1992–3; Journal of Democracy, October 1993; Keesing's 1993: 39553.

45 Bolivia
Concurrent powers
Parliamentary elections:
1989 Nationalist Revolutionary Movement   23   1,415,869   20
1993 MNR-MRTKL   35   1,647,710   21

Presidential elections:
1989 Jaime Paz Zamora (MIR)   55   1,573,000   22
1993 Sánchez de Lozada (MNR)   65   1,647,710   21

Sources: 1989 – IPU 1988–9; Europa 1991. As no candidate obtained the requisite absolute majority at the direct election (1,573,000), the National Congress elected Paz Zamora (55 per cent). *Cf*. Statistical Abstract of Latin America, Vol. 28, 1990: 256–7. 1993 – IFES 1993: No. 1; Keesing's 1993: 39505, 39593; IPU 1992–3. Since none of the presidential candidates received a majority of the votes cast (1,647,710), the Congress elected de Lozada (65 per cent).

46 Brazil
Concurrent powers
Parliamentary elections:
1990 Brazilian Democratic Movement   22   33,600,000   22

Presidential elections:
1989 Fernando Collor de Mello   53   66,166,362   45

Sources: 1989 – Europa 1991; Keesing's 1989: 37117. The second round of voting. 1990 – IPU 1990–1; Keesing's 1990: 37773, 37852. Distribution of seats.

47 Chile
Concurrent powers
Parliamentary elections:
1989 Coalition for Democracy   51   6,797,122   52
1993 Coalition for Democracy   58   6,947,547   50

Presidential elections:
1989 Patricio Alwin Azócar   55   6,978,083   54
1993 Eduardo Frei   58   6,468,406   47

Sources: 1989 – IPU 1989–90; Europa 1991. 1993 – IPU 1993–4; Keesing's 1993: 39773. Distribution of seats. See also IFES 1994: No. 2–3.

48 Colombia
Concurrent powers
Parliamentary elections:
1991 Liberal Party   53   4,950,000   15

Presidential elections:
1990 César Gaviria Trujillo   49   5,627,467   17

Sources: 1990 – Europa 1991; The World Factbook 1991–92: 67. 1991 – IPU 1991–2; Keesing's 1991: 38525. Distribution of seats.

State/Election year/Largest party or elected presidential candidate	Votes for the largest party % of total votes	Total votes Number	% of total population
49 Costa Rica Concurrent powers Parliamentary elections:			
1990 Social Christian Unity Party	51	1,328,827	44
Presidential elections:			
1990 Rafael Angel Calderón (PUSC)	51	1,328,827	44

Sources: 1990 – IPU 1989–90; Europa 1991. It is assumed that the total number of votes in the presidential election was the same as in the parliamentary elections.

50 Cuba Concurrent powers Parliamentary elections:			
1986 Communist party	100	N/A	0
1993 Communist party and independents	100	7,300,629	67
Presidential elections:			
1986 Fidel Castro	100	N/A	0
1993 Fidel Castro	100	578	0

Sources: 1986 – IPU 1986–7; Europa 1991. Indirect elections. The deputies to the National Assembly were elected by 13,256 delegates of the municipal assemblies. 1993 – IPU 1992–3; Keesing's 1993: 39311, 39360. Distribution of seats.

51 Dominican Republic Concurrent powers Parliamentary elections:			
1990 Social Christian Reform Party	35	1,965,000	27
Presidential elections:			
1990 Joaquin Balaguer (PRSC)	36	1,899,900	26

Sources: 1990: IPU 1989–90; Europa 1991; Keesing's 1990: 37529. Distribution of seats.

52 Ecuador Concurrent powers Parliamentary elections:			
1988 Democratic Left (ID)	42	3,325,772	33
1992 Social Christian Party (PSC)	27	4,161,000	39
Presidential elections:			
1988 Rodrigo Borja (ID)	46	3,325,068	33
1992 Sixto Durán Ballén	58	3,759,342	35

Sources: 1988 – IPU 1987–8. Distribution of seats; Keesing's 1988: 36097. The second round of the presidential election. *Cf.* Statistical Abstract of Latin America, Vol. 28, 1990: 266. 1992 – IPU 1991–2; IFES 1992: No. 2; Keesing's 1992: 38907–9.

53 El Salvador Concurrent powers Parliamentary elections:			
1991 Nationalist Republican Alliance	44	1,155,000	22
Presidential elections:			
1989 Alfredo Felix Cristiani	54	939,078	18

Sources: 1989 – Statistical Abstract of Latin America, Vol. 28, 1990: 267; Europa 1991. 1991 – IPU 1990–1; Keesing's 1991: 38093.

State/Election year/Largest party or elected presidential candidate	Votes for the largest party % of total votes	Total votes Number	% of total population
54 Guatemala Concurrent powers Parliamentary elections:			
1990 Union of National Centre (UCN)	26	1,762,000	19
Presidential elections:			
1990 Jorge Serrano Elias (MAS)	68	1,375,328	15
1993 Ramiro de León Carpio	92	116	0

Sources: 1990 – IPU 1990–1; The World Factbook 1991–92: 125; Keesing's 1990: 37956; Europa 1991. The second round of the presidential election. 1993 – Keesing's 1993: 39503. See also Keesing's Reference Supplement 1994: R 44.

55 Guyana Concurrent powers Parliamentary elections:			
1985 People's National Congress (PNC)	79	288,630	36
1992 People's Progressive Party (PPP)	53	303,000	38
Presidential elections:			
1985 Desmond Hoyte (PNC)	79	288,630	36
1992 Cheddi Jagan (PPP)	53	303,000	38

Sources: 1985 – IPU 1985–6. 1992 – IFES 1993: No. 3; Europa 1993; Keesing's 1992: 39137; IPU 1992–3.

56 Haiti
Executive dominance
After Duvalier's flight from the country on 7 February 1986, military-civilian governments ruled the country until 1994. See Europa 1994; Keesing's Reference Supplement 1994: R 45.

57 Honduras Concurrent powers Parliamentary elections:			
1989 National Party (PN)	51	1,799,146	36
1993 Liberal Party of Honduras (PLH)	53	1,710,737	30
Presidential elections:			
1989 Rafael Leonardo Callejas (PN)	51	1,799,146	36
1993 Carlos Roberto Reina (HLP)	53	1,710,737	30

Sources: 1989 – IPU 1989–90; Europa 1991. 1993 – IPU 1993–4; IFES 1994: No. 2–3; Keesing's 1993: 39731.

58 Jamaica Parliamentary dominance			
1989 People's National Party	56	836,814	34
1993 People's National Party	60	662,518	26

Sources: 1989 – IPU 1988–9. 1993 – IPU 1992–3; Keesing's 1993: 39360, 39409.

59 Mexico Concurrent powers Parliamentary elections:			
1991 Institutional Revolutionary Party	61	21,600,000	25

State/Election year/Largest party or elected presidential candidate	Votes for the largest party % of total votes	Total votes Number	% of total population

Presidential elections:
1988 Carlos Salinas de Gortari (PRI)   51   19,145,012 23

Sources: 1988 – Europa 1991; Statistical Abstract of Latin America, Vol. 28, 1990: 279, 282. 1991 – IPU 1991–2; Keesing's 1991: 38431.

60 Nicaragua
Concurrent powers
Parliamentary elections:
1990 Union Nacional Oppositora (UNO) 54   1,419,384 37

Presidential elections:
1990 Violeta Barrios de Chamorro (UNO) 55   1,421,000 37

Sources: 1990 – IPU 1989–90; Europa 1991.

61 Panama
Concurrent powers
Parliamentary elections:
1991 Christian Democratic Party (PDC)   42   N/A   (45)

Presidential elections:
1989 Guillermo Endara Galimany   62   1,065,000 45
    (ADOC)

Sources: 1989 – Europa 1993; Keesing's 1989: 36645. 1991 – The World Factbook 1991–92: 243. Distribution of seats.

62 Paraguay
Concurrent powers
Parliamentary elections:
1991 Colorado Party   55   744,400 17
1993 National Republican Association –
    Colorado Party (ANR)   45   1,084,237 24

Presidential elections:
1989 Andres Rodríguez (Colorado)   76   1,077,802 26
1993 Juan Carlos Washmosy (Colorado) 40   N/A   (24)

Sources: 1989 – IPU 1988–9; Europa 1991; Keesing's 1989: 36652. It is assumed that the number of valid votes in the presidential election was the same as in the parliamentary elections in 1989. 1991 – Keesing's 1991: 38674. Constituent Assembly elections. 1993 – IPU 1992–3; Keesing's 1993: 39459; Europa 1993.

63 Peru
Concurrent powers
Parliamentary elections:
1990 Democratic Front   34   6,659,076 31
1992 New Majority Change-90   37   6,187,000 28

Presidential elections:
1990 Alberto Fujimori (FREDEMO)   56   7,235,905 34

Sources: 1990 – IPU 1989–90 (distribution of seats); Europa 1991; Keesing's 1990: 37528. The second round of voting. 1992 – IPU 1992–3. *Cf.* Keesing's 1993: 39233; Europa 1993.

State/Election year/Largest party or elected presidential candidate	Votes for the largest party % of total votes	Total votes Number	% of total population

64 St Lucia
Parliamentary dominance
| 1987 United Workers' Party | 53 | 52,737 | 38 |
| 1992 United Workers' Party | 57 | 59,278 | 43 |

Sources: 1987 – Europa 1991; *cf*. IPU 1986–7. 1992 – IPU 1991–2.

65 St Vincent
Parliamentary dominance
| 1989 New Democratic Party | 66 | 43,843 | 40 |

Sources: 1989 – Europa 1991; *cf*. IPU 1988–9.

66 Suriname
Concurrent powers
Parliamentary elections:
| 1991 New Front for Democracy and Development | 59 | 170,000 | 42 |

Presidential elections:
| 1991 Runaldo Venetiaan (NF) | 79 | 817 | 0 |

Sources: 1991 – IPU 1990–1 (distribution of seats); Keesing's 1991: 37958, 38188; Keesing's 1993, Reference Supplement, R51.

67 Trinidad and Tobago
Parliamentary dominance
| 1991 People's National Movement (PNM) | 45 | 519,697 | 41 |

Sources: 1991 – IPU 1991–2; Keesing's 1991: 38671.

68 Uruguay
Concurrent powers
Parliamentary elections:
| 1989 National (*Blanco*) Party | 39 | 1,969,645 | 64 |

Presidential elections:
| 1989 Luis Alberto Lacalle Herrera | 37 | 1,969,645 | 64 |

Sources: 1989 – IPU 1989–90; Europa 1993; The World Factbook 1991–92: 327; Keesing's 1989: 37039. It is assumed that the total number of valid votes cast in the parliamentary elections was the same as in the presidential election.

69 Venezuela
Concurrent powers
Parliamentary election
| 1988 Democratic Action (AD) | 43 | 7,315,186 | 40 |
| 1993 Democratic Action (AD) | 28 | 5,616,699 | 27 |

Presidential elections:
| 1988 Carlos Andrés Pérez (AD) | 53 | 7,331,387 | 40 |
| 1993 Rafael Caldera | 30 | 5,616,699 | 27 |

Sources: 1988 – IPU 1988–9; Europa 1991. *Cf*. Statistical Abstract of Latin America, Vol. 28, 1990: 290. 1993 – IPU 1993–4; IFES 1994: No. 2–3; Journal of Democracy, January 1994; Keesing's 1993: 39774.

State/Election year/Largest party or elected presidential candidate	Votes for the largest party % of total votes	Total votes Number	% of total population

North Africa, the Middle East and Central Asia
70 Afghanistan
Executive dominance

| 1986 Najibullah (PDPA) | 100 | N/A | 0 |

A revolutionary government took power in 1992.

Sources: 1986 – Europa 1993; The World Factbook 1991–92: 1. 1992 – Keesing's 1992: 38847–8; Europa 1994.

71 Algeria
Executive dominance

| 1988 B. Chadli (FLN) | 93 | 11,369,304 | 48 |

President Chadli resigned on 11 January 1992, and a High Committee of State took power.

Sources: 1988 – Africa Research Bulletin (= ARB) 1989, January 15; Europa 1993. 1992 – Keesing's 1992: 38702.

72 Azerbaijan
Concurrent powers
Parliamentary elections:

| 1990 Communist Party | 89 | N/A | (50) |

Presidential elections:

1991 Ayaz Mutalibov	84	N/A	(40)
1992 Abulfez Elchibey	59	N/A	(40)
1993 Geidar Aliyev	99	3,966,327	54

Sources: 1990 – SWB Part 1: USSR, SU/0922, 15 November 1990; Keesing's 1991: 38015. Distribution of seats. 1991 – Keesing's 1991: 38418. According to the central electoral commission, turnout was 83.7 per cent, whereas the opposition National Democratic Front estimated that it was no more than 25 per cent. 1992 – Keesing's 1992: 38976. Direct election. Turnout 76 per cent. Elchibey was deposed by a military coup in June 1993. See Keesing's 1993: 39522, 39650; IFES 1993: No. 1. 1993 – IFES 1994: No. 2–3; Keesing's 1993: 39694; Journal of Democracy, January 1994.

73 Bahrain
Executive dominance
Bahrain is ruled by the emir and other members of the royal family without any elected legislative body. See Europa 1994; The World Factbook 1991–92: 23.

74 Cyprus
Concurrent powers
Parliamentary elections:

| 1991 Democratic Rally – Liberals | 36 | 342,038 | 48 |

Presidential elections:

| 1988 Georghios Vassiliou (Independent) | 52 | 325,062 | 47 |
| 1993 Glafkos Clerides | 50 | 355,714 | 49 |

Sources: 1988 – Europa 1991. 1991 – IPU 1990–1. 1993 – Keesing's 1993: 39338; IFES 1993: No. 4.

75 Egypt
Concurrent powers
Parliamentary elections:

| 1990 National Democratic Party (NDP) | 80 | 6,902,982 | 13 |

State/Election year/Largest party or elected presidential candidate	Votes for the largest party % of total votes	Total votes Number	% of total population
Presidential elections:			
1987 Mohammad Hosni Mubarak (NDP)	97	12,672,000	26
1993 Mohammad Hosni Mubarak (NDP)	95	15,876,000	28

Sources: 1987 – Keesing's 1987: 35673. 1990 – IPU 1990–1. 1993 – Keesing's 1993: 39711.

76 Iran
Concurrent powers
Parliamentary elections:

1988 Independents	100	16,783,531	32
1992 Pro-Rafsanjani candidates	75	18,476,051	32

Presidential elections:

1989 Ali Akbar Hashemi Rafsanjani	96	16,216,262	30
1993 Ali Akbar Rafsanjani	63	16,700,250	29

Sources: 1988 – IPU 1987–8. This election was not contested by political parties. Only independent candidates were allowed to participate in elections. 1989 – Europa 1991. 1992 – IPU 1991–2; Keesing's 1992: 38887, 38935. *Cf.* Deegan 1993: 56–9. 1993 – Keesing's 1993: 39534.

77 Iraq
Executive dominance
General Saddam Hussein's military government in 1991–3. See Europa 1994.

78 Israel
Parliamentary dominance

1988 Likud	31	2,283,123	51
1992 Labour Party	35	2,616,841	53

Sources: 1988 – IPU 1988–9. 1992 – IPU 1991–2.

79 Jordan
Concurrent powers
Parliamentary elections:

1989 Independent members of the opposition	54	552,800	17
1993 Independent centrists	55	820,116	19

Presidential elections:
Executive power is vested in the king, who shares legislative power with the National Assembly.

Sources: 1989 – IPU 1989–90 (distribution of seats); Europa 1991. Political parties were not allowed to take part in this election. 1993 – Europa 1994; SWB Part 4, ME/1842, 10 November 1993; Keesing's 1993: 39758. Distribution of seats.

80 Kazakhstan
Concurrent powers
Parliamentary elections:

1990 Communists	(95)	N/A	(50)

Presidential elections:

1991 Nursultan Nazarbayev	99	N/A	(50)

Sources: 1990 – Europa 1992. 1991 – Keesing's 1991: 38657. Turnout was 87.4 per cent.

State/Election year/Largest party or elected presidential candidate	*Votes for the largest party % of total votes*	*Total votes Number*	*% of total population*

81 Kuwait
Concurrent powers (25–75 per cent)
Parliamentary elections:
In 1986 the National Assembly was dissolved. An interim body, the National Council was established in 1990.

1990 Independents	100	N/A	4
1992 Opposition candidates	62	69,190	4

Presidential elections:
According to the 1962 constitution, executive power is vested in the Amir of Kuwait.

Sources: 1990 – IPU 1989–90; Europa 1991; The World Factbook 1991–92: 173. Political parties are outlawed. 1992 – Keesing's 1992: 39164. Distribution of seats.

82 Kyrgyzstan
Concurrent powers
Parliamentary elections:

1990 Communists	(95)	N/A	(50)

Presidential elections:

1991 Askar Akayev	95	2,100,000	47

Sources: 1990 – Europa 1992. 1991 – Keesing's 1991: 38079, 38538; Europa 1992. Turnout was 90 per cent in the presidential election, and the registered electorate was 2,341,646 in 1992.

83 Lebanon
Parliamentary dominance

1972 Maronite Christians	30	(515,000)	17
1992 Maronite Christians	27	446,302	16

Sources: 1972 – IPU 1971–2; McDowall 1984; Europa 1991. Distribution of seats. Because of the civil war that started in 1975, it was not possible to elect a new parliament in 1976. Since then the term of the parliament was extended until 1992. 1992 – IPU 1992–3; Keesing's 1992: 39117, 39165–6; Europa 1993. Distribution of seats. Maronites have 34 out of 128 seats. See also SWB 1992, Part 4, ME/1473, ME/1475, ME/1482; Bahout 1993.

84 Libya
Executive dominance
Colonel Muammar al-Qaddafi's government has ruled the country since 1969. See Europa 1994.

85 Mauritania
Military governments in 1990–1.
Concurrent powers (1992–)
Parliamentary elections:

1992 Democratic and Social Republican Party	85	450,567	21

Presidential elections:

1992 Colonel Moaouia Ould Sidi Taya	63	551,575	26

Sources: 1990–91 – See Europa 1993. 1992 – Europa 1993; Keesing's 1992: 38709; IPU 1991–2. Distribution of seats.

State/Election year/Largest party or elected presidential candidate	Votes for the largest party % of total votes	Total votes Number	% of total population
86 Morocco
Concurrent powers
Parliamentary elections:
1984 Union constitutionelle (UC)	25	4,443,004	21
1993 Socialist Union of Popular Forces	22	6,222,218	23

Presidential elections:
Executive power is in the hands of the King.

Sources: 1984 – IPU 1984–5; Europa 1991. Elections to the Chamber of Representatives, due to be held in 1990, were postponed by a referendum, held in December 1989, for two years. 1993 – IPU 1992–3; ARB (African Research Bulletin) 1993: 11040. Distribution of seats. *Cf.* Keesing's 1993: 39535, 39665; IFES 1993: No. 1.

87 Oman
Executive dominance
The Sultan has absolute power. There is no written constitution.
See Europa 1994.

88 Qatar
Executive dominance
Executive power is vested in the Amir, as Head of State. There is no elected parliament; only an appointed Advisory Council.
See Europa 1994.

89 Saudi Arabia
Executive dominance
Legislative and executive powers are in the hands of the king and the ruling dynasty.
See Europa 1994.

90 Sudan
Military governments in 1991–3.
See Europa 1994.

| 91 Syria |
| Concurrent powers |
| Parliamentary elections: |
| 1990 National Progressive Front | 66 | 3,264,616 | 27 |
| Presidential elections: |
| 1991 Hafez al-Assad | 100 | 6,727,992 | 54 |

Sources: 1990 – IPU 1989–90; Deegan 1993: 63–8; The World Factbook 1991–92: 303; Europa 1991. 1991 – SWB Part 4: Middle East, Africa, Latin America, ME/1247, 5 December 1991. See also Freedom in the World 1991–92: 586; Keesing's 1991: 38695.

| 92 Tajikistan |
| Parliamentary dominance |
| 1990 Communists | 94 | N/A | (50) |

Sources: 1990 – SWB Part 1: USSR, SU/0705, 6 March 1990. Turnout was 90 per cent. See also Eastern Europe 1992; Europa 1994.

State/Election year/Largest party or elected presidential candidate	Votes for the largest party % of total votes	Total votes Number	% of total population
93 Tunisia Concurrent powers Parliamentary elections:			
1989 Democratic Constitutional Rally	80	2,041,881	26
Presidential elections:			
1989 Ben Ali	99	2,041,881	26

Sources: 1989 – IPU 1988–9; Europa 1991; The Middle East and North Africa 1993: 850.

94 Turkey Concurrent powers Parliamentary elections:			
1991 True Path Party	27	24,416,700	43
Presidential elections:			
1989 Turgut Özal	58	450	0
1993 Süleyman Demirel	57	431	0

Sources: 1989 – Keesing's 1989: 36985. 1991 – IPU 1991–2; Keesing's 1991: 38547. 1993 – Keesing's 1993: 39482–3.

95 Turkmenistan Concurrent powers Parliamentary elections:			
1990 Communists	90	N/A	(50)
Presidential elections:			
1990 Saparmurad Niyazov	98	N/A	(50)
1992 Saparmurad Niyazov	99	N/A	(50)

Sources: 1990 – Eastern Europe 1992; Keesing's 1990: 37788; Carlson 1991. Direct popular election. 1992 – Keesing's 1992: 38969; Europa 1993.

96 United Arab Emirates
Executive dominance
Legislative and executive powers are vested in the Supreme Council, which is composed of the rulers of the seven emirates. See Europa 1994.

97 Uzbekistan Concurrent powers Parliamentary elections:			
1990 Communist Party	95	N/A	(50)
Presidential elections:			
1991 Islam Karimov	86	N/A	(50)

Sources: 1990 – Keesing's 1990: 37322 (distribution of seats). 1991 – Freedom in the World 1991–92: 587; Keesing's 1991: 38657; Eastern Europe 1992.

98 Yemen Concurrent powers Parliamentary elections:			
1990 Members of the Consultative Council of the former Yemen Arab Republic	53	N/A	0
1993 General People's Congress (GPC)	41	2,430,000	20

State/Election year/Largest party or elected presidential candidate	Votes for the largest party % of total votes	Total votes Number	% of total population

Presidential elections:
| 1990 General Ali Abdullah Saleh | 100 | N/A | 0 |
| 1993 General Ali Abdullah Saleh | 100 | 4 | 0 |

Sources: 1990 – See IPU 1989–90; Europa 1991; The World Factbook 1991–92: 341–2. Distribution of seats. The Yemen Arab Republic (North Yemen) and the People's Democratic Republic of Yemen (South Yemen) merged to form the Republic of Yemen on 22 May 1990. The parliaments of the two Yemens were amalgamated to form the 301-member House of Representatives of the Republic of Yemen. 1993 – IPU 1992–3; Keesing's 1993: 39440, 39711; Europa 1993; IFES 1993: No. 1. Distribution of seats.

Sub-Saharan Africa
99 Angola
Parliamentary dominance (1991)
1986 Popular Movement for the
        Liberation of Angola – Workers'

| Party (MPLA-PT) | 100 | N/A | 0 |

Concurrent powers (1992–3)
Parliamentary elections:
1992 Popular Movement for the
        Liberation of Angola – Workers'

| Party (MPLA-PT) | 54 | 3,952,265 | 37 |

Presidential elections:
| 1992 José Eduardo dos Santos (MPLA-PT) | 100 | 0 | 0 |

Sources: 1986 – IPU 1986–7; Europa 1991. Members of the People's Assembly were elected indirectly by provincial assemblies. 1992 – IPU 1992–3; Keesing's 1992: 39082, 39128–9; Europa 1993. A civil war broke out soon after the 1992 elections. In the 1992 direct presidential election, dos Santos received 49.6 per cent of the votes in the first round, but because it was impossible to organize the second round of the presidential election, he did not become legally elected (see Keesing's Reference Supplement 1994: R 3.

100 Benin
Concurrent powers
Parliamentary elections:
1991 Union for the Triumph of
        Democratic Renewal (UTR)

| | 19 | 1,024,485 | 21 |

Presidential elections:
| 1991 Nicephore Soglo | 68 | 1,161,781 | 24 |

Sources: 1991 – ARB (Africa Research Bulletin) 1991: 10008–11, 10044; Europa 1992. Distribution of seats in the National Assembly.

101 Botswana
Parliamentary dominance
| 1989 Botswana Democratic Party | 65 | 250,487 | 20 |

Sources: 1989 – IPU 1989–90.

102 Burkina Faso
A transitional government in 1991.
Concurrent powers (1992–3)
Parliamentary elections:
1992 Organization for Popular
        Democracy – Labour Movement

| | 48 | 1,215,419 | 13 |

State/Election year/Largest party or elected presidential candidate	Votes for the largest party % of total votes	Total votes Number	% of total population
Presidential elections:			
1991 B. Compaoré	86	854,900	9

Sources: 1991 – ARB 1991: 10161, 10383; Europa 1993; Freedom in the World 1991–92: 581. See also Keesing's 1991: 38665. 1992 – IPU 1991–2.

103 Burundi
Military governments in 1991–2.
Concurrent powers (1993)
Parliamentary elections:

1993 Front for Democracy in Burundi	73	2,110,871	35

Presidential elections:

1993 An interim presidency	100	0	0

Source: 1991–2 : See Europa 1993. 1993 ARB 1993: 11036, 11074; IPU 1992–3; IFES 1993: No. 1; Keesing's 1993: 39496–7, 39547, 39672, 39721–2. President Melchior Ndadaye, who had been elected in July 1993, was killed in an abortive military coup in October 1993, after which the interim presidency was held by the government in a collegiate capacity.

104 Cameroon
Concurrent powers
Parliamentary elections:

1988 Cameroon People's Democratic Movement	100	3,179,858	28
1992 Cameroon People's Democratic Rally	49	2,197,243	18

Presidential elections:

1988 Paul Biya (CNU)	99	3,364,090	30
1992 Paul Biya (CPDR)	40	2,965,616	24

Sources: 1988 – IPU 1987–8 (distribution of seats); ARB, June 15, 1988. 1992 – IPU 1991–2; Keesing's 1992: 38802, 39130; IFES 1992: No. 1. Distribution of seats.

105 Cape Verde
Concurrent powers
Parliamentary elections:

1991 Movement for Democracy (MPD)	68	118,127	32

Presidential elections:

1991 A. Mascarenhas Monteiro (MPD)	73	97,350	26

Sources: 1991 – IPU 1990–1; Keesing's 1991: 37948, 37994.

106 Central African Republic
Executive dominance (1991–2)

1986 General André Kolingba	92	754,807	27
1993 Central African People's Liberation Party	40	793,971	25

Presidential elections:

1993 Ange-Felix Patasse (MLPC)	53	679,232	21

Sources: 1986 – Africa Contemporary Record 1986–7: B 180. 1993 – IPU 1993–4; ARB 1993: 11142; IFES 1993: No. 1. Distribution of seats. The second round of voting in the presidential election.

State/Election year/Largest party or elected presidential candidate	Votes for the largest party % of total votes	Total votes Number	% of total population

107 Chad
Military governments in 1991–3.
See Europa 1994; Keesing's Reference Supplement 1994: R 8.

108 Comoros
Concurrent powers
Parliamentary elections:

1987 Union for Comoran Progress (UPC)	100	221,000	44
1992 Opposition members	59	N/A	(15)
1993 Rally for Democracy and Renewal	67	N/A	(15)

Presidential elections:

1990 Said Mohamed Djohar	55	187,422	35

Sources: 1987 – IPU 1986–7 (distribution of seats); ARB 1987: 8427. 1990 – Keesing's 1990: 37309; Europa 1991. 1992 – IPU 1992–3; Keesing's 1992: 39260. Low turnout. Distribution of seats. 1993 – IPU 1993–4; ARB 1993: 11264; 1994: 11295; Keesing's 1993: 39769. Distribution of seats. Turnout was poor. *Cf.* IFES 1994: No. 2–3.

109 Congo
Concurrent powers
Parliamentary elections:

1989 Congolese Labour Party (PCT)	100	870,460	40
1992 Pan-African Union for Social Democracy	31	N/A	(35)
1993 Presidential Tendency coalition	51	N/A	(35)

Presidential elections:

1989 General Denis Sassou-Nguesso	100	N/A	0
1992 Pascal Lissouba	61	825,791	35

Sources: 1989 – IPU 1989–90 (distribution of seats); Europa 1991. 1992 – IPU 1992–3; ARB 1992: 10646, 10680; Keesing's 1992: 39040–1. Distribution of seats. 1993 – IPU 1992–3; IFES 1993: No. 1. Distribution of seats. See also ARB 1993: 11181–2.

110 Côte d'Ivoire
Concurrent powers
Parliamentary elections:

1990 Democratic Party of Côte d'Ivoire	93	1,504,000	13

Presidential elections:

1990 Félix Houphouet-Boigny (PDCI)	82	2,993,806	25

Sources: 1990 – IPU 1990–1 (distribution of seats); Journal of Democracy, Winter 1991; Europa 1993.

111 Djibouti
Concurrent powers
Parliamentary elections:

1987 Popular Rally for Progress	99	91,191	24
1992 Popular Rally for Progress	100	71,827	15

Presidential elections:

1987 Hassan Gouled Aptidon	90	N/A	(24)
1993 Hassan Gouled Aptidon	61	74,838	16

Sources: 1987 – IPU 1986–7; ARB 1987: 8462. 1992 – IPU 1992–3; ARB 1993: 10852; Keesing's 1992: 39226. Distribution of seats. 1993 – Keesing's 1993: 39451; Keesing's Reference Supplement 1994: R 10.

State/Election year/Largest party or elected presidential candidate	Votes for the largest party % of total votes	Total votes Number	% of total population
112 Equatorial Guinea			
Executive dominance			
1989 Theodoro Obiang Nguema	99	N/A	(20)

Sources: 1989 – Europa 1991; Keesing's 1989: 36727. Nguema was elected unopposed. See also Keesing's Reference Supplement 1994: R 11.

113 Ethiopia			
Executive dominance			
1987 Lieutenant Colonel Mengistu	100	N/A	0
A military coup in May 1991. An interim government.			

Sources: 1987 – ARB 1987: 8394–5, 8563, 8623; Keesing's 1987: 35367–8; IPU 1986–7. 1991 – Keesing's 1991: 38174, 38276; Europa 1994.

114 Gabon			
Concurrent powers			
Parliamentary elections:			
1990 Democratic Party of Gabon (PDG)	52	N/A	(33)
Presidential elections:			
1986 Omar Bongo (PDG)	100	N/A	(33)
1993 Omar Bongo	51	417,719	33

Sources: 1986 Keesing's 1986: 35047. According to this source, the number of voters was 904,039, but it does not seem to be possible because the total population was only a little over one million. 1990 – IPU 1990–1. According to this source, the number of registered voters was approximately 600,000 in 1990. Distribution of seats. 1993 – ARB 1993: 11265; Keesing's 1993: 39767; Journal of Democracy, January 1994.

115 Gambia			
Concurrent powers			
Parliamentary elections:			
1987 People's Progressive Party (PPP)	57	207,719	26
1992 People's Progressive Party (PPP)	69	N/A	(25)
Presidential elections:			
1987 Alhaji Dawda Jawara (PPP)	59	210,156	26
1992 Alhaji Dawda Jawara (PPP)	58	223,000	25

Sources: 1987 – Europa 1991; IPU 1986–7. 1992 – ARB 1992: 10575; Keesing's 1992: 38855, 38899. Distribution of seats.

116 Ghana			
Jerry Rawling's military government in 1991.			
Concurrent powers (1992–3)			
Parliamentary elections:			
1992 National Democratic Congress	94	2,059,415	13
Presidential elections:			
1992 Jerry Rawlings	58	3,989,115	25

Sources: 1991 – See Chazan 1988; Europa 1993. 1992 – IPU 1992–3; Europa 1993; Keesing's 1992: 39180, 39228; ARB 1993: 10852. Distribution of seats.

State/Election year/Largest party or elected presidential candidate	Votes for the largest party % of total votes	Total votes Number	% of total population

117 Guinea
Military governments in 1991–2.
Concurrent powers (1993)
Parliamentary elections were not held in 1993.
Presidential elections:

| 1993 Lansana Conte (Party of Unity Progress) | 52 | 2,082,840 | 34 |

Sources: See Europa 1993. 1993 – IFES 1994: No. 2–3. Cf. ARB 1993: 11265–6; 1994: 11296; Keesing's 1993: 39767.

118 Guinea-Bissau
Parliamentary dominance

| 1989 African Party for Independence of Guinea and Cape Verde (PAIGC) | 100 | N/A | 0 |

Sources: 1989 – IPU 1988–9; ARB 1989: 9302. Indirect elections. See also Keesing's Reference Supplement 1994: R 15.

119 Kenya
Concurrent powers
Parliamentary elections:

| 1988 Kenya African National Union (KANU) | 100 | 2,231,229 | 9 |
| 1992 Kenya African National Union (KANU) | 53 | 5,425,595 | 21 |

Presidential elections:

| 1988 Daniel Arap Moi (KANU) | 100 | 0 | 0 |
| 1992 Daniel Arap Moi (KANU) | 36 | 5,400,324 | 21 |

Sources: 1988 – IPU 1987–8; Keesing's 1988: 38053; Europa 1991. Because Moi was the only presidential candidate, he was declared elected without voting. 1992 – IPU 1992–3; IFES 1993: No. 4; Europa 1993; Keesing's 1993: 39254. Distribution of seats.

120 Lesotho
Military governments in 1991–2.
Concurrent powers (1993)
Parliamentary elections:

| 1993 Basutho Congress Party (BCP) | 75 | 532,678 | 29 |

The king retained a significant part of executive power.

Sources:1991–2 See Keesing's 1991: 38132; Europa 1993. 1993 IPU 1992–3; Keesing's 1993: 39351, 40127.

121 Liberia
Interim military governments in 1991–93 and a transitional government in 1993.

Source: 1991–3: See Europa 1994; Keesing's 1993: 39582.

122 Madagascar
Concurrent powers
Parliamentary elections:

| 1989 AREMA and allied parties | 78 | 4,167,358 | 36 |
| 1993 Forces Vives Cartel and allied parties | 56 | 3,600,000 | 27 |

State/Election year/Largest party or elected presidential candidate	Votes for the largest party % of total votes	Total votes Number	% of total population
Presidential elections:			
1989 Didier Ratsiraka (AREMA)	63	4,610,624	40
1993 Albert Safy	67	4,189,780	32

Sources: 1989 – IPU 1988–9; Europa 1991; The World Factbook 1991–92: 188. 1993 – IPU 1992–3; SWB Part 4, ME/1618, 20 February 1993; Keesing's 1993: 39308–9, 39548; IFES 1993: No. 4; Journal of Democracy 1993: No. 4. Distribution of seats.

123 Malawi
Executive dominance

1971 Hastings K. Banda (MCP)	100	N/A	0

Sources: 1971 – Europa 1991. As a result of a constitutional amendment, Banda became President for Life in 1971. 1993 – See IFES 1993: No. 1; Keesing's Reference Supplement 1994: R 17.

124 Mali
A military coup in March 1991.
Concurrent powers (1992–3)
Parliamentary elections:

1992 Alliance for Democracy in Mali	65	1,008,000	10

Presidential elections:

1992 Alpha Oumar Konare (ADEMA)	69	817,000	8

Sources: 1991 – Keesing's 1991: 38138. 1992 – ARB 1992: 10541; IPU 1991–2; Keesing's 1992: 38801, 38853 (distribution of seats). Second round of the presidential election.

125 Mauritius
Parliamentary dominance

1991 MSM	48	576,000	53

Sources: 1991 – Keesing's 1991: 38427; IPU 1991–2. Distribution of seats.

126 Mozambique
Parliamentary dominance

1986 Front for the Liberation of Mozambique (Frelimo)	100	N/A	0

Sources: 1986 – IPU 1986–7; ARB 1986: 8150, 8333. Indirect elections. See also Keesing's Reference Supplement 1994: R 19.

127 Namibia
Concurrent powers
Parliamentary elections:

1989 South West Africa People's Organization (SWAPO)	57	670,830	49

Presidential elections:

1990 Sam Nujoma (SWAPO)	100	72	0

Sources: 1989 – IPU 1989–90; ARB 1989: 9472–6. 1990 – ARB 1990: 9579. Nujoma was elected by the parliament.

128 Niger
Concurrent powers
Parliamentary elections:

1989 National Movement for Developing Society (MNSD)	99	3,330,778	44

State/Election year/Largest party or elected presidential candidate	Votes for the largest party % of total votes	Total votes Number	% of total population
1993 The Alliance of the Forces of Change	60	2,240,000	27
Presidential elections:			
1989 General Ali Saibou	100	3,330,778	44
1993 Mahamane Ousmane (CDS)	54	N/A	(27)

Sources: 1989 – IPU 1989–90. 1993 – IPU 1992–3; Keesing's 1993: 39306–7, 39354. Distribution of seats.

129 Nigeria
Military governments in 1991–3.
See Europa 1994; IPU 1992–3; Keesing's 1992: 38994, 1993: 39582; ARB 1992: 10648–9. A new military coup in November 1993.

130 Rwanda
Concurrent powers
Parliamentary elections:

1988 National Revolutionary Movement for Development (MRND)	100	2,701,682	40

Presidential elections:

1988 General Juvénal Habyarimana (MRND)	100	2,701,682	40

Sources: 1988 – IPU 1988–9. See also Keesing's Reference Supplement 1994: R 22.

131 São Tomé and Príncipe
Concurrent powers
Parliamentary elections:

1991 Democratic Convergence Party	54	N/A	(29)

Presidential elections:

1991 Miguel Trovoado	81	36,000	29

Sources: 1991 – ARB 1991: 10010, 10045; Europa 1991; The World Factbook 1991–92: 272; Keesing's 1991: 37949, 38084.

132 Senegal
Concurrent powers
Parliamentary elections:

1988 Socialist Party (PS)	71	1,113,746	16
1993 Senegalese Socialist Party (PS)	57	1,064,584	14

Presidential elections:

1988 Abdou Diouf (PS)	73	1,131,468	16
1993 Abdou Diouf (PS)	58	1,297,216	17

Sources: 1988 – IPU 1987–8; Europa 1991; ARB, April 15, 1988. 1993 – IPU 1992–3; IFES 1993: No. 4; Keesing's 1993: 39354, 39449; ARB 1993: 10924.

133 Sierra Leone
Concurrent powers
Parliamentary elections:

1986 All-People's Congress (APC)	100	N/A	(25)

State/Election year/Largest party or elected presidential candidate	Votes for the largest party % of total votes	Total votes Number	% of total population
Presidential elections:			
1985 General J.S. Momoh (APC)	100	2,788,687	(25)
A military coup in 1992.			

Sources: 1985–6 – IPU 1985–6; ARB 1985: 7821; Africa Contemporary Record 1985–86: B 162. According to IPU 1985–6, the number of registered voters was approximately 2,000,000. 1992 – Keesing's 1992: 38853–4, 38900; ARB 1993: 10994; Europa 1994.

134 Somalia

President Barre was overthrown in January 1991 by rebels. Military governments and a civil war in 1991–3.

Sources: 1991–3 – See Europa 1994; Keesing's Reference Supplement 1994: R 24.

135 South Africa
Parliamentary dominance

1989 National Party (NP)	48	2,157,593	6

Sources: 1989 – IPU 1989–90. Data refer to the results of the House of Assembly election. In addition to this election, 258,186 valid votes were cast in the House of Representatives election and 153,136 votes in the House of Delegates election. Thus the total number of valid votes was 2,568,915. The degree of participation for 1989 was calculated on the basis of this total number of valid votes. See also Keesing's Reference Supplement 1994: R 25.

136 Swaziland
Executive and legislative powers are concentrated in the hands of the king and his relatives. All political parties are banned under the 1978 Constitution.
See Europa 1994; Keesing's Reference Supplement 1994: R 27. For the October 1993 parliamentary elections, see IPU 1993–4.

137 Tanzania
Concurrent powers
Parliamentary elections:

1990 Revolutionary Party of Tanzania	100	5,425,282	21

Presidential elections:

1990 Ali Hassan Mwinyi (CCM)	95	5,441,286	21

Sources: 1990 – IPU 1990–1; Keesing's 1990: 37766; ARB 1990: 9899.

138 Togo
Concurrent powers
Parliamentary elections:

1990 Rally of the Togolese People (RPT)	100	1,300,000	37

Presidential elections:

1986 General G. Eyadema (RPT)	100	1,720,654	55
1993 General G. Eyadema	96	737,237	19

Sources: 1986 – Africa Contemporary Record 1986–87: B 155. 1990 – IPU 1989–90. 1993 – IFES 1993: No. 1; Keesing's 1993: 39583.

139 Uganda
Lieutenant General Yoweri Kaguta Museveni's interim government in 1991–3.
See Europa 1994.

State/Election year/Largest party or elected presidential candidate	Votes for the largest party % of total votes	Total votes Number	% of total population

140 Zaire
Executive dominance
In December 1991, President Mobuto, who had been elected in 1984, decided to continue his term.
See Keesing's 1991: 38662; Africa Demos 1993: No. 1; Europa 1994.

141 Zambia
Concurrent powers
Parliamentary elections:
1991 Movement for Multiparty
      Democracy   75   1,273,433   15
Presidential elections:
1991 Frederick Chilubu (MMD)   76   1,283,514   15
Sources: 1991 – ARB 1991: 10341; IPU 1991–2; Keesing's 1991: 38515.

142 Zimbabwe
Concurrent powers
Parliamentary elections:
1990 ZANU-Patriotic Front (PF)   97   2,592,000   28
Presidential elections:
1990 Robert Mugabe (ZANU)   78   2,443,840   26
Sources: 1990 – IPU 1989–90; ARB 1990: 9619; Europa 1991 (distribution of seats).

South Asia
143 Bangladesh
Parliamentary dominance
1991 Bangladesh Nationalist Party (BNP) 51   32,390,000   28
Sources: 1991 – IPU 1990–1; Keesing's 1991: 38102, 38533. Distribution of seats.

144 Bhután
Bhután is an absolute monarchy.
See Europa 1994; Bhután. Background Notes, November 1987. There is no written constitution, but power is shared by the monarchy, the Council of Ministers, the National Assembly, and the Head Abbot of Bhután's Buddhist monks. Elections to the National Assembly are indirect.

145 India
Parliamentary dominance
1991 Congress (I)   45   276,000,000   32
Sources: 1991 – IPU 1990–1; Keesing's 1991, 38286–87. Distribution of seats.

146 Maldives
Executive dominance
1988 Maumoon Abdul Gayoom   96   N/A   (28)
1993 Maumoon Abdul Gayoom   92   N/A   (28)
Sources: 1988 – Europa 1991. The number of voters was 57,402 (28 per cent of the total population) in the 1989 parliamentary elections. See IPU 1989–90. 1993 – Keesing's 1993: 39691; Asian Recorder 1993: 23451; SWB Part 3: Asia – Pacific, FE/1812, 6 October 1993.

State/Election year/Largest party or elected presidential candidate	Votes for the largest party % of total votes	Total votes Number	% of total population

147 Nepal
Concurrent powers (75–25%)
Parliamentary elections:

1991 Nepali Congress Party (NCP)	38	6,969,061	35

Executive power was in the hands of the king until the constitutional reform of 1990, after which the king lost the major part of his former powers.

Sources: 1991 – IPU 1990–1; The World Factbook 1991–92: 219; Europa 1993.

148 Pakistan
Concurrent powers (75–25)
Parliamentary elections:

1990 Islamic Democratic Alliance (IDA)	37	21,163,911	19
1993 Pakistan People's Party (PPP)	43	21,402,000	18

Presidential elections:

1988 Ghulam Ishaq Khan	78	446	0
1993 Farooq Ahmeed Leghari (PPP)	62	442	0

Sources: 1988 – Europa 1991; Keesing's 1988: 37150. 1990 – IPU 1990–1. 1993 – SWB Part 3, FE/1811, 5 October 1993; FE/1815, 9 October 1993. Distribution of seats. *Cf.* Asian Recorder 1993: 23512–14, 23593–4; Keesing's 1993: 39685, 39738.

149 Sri Lanka
Concurrent powers
Parliamentary elections:

1989 United National Party (UNP)	51	5,596,318	33

Presidential elections:

1988 Ranasinghe Premadasa (UNP)	50	5,094,778	31

Sources: 1988 – Europa 1991. See also Keesing's 1993: 39467–8. 1989 – IPU 1988–9.

East Asia and Southeast Asia
150 Brunei
Sovereign authority is vested in the Sultan.
See Europa 1994.

151 Cambodia
Prince Norodom Sihanouk was reinstated as Head of State in November 1991. UN Transitional Authority 1991–1993.
Concurrent powers (1993)
Parliamentary elections:

1993 FUNCINPEC	45	4,011,327	44

Presidential elections:

1993 Prince Norodom Sihanouk	100	7	0

Sources: 1991 – Keesing's 1991: 38573–4. 1993 – IPU 1992–3; Keesing's 1993: 39513–14, 39642. Sihanouk was unanimously elected as monarch by a seven-member Throne Council.

152 China
Parliamentary dominance:

1988 Chinese Communist party	100	N/A	0
1993 Communist Party of China and allies	100	N/A	0

Sources: 1988 – IPU 1987–8; Europa 1991. Indirect elections. 1993 – IPU 1992–3. Indirect elections.

State/Election year/Largest party or elected presidential candidate	Votes for the largest party % of total votes	Total votes Number	% of total population
153 Indonesia			
Concurrent powers			
Parliamentary elections:			
1987 Golkar	73	85,885,000	52
1992 Golkar	68	95,245,000	50
Presidential elections:			
1988 General Suharto	100	N/A	0
1993 General Suharto	100	N/A	0

Sources: 1987 – IPU 1986–7. 1988 – Keesing's 1988 36024–5. 1992 – Keesing's 1992: 38964–5; IFES 1992: No. 2. 1993 – Keesing's 1993: 39372.

154 Japan			
Parliamentary dominance			
1990 Liberal-Democratic Party (LDP)	46	65,704,311	53
1993 Liberal-Democratic Party (LDP)	33	47,278,359	38

Sources: 1990 – IPU 1989–90. 1993 – IPU 1992–3. Proportional representation seats. *Cf.* Keesing's 1993: 39555; Electoral Studies 1993: 12, 4: 420.

155 Korea, North			
Concurrent powers			
Parliamentary elections:			
1990 Democratic Front of the Reunification	100	N/A	(50)
Presidential elections:			
1990 Kim II Sung	100	N/A	0

Sources: 1990 – IPU 1989–90; Europa 1993. Data on the number of votes are not available.

156 Korea, South			
Concurrent powers			
Parliamentary elections:			
1988 Democratic Justice party	34	19,642,040	47
1992 Democratic Liberal Party (DLP)	38	20,583,812	47
Presidential elections:			
1987 Roh Tae Woo (DJP)	36	23,070,748	55
1992 Kim Young Sam	42	23,775,409	54

Sources: 1987 – Keesing's 1987: 35768–9; Europa 1991. 1988 – IPU 1987–8. 1992 – IPU 1991–2; Keesing's 1992: 38798–9, 39234.

157 Laos			
Parliamentary dominance			
1989 Lao People's Revolutionary Party and allies	100	N/A	(45)
1992 Lao Front for National Construction	100	2,009,727	45

Sources: 1989 – Europa 1991. Data on the number of votes are not available. 1992 – IPU 1992–3; Keesing's 1992: 39238; Europa 1993. Distribution of seats.

State/Election year/Largest party or elected presidential candidate	Votes for the largest party % of total votes	Total votes Number	% of total population
158 Malaysia Parliamentary dominance			
1990 National Front	52	5,600,000	31

Sources: 1990 – IPU 1990–1; The World Factbook 1991–92: 191; Keesing's 1990: 37780.

159 Mongolia Concurrent powers Parliamentary elections			
1990 Mongolian People's Revolutionary Party (MPRP)	62	1,006,000	46
1992 MPRP	57	1,037,392	45
Presidential elections:			
1990 Punsalmaagiyn Ochirbat (MPRP)	100	N/A	0
1993 P. Ochirbat (Opposition Coalition)	58	1,250,000	53

Sources: 1990 – IPU 1990–1; Europa 1991; The World Factbook 1991–92: 210. Election to the People's Great Hural. 1992 – IPU 1991–2; Keesing's 1992: 38962. Election to the People's Great Hural. MPRP won 92 per cent of the seats. 1993 – IFES 1993: No. 1.

160 Myanmar (Burma)
Military governments in 1991–3.
See Europa 1994; Keesing's Reference Supplement 1994: R 65.

161 Philippines Concurrent powers Parliamentary elections:			
1987 Pro-Aquino LDP	73	23,760,000	41
1992 LDP	42	N/A	(35)
Presidential elections:			
1986 Cory Aquino (UNIDO)	(53)	(20,098,000)	(35)
1992 Fidel Ramos	24	22,646,751	35

Sources: 1986 – Keesing's 1986: 34299–302; Jackson 1989. Exact results of the 1987 presidential election are not known. Mrs Aquino was sworn in as president on 25 February, three weeks after the election, and Marcos fled the country. 1987 – IPU 1986–7; The World Factbook 1991–92: 250; Europe 1991. 1992 – Keesing's 1992: 38964; see also IPU 1991–2; Europa 1993.

162 Singapore Parliamentary dominance			
1991 People's Action Party (PAP)	61	783,612	28

Sources: 1991 – IPU 1991–92; Keesing's 1991: 38397. PAP won 77 of the 81 seats.

163 Taiwan (ROC) Concurrent powers Parliamentary elections (Legislative Branch):			
1989 Kuomintang	61	9,472,000	47
1992 Kuomintang	60	9,665,900	47
Presidential elections:			
1990 Lee Teng-hui (KMT)	100	N/A	0

Sources: 1989 and 1992 – Letter of Hung-mao Tien, President of the Chang Yung-fa Foundation, Institute for National Policy Research, March 24, 1994. See also Republic of China Yearbook 1991–92: 131–2; Keesing's 1992: 39236; Wu 1993. 1990 – Europa 1991. Lee Teng-hui was elected unopposed by the National Assembly.

State/Election year/Largest party or elected presidential candidate	Votes for the largest party % of total votes	Total votes Number	% of total population

164 Thailand
A military coup d'etat on 23 February 1991.
Concurrent powers (1992–3)
Parliamentary elections:

1992 Democrat Party	22	18,391,851	32

Presidential elections:
Executive power is in the hands of the king.

Sources: 1992 – IPU 1992–3; Keesing's 1992: 38816, 39093; Europa 1994. Distribution of seats.

165 Vietnam
Parliamentary dominance

1987 Viet Nam Fatherland Front	100	N/A	(53)
1992 Viet Nam Fatherland Front	100	36,837,427	53

Sources: 1987 – IPU 1986–7; Europa 1991. 1992 – IPU 1992–3; Keesing's 1992: 39007. Distribution of seats.

Oceania
166 Australia
Parliamentary dominance

1990 Australian Labour Party	39	9,861,075	58
1993 Australian Labour Party	45	10,576,777	59

Sources: 1990 – IPU 1989–90. 1993 – IPU 1992–3.

167 Fiji
A military government in 1991.
Parliamentary dominance (1992–3)

1992 Fijian Political Party (FPP)	43	235,969	32

Sources: 1991 – See Europa 1992. 1992–IPU 1992–3; Keesing's 1992: 38917. Distribution of seats.

168 New Zealand
Parliamentary dominance

1990 National Party	48	1,824,092	54
1993 National Party	35	1,950,000	57

Sources: 1990 – IPU 1990–1. 1993 – Keesing's 1993: 39742; Electoral Studies 1994: 197.

169 Papua New Guinea
Parliamentary dominance

1987 Pangu Pati	15	1,354,400	39
1992 Pangu Pati	20	N/A	(39)

Sources: 1987 – IPU 1987–8; Europa 1991. Distribution of seats. Each voter had to cast two votes. Therefore, it is assumed that the number of voters was 50 per cent of the number of valid votes (2,708,937). 1992 – IPU 1991–2; Keesing's 1992: 38965; Pacific Islands Monthly, August 1992: 9–10. Distribution of seats.

170 Solomon Islands
Parliamentary dominance

1989 People's Alliance Party (PAP)	57	81,239	26

State/Election year/Largest party or elected presidential candidate	Votes for the largest party % of total votes	Total votes Number	% of total population
1993 Group for National Unity and Reconciliation	45	109,550	33

Sources: 1989 – IPU 1988–9. Distribution of seats. *Cf.* Europa 1991. 1993–IPU 1992–3; Keesing's 1993: 39468; IFES 1993: No. 1; John Henderson's letter of 8 December 1994. His source is Solomon Star of 2 June 1993. Distribution of seats.

171 Vanuatu
Parliamentary dominance
1991 Union of Moderate Parties	41	52,000	37

Sources: 1991 – Keesing's 1991: 38676; John Henderson's letter of 8 December 1994. His source is Vanuatu Weekly of 7 December 1991. See also Sharma 1992.

172 Western Samoa
Parliamentary dominance
1991 Human Rights Protection Party	55	44,400	28

Sources: 1991 – IPU 1990–1. Distribution of seats.

Appendix 2

This appendix contains statistical data on Urban Population, Non Agricultural Population, Students and Literates in 172 states by regional groups in or around 1990.

Regional group/ State	Urban Population %	Non Agricul. Population %	Students per 100,000	Adult literacy %	Students as % of 5,000 %
Europe and North America					
1 Albania	35	52	679	85	14
2 Armenia	68	89	2,030	93	41
3 Austria	58	94	2,668	99	53
4 Belarus	67	81	1,700	95	34
5 Belgium	97	97	2,772	99	55
6 Bulgaria	68	88	2,096	93	42
7 Canada	77	97	7,195	99	100
8 Croatia	(56)	(78)	1,450	(93)	29
9 Czechoslovakia	77	91	1,216	97	24
10 Denmark	85	95	2,781	99	56
11 Estonia	71	91	1,636	96	33
12 Finland	60	92	3,326	99	67
13 France	74	95	2,995	99	60
14 Georgia	56	86	1,900	93	38
15 Germany	85	96	2,810	99	56
16 Greece	62	76	1,927	93	39
17 Hungary	61	88	970	97	19
18 Iceland	91	93	2,049	99	41
19 Ireland	57	86	2,578	99	52
20 Italy	69	93	2,519	97	50
21 Latvia	71	91	1,712	96	34
22 Lithuania	69	90	1,758	96	35
23 Luxembourg	84	96	1,502	99	30
24 Macedonia	(50)	(70)	1,180	(90)	22
25 Malta	87	96	882	87	18
26 Moldova	48	79	1,250	95	25
27 Netherlands	89	96	3,205	99	64
28 Norway	75	95	3,357	99	67
29 Poland	62	79	1,427	96	29
30 Portugal	34	84	1,882	85	38
31 Romania	53	80	711	95	14
32 Russia	74	80	1,900	94	38
33 Slovenia	(56)	86	1,860	(93)	37
34 Spain	78	89	3,137	97	63
35 Sweden	84	96	2,248	99	45
36 Switzerland	60	96	2,048	99	41
37 Ukraine	68	75	1,700	95	34
38 United Kingdom	89	98	2,192	99	44
39 United States	75	98	5,485	99	100
40 Yugoslavia	56	78	1,374	93	27
Latin America and the Caribbean					
41 Argentina	86	90	3,293	95	66
42 Bahamas	64	94	1,945	99	39
43 Barbados	45	93	1,657	99	33

Regional group/ State	Urban Population %	Non Agricul. Population %	Students per 100,000	Adult literacy %	Students as % of 5,000 %
44 Belize	50	63	625	95	12
45 Bolivia	51	58	1,975	77	39
46 Brazil	75	76	1,074	81	21
47 Chile	85	87	1,938	93	39
48 Colombia	70	73	1,496	87	30
49 Costa Rica	47	76	2,461	93	49
50 Cuba	75	81	2,285	94	46
51 Dominican Republic	60	64	1,929	83	39
52 Ecuador	56	70	1,958	86	39
53 El Salvador	44	63	1,512	73	30
54 Guatemala	39	49	741	55	15
55 Guyana	35	78	588	96	12
56 Haiti	28	36	107	53	2
57 Honduras	44	45	854	73	17
58 Jamaica	52	73	662	98	13
59 Mexico	73	70	1,552	87	31
60 Nicaragua	60	63	836	81	17
61 Panama	53	75	2,181	88	44
62 Paraguay	48	54	769	90	15
63 Peru	70	65	3,450	85	69
64 St Lucia	47	70	300	93	6
65 St Vincent	27	74	309	98	6
66 Suriname	47	84	1,023	95	20
67 Trinidad and Tobago	69	92	591	96	12
68 Uruguay	86	86	2,315	96	46
69 Venezuela	91	89	2,847	88	57

North Africa, the Middle East and Central Asia

70 Afghanistan	18	45	147	29	3
71 Algeria	52	76	1,146	57	23
72 Azerbaijan	53	85	1,470	93	29
73 Bahrain	83	98	1,365	77	27
74 Cyprus	53	79	1,029	87	21
75 Egypt	44	59	1,717	48	34
76 Iran	57	72	858	54	17
77 Iraq	71	79	1,240	60	25
78 Israel	92	96	2,790	95	56
79 Jordan	68	94	2,497	80	50
80 Kazakhstan	58	80	1,710	93	34
81 Kuwait	96	98	1,244	73	25
82 Kyrgyzstan	38	84	1,330	93	27
83 Lebanon	84	91	3,071	80	61
84 Libya	70	86	1,150	64	23
85 Mauritania	47	36	303	34	6
86 Morocco	48	63	958	49	19
87 Oman	11	60	391	35	8
88 Qatar	79	97	1,519	79	30
89 Saudi Arabia	77	61	1,035	62	21
90 Sudan	22	40	258	27	5
91 Syria	50	76	1,740	64	35

Regional group/ State	Urban Population %	Non Agricul. Population %	Students per 100,000	Adult literacy %	Students as % of 5,000 %
92 Tajikistan	31	86	1,280	93	26
93 Tunisia	54	76	851	65	17
94 Turkey	61	52	1,339	81	27
95 Turkmenistan	45	64	1,130	93	23
96 United Arab Emirates	78	97	642	55	13
97 Uzbekistan	40	83	1,650	93	33
98 Yemen	29	44	438	39	9
Sub-Saharan Africa					
99 Angola	27	30	71	42	1
100 Benin	38	39	235	23	5
101 Botswana	28	37	299	74	6
102 Burkina Faso	9	16	60	18	1
103 Burundi	6	9	65	50	1
104 Cameroon	41	39	288	54	6
105 Cape Verde Islands	29	57	176	66	4
106 Central African Rep.	47	37	119	38	2
107 Chad	30	25	70	30	1
108 Comoros	28	21	110	55	2
109 Congo	41	40	479	57	10
110 Côte d'Ivoire	40	44	204	54	4
111 Djibouti	81	(85)	117	19	2
112 Equatorial Guinea	29	44	50	50	1
113 Ethiopia	13	25	68	50	1
114 Gabon	46	32	368	61	7
115 Gambia	23	19	213	27	4
116 Ghana	33	50	126	60	3
117 Guinea	26	26	122	24	2
118 Guinea-Bissau	20	21	85	36	2
119 Kenya	24	23	187	69	4
120 Lesotho	20	20	100	78	2
121 Liberia	46	30	220	39	4
122 Madagascar	24	23	298	80	6
123 Malawi	12	25	63	45	1
124 Mali	19	19	73	32	1
125 Mauritius	41	77	208	80	4
126 Mozambique	27	18	11	33	0
127 Namibia	28	65	280	40	6
128 Niger	20	13	60	28	1
129 Nigeria	35	35	320	51	6
130 Rwanda	6	9	50	50	1
131 São Tomé and Prín.	26	44	200	60	4
132 Senegal	38	22	253	38	5
133 Sierra Leone	32	38	114	21	2
134 Somalia	36	30	195	24	4
135 South Africa	50	86	1,157	80	23
136 Swaziland	28	34	426	71	9
137 Tanzania	22	19	21	55	0
138 Togo	26	30	226	43	4
139 Uganda	10	19	100	48	2

Regional group/ State	Urban Population %	Non Agricul. Population %	Students per 100,000	Adult literacy %	Students as % of 5,000 %
140 Zaire	29	34	176	72	4
141 Zambia	42	31	189	73	4
142 Zimbabwe	28	32	496	67	10
South Asia					
143 Bangladesh	16	31	382	35	8
144 Bhután	5	9	130	38	3
145 India	26	33	556	48	11
146 Maldives	30	75	0	92	0
147 Nepal	10	8	479	26	10
148 Pakistan	32	50	266	35	5
149 Sri Lanka	21	48	488	88	10
East Asia and Southeast Asia					
150 Brunei	58	95	259	86	5
151 Cambodia	12	30	81	35	2
152 China	28	33	186	73	4
153 Indonesia	31	51	838	82	17
154 Japan	77	94	2,184	99	44
155 Korea, North	60	66	635	95	13
156 Korea, South	72	75	3,899	96	78
157 Laos	19	28	116	54	2
158 Malaysia	43	68	679	78	14
159 Mongolia	52	70	1,416	93	28
160 Myanmar (Burma)	25	53	459	81	9
161 Philippines	43	53	2,738	90	55
162 Singapore	100	99	963	88	19
163 Taiwan (ROC)	51	87	2,675	89	53
164 Thailand	23	36	1,763	93	35
165 Vietnam	20	39	153	88	3
Oceania					
166 Australia	85	95	2,839	99	57
167 Fiji	37	61	487	87	10
168 New Zealand	84	91	3,287	99	66
169 Papua New Guinea	16	33	146	52	3
170 Solomon Islands	9	10	127	51	3
171 Vanuatu	27	32	293	65	6
172 Western Samoa	27	36	351	92	7

Data in parentheses are the writer's estimations.

URBAN POPULATION

Sources, if not otherwise noted, UNDP, *Human Development Report* 1992, Tables 21 and 42; 1993, Tables 22 and 44; 1994, Tables 22 and 44. Urban population as percentage of the total population in 1990. *Cf. World Development Report 1993.*

Latin America and the Caribbean

Bahamas: United Nations, Statistical Yearbook 1990/91, Table 12.
St Lucia: United Nations, Statistical Yearbook 1990/91, Table 12.

212   *Tatu Vanhanen*

East Asia and Southeast Asia

Taiwan (ROC): Der Fischer Weltalmanach 1989: 111–12.

NON AGRICULTURAL POPULATION

Sources, if not otherwise noted, FAO, *Production Yearbook* 1990, Table 3; 1992, Table 3. Non agricultural population as percentage of the total economically active population in 1990.

Europe and North America

Armenia: UNDP, Human Development Report 1993 (= HDR 1993): Table 38.
Belarus: The Europa World Yearbook 1993 (= Europa 1993).
Belgium: HDR 1993: Table 38.
Estonia: HDR 1993: Table 38.
Georgia: HDR 1993: Table 38.
Germany: HDR 1993: Table 38.
Latvia: HDR 1993: Table 38.
Lithuania: HDR 1993: Table 38.
Luxembourg: HDR 1993: Table 38.
Moldova: HDR 1993: Table 38.
Russia: HDR 1994: Table 38.
Slovenia: Europa 1993.
Ukraine: Schroeder 1990: 48.

Latin America and the Caribbean

Belize: Europa 1991.
St Lucia: Europa 1991.
St Vincent: Europa 1991.

North Africa, the Middle East and Central Asia

Azerbaijan: HDR 1993: Table 38.
Kazakhstan: HDR 1993: Table 38.
Kyrgyzstan: HDR 1993: Table 38.
Qatar: HDR 1993: Table 17.
Tajikistan: HDR 1993: Table 38.
Turkmenistan: Europa 1993.
Uzbekistan: HDR 1993: Table 38.

Sub-Saharan Africa

São Tomé and Príncipe: Europa 1991.

South Asia

Maldives: Europa 1991.

East Asia and Southeast Asia

Brunei: Europa 1991.
Taiwan (ROC): The Far East and Australasia Yearbook 1991.

Oceania

Solomon Islands: Europa 1991.
Vanuatu: HDR 1993: Table 17.
Western Samoa: Europa 1991.

STUDENTS

Sources, if not otherwise noted, Unesco, *Statistical Yearbooks* 1991, Table 3.10;
1993, Table 3.10; 1994, Table 3.11. Number of students per 100,000 inhabitants.

Europa and North America

Croatia: Europa 1993.
Luxembourg: Europa 1994. Students abroad included.
Macedonia: Europa 1994.
Slovenia: Europa 1993.

Latin America and the Caribbean

Belize: Europa 1991.
St Lucia: Europa 1994. Teacher-training and technical colleges.
St Vincent: Europa 1994. Teacher-training and technical colleges.

Sub-Saharan Africa

Cape Verde Islands: Kurian 1992. Students abroad.
Comoros: Kurian 1992. Students abroad.
Djibouti: Kurian 1992.
Equatorial Guinea: Kurian 1992.
Gambia: Kurian 1992. Including students abroad.
Guinea-Bissau: Europa 1991. Teacher training and technical education.
São Tomé and Príncipe: Kurian 1992.

South Asia

Maldives: Kurian 1992; Europa 1994.
Bhután: Kurian 1992. Including students abroad.

East Asia and Southeast Asia

Cambodia: See Europa 1991. Students abroad.
Korea, North: Europa 1991. University-level.
Taiwan (ROC): The Far East and Australasia Yearbook 1991.

Oceania

Solomon Islands: Europa 1994. Students at universities overseas.
Vanuatu: John Henderson's letter of 8 December 1994.
Western Samoa: Europa 1994. Including students abroad.

LITERATES

Sources, if not otherwise noted, UNDP, *Human Development Report* 1993, Table 1;
1994, Table 1. Adult literacy rate in 1990. Cf. *World Development Report 1991*,
Table 1; Unesco, *Statistical Yearbook 1991*, Table 1.3.

East Asia and Southeast Asia

Taiwan (ROC): Der Fischer Weltalmanach 1989: 111–12.

Oceania

Solomon Islands: John Henderson's letter of 8 December 1994. His source is Tupeni Baba, *South Pacific Education Profiles*, 1992. According to Human Development Report 1994, the percentage of literates is only 24.

Appendix 3

This appendix contains statistical data on the percentage of Family Farms (FF) of total holding area in 172 states in the period 1970–91 (if not otherwise noted). (The percentage of Family Farms is calculated, if not otherwise noted, from total holding area, and the upper hectare limit of Family Farms usually refers to total holding area. Data in brackets are estimations of the writer.)

Regional group/State	Year	Criterion of Family Farms	FF %
Europe and North America			
1 Albania	1990	Private farms	(30)
2 Armenia	1991	Private farms	(40)
3 Austria	1980	100 ha	62
4 Belarus	1991	Private farms	(1)
5 Belgium	1980	100 ha	95
6 Bulgaria	1991	Private farms	(20)
7 Canada	1980	647 ha	66
8 Croatia	1991	Private farms	(75)
9 Czechoslovakia	1991	Private farms	(10)
10 Denmark	1980	100 ha	85
11 Estonia	1991	Private farms	(20)
12 Finland	1980	100 ha	98
13 France	1980	100 ha	83
14 Georgia	1991	Private farms	(40)
15 Germany	1991	100 ha	(70)
16 Greece	1971	20 ha	91
17 Hungary	1991	Private farms	(20)
18 Iceland	1967	Owner-operated farms	74
19 Ireland	1970	50 ha	68
20 Italy	1980	50 ha	55
21 Latvia	1991	Private farms	(20)
22 Lithuania	1991	Private farms	(20)
23 Luxembourg	1980	100 ha	96
24 Macedonia	1991	Private farms	(75)
25 Malta	1980	5 ha	83
26 Moldova	1991	Private farms	(5)
27 Netherlands	1980	100 ha	94
28 Norway	1969	50 ha	98
29 Poland	1978	Private farms	76
30 Portugal	1980	50 ha	44
31 Romania	1991	Private farms	(30)
32 Russia	1991	Private farms	(5)
33 Slovenia	1991	Private farms	(75)
34 Spain	1980	100 ha	39
35 Sweden	1980	100 ha	86
36 Switzerland	1980	50 ha	94
37 Ukraine	1991	Private farms	(5)
38 United Kingdom	1980	200 ha	56
39 United States	1980	809 ha	54
40 Yugoslavia	1980	20 ha	75
Latin America and the Caribbean			
41 Argentina	1969	750 ha	22
42 Bahamas	1980	40 ha	24

Regional group/State	Year	Criterion of Family Farms	FF %
43 Barbados	1971	20 ha	15
44 Belize	1985	40 ha	25
45 Bolivia	1970	100 ha and Land Reform Beneficiaries	31
46 Brazil	1980	100 ha	20
47 Chile	1972	20 Basic Irrigated Hectares	23
48 Colombia	1970	100 ha	32
49 Costa Rica	1973	100 ha	33
50 Cuba	1977	Private farms	21
51 Dominican Republic	1971	20 ha	30
52 Ecuador	1974	50 ha	36
53 El Salvador	1971	20 ha	36
54 Guatemala	1980	23 ha	29
55 Guyana	1990	Family farms	(30)
56 Haiti	1971	5 ha	52
57 Honduras	1990	Family farms	13
58 Jamaica	1980	20 ha	39
59 Mexico	1970	100 ha and 50 per cent of the area of Ejidos and Communidades Agrarias	32
60 Nicaragua	1971	70 ha	25
61 Panama	1980	100 ha	18
62 Paraguay	1980	200 ha	15
63 Peru	1972	100 ha	24
64 St Lucia	1973	20 ha	42
65 St Vincent	1973	20 ha	44
66 Suriname	1969	50 ha	32
67 Trinidad and Tobago	1963	20 ha	46
68 Uruguay	1980	500 ha	27
69 Venezuela	1971	200 ha	15

North Africa, the Middle East and Central Asia

70 Afghanistan	1990	20 ha	65
71 Algeria	1973	Private sector	35
72 Azerbaijan	1991	Private farms	(5)
73 Bahrain	1980	10 ha	62
74 Cyprus	1980	20 ha	75
75 Egypt	1965	2.1 ha	57
76 Iran	1974	10 ha	44
77 Iraq	1971	50 ha	35
78 Israel	1980	50 ha	28
79 Jordan	1980	20 ha	52
80 Kazakhstan	1991	Private farms	(5)
81 Kuwait	1970	20 ha	45
82 Kyrgyzstan	1991	Private farms	(5)
83 Lebanon	1970	20 ha	48
84 Libya	1960	100 ha	53
85 Mauritania	1984	10 ha	54
86 Morocco	1969	20 ha	66
87 Oman	1980	Holders and members of their households of the total number of permanent workers	71
88 Qatar	1970	Family-owned farms	50
89 Saudi Arabia	1980	50 ha	42

Regional group/State	Year	Criterion of Family Farms	FF %
90 Sudan	1965	60 per cent of the land in holdings of less than 10 ha	45
91 Syria	1970	50 ha	68
92 Tajikistan	1991	Private farms	(5)
93 Tunisia	1962	50 ha	60
94 Turkey	1980	50 ha	92
95 Turkmenistan	1991	Private farms	(5)
96 United Arab Emirates	1970	Family-owned holdings	40
97 Uzbekistan	1991	Private farms	(5)
98 Yemen	1980	10 ha	66
Sub-Saharan Africa			
99 Angola	1980	60 per cent of the land under de facto indigenous tenure	42
100 Benin	1980	60 per cent of the land under de facto indigenous tenure	52
101 Botswana	1980	60 per cent of the land under de facto indigenous tenure	55
102 Burkina Faso	1980	60 per cent of the land under de facto indigenous tenure	60
103 Burundi	1980	60 per cent of the land under de facto indigenous tenure	60
104 Cameroon	1980	60 per cent of the land under de facto indigenous tenure	60
105 Cape Verde Islands	1981	Area owned or held in ownerlike possession	39
106 Central African Rep.	1980	60 per cent of the land under de facto indigenous tenure	50
107 Chad	1980	60 per cent of the land under de facto indigenous tenure	60
108 Comoros	1968	Villagers' reserves and Comorian-owned land	38
109 Congo	1980	60 per cent of the land under de facto indigenous tenure	60
110 Côte d'Ivoire	1980	60 per cent of de facto indigenous land and owner-operated cultivator enterprises	53
111 Djibouti	1976	60 per cent of owner-operated and of collective tribal lands	60
112 Equatorial Guinea	1976	50 per cent of collective tribal lands	30
113 Ethiopia	1980	60 per cent of the land under de facto indigenous tenure	60
114 Gabon	1980	60 per cent of de facto indigenous land and of owner-operated lands	60
115 Gambia	1980	60 per cent of the land under de facto indigenous tenure	60
116 Ghana	1970	10 ha	67
117 Guinea	1990	60 per cent of the land under traditional tenure systems	48
118 Guinea-Bissau	1980	60 per cent of the land under de facto indigenous tenure	60
119 Kenya	1980	Small holdings (below 8 ha)	46

Regional group/State	Year	Criterion of Family Farms	FF %
120 Lesotho	1980	60 per cent of the land under de facto indigenous tenure	60
121 Liberia	1971	60 per cent of the land in holdings of less than 10 ha	26
122 Madagascar	1985	60 per cent of the agricultural land in traditional sector	56
123 Malawi	1979	60 per cent of the land under customary tenures	51
124 Mali	1980	60 per cent of the land under de facto indigenous tenure	60
125 Mauritius	1965	Owner-cultivator operated enterprises	43
126 Mozambique	1970	60 per cent of the land in holdings of less than 10 ha	29
127 Namibia	1960	60 per cent of the area in traditional sector	22
128 Niger	1980	60 per cent of the area of holdings of less than 10 ha	53
129 Nigeria	1980	60 per cent of the land under de facto indigenous tenure	60
130 Rwanda	1980	60 per cent of the land under de facto indigenous tenure	60
131 São Tomé and Prín.	1990	Family farms	20
132 Senegal	1961	60 per cent of the land in holdings of less than 10 ha	44
133 Sierra Leone	1980	60 per cent of owner-operated and partially collective enterprises	56
134 Somalia	1980	60 per cent of the area of owner-cultivator operated enterprises	49
135 South Africa	1960	171 ha and 60 per cent of tribal lands	9
136 Swaziland	1980	60 per cent of Swazi Nation Land	36
137 Tanzania	1980	60 per cent of the land under customary tenure	48
138 Togo	1980	60 per cent of the land under de facto indigenous tenure	57
139 Uganda	1980	60 per cent of the land under de facto indigenous tenure	60
140 Zaire	1980	60 per cent of the land under de facto indigenous tenure	58
141 Zambia	1980	60 per cent of the land under de facto indigenous tenure	50
142 Zimbabwe	1969	60 per cent of African area	30
South Asia			
143 Bangladesh	1977	3 ha	68
144 Bhután	1990	Family farms	(40)
145 India	1980	10 ha	68
146 Maldives	1990	Family farms	(40)
147 Nepal	1980	5 ha	61
148 Pakistan	1980	20 ha	46
149 Sri Lanka	1980	8 ha	73
East Asia and Southeast Asia			
150 Brunei	1964	10 ha	(30)

Regional group/State	Year	Criterion of Family Farms	FF %
151 Cambodia	1990	Private peasants	10
152 China	1990	Family farms	30
153 Indonesia	1963	5 ha	60
154 Japan	1980	5 ha	79
155 Korea, North	1990	Private farms	0
156 Korea, South	1980	3 ha	93
157 Laos	1990	Private farms	(50)
158 Malaysia	1960	10 ha	42
159 Mongolia	1990	Family farms	(40)
160 Myanmar (Burma)	1990	Family farms	(60)
161 Philippines	1980	10 ha	47
162 Singapore	1973	3 ha	92
163 Taiwan (ROC)	1989	Fully owned farms	86
164 Thailand	1980	22 ha	84
165 Vietnam	1990	Private plots and farms	(30)
Oceania			
166 Australia	1980	Holders and members of their household of the total number of permanent farm workers	67
167 Fiji	1980	50 ha	58
168 New Zealand	1980	2,000 ha	51
169 Papua New Guinea	1990	60% of the area of indigenous land under traditional tenure systems	(58)
170 Solomon Islands	1990	60% of the area of indigenous land under traditional tenure systems	(57)
171 Vanuatu	1990	60% of the area of indigenous land under traditional tenure systems	(50)
172 Western Samoa	1990	60 per cent of the land under customary tenure	48

NOTES BY COUNTRIES

Europe and North America

Albania
The privatization of land was started in 1991. By September 1993, 92 per cent of collective farm land and 75 per cent of state farm land had been distributed to private farmers. See Eastern Europe and the Commonwealth of Independent States 1994 (= Eastern Europe 1994): 116.

Armenia
Private farms accounted for an estimated one-third of agricultural production in 1991. By September 1992 some 90 per cent of arable land had been privatized. See Eastern Europe 1994: 136. *Cf.* Economic Review Armenia, IMF 1992a: 7.

Austria
FAO, Report on the 1980 World Census of Agriculture, Census Bulletin No. 20, 1985. Holdings classified by productive area. The average area of holdings was 24.2 ha.

Belarus
In early 1992, private farms accounted only 0.17 per cent of all agricultural land in Belarus. See Eastern Europe 1994: 170.

Belgium
FAO, Report on the 1980 World Census of Agriculture, Census Bulletin No. 11, 1984. Classified by size of agricultural area of holding. The average size of holdings was 12.4 ha.

Bulgaria
In mid-1993, as a consequence of privatization, private farms accounted for 34 per cent of arable land. See Eastern Europe 1994: 206. According to Daily News (April 17, 1995), around 60 per cent of all agricultural land in Bulgaria had been restored to pre-communist owners or their heirs in the past three years.

Canada
FAO, Report on the 1980 World Census of Agriculture, Census Bulletin No. 18, 1985. The average size of holdings was 207 ha.

Croatia
See Yugoslavia. The percentage of Family Farms in undivided Yugoslavia in 1980. Czechoslovakia: Estimation. See Eastern Europe 1994: 267–8.

Denmark
FAO, Report on the 1980 World Census of Agriculture, Census Bulletin No. 11, 1984. Classified by size of agricultural area of holding. The average size of holdings was 26.4 ha.

Estonia
Eastern Europe 1994: 293. By late 1991, 6,000 private farms had already been established.

Finland
FAO, Report on the 1980 World Census of Agriculture, Census Bulletin No. 16, 1985. Classified by size of arable area of holding. The average total area of holdings was 57 ha.

France
FAO, Report on the 1980 World Census of Agriculture, Census Bulletin No. 7. Classified by size of agricultural area of holding. The average total area of holdings was 26.7 ha.

Georgia
Estimation. According to Europa 1994: 1234, some 55 per cent of cultivated land had been transferred to private ownership in 1992. See also Eastern Europe 1994: 313.

Germany
Estimation. The share of Family Farms (below 100 ha) was 94 per cent in West Germany in 1980. See FAO, Report on the 1980 World Census of Agriculture, Census Bulletin No. 22, 1986. West Germany. Holdings classified by size of agricultural area. The average size of holdings was 17 ha. The privatization of collective farms was started in East Germany after the unification of Germany in 1990.

Greece
FAO, 1970 World Census of Agriculture, 1981: 51–3. The average size of holdings was 3.4 ha. *Cf.* World Atlas of Agriculture, 1969 Vol. 1: 198.

Hungary
See Eastern Europe 1994: 332.

Iceland
Statistical Abstract of Iceland 1967: 90. Freeholders. *Cf.* World Atlas of Agriculture, 1969 vol. 1: 224–5.

Ireland
FAO, 1970 World Census of Agriculture, 1981: 51–3. The average size of holdings was 20 ha. *Cf.* World Atlas of Agriculture, 1969 vol. 1: 231–2.

Italy
FAO, Report on the 1980 World Census of Agriculture, Census Bulletin No. 23, 1986. The average size of holdings was 7.2 ha.

Latvia
Eastern Europe 1994: 401–2. The process of land privatization began in 1990. By the end of 1992 some 80 per cent of farmland was owned by approximately 700 joint stock and share companies. The number of private farms was 52,000.

Lithuania
Eastern Europe 1994: 420. In mid-1993, land had been returned to approximately 20 per cent of the 400,000 individuals who requested it.

Luxembourg
FAO, Report on the 1980 World Census of Agriculture, Census Bulletin No. 16, 1985. Holdings classified by size of agricultural area of holding. The average total area of holdings was 25 ha.

Macedonia
Estimation.

Malta
FAO, Report on the 1980 World Census of Agriculture, Census Bulletin No. 6, 1983. Holdings classified by size of agricultural area. The average area of holdings was 1.6 ha. See also World Atlas of Agriculture, 1969 Vol. 1: 271.

Moldova
Eastern Europe 1994: 454–5. The private ownership of land was legalized in 1991, but by mid-1993 only 9 per cent of Moldovan farmland had been privatized.

Netherlands
FAO, Report on the 1980 World Census of Agriculture, Census Bulletin No. 19, 1985. The average area of holdings was 15 ha.

Norway
FAO, Report on the 1970 World Census of Agriculture, Census Bulletin No. 5, 1974. Holdings classified by size of agricultural area. The average agricultural area of holdings was 7.6 ha.

Poland
CMEA Statistical Yearbook 1979: 42. Cf. World Atlas of Agriculture, 1969 Vol. 1: 314–17; FAO, Report on the 1970 World Census of Agriculture, Census Bulletin No. 24, 1986.

Portugal
FAO, Report on the 1980 World Census of Agriculture, Census Bulletin No. 18, 1985. Holdings classified by size of productive area. The average size of holdings was 6.6 ha.

Romania
Nearly half of the agricultural land was in private hands in 1991 (The World Factbook 1991–92: 261). According to Europa 1993, by October 1992, 70 per cent of agricultural land was in private hands, although only a fraction of the new owners had received the title to their property. See also Eastern Europe 1994: 517.

Russia
Eastern Europe 1994: 556. In early 1993 there were 184,000 peasant farms, occupying 3–4 per cent of Russian farmland. The share of old household plots in total agricultural output was about 33 per cent in 1992. According to Europa 1993, by January 1993 private farms covered 7.8 million hectares of land (about 4 per cent). *Cf.* Atta 1991; Blahó 1994.

Slovenia
Estimation.

Spain
FAO, Report on the 1980 World Census of Agriculture, Census Bulletin No. 21, 1986. The average size of holdings was 18.7 ha.

Sweden
FAO, Report on the 1980 World Census of Agriculture, Census Bulletin No. 21, 1986. Holdings classified by size of arable land. The average total area of holdings was 76 ha.

Switzerland
FAO, Report on the 1980 World Census of Agriculture, Census Bulletin No. 21, 1986. Holdings classified by size of cultivated land. The average agricultural area of holdings was 10.2 ha.

Ukraine
Cf. Corney 1993, who says that 'at this point only 1 per cent of agricultural land is being cultivated by private farmers'. According to Eastern Europe 1994: 683, private plots produced over 33 per cent of total output on less than 10 per cent of the land.

United Kingdom
FAO, Report on the 1980 World Census of Agriculture, Census Bulletin No. 17, 1985. Holdings classified by size of agricultural area of holding. The average total area of holdings was 65 ha.

United States
FAO, Report on the 1980 World Census of Agriculture, Census Bulletin No. 14, 1985. The average size of holdings was 168 ha.

Yugoslavia
FAO, Report on the 1980 World Census of Agriculture, Census Bulletin No. 24, 1986. The average size of holdings was 4.2 ha.

Latin America and the Caribbean

Argentina
Land Tenure Center, Land Concentration in the Third World 1979 (=LTC 1979): 124. The average size of holdings was 396 ha.

Bahamas
FAO, Report on the 1980 World Census of Agriculture, Census Bulletin No. 8, 1984. Percentage of arable land. Holdings classified by size of cultivated area of holding. The average total area of holdings was 8.5 ha.

Barbados
LTC 1979: 126.

Belize
LTC 1979: 127. Cf. FAO, Report on the 1980 World Census of Agriculture, Census Bulletin No. 28, 1989. The average size of holdings was 23 ha.

Bolivia
Eckstein *et al.* 1978: 21–3; LTC 1979: 128–9. The average size of holdings was 88 ha. The average size of Land Reform Beneficiaries was 33 ha.

Brazil
FAO, Report on the 1980 World Census of Agriculture, Census Bulletin No. 22, 1986. The average size of holdings was 70.7 ha.

Chile
LTC 1979: 135. The average size of holdings was 7.2 Basic Irrigated Hectares. *Cf.* Kurian 1992: 376–7; Eckstein *et al.* 1978: 29–34. William Thiesenhusen, Land Tenure Center, Madison, estimated (Feb. 14, 1986) that the share of family farms might be about 20 per cent.

Colombia
LTC 1979: 137; FAO, 1970 World Census of Agriculture, 1981: 53. The average size of holdings was 26 ha. See also Kurian 1992: 402–3.

Costa Rica
FAO, 1970 World Census of Agriculture, 1981: 52; LTC 1979: 139. The average size of holdings was 38 ha.

Cuba
Nohlen and Nuscheler 1982 Vol. 3: 366; Kurian 1992: 476. *Cf.* World Atlas of Agriculture, 1970 Vol. 3: 224–5.

Dominican Republic
FAO, 1970 World Census of Agriculture, 1981: 52, 100–101; LTC 1979: 143. The average size of holdings was 9 ha.

Ecuador
LTC 1993: 144; FAO, 1970 World Census of Agriculture, 1981: 51–3. The average size of holdings was 15 ha.

El Salvador
FAO, 1970 World Census of Agriculture, 1981: 53; LTC 1979: 147. The average size of holdings was 5.4 ha. Land reform programme started in 1980 shifted the ownership of over 25 per cent of El Salvador's agricultural land (Kurian 1992: 586).

Guatemala
FAO, Report on the 1980 World Census of Agriculture, Census Bulletin No. 17, 1985. The average size of holdings was 7.8 ha. See also Kurian 1992: 715.

Guyana
Estimation. See Kurian 1992.

Haiti
LTC 1979: 154; Kurian 1992: 780. Farms cultivated by owners and their families. The average size of holdings was 1.4 ha. *Cf.* Nohlen and Nuscheler 1982 Vol. 3: 334–6.

Honduras
See Kurian 1992: 797, according to which about 60 per cent of the arable land is in the hands of the government and two United States-owned firms, United Brands and Standard Fruit. Another 27 per cent of farmland is owned by 667 large landowners. *Cf.* LTC 1979: 155.

Jamaica
FAO, Report on the 1980 World Census of Agriculture, Census Bulletin No. 15, 1985. The average size of holdings was 2.9 ha.

Mexico
LTC 1979: 159–61. The average size of private property was 70 ha. *Cf.* FAO, 1970 World Census of Agriculture, 1981: 52, 100; Nohlen and Nuscheler 1982 Vol. 3: 126–30.

Nicaragua
LTC 1979: 168. The average size of holdings was 47 ha. *Cf.* Kurian 1992: 1408.

Panama
FAO, 1980 World Census of Agriculture, Census Bulletin No. 11, 1984. The average size of holdings was 14.8 ha. Area owned or held in ownerlike possession and area of holdings operated under more than one form of tenure. See also Kurian 1992: 1501.

Paraguay
FAO, 1980 World Census of Agriculture, Census Bulletin No. 24, 1986. The average size of holdings was 88 ha.

Peru
LTC 1979: 177. The average size of holdings was 17 ha. *Cf.* FAO, 1970 World Census of Agriculture, 1981: 100–102. See also Kurian 1992: 1560.

St Lucia
LTC 1979: 180; FAO, 1970 World Census of Agriculture, 1981: 52. The average size of holdings was 2.8 ha. See also Bruce 1983.

St Vincent
LTC 1979: 181.

Suriname
LTC 1979: 182; FAO, 1970 World Census of Agriculture, 1981: 53–5, 100–1. Area owned or in ownerlike possession (57 per cent of the total area of holdings). The average size of holdings was 5.8 ha. *Cf.* Kurian 1992: 1822, according to which only 20 per cent of the farms are owned by the farmers themselves. See also FAO, Report on the 1980 World Census of Agriculture, Census Bulletin No. 20, 1986.

Trinidad and Tobago
LTC 1979: 183. The average size of holdings was 6 ha in 1963. *Cf.* Kurian 1992: 1943; FAO, Report on the 1980 World Census of Agriculture, Census Bulletin No. 16, 1985. The average size of holdings was 4.3 ha in 1980, and 75 per cent of the area of holdings was owned or in ownerlike possession.

Uruguay
FAO, 1980 World Census of Agriculture, Census Bulletin No. 8, 1984. The average size of holdings was 234 ha. *Cf.* LTC 1979: 184; Kurian 1992: 2041.

Venezuela
FAO, 1970 World Census of Agriculture, 1981: 53, 56. The average size of holdings was 91 ha. See also LTC 1979: 185–6.

North Africa, the Middle East and Central Asia

Afghanistan
Kurian 1992: 9. Cultivated land. See also Lakanwal 1980: 76–77; World Atlas of Agriculture, 1973 vol. 2: 34–5.

Algeria
Private sector covers approximately 35 per cent of the area of holdings. See Internationales Handbuch 1987. *Cf.* LTC 1979: 1; FAO, 1970 World Census of Agriculture, 1981: 51–2.

Azerbaijan
Eastern Europe 1994: 153. By mid-1992, only some 40 of the 1,200 state and collective farms had been transferred to private control, but the private sector contributed 15–20 per cent of agricultural production.

Bahrain
FAO, 1980 World Census of Agriculture, Census Bulletin No. 9, 1984. The average size of holdings was 4.4 ha. *Cf.* Kurian 1992: 103, according to which 93.5 per cent of the arable land is leased by absentee landlords for periods ranging from three to twelve years.

Cyprus
FAO, Report on the 1980 World Census of Agriculture, Census Bulletin No. 12, 1984. The average size of holdings was 4.5 ha.

Egypt
LTC 1979: 7–8; Mitwally 1980: 204. The average size of holdings was 0.8 ha. *Cf.* Kurian 1992: 561–2. In the early 1980s sharecropping was the system in 62 per cent of the farms covering 57 per cent of the farmland.

Iran
Ajami 1978: 146. Owner-operated holdings of less than 10 ha. Cultivated land. *Cf.* LTC 1979: 190–1; Nohlen and Nuscheler 1983 vol. 6: 289–94.

Iraq
FAO, 1970 World Census of Agriculture, 1981: 53, 100–102. Area owned by the holder or in ownerlike possession. The average size of holdings was 10 ha. *Cf.* LTC 1979: 192.

Israel
FAO, Report on the 1980 World Census of Agriculture, Census Bulletin No. 24, 1986. The average size of holdings was 11.3 ha. *Cf.* LTC 1979: 193.

Jordan
FAO, Report on the 1980 World Census of Agriculture, Census Bulletin No. 26, 1989. The average size of holdings was 5.9 ha. *Cf.* LTC 1979: 196.

Kazakhstan
See Eastern Europe 1994: 369.

Kuwait
FAO, Report on the 1970 World Census of Agriculture, Census Bulletin No. 12, 1975; LTC 1979: 197. The average size of holdings was 6 ha.

Kyrgyzstan
See Eastern Europe 1994: 386–7.

Lebanon
FAO, 1970 World Census of Agriculture, 1981: 51–3. The average size of holdings was 4.3 ha. *Cf.* LTC 1979: 198; Kurian 1992: 1095.

Libya
FAO, Report on the 1960 World Census of Agriculture, 1969 vol. 1/a: 118–19. The average size of holdings was 27 ha. See also LTC 1979: 27.

Mauritania
FAO, Report on the 1980 World Census of Agriculture, Census Bulletin No. 26, 1989. Holdings owned or held in ownerlike possession. The average size of holdings was 2 ha. *Cf.* Park, Baro and Ngaido 1991; Kurian 1992: 1255.

Morocco
LTC 1979: 30. The average size of holdings was 5.9 ha. *Cf.* Kurian 1992: 1316. *Oman*
FAO, Report on the 1980 World Census of Agriculture, Census Bulletin No. 12, 1984. The average size of holdings was 1 ha.

Qatar
Estimation. See Nyrop *et al.* 1977: 244; Bowen-Jones 1980: 56–9. The average holdings was 3 ha (Kurian 1992: 1603).

Saudi Arabia
FAO, Report on the 1980 World Census of Agriculture, Census Bulletin No. 17, 1985. The average size of holdings was 10.1 ha.

Sudan
LTC 1979: 54. According to World Atlas of Agriculture, 15 per cent of the area of farm land belonged to owner-operated enterprises, 44 per cent to tenant-operated enterprises, and 41 per cent to partially collective enterprises in 1967.

Syria
FAO, 1970 World Census of Agriculture, 1981: 53; Kaimowitz 1980. The average size of holdings was 10.6 ha. See also Kurian 1992: 1852–3.

Tajikistan
See Eastern Europe 1994: 652–3.

Tunisia
FAO, Report on the 1960 World Census of Agriculture, 1970 vol. 1/c: 199. The average size of holdings was 15 ha. *Cf.* LTC 1979: 58; Kurian 1992: 1959.

Turkey
FAO, Report on the 1980 World Census of Agriculture, Census Bulletin No. 13, 1985. The average size of holdings was 6.2 ha.

Turkmenistan
See Eastern Europe 1994: 665.

United Arab Emirates
Estimation. See World Atlas of Agriculture, 1973 vol. 2: 143; Nyrop *et al.* 1977: 312; Bowen-Jones 1980: 59–62.

Uzbekistan
Estimation.

Yemen
FAO, 1980 World Census of Agriculture, Census Bulletin No. 10, 1984. Yemen Arab Republic. The average size of holdings was 2.5 ha.

Sub-Saharan Africa

(Sources, if not otherwise noted, World Atlas of Agriculture, 1976 vol. 4; Riddell and Dickerman 1986.)

Angola
Estimation. According to World Atlas of Agriculture, 61 per cent of crop land and 80 per cent of grazing area belonged to partially collective enterprises (traditional tenure) in 1965.

Benin
Estimation. See World Atlas of Agriculture, 1976 vol. 4: 148–9; Riddell and Dickerman 1986. According to World Atlas, 87 per cent of the area of holdings belonged to

owner-operated enterprises (customary tenure) in 1965. *Cf.* Nohlen and Nuscheler 1982 vol. 4: 136–7.

Botswana
Estimation. According to World Atlas, 91 per cent of the total area of tribal territory and freehold land belonged to tribal territory, and, according to Riddell and Dickerman, 92 per cent. *Cf.* FAO, Report on the 1970 World Census of Agriculture, Census Bulletin No. 1, 1973; Kurian 1992: 211.

Burkina Faso
Estimation. According to World Atlas, all land belonged to owner-cultivator operated enterprises (6 per cent) or partially collective enterprises.

Burundi
Estimation. Nearly all agricultural land seems to be under customary land tenure practices.

Cameroon
Estimation. According to World Atlas, all cultivated land belonged to owner-cultivator operated enterprises or partially collective enterprises. *Cf.* FAO, Report on the 1970 World Census of Agriculture, Census Bulletin No. 21, 1978, according to which 97 per cent of the land under traditional tenure belonged to holdings of less than 10 ha; Kurian 1992: 314–15.

Cape Verde Islands
FAO, Report on the 1980 World Census of Agriculture, Census Bulletin No. 23, 1986.

Central African Republic
Estimation. According to World Atlas, 84 per cent of agricultural land belonged to partially collective enterprises (traditional tenure). *Cf.* FAO, Report on the 1970 World Census of Agriculture, Census Bulletin 21, 1978, according to which 99 per cent of cultivated land belonged to holdings of less than 10 ha.

Chad
Estimation. All land seems to be under customary land tenure practices. *Cf.* FAO, Report on the 1970 World Census of Agriculture, Census Bulletin No. 21, 1978, according to which 96 per cent of cultivated land belonged to holdings of less than 10 ha.

Comoros
Cf. Nohlen and Nuscheler 1982 vol 5: 209–10; Kurian 1992: 422.

Congo
Estimation. All land seems to be under customary land tenure practices. *Cf.* Kurian 1992: 436; FAO, Report on the 1970 World Census of Agriculture, Census Bulletin No. 21, 1978, according to which all cultivated land belonged to holdings of less than 10 ha.

Côte d'Ivoire
Estimation. According to World Atlas, 23 per cent of total area belonged to owner-operated cultivator enterprises, 65 per cent to partially collective enterprises, and 12 per cent to owner-operated capitalist enterprises. *Cf.* FAO, Report on the 1970 World Census of Agriculture, Census Bulletin No. 24, 1978, according to which 66 per cent of the total area of holdings in traditional sector belonged to holdings of less than 10 ha.

Djibouti
Estimation.

Equatorial Guinea
Estimation.

Ethiopia
FAO, Report on the 1980 World Census of Agriculture, Census Bulletin No. 5, 1983. According to Riddell and Dickerman, all rural lands were nationalized in 1975. Land was distributed on a usufructuary basis, with a 10-hectare maximum for each individual. See also Cohen and Koehn 1978; Kurian 1992: 620–1.

Gabon
See also FAO, Report on the 1970 World Census of Agriculture, Census Bulletin No. 19, 1977; LTC 1979: 13.

Gambia
Estimation. All agricultural land seems to be under customary land tenure practices.

Ghana
FAO, Report on the 1970 World Census of Agriculture, Census Bulletin No. 8, 1975; FAO, 1970 World Census of Agriculture, 1981: 52. The average size of holdings (land under crops) was 3.2 ha.

Guinea
Estimation. Kurian 1992: 736.

Guinea-Bissau
Estimation. All agricultural land seems to belong to partially collective enterprises (traditional tenure). See also LTC 1979: 15; Kurian 1992: 750.

Kenya
FAO, Report on the 1980 World Census of Agriculture, Census Bulletin No. 25, 1986. *Cf.* LTC 1979: 17–21; FAO, 1970 World Census of Agriculture, 1981: 52.

Lesotho
Estimation. All land seems to be under the customary system of tenure. *Cf.* FAO, Report on the 1970 World Census of Agriculture, Census Bulletin No. 9, 1975.

Liberia
FAO, Report on the 1970 World Census of Agriculture, Census Bulletin No. 29, 1980; LTC 1979: 24. The average size of holdings was 3 ha.

Madagascar
FAO, Report on the 1980 World Census of Agriculture, Census Bulletin No. 25, 1986. 94 per cent of agricultural land belonged to traditional sector.

Malawi
Customary land tenure system comprises 85 per cent of the land (Kurian 1992: 2187. *Cf.* Dickerman and Bloch 1991; FAO, Report on the 1980 World Census of Agriculture, Census Bulletin No. 25, 1986.

Mali
Estimation. Nearly all land seems to be under customary land tenure practices. *Cf.* LTC 1979: 29, according to which 67 per cent of the total area of holdings belonged to holdings of less than 10 ha.

Mauritius
Cf. Kurian 1992: 1270–1.

Mozambique
LTC 1979: 32–5. The average size of holdings was 1.5 ha in traditional sector. See also Kurian 1992: 1336.

Namibia
LTC 1979: 36. Bantu holdings (partially collective enterprises) covered 36 per cent of the total area of holdings and non Bantu holdings 64 per cent. Holdings of more than 1,000 ha comprised 99.9 per cent of the total area of non Bantu holdings. *Cf.* Third World Guide 93/94; Kurian 1992: 1370, according to which 'some 5,000 white ranchers covered about 80 per cent of cultivable land at independence'.

Niger
FAO, Report on the 1980 World Census of Agriculture, Census Bulletin No. 16, 1985. The average size of holdings was 4.9 ha, and 88 per cent of cultivated area of holdings belonged to holdings of less than 10 ha.

Nigeria
Estimation. According to World Atlas, 64 per cent of agricultural land belonged to owner-operated enterprises and 35 per cent to partially collective enterprises.

Rwanda
Nearly all land is under the customary system of land tenure. *Cf.* FAO, Report on the 1980 World Census of Agriculture, Census Bulletin No. 26, 1986; Kurian 1992: 1617. The average size of holdings is only 1 ha.

São Tomé and Príncipe
Estimation. Foreign companies owned 90 per cent of the land before independence. Following independence, most of these plantations were nationalized and were run as co-operatives. See Kurian 1992: 1656; Third World Guide 93/94: 513–14.

Senegal
Estimation. LTC 1979: 47. According to World Atlas, 52 per cent of agricultural area belonged to owner-operated enterprises and 48 per cent to partially collective enterprises in 1961. See also Kurian 1992: 1690–1.

Sierra Leone
Estimation. According to World Atlas, 4 per cent of the area of holdings belonged to owner-operated enterprises, 90 per cent to partially collective enterprises, and 6 per cent to tenant-operated enterprises. See also Kurian 1992: 1721.

Somalia
Estimation. According to World Atlas, 82 per cent of the area of holdings belonged to owner-cultivator operated enterprises (small cultivator farmers).

South Africa
FAO, Report on the 1960 World Census of Agriculture, 1967 vol. 1/b: 232–3. The average size of holdings was 963 ha.

Swaziland
Estimation. According to Riddell and Dickerman, over 60 per cent of the country is now Swazi Nation Land, while under 40 per cent is individual tenure (plantations). According to Kurian 1992: 1835, about 44 per cent of the land is held on freehold terms by Whites. *Cf.* LTC 1979: 55.

Tanzania
Estimation. See Kurian 1992: 1873. Approximately 80 per cent of the land is held by individuals or groups under customary rules of tenure.

Togo
Estimation. According to World Atlas, 55 per cent of the total area belonged to owner-cultivator enterprises and 49 per cent to partially collective enterprises, whereas Riddell and Dickerman estimate that 'over ninety per cent of the farms

are held according to traditional land tenure practices'. *Cf.* FAO, Report on the 1980 World Census of Agriculture, Census Bulletin No. 15, 1985.

Uganda
Estimation. Nearly all agricultural land seems to be under customary tenure systems.

Zaire
Estimation. According to Riddell and Dickerman, '97 per cent of Zairian land continues in practice to be administered under customary tenure by chiefs of land'. *Cf.* LTC 1979: 62–3.

Zambia
Estimation. According to World Atlas, 37 per cent of the total area of holdings belonged to owner-operated enterprises, 28 per cent to tenant-operated enterprises, and 35 per cent to partially collective enterprises, whereas Riddell and Dickerman estimate that in over 80 per cent of Zambia's land area, the Trust and Reserve Land, traditional tenure systems continue to operate and evolve. *Cf.* FAO, Report on the 1970 World Census of Agriculture, Census Bulletin No. 11, 1975.

Zimbabwe
Estimation. According to World Atlas, 37 per cent of the land of Rhodesia belonged to European area, 42 per cent to Tribal Trust land, and 4 per cent to African Purchase area in 1965. According to Riddell and Dickerman, European area covered 50 per cent of the land and African area also 50 per cent in 1969. *Cf.* LTC 1979: 43–6.

South Asia

Bangladesh
FAO, Report on the 1980 World Census of Agriculture, Census Bulletin No. 5, 1983. The average size of holdings was 1.3 ha. *Cf.* LTC 1979: 67–8; Nohlen and Nuscheler 1983 vol. 7: 85–6; Kurian 1992: 122.

Bhután
Estimation. See Kurian 1987 and 1992; Shah 1984: 50; Haaland 1986.

India
FAO, Report on the 1980 World Census of Agriculture, Census Bulletin No. 22, 1986. Area owned or held in ownerlike possession. The average size of holdings was 2 ha.

Maldives
Estimation.

Nepal
FAO, Report on the 1980 World Census of Agriculture, Census Bulletin No. 20, 1985. Area owned or held in ownerlike possession. The average size of holdings was 1.1 ha. See also Kurian 1992: 1390.

Pakistan
FAO, Report on the 1980 World Census of Agriculture, Census Bulletin No. 9, 1984. Area owned or held in ownerlike possession. The average size of holdings was 4.7 ha. *Cf.* Kurian 1992: 1479.

Sri Lanka
FAO, 1980 World Census of Agriculture, Census Bulletin No. 14, 1985. The average size of holdings was 1.1 ha.

East Asia and Southeast Asia

Brunei
Estimation. See Kurian 1992: 252–3.

Cambodia
Estimation. See Kurian 1992: 298; Nohlen and Nuscheler 1983 vol. 7: 349–58. In 1975 the Khmer Rouge government abolished private ownership of land, and all landholdings were transferred to the state. Heng Samrin officials claimed that 90 per cent of Khmer peasants were organized into 'solidarity production' teams.

China
Estimation. See China, a country study 1988: 125–8; Bruce and Harrell 1989; The Far East and Australasia 1991: 306–7, 310; Womack 1992.

Indonesia
FAO, Report on the 1960 World Census of Agriculture, 1970 vol. 1/c: 72–3; LTC 1979: 95. Area owned or in ownerlike possession. The average size of holdings was 1.1 ha.

Japan
FAO, Report on the 1980 World Census of Agriculture, Census Bulletin No. 12, 1984. The average size of holdings was 1 ha.

Korea, North
Kurian 1992: 1075. All private ownership of land was abolished in 1959.

Korea, South
FAO, Report on the 1980 World Census of Agriculture, Census Bulletin No. 15, 1985. Agricultural area. The average size of holdings was 0.9 ha.

Laos
Estimation. See Kurian 1992: 1075. More than 80 per cent of rural families own their own rice-fields. The average farm size was 2 ha.

Malaysia
FAO, Report on the 1960 World Census of Agriculture, 1967 vol. 1/b. The average size of farm households was 2 ha. Large estates comprised 53 per cent of the total area of holdings.

Mongolia
Estimation.

Myanmar (Burma)
Estimation. See Report to the Pyithu Hluttaw on The Financial, Economic and Social Conditions of The Socialist Republic of the Union of Burma for 1978–79: 40; Kurian 1992: 1354. The government holds formal title to all land. The average holding is about 2 ha.

Philippines
FAO, Report on the 1980 World Census of Agriculture, Census Bulletin No. 23, 1986. Area owned or held in ownerlike possession. The average size of holdings was 2.8 ha.

Singapore
FAO, Report on the 1970 World Census of Agriculture, Census Bulletin No. 29, 1980; LTC 1979: 117. The average size of holdings was 0.7 ha.

Taiwan (ROC)
Nohlen and Nuscheler 1983 vol. 8: 159–60; Republic of China Yearbook 1991–92: 203–4. The average size of holdings was 1.1 ha.

Thailand
FAO, 1980 World Census of Agriculture, Census Bulletin No. 10, 1984. Area owned
or held in ownerlike possession. The average size of holdings was 3.7 ha.

Vietnam
Estimation. Kurian 1992: 2091, 2093. In the North the socialist sector covers 95 per
cent of the farmlands, whereas in the South individual ownership is still widespread,
and production collectives are limited to 21 per cent of the farm households and 15
per cent of the arable land area.

Oceania

Australia
FAO, Report on the 1980 World Census of Agriculture, Census Bulletin No. 27,
1989. The average size of holdings was 2,820 ha.

Fiji
FAO, Report on the 1980 World Census of Agriculture, Census Bulletin No. 11,
1984. The average size of holdings was 4.2 ha.

New Zealand
FAO, Report on the 1980 World Census of Agriculture, Census Bulletin No. 27,
1989. The average size of holdings was 297 ha.

Papua New Guinea
Estimation. Kurian 1992: 1519. Most indigenous land is communally held. See
World Atlas of Agriculture, 1973 vol. 2: 657–8.

Solomon Islands
Estimation. See World Atlas of Agriculture, 1973 vol. 2: 664. Native land comprised
94 per cent of the total land area. See also Kurian 1992: 1753.

Vanuatu
Estimation. See Kurian 1992: 2055.

Western Samoa
Estimation. See Kurian 1992: 2107. About 80 per cent of the total arable land is held
in customary tenure.

Appendix 4

This appendix contains statistical data on the estimated degree of concentration (DC) and decentralization (DD) of non agricultural economic resources in 172 states in or around 1990.

VARIABLES

CPE = centrally planned economy (command economy) with a high degree of public ownership

PSD = public sector dominated economy with a significant private sector and/or with significant foreign ownership

CPS = market oriented economy with a concentrated private sector and/or with a large public sector and/or with significant foreign ownership

MOE = market oriented economy with diversified ownership

DC = degree of concentration of non agricultural economic resources

DD = degree of decentralization of non agricultural economic resources (100 – DC)

Regional group/State	Degree of concentration of non agricultural economic resources (DC)				DD
	CPE %	PSD %	CPS %	MOE %	
Europe and North America					
1 Albania	90	—	—	—	10
2 Armenia	90	—	—	—	10
3 Austria	—	—	—	30	70
4 Belarus	95	—	—	—	5
5 Belgium	—	—	—	30	70
6 Bulgaria	90	—	—	—	10
7 Canada	—	—	40	—	60
8 Croatia	—	80	—	—	20
9 Czechoslovakia	—	80	—	—	20
10 Denmark	—	—	—	30	70
11 Estonia	—	80	—	—	20
12 Finland	—	—	—	30	70
13 France	—	—	—	30	70
14 Georgia	90	—	—	—	10
15 Germany	—	—	40	—	60
16 Greece	—	—	—	30	70
17 Hungary	—	70	—	—	30
18 Iceland	—	—	—	20	80
19 Ireland	—	—	—	30	70
20 Italy	—	—	—	30	70
21 Latvia	—	80	—	—	20
22 Lithuania	—	80	—	—	20
23 Luxembourg	—	—	—	30	70
24 Macedonia	—	80	—	—	20
25 Malta	—	—	—	30	70
26 Moldova	90	—	—	—	10
27 Netherlands	—	—	—	30	70
28 Norway	—	—	—	30	70
29 Poland	—	70	—	—	30

Regional group/State	Degree of concentration of non agricultural economic resources (DC)				DD
	CPE %	PSD %	CPS %	MOE %	
30 Portugal	—	—	40	—	60
31 Romania	—	80	—	—	20
32 Russia	90	—	—	—	10
33 Slovenia	—	70	—	—	30
34 Spain	—	—	—	30	70
35 Sweden	—	—	—	30	70
36 Switzerland	—	—	—	30	70
37 Ukraine	90	—	—	—	10
38 United Kingdom	—	—	—	30	70
39 United States	—	—	40	—	60
40 Yugoslavia	—	70	—	—	30
Latin America and the Caribbean					
41 Argentina	—	—	50	—	50
42 Bahamas	—	—	50	—	50
43 Barbados	—	—	50	—	50
44 Belize	—	—	50	—	50
45 Bolivia	—	—	70	—	30
46 Brazil	—	—	60	—	40
47 Chile	—	—	50	—	50
48 Colombia	—	—	60	—	40
49 Costa Rica	—	—	50	—	50
50 Cuba	95	—	—	—	5
51 Dominican Republic	—	—	60	—	40
52 Ecuador	—	—	60	—	40
53 El Salvador	—	—	60	—	40
54 Guatemala	—	—	80	—	20
55 Guyana	—	80	—	—	20
56 Haiti	—	—	60	—	40
57 Honduras	—	—	60	—	40
58 Jamaica	—	—	60	—	40
59 Mexico	—	—	60	—	40
60 Nicaragua	—	60	—	—	40
61 Panama	—	—	70	—	30
62 Paraguay	—	—	80	—	20
63 Peru	—	—	60	—	40
64 St Lucia	—	—	60	—	40
65 St Vincent	—	—	60	—	40
66 Suriname	—	—	70	—	30
67 Trinidad and Tobago	—	—	50	—	50
68 Uruguay	—	—	50	—	50
69 Venezuela	—	—	60	—	40
North Africa, the Middle East and Central Asia					
70 Afghanistan	—	70	—	—	30
71 Algeria	—	70	—	—	30
72 Azerbaijan	95	—	—	—	5
73 Bahrain	—	—	75	—	25
74 Cyprus	—	—	—	30	70

Regional group/State	Degree of concentration of non agricultural economic resources (DC)				DD
	CPE %	PSD %	CPS %	MOE %	
75 Egypt	—	70	—	—	30
76 Iran	—	—	70	—	30
77 Iraq	—	75	—	—	25
78 Israel	—	—	—	40	60
79 Jordan	—	—	70	—	30
80 Kazakhstan	95	—	—	—	5
81 Kuwait	—	—	80	—	20
82 Kyrgyzstan	95	—	—	—	5
83 Lebanon	—	—	—	40	60
84 Libya	—	80	—	—	20
85 Mauritania	—	—	85	—	15
86 Morocco	—	—	60	—	40
87 Oman	—	—	80	—	20
88 Qatar	—	—	80	—	20
89 Saudi Arabia	—	—	80	—	20
90 Sudan	—	80	—	—	20
91 Syria	—	75	—	—	25
92 Tajikistan	95	—	—	—	5
93 Tunisia	—	—	60	—	40
94 Turkey	—	—	50	—	50
95 Turkmenistan	99	—	—	—	1
96 United Arab Emirates	—	—	80	—	20
97 Uzbekistan	95	—	—	—	5
98 Yemen	—	—	70	—	30
Sub-Saharan Africa					
99 Angola	—	80	—	—	20
100 Benin	—	80	—	—	20
101 Botswana	—	—	70	—	30
102 Burkina Faso	—	80	—	—	20
103 Burundi	—	—	85	—	15
104 Cameroon	—	—	80	—	20
105 Cape Verde	—	—	70	—	30
106 Central African Rep.	—	—	80	—	20
107 Chad	—	—	80	—	20
108 Comoros	—	—	70	—	30
109 Congo	—	80	—	—	20
110 Côte d'Ivoire	—	—	80	—	20
111 Djibouti	—	—	80	—	20
112 Equatorial Guinea	—	—	70	—	30
113 Ethiopia	—	90	—	—	10
114 Gabon	—	—	80	—	20
115 Gambia	—	—	70	—	30
116 Ghana	—	—	60	—	40
117 Guinea	—	85	—	—	15
118 Guinea-Bissau	—	80	—	—	20
119 Kenya	—	—	60	—	40
120 Lesotho	—	—	80	—	20

Regional group/State	Degree of concentration of non agricultural economic resources (DC)				DD
	CPE %	PSD %	CPS %	MOE %	
121 Liberia	—	—	85	—	15
122 Madagascar	—	80	—	—	20
123 Malawi	—	—	90	—	10
124 Mali	—	85	—	—	15
125 Mauritius	—	—	50	—	50
126 Mozambique	—	85	—	—	15
127 Namibia	—	—	80	—	20
128 Niger	—	—	80	—	20
129 Nigeria	—	—	70	—	30
130 Rwanda	—	—	80	—	20
131 São Tomé and Príncipe	—	—	80	—	20
132 Senegal	—	—	70	—	30
133 Sierra Leone	—	—	70	—	30
134 Somalia	—	80	—	—	20
135 South Africa	—	—	70	—	30
136 Swaziland	—	—	80	—	20
137 Tanzania	—	80	—	—	20
138 Togo	—	—	80	—	20
139 Uganda	—	—	80	—	20
140 Zaire	—	—	80	—	20
141 Zambia	—	80	—	—	20
142 Zimbabwe	—	—	70	—	30
South Asia					
143 Bangladesh	—	75	—	—	25
144 Bhután	—	—	50	—	40
145 India	—	—	50	—	50
146 Maldives	—	—	50	—	40
147 Nepal	—	—	70	—	30
148 Pakistan	—	—	60	—	40
149 Sri Lanka	—	—	50	—	50
East Asia and Southeast Asia					
150 Brunei	—	90	—	—	10
151 Cambodia	90	—	—	—	10
152 China	—	70	—	—	30
153 Indonesia	—	—	60	—	40
154 Japan	—	—	—	40	60
155 Korea, North	95	—	—	—	5
156 Korea, South	—	—	50	—	50
157 Laos	85	—	—	—	15
158 Malaysia	—	—	60	—	40
159 Mongolia	90	—	—	—	10
160 Myanmar (Burma)	—	70	—	—	30
161 Philippines	—	—	60	—	40
162 Singapore	—	—	60	—	40
163 Taiwan (ROC)	—	—	—	40	60
164 Thailand	—	—	60	—	40
165 Vietnam	85	—	—	—	5

Regional group/State	Degree of concentration of non agricultural economic resources (DC)				DD
	CPE %	PSD %	CPS %	MOE %	
Oceania					
166 Australia	—	—	—	30	70
167 Fiji	—	—	50	—	50
168 New Zealand	—	—	—	30	70
169 Papua New Guinea	—	—	70	—	30
170 Solomon Islands	—	—	—	50	50
171 Vanuatu	—	—	—	40	60
172 Western Samoa	—	—	50	—	50

NOTES BY COUNTRIES:

Estimates on the nature of economic systems and on the degree of concentration of non agricultural economic resources (DC), if not otherwise indicated, are based on Nohlen and Nuscheler 1982; Kurian 1987 and 1992; Vanhanen 1990a: Appendix 4; Lane and Ersson 1990: 229–53; *The Europa World Year Book* (1991–4). All data on DC given in this Appendix are estimations made by the writer.

Europe and North America

Albania
All the major means of production were owned by the state in 1990, but in 1991 measures of privatization were initiated. See also Eastern Europe and the Commonwealth of Independent States 1992 (= Eastern Europe 1992); Freedom in the World 1991–92.

Armenia
A law on privatization was adopted in mid-1992. See also International Monetary Fund (IMF) 1992a; 1992b: 46, according to which 2.3 per cent of employment was provided by leased enterprises, joint stock companies, and economic associations (= private sector enterprises) in 1990–1.

Belarus
Nearly all the means of production were still owned by the state in 1991, although some steps toward privatization had been taken. See IMF 1992b: 46, according to which 8.8 per cent of employment was provided by private sector enterprises in 1990–1. According to Eastern Europe 1994: 171, only 1.8 per cent of the labour force was employed by the private sector.

Bulgaria
Eastern Europe 1994: 209–10. In 1991 the state still owned some 93 per cent of the country's capital stock, but privatization had been started, and Bulgaria was gradually replacing a centrally planned economy by a market oriented economy. See Bulgarian Economic Review, April 8–21, 1992.

Canada
Time (6 October 1986) refers to Diane Francis' book *Controlling Interest: Who Owns Canada?*, according to which thirty-two families and five conglomerates control a third of Canadian non financial assets.

Croatia
All the major means of production were still state-owned in 1991, but the transfer of state-owned enterprises to private ownership was taking place. See Eastern Europe 1992.

Czechoslovakia
Eastern Europe 1994: 267–8. In 1993, 85 per cent of industrial production was still in the hands of state-owned firms, whereas the private sector accounted for 58 per cent of construction and 72 per cent of retailing.

Estonia
Eastern Europe 1994: 294. Privatization was launched in 1990. In 1991 Estonia was transforming its centrally planned economy toward a market oriented economic system. In 1993 some 80 per cent of small state enterprises and thirty major concerns had been privatized.

Finland
According to Koste (1969: 64–83), large enterprises controlled by the so-called ten families produced 25 per cent of the total industrial production and paid 28 per cent of the wages. It seems reasonable to assume that the degree of concentration has not increased since the 1960s.

France
For its economic system, see Gardner 1988: 165–85.

Georgia
All the major means of production were still state-owned in 1991. The privatization of industry had not made much progress by the end of 1993. See Eastern Europe 1994: 314.

Germany
The transfer of state-owned enterprises to private ownership was started in former East Germany in 1990. For West Germany's economic system, see Gardner 1988: 127–47.

Hungary
The transition to a market oriented economy was launched in 1988, but in 1989 state-related businesses still accounted for about 90 per cent of economic output. A comprehensive privatization programme was initiated in 1990. The government intended to reduce the proportion of state-controlled companies from 90 per cent to 40 per cent within five years. See Eastern Europe 1994: 333–4.

Latvia
See Eastern Europe 1994. The transition to a market economy was launched in 1991.

Lithuania
The transition to a market economy was started in 1990. According to Europa 1992: 1806, 24 per cent of state capital had been privatized by late 1992.

Macedonia
Transition to a market economy was started in 1991, although nearly all the means of production were still state-owned. See Eastern Europe 1992.

Malta
Most industrial enterprises are small or medium-size, and public enterprises accounted for only 6 per cent of gross fixed capital formation in 1978–80. See Commonwealth Fact Sheet: Malta, 1976; Short 1984.

Moldova
8.9 per cent of employment was provided by private sector enterprises in 1990–1 (IMF 1992b: 46). See also Eastern Europe 1994: 455.

Poland
See Human Development Report (= HDR) 1993: 62. According to Europa 1993: 2320, 'by late 1992 the private sector accounted for about 50 per cent of total economic activity' (*cf.* Blanchard 1994). Kenneth Ka-lok Chan (1994) estimates that Poland's private sector now accounts for one-third of the country's gross domestic product (GDP) and that its 1.5 million firms employ about 60 per cent of the work force. The privatization of state-owned enterprises was started in 1990.

Portugal
In 1974-5 many sectors of non agricultural economy were nationalized completely or partly, but the privatization of state-owned companies has been taking place since the 1980s.

Romania
Nearly all means of production were under public sector control in 1990, but the government started to privatize state-owned industries in 1991. In 1992 the private sector contributed in excess of 25 per cent of GDP (Europa 1993: 2379). See also The World Factbook 1991-2: 261; Eastern Europe 1994: 517.

Russia
See HDR 1993: 63. The transition from a centrally planned economy to a market economy was started in 1991, but 90 per cent of Russia's production, distribution and retail outlets were still in the hands of the state in 1992 (Greenwald 1992). Private sector enterprises provided 9.7 per cent of employment in 1990-1 (IMF 1992b: 46) and about 33 per cent by the end of 1993 (Roland 1994). See also Blahó 1994.

Slovenia
Eastern Europe 1994: 633. The privatization of state-owned and co-operative enterprises was launched in 1990.

Sweden
According to a Swedish study, seventeen large industrial groups generated 36 per cent of the value of industrial production in the 1960s (Bruun 1969: 15-20). See also Gardner 1988: 149-63.

Ukraine
All the major means of production were still state-owned in 1991, but the aim was to establish a market economy. Private sector enterprises provided 8.1 per cent of employment in 1990-1 (IMF 1992b: 46). See also Eastern Europe 1994: 685.

United Kingdom
For its economic system, see Gardner 1988: 101-25.

United States
According to Hurst (1979: 24-9), the top 10 per cent US adults held 50 per cent of the personal wealth and the top 1 per cent about 21 per cent in 1962. The largest 100 corporations controlled 48 per cent of the corporate assets in 1972 (*cf.* Gardner 1988: 79-83).

Yugoslavia
See Eastern Europe 1994: 730, according to which the informal sector accounted for 23.7 per cent of real GNP in Yugoslavia in 1991. Most of the major means of production were state-owned, but decision-making power was decentralized to some extent by its unique workers' self-management system. See Dahl 1985: 144-7; Gardner 1988: 320-33, 466.

Latin America and the Caribbean

Argentina
Foreign sector provided about 40 per cent of the production of manufacturing enterprises in 1980 (Länder der Erde 1981: 45). Privatization programme was taking place in the beginning of the 1990s (HDR 1993: 54).

Bahamas
Tourism is the major industry, and many hotels are owned by foreign companies. See Graham and Edwards 1984: 25–6; Third World Guide 93/94: 153–4.

Belize
A mixed economy in which the government co-operates with the private sector. Foreign sector is large.

Bolivia
Since the 1952 popular revolution, the state has played a significant role in directing the economy, particularly in mining, which contributes 75–90 per cent of the country's export earnings. The central government controls the seven largest public enterprises in the country, whose combined output represents 30 per cent of the GDP (Kurian 1992: 193).

Brazil
Earlier the public sector played a dominant role in the economy, but since the 1980s state-owned companies have been transferred to the private sector. See also HDR 1993: 55; Kurian 1992: 233.

Chile
See also Kurian 1992: 377–8.

Colombia
A market economy in which the dominant sector is private. Ten monopolies controlled 67 per cent of the production capital in the 1970s (Länder der Erde 1981: 346). *Cf.* Kurian 1992: 403–4, according to which the bulk of the industrial establishments are small-scale family-owned enterprises.

Cuba
The share of the socialist sector of gross industrial production was 100 per cent in 1978 (CMEA 1979: 41. See also Gardner 1988: 466). Cuba's economic system in 1990 was approximately the same as in 1978. See also The World Factbook 1991–92: 76; Kurian 1992: 477.

Ecuador
The petroleum sector is completely owned and controlled by the state and foreign companies. The manufacturing industries are dominated by private domestic and foreign enterprises. See Latin America and Caribbean Review 1986: 69–73.

Guatemala
Most of the large enterprises are owned and run by the richest 2 per cent of Guatemalans and foreigners who dominate not only agriculture but also commerce and finance.

Guyana
Economy has been dominated by the public sector, which, as a consequence of a nationalization programme carried out in the mid-1970s, controlled about 80 per cent of the total productive capacity at the beginning of the 1980s. See Länder der Erde 1981: 238–9; Third World Guide 93/94: 314–15.

Haiti
Most of the largest industrial enterprises are wholly or partly foreign-owned. See also Kurian 1992: 780–1.

Honduras
A significant part of industry is owned by foreign companies. See also Kurian 1992: 403–4.

Jamaica
See Kurian 1992.

Mexico
According to *Time* (25 August 1986), the Institutional Revolutionary Party (PRI) employs 3 million bureaucrats and controls about half of the economy.

Nicaragua
The dominant sector was public in the 1980s, but the Chamorro government has pledged to reduce it. However, over 50 per cent of the agricultural and industrial firms are still state-owned (The World Factbook 1991–92: 227).

Paraguay
Foreign capital has controlled about 80 per cent of the industrial production in Paraguay (Länder der Erde 1981: 478). *Cf.* Kurian 1992: 1539.

Peru
Mining is dominated by large establishments owned by the state and foreign companies. See also Kurian 1992: 1561–2.

St Lucia
See Third World Guide 93/94: 509.

St Vincent
See Third World Guide 93/94: 510.

Suriname
The bauxite industry is the dominant sector of non agricultural economy. It is controlled by foreign-owned companies. It accounts for about 70 per cent of export earnings and 40 per cent of tax revenues (The World Factbook 1991–92: 295).

Venezuela
Petroleum production is the most important industry in Venezuela. It is dominated by a state-owned company, but small and medium-size enterprises (less than 100 workers) employed 43 per cent of the workers and produced 25 per cent of the value of production in 1976 (Annuario Estadistico 1977: 329).

North Africa, the Middle East and Central Asia

Afghanistan
Since the 1978 revolution, the government has controlled most sectors of non agricultural economy.

Algeria
The government controls all the key sectors of non agricultural economy, particularly petroleum and natural gas industries. State industries dominate the economy and employ over 66 per cent of the labour force (Kurian 1992: 28).

Azerbaijan
As in the other regions of the former Soviet Union, privatization programmes have been started in Azerbaijan, too. In 1990–1, private sector enterprises provided 3 per cent of employment (IMF 1992b: 46).

Bahrain
The petroleum sector, which is the dominant sector of the economy, is completely owned and controlled by the government and foreign companies.

Cyprus
At the beginning of independence, the manufacturing sector consisted almost entirely of small, family-owned enterprises having fewer than five workers. According to a census, conducted in 1972, over four-fifths of the 7,612 plants in manufacturing still had from one to four employees; only thirty establishments had more than 100. See Cyprus: A Country Study 1980: 126–30.

Egypt
The public sector has dominated Egypt's economy since the 1960s. It accounted for 70 per cent of the industrial sector in the beginning of the 1990s (HDR 1993: 57). See also Short 1984; The World Factbook 1991–92: 90.

Iran
After the 1979 revolution, a significant number of banks and insurance companies and manufacturing industries were nationalized, but the new five-year plan, passed in January 1990, calls for the transfer of many government-controlled enterprises to the private sector (The World Factbook 1991–92: 147).

Iraq
The economy is dominated by state enterprises. Public enterprises accounted for 97 per cent of gross domestic fixed capital formation in manufacturing in 1979 (Short 1984). Small-scale industry and services have been left to private enterprise (The World Factbook 1991–92: 149; *cf.* Perthes 1994: 250).

Israel
Nearly all industrial establishments are operated by private owners. One hundred of the largest plants, employing more than 300 workers, accounted for about 40 per cent of industrial output and over 80 per cent of industrial exports in 1977 (Israel: A Country Study 1978: 206).

Jordan
In the 1970s, only 33 per cent of the national economy could be regarded as actually subject to free-market conditions, the rest being part of a more or less protected public or joint private–public sector (Perthes 1994: 245).

Kazakhstan
The government announced its proposal for transition to market economy, including privatization, in October 1990. Private sector enterprises accounted for 10.9 per cent of employment in 1990–1 (IMF 1992b: 46). See also Eastern Europe 1994: 369.

Kuwait
The petroleum industry is completely owned and controlled by the state and foreign companies.

Kyrgyzstan
Eastern Europe 1994: 387. The privatization programme began in 1991. In January 1993, the private sector comprised 11 per cent of the economy and 26 per cent by the end of 1993. Its economy is still dominated by state enterprises. Private sector enterprises provided for 3.6 per cent of employment in 1990–1 (IMF 1992b: 46).

Lebanon
Its non agricultural economy is very diversified. Most enterprises are small or medium-sized, and they employ most of the workers.

Libya
Many manufacturing enterprises are privately owned, but the dominant petroleum industry is completely controlled by the state and foreign oil companies.

Mauritania
Mining, which is the most important non agricultural sector of economy, is completely dominated by the state and foreign companies.

Morocco
Small-scale industry, employing between ten and fifty workers, accounts for three quarters of industrial employment and 40 per cent of the value of industrial production.

Oman
The economy is based on the production and export of petroleum. The state and foreign companies dominate these sectors of economy.

Qatar
As in the other Arab countries, the dominant petroleum production is wholly owned and controlled by the state and foreign companies.

Saudi Arabia
The production of petroleum and petroleum products is the most important sector of economy. It is dominated by the state and foreign companies.

Sudan
The economy is dominated by governmental entities that account for more than 70 per cent of new investment (The World Factbook 1991–92: 294). See also Marsden and Bélot 1988: 11–12; Nellis 1988: 7.

Syria
According to Kurian (1992: 1853), the state-owned sector provides 75 per cent of the value of industrial production, whereas according to Perthes (1994: 249), the private sector now contributes 55 per cent of Syria's domestic product and 37 per cent of manufacturing industries.

Tajikistan
In 1991, nearly all means of production were still owned and controlled by the government. Private sector enterprises provided 5.3 per cent of employment in 1990–91 (IMF 1992b: 46).

Tunisia
The public sector has been restricted to heavy industry, whereas most of the more than 1,000 manufacturing establishments are owned by private Tunisian firms. In 1988, the privatization of state-owned companies was started. See also Kurian 1992: 1960.

Turkmenistan
In 1991, nearly all means of production were still owned and controlled by the government. Private sector enterprises provided 0.7 per cent of employment in 1990–91 (IMF 1992b: 46). See also Eastern Europe 1994: 666.

United Arab Emirates
The dominant petroleum industry is completely owned and controlled by the state and foreign companies. See also Kurian 1992: 2025.

Uzbekistan
In 1991, nearly all means of production were still owned and controlled by the government. Private sector enterprises provided 3.9 per cent of employment in

1990–91 (IMF 1992b: 46). By 1992 the private sector contributed 15.7 per cent of GDP. The number of private enterprises was increasing (Eastern Europe 1994: 705).

Yemen
Most large enterprises are owned by the government, whereas most small and medium-size enterprises belong to the private sector.

Sub-Saharan Africa

Angola
Nationalized industries accounted for 58 per cent of the total production in 1982, the private sector 29 per cent, and joint ventures 13 per cent (Africa South of the Sahara 1982–83: 197), but in 1988 the government started to transfer some state enterprises to private ownership.

Benin
The key sectors of non agricultural economy were nationalized in 1972–4, but the government changed its economic policy at the end of the 1980s and started to promote private enterprises.

Botswana
Mining enterprises are nearly completely owned and controlled by the state and foreign companies, but the ownership of other sectors of non agricultural economy is more diversified.

Burkina Faso
The state controls some large enterprises, but most industrial firms are wholly or partly foreign-owned.

Burundi
Europeans own about 40 per cent of industrial enterprises. They account for more than 98 per cent of the volume of business and 96 per cent of industrial employment (Kurian 1992: 280–1). Therefore, the degree of concentration can be regarded to be high.

Cameroon
The public sector accounted for 39 per cent and the foreign sector 57 per cent of the total capital in all industries in 1976 (see L'economie Camerounaise. Numero spécial du bulletin de l'Afrique noire, 1977). Since then the share of domestic private ownership in industries has probably increased.

Cape Verde
See Kurian 1992.

Central African Republic
Most large enterprises are partly owned by the state. The private sector is dominated by foreign capital. Therefore, the degree of concentration can be regarded to be high.

Chad
Most of the industrial enterprises are owned by the state or are joint ventures by the state and foreign participants.

Comoros
The government has been the most important employer of non agricultural labour, although the dominant sector is private.

Congo
State-owned enterprises played a major part in the modernized sectors of the economy since the 1960s, but in 1990 the ruling party abandoned its Marxist–Leninist ideology. Since then the role of the private sector has increased.

Côte d'Ivoire
In 1979, 32 per cent of the industry was owned by the state, 55 per cent by foreign interests, and 13 per cent by domestic participants (see Worldmark 1984 vol. 2: 137).

Equatorial Guinea
Industrial and mining enterprises are mainly owned by the state or foreign companies.

Ethiopia
The government took over ownership of over 100 private manufacturing enterprises during the 1970s. As a consequence, public enterprises accounted for 96 per cent of the total value added in enterprises with ten or more workers (Marsden and Bélot 1988: 10–11. See also Ethiopia: A Country Study 1981: 166–70, 181–3). After the fall of Mengistu's regime, Ethiopia started to move toward a market economy.

Gabon
Most manufacturing establishments and mining and petroleum enterprises in particular are owned by foreign companies and the state. See Third World Guide 93/94.

Gambia
Tourism, which is the most dynamic sector of economy, is almost entirely under foreign control.

Ghana
Most large industrial enterprises are owned by the state and foreign participants, but small industrial enterprises are under more diversified ownership. See also HDR 1993: 58; Worldmark 1984 vol. 2: 117; Marsden and Bélot 1988: 12.

Guinea
Manufacturing activity is dominated by the public sector, which accounts for nearly 90 per cent of the output (Kurian 1992: 737). See also Marsden and Bélot 1988: 11; Nellis 1986: 7–11.

Guinea-Bissau
A centrally planned socialist economy was established in Guinea-Bissau in the 1970s. In 1980 about 80 per cent of the work force were employed in the public sector. See EIU, The Economist Intelligence Review of Senegal, The Gambia, Guinea-Bissau, Cape Verde. Annual Supplement 1985: 58. However, since the mid-1980s the role of private sector has increased.

Kenya
The private sector is dominant. The major part of industrial production seems to be under foreign control. See also HDR 1993: 60; Länder der Erde 1981: 343.

Lesotho
The few mining and manufacturing enterprises are mostly owned by foreign companies or they are joint ventures with the state. South Africa is the major source of employment for a very large part of its labour force.

Liberia
The dominant private sector consists mainly of foreign companies. According to Nohlen and Nuscheler (1982 vol. 4: 230–1), three-quarters of all the enterprises are foreign-owned. See also Third World Guide 93/94.

Madagascar
As a consequence of nationalization, the government controlled over 70 per cent of the national economy in 1979. The state sector and public enterprises employed 72 per cent of the labour force in the modern sector in 1980 (Pryor 1988a: 48, 70). See also Kurian 1992: 1171.

Malawi
Its non agricultural economy was nearly completely dominated by foreign companies and the Press (Holding) Ltd., which was owned by President Banda. See Länder der Erde 1981: 394; Pryor 1988b: 77.

Mali
About 85 per cent of industrial product was accounted by state companies in the 1980s, but in the latter half of the 1980s the government started to promote the private sector. Unprofitable state-owned enterprises have been transferred to private ownership.

Mauritius
The private sector is dominant. About half of the industrial enterprises may be locally owned. The rest are foreign-owned.

Mozambique
In 1982 the government controlled 67 per cent of industry, the private sector 22 per cent, and the remaining 11 per cent were mixed state/private enterprises. However, in 1989 the ruling party abandoned its Marxist-Leninist ideology and started to stimulate private enterprises. See also Ramsay 1991: 148.

Namibia
Most of the non agricultural means of production are owned by the white minority and foreign companies.

Niger
Most industrial enterprises are owned by French companies. Mining is completely controlled by the state and foreign companies.

Nigeria
The petroleum sector is completely controlled by the state and foreign companies, but in the other sectors of non agricultural economy the pattern of ownership is more diversified. See also Marsden and Bélot 1988: 12. However, at least 70 per cent of vital economic sectors are still in the hands of foreigners (Kurian 1992: 1444).

Rwanda
Foreign companies dominate the mining and manufacturing sectors.

São Tomé and Príncipe
The manufacturing sector consists of some small enterprises, which are mostly owned by the state or foreigners.

Senegal
Much of the industry is foreign-owned, especially by French firms.

Sierra Leone
Large mining and manufacturing enterprises are owned by the state and foreign companies, but many small enterprises are locally owned.

Somalia
According to one estimate (Länder der Erde 1981: 556), the public sector controls about 70 per cent of industrial production. Kurian (1987) estimates that 89 per cent of the value added in manufacturing is accounted for by the public sector.

South Africa
The white minority controls nearly all the means of production in South Africa.

Swaziland
Its market-oriented economy is dominated by foreign companies. Foreign companies contribute about 80 per cent to the GDP and employ one-third of the labour force (Nohlen and Nuscheler 1982 vol. 5: 383).

Tanzania
The public sector has been dominant in the non agricultural sectors of economy since the 1970s. Most of the private sector enterprises are in the hands of Europeans and Asians.

Togo
Large industrial enterprises, which employ most of the industrial workers, are owned by the state and foreign companies. See also Worldmark 1984 vol. 2: 325.

Uganda
Foreign-owned enterprises seem to dominate Uganda's non agricultural economy.

Zaire
The mining sector, which is the most important non agricultural sector of economy, is completely controlled by the state and foreign companies. Manufacturing is mostly dominated by foreign-owned companies. See also Marsden and Bélot 1988: 13–14.

Zambia
In the 1980s, about 80 per cent of industrial production originated in parastatal enterprises. Public enterprises accounted for 61 per cent of gross fixed capital formation (Short 1984) and 38 per cent of GDP at factor cost (Nellis 1988: 7).

Zimbabwe
The private sector has remained dominant in Zimbabwe, but most manufacturing enterprises are owned by local white entrepreneurs and foreign companies.

South Asia

Bangladesh
By 1975 about 80 per cent of the manufacturing enterprises had been nationalized as well as foreign trade and most banks, but since the 1980s many state enterprises have been privatized and the role of the private sector has become stronger.

Bhután
The private sector is dominant. All industrial enterprises are small, and their ownership seems to be relatively diversified.

India
The government has supported public enterprises with very large investments since the 1950s, but the private sector has remained dominant. It has been, however, under very complicated state regulation and control. Most industrial workers (70–80 per cent) are employed by village and small industries. Therefore, the control of non agricultural employment is diversified. The private sector's share of total investment was 56 per cent in 1990 (HDR 1993: 59). See also Lucas and Papanek 1988.

Maldives
There are only a small number of 'modern' manufacturing enterprises in Maldives. Cottage industries employ nearly one-quarter of the total labour force. However, the degree of resource concentration may be higher than estimated in this study (see Maloney 1995).

Nepal
The private sector is dominant. According to one estimate (Länder der Erde 1981: 432), about 80 per cent of industrial enterprises are controlled by Indian investors. See also Shrestha 1982: 15–20.

Pakistan

Pakistan's manufacturing activity is composed of a large private and a small public sector (Kurian 1992: 1480), but the government controls industry through its licensing system. See also The World Factbook 1991–92: 241.

Sri Lanka

The public and private sectors were roughly in balance in the 1980s. The public sector corporations accounted for 40 per cent of the industrial production, but a large number of small private enterprises contributed the other half and employed considerably more industrial workers than the public sector. See also Lakshman 1980: 18–20.

East Asia and Southeast Asia

Brunei

Oil and natural gas dominate Brunei's economy, (82 per cent of GDP). These sectors of economy are completely controlled by the government and foreign companies. Small manufacturing enterprises are mostly owned by Chinese entrepreneurs.

Cambodia

The Pol Pot government nationalized all businesses in 1975. There was then a centrally planned economy in Cambodia until the establishment of Prince Sihanouk's interim coalition government in 1991. It started to transform the economic system toward a market economy.

China

A centrally planned socialist economy, but since 1978 the control of economy has been decentralized and the share of the private sector has increased significantly. See also HDR 1993: 56; Prybula 1992: 262–7; Womack 1992; People's Republic of China Yearbook 1991/92: 129–30. According to the State Economic Information Center, the output value ratio of private economy in the GNP grew from merely 0.5 per cent in 1980 to 11.8 per cent in 1991 (Issues & Studies 1993, vol 29, No 2: 132). According to Chang Chen-pang (1994), the output of the 'capitalist' sector, when collective enterprises are included, is now equal to that of the state-owned economy.

Indonesia

Most large industries are owned by the state or partly foreign-owned, but cottage industries (less than five workers) employ about 80 per cent of the industrial work force, although they produce only 13 per cent of the value of production (EIU, Indonesia. Annual 1985: 38).

Japan

Three largest monopoly groups control over 40 per cent of industrial production, but small industrial enterprises employ 75 per cent of industrial workers. See Gardner 1988: 195; Länder der Erde 1981: 301; Japan Statistical Yearbook 1982: 188–9.

Korea, North

A centrally planned economy. Nearly all the means of production are owned by the government. State-owned industry produces 95 per cent of manufactured goods (The World Factbook 1991–92: 170).

Korea, South

Most industries are family-owned. Small and medium-scale manufacturing establishments (less than 200 workers) provide 54 per cent of employment and account for 36 per cent of the value added in manufacturing (Kurian 1992: 1032).

Laos
Laos has a centrally planned economy with government ownership and control of productive enterprises of any size, but recently the government has started to decentralize control and encourage private enterprise (The World Factbook 1991–92: 175). See also EIU, Indochina: Vietnam, Laos, Cambodia. Annual 1985: 30.

Malaysia
Private sector is dominant. In 1980, foreigners owned 62 per cent of corporate assets, but in 1985 their share had dropped to 25 per cent (HDR 1993: 61).

Mongolia
A centrally planned economy. In 1978 the share of the socialist sector of gross industrial production was 100 per cent (CMEA 1979: 41), but since 1990 private enterprises have been encouraged, and Mongolia's economic system is being transformed toward a market economy.

Myanmar
The key sectors of industry were nationalized in 1963. Public enterprises accounted for 60 per cent of gross fixed capital formation in 1978–80 and 56 per cent of gross domestic product in manufacturing in 1980 (Short 1984).

Philippines
Manufacturing is dominated by the private sector. Firms employing over 100 workers together contribute 70 per cent of the value added in manufacturing (Kurian 1992: 1587).

Singapore
The private sector is dominant. In manufacturing foreign firms employed 55 per cent of the work force in 1980.

Taiwan (ROC)
The private sector is dominant, and its ownership seems to be relatively diversified. See The Republic of China Yearbook 1991–92: 213–19; The Taiwan Development Experiment and its Relevance to Other Countries 1988; San 1992.

Thailand
The private sector is dominant. Previously the country's Chinese minority controlled over 90 per cent of manufacturing, but now the ownership structure of manufacturing industries is much more diversified.

Vietnam
A centrally planned economy, but since 1986 the government has sponsored a reform programme that seeks to turn more economic activity to the private sector. See HDR 1993: 64; The World Factbook 1991–92: 332.

Oceania

Fiji
The dominant sector is private. Many of the industrial enterprises are owned and controlled by foreign investors. See also Ward 1971: 261; Browne 1989: 33–59.

Papua New Guinea
The dominant sector is private. Most industrial enterprises are foreign-owned. See also Browne 1989: 84–107.

Solomon Islands
The industrial sector is very small. Nearly all establishments are small, and their ownership is diversified. See also Browne 1989: 109–33.

Vanuatu

The dominant sector is private. The non agricultural economy is dominated by service activities, which accounts for more than 50 per cent of GDP. See Browne 1989: 157–79.

Western Samoa

The dominant sector is private, but, according to Browne (1989: 184–5), the central government plays a major role in the economy, with receipts and expenditure each equivalent to about 50 per cent of GDP.

Appendix 5

This appendix contains statistical data on the decennial values of political and explanatory variables and the results of regression analysis of ID on IPR in the total comparison group of 1,139 decennial observation units of the period 1850–1993 for the 967 observation units of the period 1850–1980.

VARIABLES

Com = Competition
Par = Participation
ID = Index of Democratization
IOD = Index of Occupational Diversification
IKD = Index of Knowledge Distribution
FF = Family Farms
IPR = Index of Power Resources
Res = Residual produced by the regression equation of ID on IPR
Pre = Predicted value of ID produced by the regression equation of ID on IPR

State/decade	Com	Par	ID	IOD	IKD	FF	IPR	Res	Pre
Asian and Australasian countries									
Afghanistan									
1 1920–29	0	0	0	9.0	0.5	20.0	0	−1.5	1.5
2 1930–39	0	0	0	8.5	0.5	20.0	0	−1.5	1.5
3 1940–49	0	0	0	9.0	1.0	23.0	0	−1.5	1.5
4 1950–59	0	0	0	9.0	1.5	27.0	0	−1.5	1.5
5 1960–69	0	0.8	0	10.5	2.5	27.0	0.1	−1.6	1.6
6 1970–79	0	1.3	0	13.5	4.5	27.0	0.2	−1.6	1.6
Australia									
7 1901–09	61.8	18.9	11.7	54.0	46.5	67.0	16.8	−2.3	14.0
8 1910–19	49.5	35.2	17.4	60.0	49.0	67.0	19.7	1.2	16.2
9 1920–29	55.4	39.0	21.6	63.5	51.5	67.0	21.9	3.8	17.8
10 1930–39	58.6	50.8	29.8	64.5	55.0	71.0	25.2	9.5	20.3
11 1940–49	53.5	56.9	30.4	68.5	56.0	70.0	26.9	8.9	21.5
12 1950–59	53.9	51.7	27.9	72.5	56.5	70.0	28.7	5.0	22.9
13 1960–69	55.7	50.0	27.8	77.5	68.0	70.0	36.9	−1.2	29.0
14 1970–79	55.3	54.4	30.1	82.0	88.5	70.0	50.8	−9.2	39.3
Bangladesh									
15 1971–79	13.7	13.7	1.9	17.0	20.5	69.0	2.4	−1.4	3.3
Burma									
16 1948–49	20.0	5.0	1.0	20.5	24.5	31.0	1.6	−1.7	2.7
17 1950–59	42.9	12.3	5.3	21.5	29.0	36.0	2.2	2.2	3.1
18 1960–69	8.6	5.3	0.5	21.0	31.0	46.0	3.0	−3.2	3.7
19 1970–79	0	12.2	0	26.0	38.0	60.0	5.9	−5.9	5.9
China									
20 1850–59	0	0	0	7.5	1.0	45.0	0	−1.5	1.5
21 1860–69	0	0	0	7.5	1.0	45.0	0	−1.5	1.5
22 1870–79	0	0	0	7.5	1.0	45.0	0	−1.5	1.5
23 1880–89	0	0	0	7.5	1.0	45.0	0	−1.5	1.5
24 1890–99	0	0	0	7.5	1.0	45.0	0	−1.5	1.5
25 1900–09	0	0	0	7.5	1.0	45.0	0	−1.6	1.6

State/decade	Com	Par	ID	IOD	IKD	FF	IPR	Res	Pre
26 1910–19	7.2	0	0	10.0	2.0	45.0	0.1	−1.6	1.6
27 1920–29	0	0	0	12.5	3.5	45.0	0.2	−1.6	1.6
28 1930–39	0	0	0	15.5	8.5	45.0	0.6	−1.9	1.9
29 1940–49	1.1	0	0	16.5	10.5	40.0	0.7	−2.0	2.0
30 1950–59	0	0	0	17.0	13.5	43.0	1.0	−2.2	2.2
31 1960–69	0	0	0	19.0	21.0	2.0	0.1	−1.6	1.6
32 1970–79	0	0	0	25.0	23.5	2.0	0.1	−1.6	1.6
Fiji									
33 1970–79	43.0	30.9	13.3	31.5	43.0	30.0	4.1	8.8	4.5
India									
34 1947–49	27.7	6.4	1.8	17.0	9.0	25.0	0.4	0.0	1.8
35 1950–59	48.7	19.3	9.4	19.0	15.0	47.0	1.3	6.9	2.5
36 1960–69	55.8	26.4	14.7	20.5	27.0	53.0	2.9	11.1	3.6
37 1970–79	57.3	28.1	16.1	22.0	29.5	63.0	4.1	11.6	4.5
Indonesia									
38 1950–59	39.5	11.5	4.5	17.0	8.5	44.0	0.6	2.6	1.9
39 1960–69	0	0	0	18.0	20.0	54.0	1.9	−2.9	2.9
40 1970–79	16.8	20.8	3.5	22.5	32.5	54.0	3.9	−0.9	4.4
Iran									
41 1850–59	0	0	0	10.0	0.5	10.0	0	−1.5	1.5
42 1860–69	0	0	0	10.0	0.5	10.0	0	−1.5	1.5
43 1870–79	0	0	0	11.0	0.5	10.0	0	−1.5	1.5
44 1880–89	0	0	0	11.0	0.5	10.0	0	−1.5	1.5
45 1890–99	0	0	0	11.0	1.0	10.0	0	−1.5	1.5
46 1900–09	0	0	0	11.0	1.5	10.0	0	−1.5	1.5
47 1910–19	0	0.1	0	13.5	1.5	10.0	0	−1.5	1.5
48 1920–29	0	0.2	0	14.0	2.0	10.0	0	−1.5	1.5
49 1930–39	0	0	0	18.0	3.0	10.0	0.1	−1.6	1.6
50 1940–49	3.5	0.8	0	23.0	4.0	10.0	0.1	−1.6	1.6
51 1950–59	2.0	1.5	0	30.0	6.0	10.0	0.2	−1.6	1.6
52 1960–69	4.0	3.2	0.2	36.5	10.0	16.0	0.6	−1.7	1.9
53 1970–79	5.0	6.4	0.3	43.5	21.0	40.0	3.7	−3.9	4.2
Iraq									
54 1932–39	0	0	0	15.5	2.5	15.0	0.1	−1.6	1.6
55 1940–49	1.5	0	0	18.5	3.5	15.0	0.1	−1.6	1.6
56 1950–59	4.4	2.3	0.1	20.5	6.5	15.0	0.2	−1.6	1.7
57 1960–69	0	0	0	39.5	8.0	18.0	0.6	−1.9	1.9
58 1970–79	0	0	0	47.5	13.0	35.0	2.2	−3.1	3.1
Israel									
59 1948–49	32.1	20.3	6.5	59.5	38.5	46.0	10.5	−2.8	9.3
60 1950–59	64.8	46.4	30.1	72.0	50.5	46.0	16.7	16.2	13.9
61 1960–69	63.0	47.4	30.0	73.5	62.0	46.0	21.0	12.9	17.1
62 1970–79	60.3	48.8	29.4	77.5	82.0	46.0	29.2	6.2	23.2
Japan									
63 1850–59	0	0	0	7.5	5.0	0	0	−1.5	1.5
64 1860–69	0	0	0	7.5	5.0	0	0	−1.5	1.5
65 1870–79	0	0	0	11.0	7.5	0	0	−1.5	1.5
66 1880–89	0	0	0	14.5	10.0	35.0	0.5	−1.9	1.9
67 1890–99	22.3	0.5	0.1	18.0	18.0	30.0	1.0	−2.1	2.2

State/decade	Com	Par	ID	IOD	IKD	FF	IPR	Res	Pre
68 1900–09	23.0	0.8	0.2	21.5	26.0	30.0	1.7	−2.5	2.7
69 1910–19	26.2	1.2	0.3	27.5	31.5	27.0	2.3	−2.9	3.2
70 1920–29	26.5	3.6	1.0	35.0	41.0	28.0	4.0	−3.5	4.5
71 1930–39	27.3	7.7	2.1	40.0	51.0	28.0	5.7	−3.6	5.7
72 1940–49	34.2	17.0	5.8	47.5	60.5	40.0	11.5	−4.2	10.0
73 1950–59	56.1	40.7	22.8	45.0	65.5	67.0	19.7	6.6	16.2
74 1960–69	46.6	43.4	20.2	65.0	72.5	71.0	33.5	−6.2	26.4
75 1970–79	54.7	48.4	26.5	76.5	87.0	74.0	49.3	−11.7	38.2
Jordan									
76 1946–49	0	0	0	41.5	3.5	34.0	0.5	−1.9	1.9
77 1950–59	8.3	4.0	0.3	44.0	8.5	34.0	1.3	−2.2	2.5
78 1960–69	1.2	4.9	0.1	42.5	15.5	34.0	2.2	−3.0	3.1
79 1970–79	1.6	2.4	0	48.0	22.0	36.0	3.8	−4.3	4.3
Kampuchea (Cambodia)									
80 1953–59	7.3	17.0	1.2	13.0	11.5	76.0	1.1	−1.1	2.3
81 1960–69	0	34.9	0	14.0	17.0	66.0	1.6	−2.7	2.7
82 1970–79	8.8	8.1	0.7	22.0	21.0	66.0	3.0	−3.0	3.7
Korea, North									
83 1948–49	1.5	49.0	0.7	19.0	12.0	26.0	0.6	−1.2	1.9
84 1950–59	0	49.0	0	27.0	34.0	26.0	2.4	−3.3	3.3
85 1960–69	0	49.0	0	33.5	46.5	0	0	−1.5	1.5
86 1970–79	0	49.0	0	43.5	84.5	0	0	−1.5	1.5
Korea, South									
87 1948–49	9.0	0	0	19.0	11.0	37.0	0.8	−2.1	2.1
88 1950–59	30.6	29.5	9.0	24.0	31.5	50.0	3.8	4.7	4.3
89 1960–69	40.8	32.2	13.1	31.0	44.5	84.0	11.6	3.0	10.1
90 1970–79	10.0	7.8	0.8	38.0	64.0	84.0	20.4	−15.9	16.7
Kuwait									
91 1961–69	0	1.6	0	76.0	26.5	19.0	3.8	−4.3	4.3
92 1970–79	2.0	1.1	0	79.5	27.5	19.0	4.2	−4.6	4.6
Lebanon									
93 1946–49	45.5	11.9	5.4	32.0	25.5	40.0	3.3	1.5	3.9
94 1950–59	45.5	23.7	10.8	37.0	36.5	40.0	5.4	5.3	5.5
95 1960–69	45.5	25.7	11.7	40.0	42.0	53.0	8.9	3.6	8.1
96 1970–79	45.5	11.0	5.0	44.0	60.0	53.0	14.0	−6.9	11.9
Malaysia									
97 1957–59	28.3	18.9	5.3	28.5	20.5	33.0	1.9	2.4	2.9
98 1960–69	45.2	22.7	10.3	34.5	25.0	33.0	2.8	6.7	3.6
99 1970–79	45.3	22.4	10.1	34.5	32.5	33.0	3.7	5.9	4.2
Mongolia									
100 1921–29	0	0	0	16.5	0.5	20.0	0	−1.5	1.5
101 1930–39	0	0	0	16.5	2.5	20.0	0.1	−1.6	1.6
102 1940–49	0	0	0	16.5	5.0	20.0	0.2	−1.6	1.6
103 1950–59	0	45.3	0	20.0	28.5	0	0	−1.5	1.5
104 1960–69	0	49.7	0	24.0	46.0	0	0	−1.5	1.5
105 1970–79	0	46.3	0	39.0	58.0	0	0	−1.5	1.5
Nepal									
106 1920–29	0	0	0	3.5	1.0	20.0	0	−1.5	1.5
107 1930–39	0	0	0	3.5	1.0	20.0	0	−1.5	1.5

State/decade	Com	Par	ID	IOD	IKD	FF	IPR	Res	Pre
108 1940–49	0	0	0	3.5	1.5	20.0	0	−1.5	1.5
109 1950–59	6.3	2.0	0.1	4.0	3.0	20.0	0	−1.4	1.5
110 1960–69	0	0	0	4.0	5.0	37.0	0.1	−1.6	1.6
111 1970–79	0	0	0	5.5	9.0	37.0	0.2	−1.6	1.6
New Zealand									
112 1890–99	46.8	26.7	12.5	45.5	49.5	46.0	10.4	3.3	9.2
113 1900–09	46.0	41.0	18.9	47.5	52.0	42.0	10.4	9.7	9.2
114 1910–19	54.6	46.4	25.4	53.0	52.5	48.0	13.4	13.9	11.5
115 1920–29	59.9	47.8	28.6	53.0	56.0	57.0	16.9	14.5	14.1
116 1930–39	53.5	50.7	27.1	56.5	64.5	57.0	20.8	10.1	17.0
117 1940–49	48.2	57.7	27.8	62.5	65.0	60.0	24.4	8.1	19.7
118 1950–59	50.8	53.5	27.2	69.9	66.0	61.0	27.8	5.0	22.2
119 1960–69	54.0	47.3	25.5	72.5	79.5	62.0	35.7	−2.6	28.1
120 1970–79	54.2	50.8	27.5	76.0	83.0	56.0	35.3	−0.3	27.8
Pakistan									
121 1947–49	29.0	0	0	15.0	9.0	35.0	0.5	−1.9	1.9
122 1950–59	35.2	0	0	16.0	14.0	40.0	0.9	−2.2	2.2
123 1960–69	17.1	0.1	0	18.0	14.0	42.0	1.1	−2.3	2.3
124 1970–79	30.7	13.2	4.1	23.0	18.5	36.0	1.5	1.5	2.6
Philippines									
125 1946–49	46.8	14.2	6.6	19.5	25.5	33.0	1.6	3.9	2.7
126 1950–59	44.7	20.1	9.0	22.0	58.5	33.0	4.2	4.4	4.6
127 1960–69	46.9	22.8	10.7	26.0	73.0	33.0	6.3	4.5	6.2
128 1970–79	11.3	6.8	0.8	37.0	82.5	33.0	10.1	−8.2	9.0
Saudi Arabia									
129 1927–29	0	0	0	7.5	0.5	25.0	0	−1.5	1.5
130 1930–39	0	0	0	7.5	0.5	25.0	0	−1.5	1.5
131 1940–49	0	0	0	10.0	1.0	25.0	0	−1.5	1.5
132 1950–59	0	0	0	13.5	1.5	25.0	0.1	−1.6	1.6
133 1960–69	0	0	0	20.0	3.5	25.0	0.2	−1.6	1.6
134 1970–79	0	0	0	27.0	8.0	25.0	0.5	−1.9	1.9
Sri Lanka									
135 1948–49	60.1	27.6	16.6	29.5	30.0	47.0	4.2	12.0	4.6
136 1950–59	58.6	28.9	16.9	29.0	34.0	47.0	4.6	12.0	4.9
137 1960–69	61.3	33.5	20.5	30.0	39.5	51.0	6.0	14.5	6.0
138 1970–79	45.5	36.6	16.6	30.0	42.5	51.0	6.5	10.3	6.3
Syria									
139 1946–49	34.5	8.0	2.8	31.5	13.0	30.0	1.2	0.4	2.4
140 1950–59	22.0	10.8	2.4	34.5	15.0	32.0	1.7	−0.3	2.7
141 1960–69	0	0	0	39.0	19.5	34.0	2.6	−3.4	3.4
142 1970–79	0.6	30.9	0.2	43.0	35.5	36.0	5.5	−5.4	5.6
Thailand									
143 1850–59	0	0	0	4.5	0.5	10.0	0	−1.5	1.5
144 1860–69	0	0	0	4.5	0.5	10.0	0	−1.5	1.5
145 1870–79	0	0	0	4.5	1.0	10.0	0	−1.5	1.5
146 1880–89	0	0	0	5.0	1.5	15.0	0	−1.5	1.5
147 1890–99	0	0	0	5.0	2.0	15.0	0	−1.5	1.5
148 1900–09	0	0	0	6.0	2.5	20.0	0	−1.5	1.5
149 1910–19	0	0	0	7.5	5.0	35.0	0.1	−1.6	1.6

State/decade	Com	Par	ID	IOD	IKD	FF	IPR	Res	Pre
150 1920–29	0	0	0	6.5	7.5	40.0	0.2	−1.6	1.6
151 1930–39	0	1.0	0	8.0	12.5	50.0	0.5	−1.9	1.9
152 1940–49	0	1.8	0	10.5	17.5	55.0	1.0	−2.2	2.2
153 1950–59	2.0	2.4	0	9.0	30.5	60.0	1.6	−2.7	2.7
154 1960–69	5.0	1.9	0.1	13.5	41.0	66.0	3.7	−4.1	4.2
155 1970–79	19.6	4.7	0.9	19.0	48.5	66.0	6.1	−5.1	6.0
Turkey									
156 1850–59	0	0	0	11.5	1.0	20.0	0	−1.5	1.5
157 1860–69	0	0	0	11.5	1.0	20.0	0	−1.5	1.5
158 1870–79	0	0	0	12.5	1.5	20.0	0	−1.5	1.5
159 1880–89	0	0	0	12.5	1.5	20.0	0	−1.5	1.5
160 1890–99	0	0	0	13.0	2.0	20.0	0.1	−1.6	1.6
161 1900–09	0	0.1	0	14.0	2.0	20.0	0.1	−1.6	1.6
162 1910–19	0.2	0.2	0	15.0	2.5	25.0	0.1	−1.6	1.6
163 1920–29	0	0.3	0	17.0	5.0	25.0	0.2	−1.6	1.6
164 1930–39	0	0.5	0	15.0	7.5	30.0	0.3	−1.7	1.7
165 1940–49	18.0	15.5	2.8	17.0	12.5	40.0	0.8	0.7	2.1
166 1950–59	46.9	37.8	17.7	18.5	18.5	49.0	1.7	15.0	2.7
167 1960–69	50.1	29.5	14.8	23.0	26.0	59.0	3.5	10.7	4.1
168 1970–79	60.3	30.0	18.1	28.0	37.0	63.0	6.5	11.8	6.3
Vietnam									
169 1954–59	0	0	0	10.0	25.5	40.0	1.0	−2.2	2.2
170 1960–69	0	41.7	0	14.5	33.0	14.0	0.7	−2.0	2.0
171 1970–79	0	45.1	0	16.0	41.5	5.0	0.3	−1.7	1.7
Yemen, North									
172 1921–29	0	0	0	5.5	0.5	10.0	0	−1.5	1.5
173 1930–39	0	0	0	5.5	0.5	10.0	0	−1.5	1.5
174 1940–49	0	0	0	5.5	1.0	10.0	0	−1.5	1.5
175 1950–59	0	0	0	8.5	1.0	10.0	0	−1.5	1.5
176 1960–69	0	0	0	10.0	2.0	10.0	0	−1.5	1.5
177 1970–79	0	0	0	15.0	3.5	10.0	0.1	−1.6	1.6
Yemen, South									
178 1967–69	0	0	0	22.0	10.0	10.0	0.2	−1.6	1.6
179 1970–79	0	0	0	28.0	10.0	10.0	0.3	−1.7	1.7
European countries									
Albania									
180 1920–29	23.4	0	0	10.0	10.0	20.0	0.2	−1.6	1.6
181 1930–39	0	0	0	12.0	12.5	25.0	0.4	−1.8	1.8
182 1940–49	6.8	48.3	3.3	13.0	15.0	30.0	0.6	1.4	1.9
183 1950–59	0.8	52.3	0.4	14.5	23.0	40.0	1.3	−2.1	2.5
184 1960–69	0	51.7	0	24.5	39.5	9.0	0.9	−2.2	2.2
185 1970–79	0	49.6	0	31.0	59.0	6.0	1.0	−2.2	2.2
Austria									
186 1850–59	0	0	0	18.0	20.0	35.0	1.3	−2.5	2.5
187 1860–69	6.0	0.1	0	19.0	23.0	35.0	1.5	−2.6	2.6
188 1870–79	21.8	0.3	0.1	22.0	32.5	40.0	2.9	−3.5	3.6
189 1880–89	28.7	0.4	0.1	23.0	35.5	40.0	3.3	−3.8	3.9
190 1890–99	35.8	1.0	0.4	24.0	38.5	40.0	3.7	−3.8	4.2
191 1900–09	43.0	4.1	1.8	27.0	41.5	41.0	4.6	−3.1	4.9

State/decade	Com	Par	ID	IOD	IKD	FF	IPR	Res	Pre
192 1910–19	45.2	11.8	5.3	30.0	46.0	41.0	5.7	−0.4	5.7
193 1920–29	55.0	59.6	27.8	51.5	55.0	45.0	12.7	16.9	10.9
194 1930–37	29.3	27.6	8.1	52.0	65.5	45.0	15.3	−4.8	12.9
195 1945–49	51.4	49.9	25.6	49.0	65.0	50.0	15.9	12.3	13.3
196 1950–59	56.2	61.8	34.7	54.0	56.0	60.0	18.1	19.7	15.0
197 1960–69	53.7	62.3	33.5	57.0	65.5	59.0	22.0	15.6	17.9
198 1970–79	49.9	61.7	30.8	61.0	73.0	59.0	26.3	9.7	21.1
Belgium									
199 1850–59	44.2	1.5	0.7	33.5	26.5	22.0	2.0	−2.3	3.0
200 1860–69	44.9	1.6	0.7	35.5	29.5	22.0	2.3	−2.5	3.2
201 1870–79	43.6	1.4	0.6	39.9	33.5	22.0	2.9	−3.0	3.6
202 1880–89	45.2	1.6	0.7	43.0	37.0	22.0	3.5	−3.4	4.1
203 1890–99	49.3	12.8	6.3	46.5	41.0	21.0	4.0	1.8	4.5
204 1900–09	49.6	20.9	10.4	53.0	45.0	21.0	5.0	5.2	5.2
205 1910–19	54.1	22.1	12.0	56.0	47.5	22.0	5.9	6.1	5.9
206 1920–29	62.2	26.1	16.2	64.0	51.5	30.0	9.9	7.3	8.9
207 1930–39	64.5	28.3	18.3	67.0	53.0	40.0	14.2	6.2	12.1
208 1940–49	59.2	34.2	20.2	68.0	54.5	60.0	22.2	2.2	18.0
209 1950–59	55.2	58.0	32.0	70.0	56.5	90.0	35.6	4.0	28.0
210 1960–69	61.1	56.0	34.2	72.0	60.5	90.0	39.2	3.5	30.7
211 1970–79	68.0	55.9	38.0	74.0	66.0	90.0	44.0	3.7	34.3
Bulgaria									
212 1908–09	19.0	5.5	1.0	12.5	18.0	52.0	1.2	−1.4	2.4
213 1910–19	27.4	6.9	1.9	12.5	19.0	53.0	1.3	−0.6	2.5
214 1920–29	22.7	10.3	2.3	13.5	27.5	60.0	2.2	−0.8	3.1
215 1930–39	22.2	8.9	2.0	15.5	36.0	75.0	4.2	−2.6	4.6
216 1940–49	8.5	25.1	2.1	18.5	41.5	73.0	5.6	−3.6	5.7
217 1950–59	1.0	66.8	0.7	23.5	47.5	60.0	6.7	−5.8	6.5
219 1970–79	0.1	72.1	0.1	49.0	75.5	1.0	0.4	−1.7	1.8
Czechoslovakia									
220 1920–29	56.1	24.4	13.7	38.5	49.0	40.0	7.5	6.6	7.1
221 1930–39	51.2	24.4	12.5	41.5	53.0	65.0	14.3	0.4	12.1
222 1940–49	21.6	34.4	7.4	41.5	57.5	65.0	15.5	−5.6	13.0
223 1950–59	5.6	63.5	3.6	42.0	57.0	60.0	14.4	−8.6	12.2
224 1960–69	0.2	66.8	0.1	49.5	66.5	12.0	4.0	−4.4	4.5
225 1970–79	0.2	70.7	0.1	54.5	83.0	10.0	4.5	−4.7	4.8
Denmark									
226 1850–59	29.1	1.7	0.5	30.0	47.5	35.0	5.0	−4.7	5.2
227 1860–69	29.7	2.3	0.7	30.5	48.5	35.0	5.2	−4.7	5.4
228 1870–79	26.9	3.4	0.9	31.0	49.5	35.0	5.4	−4.6	5.5
229 1880–89	22.2	4.3	1.0	32.5	50.0	35.0	5.7	−4.7	5.7
230 1890–99	29.0	5.0	1.4	37.5	50.5	38.0	7.2	−5.4	6.8
231 1900–09	58.8	9.3	5.5	40.0	50.5	40.0	8.1	−2.0	7.5
232 1910–19	69.6	14.8	10.3	42.5	52.0	44.0	9.7	1.6	8.7
233 1920–29	63.7	38.1	24.3	48.5	52.5	49.0	12.5	13.5	10.8
234 1930–39	56.1	43.2	24.2	49.5	53.0	60.0	15.7	11.0	13.2
235 1940–49	59.7	48.8	29.1	56.0	55.5	70.0	21.8	11.4	17.7
236 1950–59	59.8	49.7	29.7	60.0	57.5	87.0	30.0	5.9	23.8
237 1960–69	60.3	55.8	33.6	65.0	63.0	87.0	35.6	5.6	28.0
238 1970–79	66.8	60.4	40.3	70.5	65.5	87.0	40.2	8.9	31.4

State/decade	Com	Par	ID	IOD	IKD	FF	IPR	Res	Pre
Finland									
239 1917–19	47.1	21.2	10.0	20.5	42.0	34.0	2.9	6.4	3.6
240 1920–29	62.0	18.6	11.5	21.5	46.5	47.0	4.7	6.5	5.0
241 1930–39	71.8	29.4	21.1	24.5	50.5	60.0	7.4	14.1	7.0
242 1940–49	41.8	20.4	8.5	31.0	57.0	68.0	12.0	−1.9	10.4
243 1950–59	64.1	43.7	28.0	38.0	61.0	87.0	20.2	11.5	16.5
244 1960–69	59.4	48.2	28.6	47.0	66.0	93.0	28.8	5.7	22.9
245 1970–79	48.2	40.3	19.4	57.5	75.0	94.0	40.5	−12.2	31.6
France									
246 1850–59	11.1	9.7	1.1	28.5	29.0	28.0	2.3	−2.1	3.2
247 1860–69	11.6	9.3	1.1	31.5	33.0	29.0	3.0	−2.6	3.7
248 1870–79	45.3	19.5	8.8	33.5	35.5	29.0	3.4	4.8	4.0
249 1880–89	37.0	19.7	7.3	35.0	38.0	29.0	3.9	2.9	4.4
250 1890–99	53.0	19.6	10.4	37.0	41.0	29.0	4.4	5.6	4.8
251 1900–09	68.2	21.6	14.7	40.5	44.0	29.0	5.2	9.3	5.4
252 1910–19	80.2	21.2	17.0	42.5	48.0	29.0	5.9	11.1	5.9
253 1920–29	72.6	22.1	16.0	48.0	50.5	35.0	8.5	8.2	7.8
254 1930–39	79.4	23.4	18.6	51.5	52.5	45.0	12.2	8.0	10.6
255 1940–49	71.9	48.0	34.5	54.5	57.5	55.0	17.2	20.2	14.3
256 1950–59	68.8	41.9	28.8	56.5	57.5	70.0	22.7	10.4	18.4
257 1960–69	52.1	32.9	17.1	63.0	65.5	70.0	28.9	−5.9	23.0
258 1970–79	66.1	50.5	33.4	68.0	71.5	67.0	32.6	7.6	25.8
German Democratic Republic									
259 1950–59	0.2	70.8	0.1	57.5	53.0	60.0	18.3	−15.0	15.1
260 1960–69	0.1	71.3	0.1	59.0	63.5	8.0	3.0	−3.6	3.7
261 1970–79	0.1	70.6	0.1	63.0	82.0	6.0	3.1	−3.7	3.8
Germany/Federal Republic of Germany									
262 1871–79	35.5	5.7	2.0	31.5	41.5	48.0	6.3	−4.2	6.2
263 1880–89	38.5	6.5	2.5	34.5	44.5	48.0	7.4	−4.5	7.0
264 1890–99	38.5	7.3	2.8	39.0	47.5	49.0	9.1	−5.5	8.3
265 1900–09	35.2	8.0	2.8	45.0	50.5	50.0	11.4	−7.2	10.0
266 1910–19	33.8	10.7	3.6	49.5	52.0	51.0	13.1	−7.6	11.2
267 1920–29	54.3	35.6	19.3	53.0	54.0	54.0	15.5	6.3	13.0
268 1930–39	18.4	15.7	2.9	56.0	58.5	54.0	17.7	−11.8	14.7
269 1940–49	11.5	8.4	1.0	59.5	59.5	64.0	22.7	−17.4	18.4
270 1950–59	57.6	54.9	31.6	61.5	53.0	90.0	29.3	8.3	23.3
271 1960–69	53.2	57.5	30.7	69.0	61.5	90.0	38.2	0.8	29.9
272 1970–79	53.0	61.9	32.8	73.0	67.5	87.0	42.9	− 0.6	33.4
Greece									
273 1850–59	17.0	5.0	0.8	21.5	16.0	35.0	1.2	−1.6	2.4
274 1860–69	26.0	5.0	1.3	22.5	16.5	35.5	1.3	−1.2	2.5
275 1870–79	21.3	5.0	1.1	24.5	17.6	35.0	1.5	−1.5	2.6
276 1880–89	23.4	7.5	1.8	26.5	18.5	35.0	1.7	−0.9	2.7
277 1890–99	19.7	7.8	1.5	29.0	21.0	26.0	1.6	−1.2	2.7
278 1900–09	28.3	7.5	2.1	31.5	23.0	28.0	2.0	−0.9	3.0
279 1910–19	16.9	7.5	1.3	33.5	24.0	30.0	2.4	−2.0	3.3
280 1920–29	39.3	10.9	4.3	34.0	28.0	28.0	2.7	0.8	3.5
281 1930–39	32.2	10.0	3.3	35.0	32.0	45.0	5.0	−1.9	5.2
282 1940–49	25.7	8.5	2.2	37.0	37.5	55.0	7.6	−4.9	7.1
283 1950–59	57.1	30.5	17.4	39.5	42.0	75.0	12.4	6.7	10.7

State/decade	Com	Par	ID	IOD	IKD	FF	IPR	Res	Pre
284 1960–69	35.7	37.4	13.4	40.5	49.5	83.0	16.6	−0.4	13.8
285 1970–79	31.1	33.0	10.3	47.5	58.0	83.0	22.9	−8.2	18.5
Hungary									
286 1870–79	35.0	4.0	1.4	19.0	16.5	39.0	1.2	−1.0	2.4
287 1880–89	30.0	4.0	1.2	20.5	21.5	39.0	1.7	−1.5	2.7
288 1890–99	38.0	4.0	1.5	21.5	27.0	39.0	2.3	−1.7	3.2
289 1900–09	41.7	4.0	1.7	22.5	31.5	39.0	2.8	−1.9	3.6
290 1910–19	47.7	4.0	1.9	26.0	37.0	40.0	3.8	−2.4	4.3
291 1920–29	25.0	11.6	2.9	37.0	47.0	40.0	7.0	−3.8	6.7
292 1930–39	19.7	11.8	2.3	40.0	53.0	41.0	8.7	−5.7	8.0
293 1940–49	40.2	31.6	12.7	41.5	54.5	41.0	9.3	4.3	8.4
294 1950–59	2.4	64.9	1.6	41.0	53.5	68.0	14.9	−11.0	12.6
295 1960–69	1.3	68.0	0.9	49.0	62.5	18.0	5.5	−4.7	5.6
296 1970–79	0.7	71.0	0.5	57.5	63.5	2.0	0.7	−1.5	2.0
Ireland									
297 1922–29	61.2	34.9	21.4	33.5	46.5	40.0	6.2	15.3	6.1
298 1930–39	53.0	44.2	23.4	35.5	52.5	58.0	10.8	13.9	9.5
299 1940–49	52.3	43.0	22.5	38.0	56.5	60.0	12.9	11.4	11.1
300 1950–59	54.4	44.2	24.0	43.5	59.0	74.0	19.9	8.4	15.6
301 1960–69	54.0	42.7	23.1	48.0	62.5	82.0	24.6	3.3	19.8
302 1970–79	52.6	46.0	24.2	54.5	68.0	82.0	30.4	0.1	24.1
Italy									
303 1861–69	40.0	1.1	0.4	27.5	14.0	18.0	0.7	−1.6	2.0
304 1870–79	34.4	1.1	0.4	29.5	17.0	18.0	0.9	−1.8	2.2
305 1880–89	25.0	3.3	1.0	31.0	21.5	18.0	1.2	−1.4	2.4
306 1890–99	21.8	4.5	1.0	32.0	24.5	18.0	1.4	−1.5	2.5
307 1900–09	31.9	4.4	1.4	33.5	28.5	18.0	1.7	−1.3	2.7
308 1910–19	44.5	11.7	5.2	37.0	34.5	18.0	2.3	2.0	3.2
309 1920–29	32.8	8.7	2.9	38.0	39.5	22.0	3.3	−1.0	3.9
310 1930–39	0	0	0	44.0	44.5	27.0	5.4	−5.5	5.5
311 1940–49	23.3	21.7	5.1	45.5	46.0	30.0	6.3	−1.1	6.2
312 1950–59	56.9	57.8	32.9	49.5	57.5	33.0	9.4	24.4	8.5
313 1960–69	60.4	60.5	36.5	58.0	61.0	45.0	15.9	23.2	13.3
314 1970–79	61.2	62.7	38.4	65.0	67.0	50.0	21.8	20.7	17.7
Netherlands									
315 1850–59	33.0	1.0	0.3	38.0	37.5	25.0	3.6	−3.9	4.2
316 1860–69	37.7	1.2	0.5	43.0	38.5	25.0	4.1	−4.0	4.5
317 1870–79	54.4	2.0	1.1	45.5	41.0	25.0	4.7	−3.9	5.0
318 1880–89	54.6	2.9	1.6	47.0	42.0	25.0	4.9	−3.5	5.1
319 1890–99	59.5	5.4	3.2	49.5	44.5	25.0	5.5	−2.4	5.6
320 1900–09	71.8	9.9	7.1	53.5	47.5	25.0	6.4	0.9	6.2
321 1910–19	74.8	12.5	9.3	56.5	49.5	26.0	7.3	2.4	6.9
322 1920–29	70.6	37.6	26.5	61.0	51.5	40.0	12.6	15.6	10.9
323 1930–39	71.3	45.2	32.2	64.0	53.0	50.0	17.0	18.1	14.1
324 1940–49	69.1	50.4	34.8	65.5	56.5	60.0	22.2	16.8	18.0
325 1950–59	69.2	51.9	35.9	69.0	58.0	92.0	36.8	7.0	28.9
326 1960–69	69.8	53.2	37.1	74.5	64.0	93.0	44.3	2.6	34.5
327 1970–79	71.1	56.0	39.8	78.5	67.0	91.0	47.9	2.6	37.2
Norway									
328 1850–59	30.0	1.2	0.3	16.5	42.5	64.0	4.5	−4.5	4.8

State/decade	Com	Par	ID	IOD	IKD	FF	IPR	Res	Pre
329 1860–69	27.5	1.1	0.3	19.5	44.0	64.0	5.5	−5.3	5.6
330 1870–79	25.7	1.0	0.3	25.0	46.0	67.0	7.7	−6.9	7.2
331 1880–89	34.7	3.3	1.1	30.5	48.5	71.0	10.5	−8.2	9.3
332 1890–99	49.7	6.6	3.3	32.0	48.5	74.0	11.5	−6.7	10.0
333 1900–09	52.7	11.5	6.1	38.0	51.5	77.0	15.1	−6.6	12.7
334 1910–19	63.4	22.1	14.0	39.5	51.5	80.0	16.3	0.4	13.6
335 1920–29	66.1	34.2	22.6	43.0	52.5	82.0	18.5	7.3	15.3
336 1930–39	61.6	45.9	28.3	45.5	54.5	84.0	20.8	11.3	17.0
337 1940–49	58.1	49.7	28.9	48.0	57.5	86.0	23.7	9.8	19.1
338 1950–59	53.2	52.9	28.1	52.0	59.5	88.0	27.2	6.4	21.7
339 1960–69	54.6	53.1	29.0	57.5	61.0	91.0	31.9	3.8	25.2
340 1970–79	59.2	55.6	32.9	64.5	63.0	90.0	36.6	4.2	28.7
Poland									
341 1920–29	63.2	23.7	15.0	17.5	37.5	53.0	3.5	10.9	4.1
342 1930–39	43.9	9.9	4.3	23.5	43.0	65.0	6.6	−2.1	6.4
343 1940–49	12.0	28.7	3.4	27.0	48.5	70.0	9.2	−4.9	8.3
344 1950–59	4.6	56.4	2.6	34.5	57.0	81.0	15.9	−10.7	13.3
345 1960–69	1.4	59.9	0.8	42.0	71.0	79.0	23.6	−18.3	19.1
346 1970–79	0.4	66.6	0.3	51.5	67.0	76.0	26.2	−20.7	21.0
Portugal									
347 1850–59	5.0	2.5	0.1	18.0	9.5	20.0	0.3	−1.6	1.7
348 1860–69	5.0	2.5	0.1	18.5	9.0	20.0	0.3	−1.6	1.7
349 1870–79	5.0	2.5	0.1	19.0	9.5	20.0	0.4	−1.7	1.8
350 1880–89	10.0	2.5	0.2	20.5	10.0	20.0	0.4	−1.6	1.8
351 1890–99	10.0	2.5	0.2	22.0	13.0	20.0	0.6	−1.7	1.9
352 1900–09	22.2	2.5	0.6	23.0	14.5	20.0	0.7	−1.4	2.0
353 1910–19	25.0	5.1	1.3	27.5	16.5	20.0	0.9	−0.9	2.2
354 1920–29	29.8	3.6	1.1	30.5	18.5	20.0	1.1	−1.2	2.3
355 1930–39	0	4.9	0	32.5	22.0	20.0	1.4	−2.5	2.5
356 1940–49	0	7.0	0	33.0	28.0	23.0	2.1	−3.0	3.0
357 1950–59	4.8	7.9	0.4	34.0	34.0	26.0	3.0	−3.3	3.7
358 1960–69	13.1	5.7	0.7	37.0	39.0	28.0	4.0	−3.8	4.5
359 1970–79	21.7	21.0	4.6	42.0	46.5	30.0	5.9	−1.3	5.9
Romania									
360 1880–89	15.0	0.4	0.1	13.5	8.0	26.0	0.3	−1.6	1.7
361 1890–99	15.0	0.5	0.1	14.0	9.5	29.0	0.4	−1.7	1.8
362 1900–09	14.7	0.5	0.1	15.0	12.5	30.0	0.6	−1.8	1.9
363 1910–19	15.2	1.6	0.2	14.0	21.5	35.0	1.1	−2.1	2.3
364 1920–29	22.9	7.2	1.6	16.5	25.0	41.0	1.7	−1.1	2.7
365 1930–39	29.7	6.4	1.9	17.0	34.0	54.0	3.1	−1.9	3.8
366 1940–49	3.6	14.0	0.5	21.5	44.0	54.0	5.1	−4.8	5.3
367 1950–59	2.5	60.2	1.5	23.5	46.5	60.0	6.6	−4.9	6.4
368 1960–69	0.3	67.0	0.2	28.5	61.5	18.0	3.2	−3.7	3.9
369 1970–79	0.7	69.3	0.5	40.5	68.0	9.0	2.5	−2.8	3.3
Spain									
370 1850–59	13.7	0.3	0	19.0	12.5	15.0	0.4	−1.8	1.8
371 1860–69	13.7	1.2	0.2	20.0	15.0	15.0	0.4	−1.6	1.8
372 1870–79	8.2	5.5	0.5	22.0	18.0	15.0	0.6	−1.4	1.9
373 1880–89	12.6	1.8	0.2	23.0	21.5	15.0	0.7	−1.8	2.0
374 1890–99	16.7	6.5	1.1	25.0	23.5	15.0	0.9	−1.1	2.2

State/decade	Com	Par	ID	IOD	IKD	FF	IPR	Res	Pre
375 1900–09	20.9	7.8	1.6	26.5	24.5	16.0	1.0	−0.6	2.2
376 1910–19	26.0	6.0	1.6	33.5	28.0	18.0	1.7	−1.1	2.7
377 1920–29	26.5	1.6	0.4	35.0	33.0	20.0	2.3	−2.8	3.2
378 1930–39	39.0	14.5	5.7	38.5	39.5	22.0	3.3	1.8	3.9
379 1940–49	0	0	0	42.0	46.0	22.0	4.3	−4.7	4.7
380 1950–59	0	0	0	45.5	48.5	22.0	4.9	−5.1	5.1
381 1960–69	0	0	0	51.5	52.5	24.0	6.5	−6.3	6.3
382 1970–79	19.8	15.0	3.0	58.0	57.5	24.0	8.0	−4.4	7.4
Sweden									
383 1850–59	37.5	0.5	0.2	18.5	47.0	35.0	3.0	−3.5	3.7
384 1860–69	34.3	0.5	0.2	20.0	47.5	35.0	3.3	−3.7	3.9
385 1870–79	21.3	0.5	0.1	22.5	48.5	35.0	3.8	−4.2	4.3
386 1880–89	23.8	0.8	0.2	24.0	49.0	35.0	4.1	−4.3	4.5
387 1890–99	27.2	1.3	0.4	26.0	50.5	35.0	4.6	−4.5	4.9
388 1900–09	39.1	3.2	1.3	29.5	51.5	35.0	5.3	−4.1	5.4
389 1910–19	63.0	10.3	6.5	35.0	51.5	41.0	7.4	−0.5	7.0
390 1920–29	61.3	29.4	18.0	39.5	52.5	50.0	10.4	8.8	9.2
391 1930–39	57.6	42.6	24.5	43.0	54.0	60.0	13.9	12.7	11.8
392 1940–49	50.7	48.1	24.4	48.5	57.0	70.0	19.4	8.5	15.9
393 1950–59	54.2	53.6	29.1	57.4	58.0	79.0	26.3	8.0	21.1
394 1960–69	51.9	57.1	29.6	63.5	61.5	78.0	30.5	5.4	24.2
395 1970–79	56.2	63.8	35.9	70.5	74.0	75.0	39.1	5.3	30.6
Switzerland									
396 1850–59	32.7	4.0	1.3	23.0	43.5	45.0	4.5	−3.5	4.8
397 1860–69	52.7	5.0	2.6	32.0	45.0	45.0	6.5	−3.7	6.3
398 1870–79	51.0	6.6	3.4	32.0	47.0	45.0	6.8	−3.1	6.5
399 1880–89	49.3	11.8	5.8	33.5	48.5	45.0	7.3	−1.1	6.9
400 1890–99	46.3	11.9	5.5	37.5	50.5	45.0	8.5	−2.3	7.8
401 1900–09	49.6	11.7	5.8	42.0	51.5	48.0	10.4	−3.4	9.2
402 1910–19	51.9	11.5	6.0	47.0	54.5	55.0	14.1	−6.0	12.0
403 1920–29	71.9	19.1	13.7	48.5	57.5	60.0	16.7	−0.2	13.9
404 1930–39	72.0	20.8	15.0	52.0	58.5	69.0	21.0	−2.1	17.1
405 1940–49	73.0	19.0	13.9	53.5	60.0	69.0	22.1	−4.0	17.9
406 1950–59	73.6	20.8	14.7	56.0	63.5	85.0	30.2	−9.3	24.0
407 1960–69	74.4	17.3	12.9	59.5	67.0	90.0	35.9	−15.3	28.2
408 1970–79	76.1	29.3	22.3	62.5	69.5	90.0	39.1	−8.3	30.6
United Kingdom									
409 1850–59	52.8	2.5	1.3	53.5	30.0	5.0	0.8	−0.8	2.1
410 1860–69	55.7	2.8	1.6	57.0	33.5	5.0	1.0	−0.6	2.2
411 1870–79	49.4	5.5	2.7	61.0	38.0	5.0	1.2	0.3	2.5
412 1880–89	50.2	7.0	3.5	65.0	41.5	8.0	2.2	0.4	3.1
413 1890–99	51.1	9.5	4.9	70.0	46.5	12.0	3.9	0.5	4.4
414 1900–09	50.1	9.6	4.8	72.0	48.0	16.0	5.5	−0.8	5.6
415 1910–19	54.8	13.2	7.2	75.0	50.0	20.0	7.5	0.1	7.0
416 1920–29	57.2	32.2	18.4	78.5	50.0	25.0	9.8	9.6	8.8
417 1930–39	50.0	46.0	23.0	81.5	53.5	30.0	13.1	11.8	11.2
418 1940–49	52.0	52.9	27.5	81.5	54.5	35.0	15.5	14.5	13.0
419 1950–59	51.1	54.8	28.0	82.0	53.0	48.0	20.9	11.0	17.0
420 1960–69	52.2	51.6	26.9	82.5	57.0	52.0	24.5	7.2	19.7
421 1970–79	57.4	52.2	30.0	83.0	61.5	49.0	25.0	9.9	20.1

State/decade	Com	Par	ID	IOD	IKD	FF	IPR	Res	Pre
Russia/USSR									
422 1850–59	0	0	0	9.0	2.5	1.0	0	−1.5	1.5
423 1860–69	0	0	0	9.5	3.5	1.0	0	−1.5	1.5
424 1870–79	0	0	0	10.0	5.5	31.0	0.2	−1.6	1.6
425 1880–89	0	0	0	10.5	7.5	33.0	0.3	−1.7	1.7
426 1890–99	0	0	0	11.0	9.5	36.0	0.4	−1.8	1.8
427 1900–09	13.0	0	0	11.0	15.5	39.0	0.7	−2.0	2.0
428 1910–19	25.8	0	0	12.0	23.0	43.0	1.2	−2.4	2.4
429 1920–29	0	0	0	12.5	24.0	50.0	1.5	−2.6	2.6
430 1930–39	0.4	16.3	0.1	16.0	36.0	18.0	1.0	−2.1	2.2
431 1940–49	1.1	56.0	0.6	28.0	50.5	1.0	0.1	−1.0	1.6
432 1950–59	0.3	64.0	0.2	36.0	69.0	1.0	0.2	−1.4	1.6
433 1960–69	0.4	63.0	0.3	47.0	73.0	0	0	−1.2	1.5
434 1970–79	0.2	63.9	0.1	60.0	82.0	0	0	−1.4	1.5
Yugoslavia									
435 1920–29	66.7	14.9	9.9	12.3	29.0	29.0	2.2	6.8	3.1
436 1930–39	20.5	8.2	1.7	15.0	32.5	72.0	3.5	−2.4	4.1
437 1940–49	11.8	42.3	5.0	16.0	37.0	72.0	4.3	0.3	4.7
438 1950–59	4.9	56.2	2.8	19.0	41.0	77.0	6.0	−3.2	6.0
439 1960–69	3.8	58.4	2.2	27.0	57.0	77.0	11.9	−8.1	10.3
440 1970–79	2.8	22.7	0.6	35.0	71.5	77.0	19.3	−15.3	15.9
American countries									
Argentina									
441 1850–59	6.6	0.7	0	18.5	7.0	5.0	0.1	−1.6	1.6
442 1860–69	8.6	0.9	0.1	21.5	9.0	5.0	0.1	−1.5	1.6
443 1870–79	36.3	1.2	0.4	24.0	12.5	5.0	0.1	−1.2	1.6
444 1880–89	27.1	2.0	0.5	27.0	18.0	6.0	0.3	−1.2	1.7
445 1890–99	8.6	2.0	0.2	33.5	23.0	7.0	0.5	−1.7	1.9
446 1900–09	17.2	2.3	0.4	39.0	27.0	8.0	0.8	−1.7	2.1
447 1910–19	19.4	5.2	1.0	43.0	33.0	10.0	1.4	−1.5	2.5
448 1920–29	44.8	9.6	4.3	50.0	39.0	11.0	2.1	1.3	3.0
449 1930–39	34.5	10.9	3.8	52.5	46.5	12.0	2.9	0.2	3.6
450 1940–49	30.7	11.1	3.4	57.5	50.0	12.0	3.4	−0.6	4.0
451 1950–59	30.1	27.8	8.4	62.5	56.0	18.0	6.3	2.2	6.2
452 1960–69	33.2	22.4	7.4	67.0	68.5	22.0	10.1	−1.6	9.0
453 1970–79	11.5	15.0	1.7	72.0	87.0	24.0	15.0	−11.0	12.7
Bolivia									
454 1850–59	0	0	0	7.2	4.0	2.0	0	−1.5	1.5
455 1860–69	0	0	0	8.0	4.0	2.0	0	−1.5	1.5
456 1870–79	0	0	0	9.5	4.5	2.0	0	−1.5	1.5
457 1880–89	28.4	0.9	0.3	11.0	5.0	2.0	0	−1.2	1.5
458 1890–99	41.3	1.6	0.7	12.0	7.0	2.0	0	−0.8	1.5
459 1900–09	6.0	1.2	0.1	16.0	9.0	2.0	0	−1.4	1.5
460 1910–19	10.3	3.1	0.3	18.0	10.0	2.0	0	−1.2	1.5
461 1920–29	5.4	1.6	0.1	19.0	10.0	2.0	0	−1.4	1.5
462 1930–39	3.0	0.5	0	22.0	13.0	2.0	0.1	−1.6	1.6
463 1940–49	20.2	1.8	0.4	25.5	16.5	3.0	0.1	−1.2	1.6
464 1950–59	35.0	13.2	4.6	28.0	20.5	3.0	0.2	3.0	1.6
465 1960–69	21.7	17.0	3.7	30.5	28.0	20.0	1.7	1.0	2.7
466 1970–79	0	0	0	33.0	40.5	25.0	3.3	−3.9	3.9

State/decade	Com	Par	ID	IOD	IKD	FF	IPR	Res	Pre
Brazil									
467 1850–59	0	0	0	11.0	5.5	3.0	0	−1.5	1.5
468 1860–69	0	0	0	12.0	8.0	3.0	0	−1.5	1.5
469 1870–79	0	0	0	13.5	10.0	3.0	0	−1.5	1.5
470 1880–89	0	0	0	16.5	10.0	3.0	0	−1.5	1.5
471 1890–99	13.7	1.4	0.2	19.0	10.0	3.0	0.1	−1.4	1.6
472 1900–09	8.9	2.4	0.2	23.0	18.5	4.0	0.2	−1.4	1.6
473 1910–19	20.4	2.2	0.4	22.5	19.0	5.0	0.2	−1.2	1.6
474 1920–29	22.1	2.3	0.5	21.5	19.5	7.0	0.3	−1.2	1.7
475 1930–39	7.6	0	0	23.5	21.5	10.0	0.5	−1.9	1.9
476 1940–49	23.8	6.7	1.6	24.5	25.0	14.0	0.9	−0.6	2.2
477 1950–59	59.7	15.5	9.3	30.5	27.0	14.0	1.2	6.9	2.4
478 1960–69	22.1	7.2	1.6	38.5	34.0	18.0	2.4	−1.7	3.3
479 1970–79	8.0	0	0	48.0	42.9	19.0	3.8	−4.3	4.3
Canada									
480 1867–69	49.9	12.0	6.0	24.5	40.0	63.0	6.2	−0.1	6.1
481 1870–79	47.8	12.2	5.8	27.4	42.0	63.0	7.3	−1.1	6.9
482 1880–89	47.4	13.2	6.3	31.0	44.0	63.0	8.6	−1.6	7.9
483 1890–99	50.1	16.6	8.3	34.0	46.5	63.0	10.0	−0.6	8.9
484 1900–09	48.1	17.6	8.5	37.5	47.0	64.0	11.3	−1.4	9.9
485 1910–19	45.0	18.5	8.3	43.0	53.0	58.0	13.2	−3.0	11.3
486 1920–29	55.0	32.5	17.9	49.5	56.0	55.0	15.2	5.1	12.8
487 1930–39	55.6	40.6	22.6	54.0	68.0	62.0	22.8	4.1	18.5
488 1940–49	51.5	41.4	21.3	57.0	66.0	65.0	24.5	1.6	19.7
489 1950–59	50.9	41.1	20.9	64.0	70.0	64.0	28.7	−2.0	22.9
490 1960–69	56.3	40.7	22.9	70.0	85.0	64.0	38.1	−7.0	29.9
491 1970–79	57.6	42.3	24.4	75.0	81.5	64.0	39.1	−6.2	30.6
Chile									
492 1850–59	9.3	1.8	0.2	13.0	8.5	1.0	0	−1.3	1.5
493 1860–69	4.8	1.7	0.1	16.5	10.0	1.0	0	−1.4	1.5
494 1870–79	13.4	2.2	0.3	20.5	13.0	1.0	0	−1.2	1.5
495 1880–89	9.4	4.1	0.4	24.0	14.5	1.0	0	−1.1	1.5
496 1890–99	19.9	3.7	0.7	28.5	20.0	1.0	0.1	−0.9	1.6
497 1900–09	28.7	3.9	1.1	32.5	24.0	2.0	0.2	−0.5	1.6
498 1910–19	25.0	4.1	1.0	39.0	28.5	3.0	0.3	−0.7	1.7
499 1920–29	36.1	4.9	1.8	45.5	35.0	4.0	0.6	−0.1	1.9
500 1930–39	37.1	7.4	2.7	47.0	44.0	5.0	1.0	0.5	2.2
501 1940–49	51.4	8.7	4.5	50.5	43.0	6.0	1.3	2.0	2.5
502 1950–59	57.6	14.1	8.1	56.0	46.0	6.0	1.5	5.5	2.6
503 1960–69	53.7	24.5	13.2	61.5	51.0	7.0	2.2	10.1	3.1
504 1970–79	19.0	9.9	1.9	66.5	61.0	17.0	6.9	−4.7	6.6
Colombia									
505 1850–59	33.8	3.3	1.1	6.5	4.0	3.0	0	−0.4	1.5
506 1860–69	15.0	0	0	7.5	4.0	3.0	0	−1.5	1.5
507 1870–79	24.1	0	0	9.0	4.5	3.0	0	−1.5	1.5
508 1880–89	13.3	0	0	10.0	5.0	3.0	0	−1.5	1.5
509 1890–99	15.4	4.0	0.6	11.5	6.5	4.0	0	−0.9	1.5
510 1900–09	9.0	0.5	0	13.0	9.0	5.0	0.1	−1.6	1.6
511 1910–19	32.3	3.9	1.3	14.0	15.5	7.0	0.2	−0.3	1.6
512 1920–29	24.7	7.7	1.9	16.0	23.0	10.0	0.4	0.1	1.8
513 1930–39	22.1	10.2	2.3	17.0	28.0	13.0	0.6	0.4	1.9

State/decade	Com	Par	ID	IOD	IKD	FF	IPR	Res	Pre
514 1940–49	35.8	11.0	3.9	20.0	30.0	15.0	0.9	1.7	2.2
515 1950–59	8.9	7.4	0.7	33.5	33.5	17.0	1.9	−2.2	2.9
516 1960–69	30.6	16.4	5.0	40.0	41.0	20.0	3.3	1.1	3.9
517 1970–79	51.7	19.5	10.1	48.0	46.5	22.0	4.9	5.0	5.1
Costa Rica									
518 1850–59	0	0.2	0	17.5	7.5	25.0	0.3	−1.7	1.7
519 1860–69	6.1	0.1	0	18.5	8.5	25.0	0.4	−1.8	1.8
520 1870–79	0	0.1	0	19.0	9.5	20.0	0.4	−1.8	1.8
521 1880–89	0	0.2	0	19.5	11.0	15.0	0.3	−1.7	1.7
522 1890–99	22.9	0.2	0	19.5	15.0	15.0	0.4	−1.8	1.8
523 1900–09	32.0	0.2	0.1	19.0	21.0	15.0	0.6	−1.8	1.9
524 1910–19	5.1	1.2	0.1	20.0	27.0	15.0	0.8	−2.0	2.1
525 1920–29	40.4	14.2	5.7	23.0	32.5	15.0	1.1	3.4	2.3
526 1930–39	45.4	15.0	6.8	25.0	37.5	15.0	1.4	4.3	2.5
527 1940–49	24.8	15.4	3.8	28.0	40.5	20.0	2.4	0.5	3.3
528 1950–59	43.1	18.2	7.8	34.0	45.5	25.0	3.9	3.4	4.4
529 1960–69	51.6	27.4	14.1	36.0	51.0	27.0	5.0	8.9	5.2
530 1970–79	52.2	35.6	18.6	41.0	59.0	27.0	6.5	12.3	6.3
Cuba									
531 1902–09	4.4	9.5	0.4	38.5	23.5	10.0	0.9	−1.8	2.2
532 1910–19	27.2	16.6	4.5	39.5	30.0	10.0	1.2	2.1	2.4
533 1920–29	35.5	10.2	3.6	37.0	33.5	9.0	1.1	1.3	2.3
534 1930–39	0	3.0	0	41.0	39.5	9.0	1.5	−2.6	2.6
535 1940–49	46.5	31.0	14.4	45.5	43.5	8.0	1.6	11.7	2.7
536 1950–59	18.1	15.4	2.8	46.5	49.5	8.0	1.8	−0.0	2.8
537 1960–69	0	0	0	50.5	54.0	26.0	7.1	−6.8	6.8
538 1970–79	0	0	0	55.5	58.5	20.0	6.4	−6.2	6.2
Dominican Republic									
539 1850–59	2.6	0	0	5.0	2.5	10.0	0	−1.5	1.5
540 1860–69	3.4	0.4	0	6.0	2.5	10.0	0	−1.5	1.5
541 1870–79	4.4	1.4	0.1	7.0	2.5	10.0	0	−1.4	1.5
542 1880–89	17.7	10.0	1.8	8.5	3.0	10.0	0	0.3	1.5
543 1890–99	9.4	0.1	0	13.5	4.0	10.0	0.1	−1.6	1.6
544 1900–09	2.2	0.1	0	14.5	5.5	10.0	0.1	−1.6	1.6
545 1910–19	9.7	0	0	15.5	7.5	10.0	0.1	−1.6	1.6
546 1920–29	12.1	0	0	18.0	9.5	13.0	0.2	−1.6	1.6
647 1930–39	0.3	18.3	0.1	19.0	13.0	16.0	0.4	−1.7	1.8
548 1940–49	2.1	33.1	0.7	21.0	17.0	19.0	0.7	−1.3	2.0
549 1950–59	1.4	45.1	0.6	22.5	23.5	20.0	1.1	−1.7	2.3
550 1960–69	21.4	27.4	5.9	26.0	37.5	24.0	2.3	2.7	3.2
551 1970–79	31.2	26.3	8.2	33.0	38.0	26.0	3.3	4.3	3.9
Ecuador									
552 1850–59	0	0	0	8.0	3.5	10.0	0	−1.5	1.5
553 1860–69	14.0	1.2	0.2	9.0	3.5	10.0	0	−1.3	1.5
554 1870–79	1.3	0.5	0	10.0	3.5	10.0	0	−1.5	1.5
555 1880–89	16.0	1.0	0.2	12.0	4.5	10.0	0.1	−1.4	1.6
556 1890–99	25.7	2.5	0.6	14.0	5.5	10.0	0.1	−1.0	1.6
557 1900–09	9.9	4.0	0.4	15.5	8.0	10.0	0.1	−1.2	1.6
558 1910–19	9.0	4.5	0.4	18.5	11.0	10.0	0.2	−1.2	1.7
559 1920–29	5.0	3.2	0.2	21.5	15.0	14.0	0.5	−1.7	1.9

State/decade	Com	Par	ID	IOD	IKD	FF	IPR	Res	Pre
560 1930–39	1.9	0.5	0	23.5	20.0	16.0	0.8	−2.1	2.1
561 1940–49	32.3	3.0	1.0	27.0	24.5	20.0	1.3	−1.5	2.5
562 1950–59	63.0	12.4	7.8	32.5	32.5	23.0	2.4	4.5	3.3
563 1960–69	28.8	8.3	2.4	34.0	40.0	25.0	3.4	−1.6	4.0
564 1970–79	16.6	4.8	0.8	39.0	47.0	29.0	5.3	−4.6	5.4
El Salvador									
565 1850–59	0	0	0	5.0	2.5	15.0	0	−1.5	1.5
566 1860–69	1.5	0.9	0	6.0	3.5	15.0	0	−1.5	1.5
567 1870–79	0	0	0	7.0	3.5	15.0	0	−1.5	1.5
568 1880–89	6.0	0.9	0.1	9.5	5.0	15.0	0.1	−1.5	1.6
569 1890–99	0	1.8	0	10.5	6.0	15.0	0.1	−1.6	1.6
570 1900–09	0	2.1	0	13.0	8.0	15.0	0.2	−1.6	1.6
571 1910–19	0	3.4	0	16.0	9.5	18.0	0.3	−1.7	1.7
572 1920–29	0	5.0	0	17.5	11.5	22.0	0.4	−1.8	1.8
573 1930–39	0	4.0	0	20.0	15.5	26.0	0.8	−2.1	2.1
574 1940–49	0.1	5.4	0	22.5	18.0	30.0	1.2	−2.4	2.4
575 1950–59	11.4	34.0	3.9	25.0	20.5	34.0	1.7	1.2	2.7
576 1960–69	16.4	11.1	1.8	28.0	27.5	34.0	2.6	−1.6	3.4
577 1970–79	48.3	16.8	8.1	35.0	33.0	34.0	3.9	3.7	4.4
Guatemala									
578 1850–59	0	0	0	7.5	3.0	10.0	0	−1.5	1.5
579 1860–69	4.0	0	0	8.5	3.0	10.0	0	−1.5	1.5
580 1870–79	7.0	0	0	10.0	3.0	10.0	0	−1.5	1.5
581 1880–89	0	1.5	0	11.0	4.0	10.0	0	−1.5	1.5
582 1890–99	24.0	2.4	0.6	13.5	6.0	10.0	0.1	−1.0	1.6
583 1900–09	0	2.4	0	14.5	6.0	10.0	0.1	−1.6	1.6
584 1910–19	0	4.0	0	15.5	6.5	10.0	0.1	−1.6	1.6
585 1920–29	5.0	13.0	0.6	16.5	7.5	12.0	0.1	−1.0	1.6
586 1930–39	0	25.1	0	18.0	10.0	15.0	0.3	−1.7	1.7
587 1940–49	7.7	10.7	0.8	19.5	18.0	17.0	0.6	−1.1	1.9
588 1950–59	27.0	8.7	2.3	21.5	16.5	20.0	0.7	0.3	2.0
589 1960–69	42.6	8.8	3.7	24.5	23.0	29.0	1.6	1.0	2.7
590 1970–79	59.4	11.3	6.7	28.5	29.0	29.0	2.4	3.4	3.3
Guyana									
591 1966–69	49.2	40.2	19.8	38.0	44.0	15.0	2.5	16.5	3.3
592 1970–79	34.2	44.8	15.3	48.4	46.5	25.0	5.6	9.6	5.7
Haiti									
593 1850–59	0	0	0	6.5	2.5	20.0	0	−1.5	1.5
594 1860–69	0	0	0	6.5	2.5	20.0	0	−1.5	1.5
595 1870–79	0	1.0	0	6.5	2.5	20.0	0	−1.5	1.5
596 1880–89	0	1.6	0	6.5	3.0	20.0	0	−1.5	1.5
597 1890–99	0	0.8	0	8.5	3.0	20.0	0.1	−1.6	1.6
598 1900–09	0	0.4	0	9.0	4.5	20.0	0.1	−1.6	1.6
599 1910–19	0	0	0	9.0	4.5	20.0	0.1	−1.6	1.6
600 1920–29	0	0	0	8.5	5.5	22.0	0.1	−1.6	1.6
601 1930–39	5.0	1.5	0.1	9.0	5.5	24.0	0.1	−1.5	1.6
602 1940–49	1.6	2.7	0	9.0	6.0	28.0	0.2	−1.6	1.6
603 1950–59	9.2	10.3	0.9	10.5	6.0	32.0	0.2	−0.7	1.6
604 1960–69	2.8	3.3	0.1	12.0	11.0	36.0	0.5	−1.8	1.9
605 1970–79	0	0	0	17.5	14.0	44.0	1.1	−2.3	2.3

State/decade	Com	Par	ID	IOD	IKD	FF	IPR	Res	Pre
Honduras									
606 1850–59	22.0	4.8	1.1	5.0	5.0	10.0	0	−0.4	1.5
607 1860–69	10.5	6.1	0.6	5.0	6.0	10.0	0	−0.9	1.5
608 1870–79	6.8	3.0	0.2	5.0	6.0	10.0	0	−1.3	1.5
609 1880–89	12.8	12.3	1.6	5.5	8.5	10.0	0	0.1	1.5
610 1890–99	12.0	11.4	1.4	6.5	9.5	10.0	0.1	−0.2	1.6
611 1900–09	13.7	4.6	0.6	10.5	11.0	10.0	0.1	−1.0	1.6
612 1910–19	7.9	10.5	0.8	10.5	14.0	10.0	0.1	−0.8	1.6
613 1920–29	19.8	14.8	2.9	10.5	16.0	13.0	0.2	1.3	1.6
614 1930–39	25.9	9.1	2.4	10.5	17.5	17.0	0.3	0.7	1.7
615 1940–49	0	3.8	0	11.0	18.5	20.0	0.4	−1.8	1.8
616 1950–59	10.2	7.5	0.8	12.5	19.0	25.0	0.6	−1.1	1.9
617 1960–69	10.2	0	0	20.5	26.5	30.0	1.6	−2.7	2.7
618 1970–79	5.0	7.7	0.4	25.5	32.0	30.0	2.4	−2.9	3.3
Jamaica									
619 1961–69	50.0	30.7	15.3	43.0	42.5	32.0	5.8	9.5	5.8
620 1970–79	44.5	29.2	13.0	52.5	46.5	35.0	8.5	5.2	7.8
Mexico									
621 1850–59	15.5	0	0	11.5	6.0	2.0	0	−1.5	1.5
622 1860–69	21.2	0.1	0	11.5	7.5	2.0	0	−1.5	1.5
623 1870–79	12.0	0.1	0	14.0	7.5	2.0	0	−1.5	1.5
624 1880–89	5.8	0.1	0	15.5	10.0	2.0	0	−1.5	1.5
625 1890–99	1.0	0	0	17.0	13.5	1.0	0	−1.5	1.5
626 1900–09	1.0	0	0	19.5	16.5	1.0	0	−1.5	1.5
627 1910–19	0.8	1.2	0	23.5	17.0	1.0	0	−1.5	1.5
628 1920–29	8.7	10.0	0.9	25.0	19.5	5.0	0.2	−0.7	1.6
629 1930–39	3.7	12.7	0.5	24.0	22.5	12.0	0.6	−1.4	1.9
630 1940–49	12.4	11.9	1.5	26.5	26.0	25.0	1.7	−1.2	2.7
631 1950–59	21.8	14.3	3.1	33.0	34.0	29.0	3.3	−0.8	3.9
632 1960–69	10.6	22.6	2.4	37.0	38.0	33.0	4.6	−2.5	4.9
633 1970–79	11.5	29.2	3.4	44.0	48.0	42.0	8.9	−4.7	8.1
Nicaragua									
634 1850–59	18.0	0.1	0	5.0	3.0	10.0	0	−1.5	1.5
635 1860–69	7.0	0.2	0	6.0	3.0	10.0	0	−1.5	1.5
636 1870–79	10.0	0.2	0	7.0	4.0	10.0	0	−1.5	1.5
637 1880–89	13.0	0.2	0	10.0	5.5	10.0	0.1	−1.6	1.6
638 1890–99	6.0	0.1	0	12.0	6.5	10.0	0.1	−1.6	1.6
639 1900–09	0	0	0	13.5	8.0	10.0	0.1	−1.6	1.6
640 1910–19	0	2.2	0	15.5	11.0	10.0	0.2	−1.6	1.6
641 1920–29	22.5	12.3	2.8	17.5	14.0	12.0	0.3	1.1	1.7
642 1930–39	25.1	17.4	4.4	21.5	17.5	14.0	0.5	2.5	1.9
643 1940–49	0	0	0	24.5	20.0	16.0	0.8	−2.1	2.1
644 1950–59	9.2	18.4	1.7	23.5	22.0	19.0	1.0	−0.5	2.2
645 1960–69	15.1	29.1	4.4	30.5	29.0	17.0	1.5	1.8	2.6
646 1970–79	10.1	25.3	2.6	40.0	33.0	17.0	2.2	−0.5	3.1
Panama									
647 1903–09	8.6	1.7	0.1	13.5	9.5	15.0	0.2	−1.5	1.6
648 1910–19	20.0	3.6	0.7	19.0	14.0	15.0	0.4	−1.1	1.8
649 1920–29	8.0	6.0	0.5	26.0	19.5	15.0	0.8	−1.6	2.1
650 1930–39	24.0	10.5	2.5	30.0	27.5	15.0	1.2	0.1	2.4

State/decade	Com	Par	ID	IOD	IKD	FF	IPR	Res	Pre
651 1940–49	22.3	5.2	1.2	36.0	37.5	17.0	2.3	−2.0	3.2
652 1950–59	37.5	24.8	9.3	33.5	41.0	21.0	2.8	5.7	3.6
653 1960–69	47.1	20.0	9.4	41.0	49.5	17.0	3.5	5.3	4.1
654 1970–79	0	0	0	47.5	54.0	19.0	4.9	−5.1	5.1
Paraguay									
655 1850–59	0	0	0	5.0	2.5	4.0	0	−1.5	1.5
656 1860–69	0	0	0	6.0	5.0	4.0	0	−1.5	1.5
657 1870–79	0	1.8	0	7.0	5.0	4.0	0	−1.5	1.5
658 1880–89	0	2.4	0	10.5	7.5	4.0	0	−1.5	1.5
659 1890–99	0	2.7	0	13.5	10.0	4.0	0.1	−1.6	1.6
660 1900–09	0	2.2	0	17.0	16.0	4.0	0.1	−1.6	1.6
661 1910–19	0	4.5	0	21.5	21.0	4.0	0.2	−1.6	1.6
662 1920–29	4.0	5.8	0.2	24.0	27.0	4.0	0.3	−1.5	1.7
663 1930–39	4.0	6.0	0.2	24.0	33.0	5.0	0.4	−1.6	1.8
664 1940–49	0	6.5	0	28.0	33.5	5.0	0.5	−1.9	1.9
665 1950–59	4.6	21.2	1.0	32.0	38.5	6.0	0.8	−1.1	2.1
666 1960–69	19.1	29.1	5.6	33.5	43.5	7.0	1.0	3.4	2.2
667 1970–79	23.0	31.5	7.2	37.5	49.0	7.0	1.3	4.7	2.5
Peru									
668 1850–59	21.5	4.9	1.1	10.5	4.0	2.0	0	−0.4	1.5
669 1860–69	15.9	4.8	0.8	10.5	6.0	2.0	0	−0.7	1.5
670 1870–79	18.9	0.1	0	11.0	8.0	2.0	0	−1.5	1.5
671 1880–89	0	0	0	11.5	10.5	2.0	0	−1.5	1.5
672 1890–99	5.9	0.3	0	12.0	11.5	2.0	0	−1.5	1.5
673 1900–09	1.9	2.5	0	13.0	11.5	2.0	0	−1.5	1.5
674 1910–19	11.2	2.7	0.3	14.5	11.5	2.0	0	−1.2	1.5
675 1920–29	15.1	3.8	0.6	16.0	12.5	2.0	0	−0.9	1.5
676 1930–39	15.3	1.6	0.2	20.5	17.5	3.0	0.1	−1.4	1.6
677 1940–49	21.2	4.3	0.9	25.0	23.5	5.0	0.3	−0.8	1.7
678 1950–59	22.7	10.0	2.3	29.5	26.0	7.0	0.5	0.4	1.9
679 1960–69	43.3	11.8	5.1	37.0	39.5	8.0	1.2	2.7	2.4
680 1970–79	0	0	0	44.5	51.0	13.0	3.0	−3.7	3.7
Trinidad and Tobago									
681 1961–69	45.2	35.0	15.8	48.0	45.5	31.0	6.8	9.3	6.5
682 1970–79	31.5	20.9	6.6	56.5	49.5	31.0	8.7	−1.4	8.0
United States									
683 1850–59	52.1	13.4	7.0	24.0	43.5	60.0	6.1	1.0	6.0
684 1860–69	51.1	13.7	7.0	28.0	43.5	60.0	7.3	0.1	6.9
685 1870–79	48.1	15.1	7.3	34.0	46.5	60.0	9.5	−1.3	8.6
686 1880–89	51.7	18.4	9.5	35.0	53.0	60.0	11.1	−0.2	9.7
687 1890–99	51.5	19.0	10.0	41.0	56.0	60.0	13.8	−1.8	11.8
688 1900–09	46.3	17.2	8.0	45.5	60.0	60.0	16.4	−5.7	13.7
689 1910–19	53.1	17.0	9.0	51.0	65.0	60.0	19.9	−7.3	16.3
690 1920–29	42.6	26.4	11.2	57.5	66.0	60.0	22.8	−7.3	18.5
691 1930–39	41.2	33.2	13.7	62.5	75.5	61.0	28.8	−9.2	22.9
692 1940–49	46.9	35.4	16.6	65.5	92.5	65.0	39.4	−14.2	30.8
693 1950–59	45.2	37.0	16.7	69.5	98.0	72.0	49.0	−21.3	38.0
694 1960–69	47.0	37.3	17.5	75.5	98.5	72.0	53.5	−23.8	41.3
695 1970–79	47.0	37.4	17.6	78.0	99.0	72.0	55.6	−25.3	42.9

State/decade	Com	Par	ID	IOD	IKD	FF	IPR	Res	Pre
Uruguay									
696 1850–59	11.7	1.3	0.2	16.5	7.5	8.0	0.1	−1.4	1.6
697 1860–69	3.2	1.5	0	22.0	10.0	8.0	0.2	−1.6	1.7
698 1870–79	8.0	1.3	0.1	29.5	14.5	8.0	0.3	−1.6	1.7
699 1880–89	1.3	4.5	0.1	27.0	28.0	10.0	0.8	−2.0	2.1
700 1890–99	19.1	4.0	0.8	33.0	30.0	10.0	1.0	−1.4	2.2
701 1900–09	29.3	4.3	1.3	35.5	34.0	10.0	1.2	−1.1	2.4
702 1910–19	33.7	7.9	2.7	38.0	35.5	13.0	1.8	−0.1	2.8
703 1920–29	51.6	15.6	8.0	41.5	41.0	15.0	2.6	4.6	3.4
704 1930–39	41.6	13.2	5.5	48.0	43.0	17.0	3.5	1.4	4.1
705 1940–49	46.9	25.7	12.1	51.5	44.0	19.0	4.3	7.4	4.7
706 1950–59	48.9	38.3	18.7	58.5	57.5	21.0	7.1	11.9	6.8
707 1960–69	51.5	41.7	21.5	67.5	72.0	21.0	10.2	12.4	9.1
708 1970–79	16.8	15.2	2.6	76.5	77.0	24.0	14.1	−9.4	12.0
Venezuela									
709 1850–59	18.9	0	0	11.0	5.0	2.0	0	−1.5	1.5
710 1860–69	3.3	1.3	0	12.0	5.0	2.0	0	−1.5	1.5
711 1870–79	5.7	6.6	0.4	13.5	6.0	2.0	0	−1.1	1.5
712 1880–89	0	0	0	14.5	8.5	2.0	0	−1.5	1.5
713 1890–99	0.2	9.6	0	15.5	10.5	2.0	0	−1.5	1.5
714 1900–09	0	0	0	17.0	11.0	2.0	0	−1.5	1.5
715 1910–19	0	0	0	18.0	11.0	2.0	0	−1.5	1.5
716 1920–29	0	0	0	22.0	13.5	2.0	0.1	−1.6	1.6
717 1930–39	0	0	0	29.5	18.5	2.0	0.1	−1.6	1.6
718 1940–49	6.2	2.7	0.2	38.5	22.0	3.0	0.3	−1.5	1.7
719 1950–59	10.6	8.0	0.8	44.0	28.5	4.0	0.5	−1.1	1.9
720 1960–69	64.5	38.9	25.1	56.5	38.0	5.0	1.1	22.8	2.3
721 1970–79	57.3	38.8	22.2	65.0	52.5	17.0	5.8	16.4	5.8
African countries									
Algeria									
722 1962–69	0	18.4	0	28.5	12.0	42.0	1.4	−2.5	2.5
723 1970–79	0.2	16.9	0	36.0	16.5	42.0	2.5	−3.3	3.3
Benin									
724 1960–69	9.4	14.0	1.3	27.5	6.5	25.0	0.4	−0.5	1.8
725 1970–79	0	0	0	30.0	7.5	25.0	0.6	−1.9	1.9
Botswana									
726 1966–69	22.0	21.6	4.8	5.5	11.5	40.0	0.3	3.1	1.7
727 1970–79	26.5	11.6	3.1	8.5	16.5	40.0	0.6	1.2	1.9
Burundi									
728 1962–69	7.1	9.8	0.7	6.0	4.0	20.0	0	−0.8	1.5
729 1970–79	0	0	0	8.0	7.0	20.0	0.1	−1.6	1.6
Cameroon									
730 1960–69	16.2	32.4	5.2	9.5	4.0	20.0	0.1	3.6	1.6
731 1970–79	0	53.5	0	15.0	10.0	20.0	0.3	−1.7	1.7
Central African Republic									
732 1960–69	0.6	15.5	0.1	8.0	5.0	25.0	0.1	−1.5	1.6
733 1970–79	0	0	0	13.0	7.5	25.0	0.2	−1.6	1.6
Chad									
734 1960–69	6.8	24.8	1.7	5.5	2.5	20.0	0	0.2	1.5
735 1970–79	0	22.2	0	8.0	5.0	20.0	0.1	−1.6	1.6

State/decade	Com	Par	ID	IOD	IKD	FF	IPR	Res	Pre
Congo									
736 1960–69	7.5	30.1	2.3	34.5	7.0	20.0	0.5	0.4	1.9
737 1970–79	6.4	13.3	0.9	45.0	12.5	20.0	1.1	−1.4	2.3
Egypt									
738 1922–29	12.0	1.5	0.2	24.5	5.0	30.0	0.4	−1.6	1.8
739 1930–39	5.4	1.0	0.1	30.5	8.0	30.0	0.7	−1.9	2.0
740 1940–49	17.3	2.5	0.4	26.5	9.5	33.0	0.8	−1.7	2.1
741 1950–59	2.9	9.6	0.3	33.5	13.5	29.0	1.3	−2.2	2.5
742 1960–69	0	24.1	0	39.0	21.0	36.0	2.9	−3.6	3.6
743 1970–79	6.1	22.6	1.4	41.5	37.0	45.0	6.9	−5.2	6.6
Ethiopia									
744 1910–19	0	0	0	3.0	0.5	15.0	0	−1.5	1.5
745 1920–29	0	0	0	3.5	0.5	15.0	0	−1.5	1.5
746 1930–39	0	0	0	4.5	0.5	15.0	0	−1.5	1.5
747 1940–49	0	0	0	5.5	1.0	15.0	0	−1.5	1.5
748 1950–59	0	1.9	0	6.5	1.5	17.0	0	−1.5	1.5
749 1960–69	0	6.9	0	8.0	2.0	20.0	0	−1.5	1.5
750 1970–79	0	3.1	0	10.0	3.5	20.0	0.1	−1.6	1.6
Ghana									
751 1957–59	42.9	11.6	5.0	18.0	11.0	35.0	0.7	3.0	2.0
752 1960–69	10.7	11.7	1.3	25.0	13.5	35.0	1.2	−1.1	2.4
753 1970–79	12.1	5.0	0.6	32.5	17.0	35.0	1.9	−2.3	2.9
Guinea									
754 1958–59	0	0	0	5.0	4.5	15.0	0	−1.5	1.5
755 1960–69	0	45.4	0	8.5	4.5	15.0	0.1	−1.6	1.6
756 1970–79	0	55.1	0	13.0	5.5	15.0	0.1	−1.6	1.6
Ivory Coast									
757 1960–69	0	49.3	0	10.5	3.5	25.0	0.1	−1.6	1.6
758 1970–79	0.1	47.5	0	19.5	10.5	25.0	0.5	−1.9	1.9
Kenya									
759 1963–69	5.9	11.7	0.7	10.0	12.5	30.0	0.4	−1.1	1.8
760 1970–79	0	9.2	0	14.0	17.5	30.0	0.7	−2.0	2.0
Lesotho									
761 1965–69	58.4	40.0	23.4	4.5	22.5	33.0	0.3	21.7	1.7
762 1970–79	0	0	0	6.5	31.0	33.0	0.7	−2.0	2.0
Liberia									
763 1910–19	0	1.0	0	5.0	1.0	5.0	0	−1.5	1.5
764 1920–29	0	1.6	0	5.0	1.0	5.0	0	−1.5	1.5
765 1930–39	0	2.0	0	6.0	3.0	5.0	0	−1.5	1.5
766 1940–49	0	2.0	0	6.0	4.0	10.0	0	−1.5	1.5
767 1950–59	0	24.2	0	8.5	4.5	15.0	0.1	−1.6	1.6
768 1960–69	0	53.0	0	13.0	7.0	20.0	0.2	−1.6	1.6
769 1970–79	0	51.7	0	19.0	8.5	20.0	0.3	−1.7	1.7
Libya									
770 1951–59	7.1	11.6	0.8	29.5	6.5	32.0	0.6	−1.1	1.9
771 1960–69	0	11.7	0	32.0	11.0	32.0	1.1	−2.3	2.3
772 1970–79	0	0	0	48.0	27.5	32.0	4.2	−4.6	4.6

State/decade	Com	Par	ID	IOD	IKD	FF	IPR	Res	Pre
Madagascar									
773 1960–69	12.0	28.8	3.5	7.5	18.5	57.0	0.8	1.4	2.1
774 1970–79	3.6	29.8	1.1	11.0	26.0	57.0	1.6	−1.6	2.7
Malawi									
775 1964–69	0	0	0	5.0	5.0	20.0	0.1	−1.6	1.6
776 1970–79	0	0	0	9.5	11.0	20.0	0.2	−1.6	1.6
Mali									
777 1960–69	0	10.8	0	5.0	1.0	31.0	0	−1.5	1.5
778 1970–79	0	5.1	0	7.5	3.0	31.0	0.1	−1.6	1.6
Mauritania									
779 1960–69	3.1	41.4	1.3	5.0	1.0	25.0	0	−0.2	1.5
780 1970–79	0.1	34.2	0	10.0	5.5	25.0	0.1	−1.6	1.6
Morocco									
781 1956–59	0	0	0	25.5	7.0	50.0	0.9	−2.2	2.2
782 1960–69	6.5	2.6	0.2	30.0	7.5	53.0	1.2	−2.2	2.4
783 1970–79	11.7	6.7	0.8	34.5	12.5	53.0	2.3	−2.4	3.2
Niger									
784 1960–69	0	24.2	0	4.0	0.5	28.0	0	−1.5	1.5
785 1970–79	0	19.0	0	7.0	1.0	28.0	0	−1.5	1.5
Nigeria									
786 1960–69	40.1	9.8	3.9	20.0	8.5	35.0	0.6	2.0	1.9
787 1970–79	6.6	2.3	0.2	26.5	13.0	35.0	1.2	−2.2	2.4
Rwanda									
788 1962–69	1.0	26.1	0.3	3.0	5.0	20.0	0	−1.2	1.5
789 1970–79	0.2	18.4	0	5.0	8.0	20.0	0.1	−1.6	1.6
Senegal									
790 1960–69	5.3	32.0	1.7	17.5	3.5	22.0	0.1	0.1	1.6
791 1970–79	3.6	29.1	1.0	24.0	7.0	22.0	0.4	−0.8	1.8
Sierra Leone									
792 1961–69	54.7	22.9	12.5	14.0	4.0	25.0	0.1	10.9	1.6
793 1970–79	21.3	15.0	3.2	18.0	6.0	25.0	0.3	1.5	1.7
Somalia									
794 1960–69	35.7	29.4	10.5	9.5	2.5	20.0	0	9.0	1.5
795 1970–79	0	0	0	14.5	2.5	20.0	0.1	−1.6	1.6
South Africa									
796 1910–19	56.9	4.1	2.3	25.0	15.5	1.0	0	0.8	1.5
797 1920–29	53.3	4.2	2.2	24.0	17.5	1.0	0	0.7	1.5
798 1930–39	58.8	4.7	2.8	33.0	19.5	1.0	0.1	1.2	1.6
799 1940–49	49.6	8.5	4.2	38.5	25.0	2.0	0.2	2.6	1.6
800 1950–59	49.7	8.8	4.4	49.0	27.0	3.0	0.4	2.6	1.8
801 1960–69	47.7	6.0	2.9	52.0	39.5	2.0	0.4	1.1	1.8
802 1970–79	44.5	5.6	2.5	53.0	50.5	2.0	0.5	0.6	1.9
Sudan									
803 1956–59	24.5	4.0	1.0	9.0	2.0	30.0	0.1	−0.6	1.6
804 1960–69	21.8	4.8	1.0	10.0	3.0	30.0	0.1	−0.6	1.6
805 1970–79	1.1	21.7	0.2	14.5	9.0	30.0	0.4	−1.6	1.8
Tanzania									
806 1961–69	2.7	16.3	0.4	8.0	5.0	15.0	0.1	−1.2	1.6
807 1970–79	5.8	28.8	1.7	10.0	14.0	15.0	0.2	0.1	1.6

State/decade	Com	Par	ID	IOD	IKD	FF	IPR	Res	Pre
Togo									
808 1960–69	4.6	21.6	1.0	13.0	5.0	20.0	0.1	−0.6	1.6
809 1970–79	0	5.2	0	19.0	6.0	20.0	0.2	−1.6	1.6
Tunisia									
810 1956–59	1.0	18.5	0.2	31.0	8.0	45.0	1.1	−2.1	2.3
811 1960–69	0.2	27.7	0.1	40.5	12.5	51.0	2.6	−3.3	3.4
812 1970–79	0.1	27.5	0	48.5	19.5	51.0	4.8	−5.1	5.1
Uganda									
813 1962–69	23.9	7.4	1.8	7.0	12.5	25.0	0.2	0.2	1.6
814 1970–79	0	0	0	9.5	15.5	25.0	0.4	−1.8	1.8
Upper Volta									
815 1960–69	0	4.4	0	6.0	4.0	25.0	0.1	−1.6	1.6
816 1970–79	15.7	7.0	1.1	7.5	4.5	25.0	0.1	−0.5	1.6
Zaire									
817 1960–69	23.9	4.9	1.2	12.0	8.0	20.0	0.2	−0.4	1.6
818 1970–79	0.5	44.9	0.2	18.5	16.0	20.0	0.6	−1.7	1.9
Zambia									
819 1964–69	6.1	11.0	0.7	19.0	20.5	22.0	0.9	−1.5	2.2
820 1970–79	17.3	21.2	3.7	28.0	23.5	22.0	1.4	1.2	2.5
147 countries in 1980 (Vanhanen 1990a)						*DER*			
821 Afghanistan	0	0	0	18.5	11.0	45.6	0.9	−2.2	2.2
822 Albania	0	56.0	0	38.5	40.5	0	0	−1.5	1.5
823 Algeria	0.7	41.4	0.3	47.0	26.5	30.0	3.7	−3.9	4.2
824 Angola	0	0	0	31.5	15.5	29.1	1.4	−2.5	2.5
825 Argentina	0	0	0	84.5	65.0	32.3	17.7	−14.7	14.7
826 Australia	54.9	56.5	31.0	91.5	71.5	68.9	45.1	−4.1	35.1
827 Austria	49.0	63.7	31.2	72.5	67.5	69.3	33.9	4.5	26.7
828 Bahamas	45.0	31.9	14.4	73.5	52.0	40.7	15.6	1.3	13.1
829 Bahrain	0	0	0	87.5	45.0	10.7	4.2	−4.6	4.6
830 Bangladesh	22.3	24.0	5.4	13.5	17.5	59.5	1.4	2.9	2.5
831 Barbados	47.8	40.4	19.3	63.0	64.5	35.8	14.5	7.0	12.3
832 Belgium	63.8	56.2	35.9	84.5	70.5	70.3	41.9	3.2	32.7
833 Benin	0	0	0	34.0	15.5	29.3	1.5	−2.6	2.6
834 Bhután	0	0	0	5.5	11.5	67.9	0.4	−1.8	1.8
835 Bolivia	0	0	0	41.5	48.5	30.5	6.1	−6.0	6.0
836 Botswana	24.6	16.8	4.1	18.0	31.0	45.6	2.5	0.8	3.3
837 Brazil	44.8	8.4	3.8	65.0	49.5	26.2	8.4	−3.9	7.7
838 Bulgaria	0	72.8	0	65.5	59.0	0	0	−1.5	1.5
839 Burkina Faso	0	0	0	14.5	6.0	50.5	0.4	−1.8	1.8
840 Burma	0	43.5	0	37.5	35.0	36.6	4.8	5.1	5.1
841 Burundi	0	0	0	9.5	14.0	51.5	0.7	−2.0	2.0
842 Cameroon	0	39.0	0	27.0	25.5	36.7	2.5	−3.3	3.3
843 Canada	55.9	45.8	25.6	87.5	86.5	59.5	45.0	−9.4	35.0
844 Cape Verde	7.6	32.2	2.4	32.0	23.0	37.4	2.8	−1.2	3.6
845 Central Af. Rep.	0	0	0	27.0	17.5	53.5	2.5	−3.3	3.3
846 Chad	0	0	0	8.5	24.0	52.0	1.1	−2.3	2.3
847 Chile	0	0	0	81.0	59.0	36.4	17.4	−14.4	14.4
848 China	0	0	0	26.5	33.5	1.4	0.1	−1.6	1.6
849 Colombia	50.3	19.6	9.9	71.5	53.0	28.6	10.8	0.4	9.5

State/decade	Com	Par	ID	IOD	IKD	DER	IPR	Res	Pre
850 Comoros	0	54.7	0	23.5	30.0	20.9	1.5	−2.6	2.6
851 Congo	0	0	0	55.5	30.0	33.6	5.6	−5.7	5.7
852 Costa Rica	51.2	40.7	20.8	54.0	70.5	43.7	16.6	7.0	13.8
853 Cuba	0	0.1	0	71.0	63.5	4.2	1.9	−2.9	2.9
854 Cyprus	30.0	37.5	11.2	54.0	47.5	71.7	18.4	−4.0	15.2
855 Czechoslovakia	0	71.1	0	76.5	62.5	0.5	0.2	−1.6	1.6
856 Denmark	61.7	61.9	38.2	88.5	70.0	71.0	44.0	3.9	34.3
857 Djibouti	0	30.0	0	50.0	10.0	40.0	2.0	−3.0	3.0
858 Dominican Rep.	51.4	30.1	15.5	47.5	45.5	31.8	6.9	8.9	6.6
859 Ecuador	31.5	19.0	6.0	50.0	72.5	32.2	11.7	−4.2	10.2
860 Egypt	0.1	24.0	0	47.5	38.0	30.0	5.4	−5.5	5.5
861 El Salvador	0	0	0	45.5	37.5	27.5	4.7	−5.0	5.0
862 Eq. Guinea	0	0	0	38.0	18.5	23.7	1.7	−2.7	2.7
863 Ethiopia	0	0	0	17.5	15.5	12.4	0.3	−1.7	1.7
864 Fiji	47.7	30.0	14.3	51.0	44.0	35.2	7.9	6.9	7.4
865 Finland	46.8	56.2	26.3	74.5	76.0	73.2	41.4	−6.0	32.3
866 France	63.3	51.3	32.5	84.5	69.5	71.2	41.8	−0.1	32.6
867 Gabon	0.2	54.1	0.1	30.0	27.5	44.3	3.7	−4.1	4.2
868 Gambia	30.4	32.0	9.7	20.0	10.5	45.0	0.9	7.5	2.2
869 German D.R.	0.1	67.9	0.1	83.5	73.5	2.3	1.4	−2.4	2.5
870 Germany, F.R.	57.1	61.6	35.2	90.5	69.5	70.4	44.3	0.7	34.5
871 Ghana	48.0	16.1	7.7	42.5	24.0	48.9	5.0	2.5	5.2
872 Greece	58.2	55.3	32.2	62.5	58.5	59.2	21.6	14.6	17.6
873 Guatemala	57.7	9.7	5.6	42.0	32.5	28.2	3.8	1.3	4.3
874 Guinea	0	56.4	0	19.5	16.0	42.6	1.3	−2.5	2.5
875 Guinea-Bissau	0	0	0	21.5	10.0	44.4	1.0	−2.2	2.2
876 Guyana	26.3	46.6	12.3	58.0	50.0	17.4	5.0	7.1	5.2
877 Haiti	0	0	0	30.5	16.0	48.1	2.3	−3.2	3.2
878 Honduras	0	0	0	36.5	37.0	36.3	4.9	−5.1	5.1
879 Hungary	0	70.2	0	69.0	59.0	1.2	0.5	−1.9	1.9
880 Iceland	64.4	54.4	35.0	88.0	73.0	79.3	50.9	−4.4	39.4
881 India	57.3	29.6	17.0	29.5	26.0	58.2	4.5	12.2	4.8
882 Indonesia	9.5	11.7	1.1	30.5	37.0	37.7	4.3	−3.6	4.7
883 Iran	22.1	36.0	8.0	55.5	25.0	41.6	5.8	2.2	5.8
884 Iraq	0	0	0	66.0	31.5	26.0	5.4	−5.5	5.5
885 Ireland	49.4	49.0	24.2	65.8	65.0	73.4	32.7	−1.6	25.8
886 Israel	66.6	48.4	32.2	91.0	72.5	58.6	38.7	1.9	30.3
887 Italy	61.7	65.0	40.1	79.0	68.0	68.3	36.7	11.3	28.8
888 Ivory Coast	0	34.2	0	30.5	20.0	48.4	3.0	−3.7	3.7
889 Jamaica	42.4	34.5	14.6	60.0	54.5	31.0	10.1	5.6	9.0
890 Japan	55.4	50.5	28.0	83.5	70.0	62.1	36.3	−0.5	28.5
891 Jordan	0	0	0	65.0	45.0	34.2	10.0	−8.9	8.9
892 Kampuchea	0	0	0	21.0	24.0	7.4	0.4	−1.8	1.8
893 Kenya	0	24.4	0	18.0	24.5	48.1	2.1	−3.1	3.1
894 Korea, North	0	50.0	0	57.0	65.5	0	0	−1.5	1.5
895 Korea, South	17.2	10.0	1.7	58.0	62.5	60.7	22.0	−16.2	17.9
896 Kuwait	0	0.6	0	93.0	44.0	10.1	4.1	−4.5	4.5
897 Laos	0	0	0	20.0	22.5	27.2	1.2	−2.4	2.4
898 Lebanon	54.5	17.4	9.5	83.0	68.0	58.8	33.2	−16.7	26.2
899 Lesotho	0	0	0	14.0	36.5	52.0	2.7	−3.5	3.5
900 Liberia	0	0	0	31.5	17.0	36.1	1.9	−2.9	2.9

State/decade	Com	Par	ID	IOD	IKD	DER	IPR	Res	Pre
901 Libya	0	0	0	68.0	34.5	14.8	3.5	−4.1	4.1
902 Luxembourg	65.5	48.4	31.7	87.5	52.0	69.7	31.7	6.6	25.1
903 Madagascar	5.3	44.2	2.3	18.5	27.5	49.9	2.5	−1.0	3.3
904 Malawi	0	0	0	13.0	18.0	37.7	0.9	−2.2	2.2
905 Malaysia	42.8	26.9	11.5	40.5	38.0	41.0	6.3	5.3	6.2
906 Mali	0	47.8	0	16.5	7.0	53.5	0.1	−1.6	1.6
907 Malta	48.5	62.3	30.2	77.5	44.5	60.7	20.9	13.2	17.0
908 Mauritania	0	0	0	20.0	9.0	51.5	0.9	−2.2	2.2
909 Mauritius	59.9	43.7	26.2	57.5	40.5	41.7	9.7	17.5	8.7
910 Mexico	5.6	30.2	1.7	65.5	54.5	34.0	12.1	−8.8	10.5
911 Mongolia	0	45.9	0	51.0	47.0	0	0	−1.5	1.5
912 Morocco	13.8	6.9	1.0	45.0	20.5	37.1	3.4	−3.0	4.0
913 Mozambique	0	0	0	22.5	13.0	31.1	0.9	−2.2	2.2
914 Nepal	0	0	0	6.0	14.0	58.1	0.5	−1.9	1.9
915 Netherlands	66.2	60.0	39.7	85.5	75.0	70.7	45.3	4.5	35.2
916 New Zealand	59.6	54.8	32.7	88.0	73.5	69.5	45.0	−2.3	35.0
917 Nicaragua	0	0	0	55.0	50.0	17.0	4.7	−5.0	5.0
918 Niger	0	0	0	12.5	5.5	52.9	0.4	−1.8	1.8
919 Nigeria	66.2	21.6	14.3	33.5	19.0	41.2	2.6	10.9	3.4
920 Norway	57.7	56.9	32.8	72.5	69.0	71.6	35.8	4.7	28.1
921 Oman	0	0	0	22.5	10.5	34.8	0.8	−2.1	2.1
922 Pakistan	0	0	0	37.5	15.0	33.7	1.9	−2.9	2.9
923 Panama	10.5	0	0	59.5	64.0	24.9	9.5	−8.6	8.6
924 PNG	64.0	33.0	21.9	18.0	21.5	53.0	2.1	18.9	3.0
925 Paraguay	10.4	33.4	3.5	45.0	51.0	16.1	3.7	−0.7	4.2
926 Peru	54.6	23.3	12.7	65.0	57.5	25.6	9.6	4.1	8.6
927 Philippines	0	0	0	45.0	69.0	42.9	13.3	−11.4	11.4
928 Poland	0.5	69.7	0	63.5	65.5	24.2	10.1	−9.0	9.0
929 Portugal	48.8	58.9	28.7	52.5	51.5	41.0	11.1	19.0	9.7
930 Qatar	0	0	0	79.0	35.5	15.5	4.3	−4.7	4.7
931 Romania	1.5	70.4	1.1	51.5	57.5	4.2	1.2	−1.3	2.4
932 Rwanda	1.0	42.8	0.4	7.0	25.0	60.2	1.1	−1.9	2.3
933 Saudi Arabia	0	0	0	53.5	19.0	29.2	3.0	−3.7	3.7
934 Senegal	18.2	18.1	3.3	25.5	15.0	41.1	1.6	0.6	2.7
935 Sierra Leone	0	0	0	28.5	13.0	49.5	1.8	−2.8	2.8
936 Singapore	22.3	26.3	5.9	99.0	51.0	29.5	14.9	−6.7	12.6
937 Solomon Is.	58.2	25.8	15.0	12.0	28.0	57.3	1.9	12.1	2.9
938 Somalia	0	0	0	25.0	3.5	50.0	0.4	−1.8	1.8
939 South Africa	33.9	3.9	1.3	60.5	30.0	17.1	3.1	−2.5	3.8
940 Spain	65.0	48.2	31.3	78.5	65.0	63.4	32.3	5.8	25.5
941 Sri Lanka	24.2	21.9	5.3	37.0	46.0	57.5	9.8	−3.5	8.8
942 Sudan	0.9	33.6	0.3	24.0	11.5	44.6	1.2	−2.1	2.4
943 Suriname	0	0	0	66.0	39.0	11.1	2.9	−3.6	3.6
944 Swaziland	0	0	0	20.5	34.5	27.5	1.9	−2.9	2.9
945 Sweden	56.8	65.7	37.3	91.0	74.0	65.3	44.0	3.0	34.3
946 Switzerland	75.1	28.8	21.6	76.5	63.0	71.2	34.3	−5.4	27.0
947 Syria	0.4	49.0	0.2	51.0	42.0	29.6	6.3	−6.0	6.2
948 Tanzania	7.0	29.2	2.0	15.5	33.5	38.6	2.0	−1.0	3.0
949 Thailand	36.4	9.7	3.5	19.5	57.0	56.2	6.2	−2.6	6.1
950 Togo	0	52.1	0	26.0	18.0	47.2	2.2	−3.1	3.1
951 Trinidad & T.	47.0	30.5	14.3	52.5	53.0	31.3	8.7	6.3	8.0

State/decade	Com	Par	ID	IOD	IKD	DER	IPR	Res	Pre
952 Tunisia	0	0	0	55.5	28.5	31.5	5.0	−5.2	5.2
953 Turkey	0	0	0	46.5	40.0	50.5	9.4	−8.5	8.5
954 Uganda	52.8	31.9	16.8	14.0	26.5	52.4	1.9	13.9	2.9
955 USSR	0.1	66.4	0.1	73.0	69.5	0	0	−1.4	1.5
956 United A. E.	0	0	0	78.5	31.0	10.2	2.5	−3.3	3.3
957 United Kingdom	56.1	55.9	31.4	94.5	64.5	69.3	42.2	−1.5	32.9
958 United States	49.3	38.0	18.7	87.5	99.5	60.0	52.2	−21.7	40.4
959 Uruguay	0	0	0	86.0	59.5	40.4	20.7	−16.9	16.9
960 Venezuela	53.4	37.6	20.1	82.5	62.5	26.4	13.6	8.5	11.6
961 Vietnam	0	46.5	0	24.0	44.0	5.0	0.5	−1.9	1.9
962 Yemen, North	0	0	0	17.5	5.5	37.0	0.4	−1.8	1.8
963 Yemen, South	0	32.2	0	39.0	22.0	10.0	0.9	−2.2	2.2
964 Yugoslavia	0	59.7	0	52.5	64.0	46.6	15.7	−13.2	13.2
965 Zaire	0	44.5	0	30.0	28.5	41.1	3.5	−4.1	4.1
966 Zambia	20.0	20.0	4.0	38.0	35.5	41.4	5.6	−1.7	5.7
967 Zimbabwe	37.4	37.6	14.1	32.0	35.5	25.9	2.9	10.5	3.6

Part II

Comments

6 Tatu Vanhanen thesis and the prospects of democracy in Latin America

Mitchell A. Seligson

No serious student of democracy has been able to conduct work on the empirical theory of democracy since Tatu Vanhanen first began publishing his compilations of data without making reference to that work. The material contained in this collection of monographs, books and papers provides the raw data upon which so many of us rely for our work. Moreover, the collection of historical material, taking us back to the middle of the last century in a number of cases, is a unique resource, found nowhere else.

In the material covered in this book, Vanhanen has attempted to make sense of his own data, proposing a refinement of both theory and method that takes us beyond his previous works and updates the series to provide us with data for the 1990s. Those of us who have been asked to write region-specific chapters to accompany the Vanhanen world-wide analysis have a dual task. We must determine the extent to which the overall theory helps in the prediction of democracy for our region and we must determine the extent to which the data base provides an accurate reflection of the conditions in that region. In this paper I attempt to respond to both challenges. At the outset, however, it should be noted that I am very sympathetic to the enterprise that Vanhanen has undertaken and therefore my critique should be viewed as one that is coming from an analyst who applauds the method but disagrees with some of its specific points and applications.

A substantial number of Vanhanen's 172 cases are located in Latin America; in this analysis a total of twenty-nine cases. Critiquing the analysis becomes a major challenge when one is limited to these cases for a variety of reasons. First, as shown on Vanhanen's Table 3.7, not a single case of these twenty-nine deviates so much from the theory that they violate it. All but five cases are located above the democracy threshold of above 6.3 in the IPR index, and all of them were democracies based upon his democracy index (ID). Second, most of the five cases that range in the transition zone (an IPR of from 3.3 to 6.3) are clearly the least democratic countries by the ID standard. Thus, not a single case (at least at first analysis) in the Latin America region seems to violate the theory Vanhanen has proposed. Third, deviations from the arithmetic means of regression residuals are quite low for the Latin American region as a whole. As shown on Vanhanen's Table

4.2, the mean deviation from the IPR index for Latin America and the Caribbean is only 2.4, compared to more than double that for Europe and North America (6.7) and nearly quadruple that for the Australia and Pacific region (9.3). Indeed, only sub-Saharan Africa (0.8) and East Asia and Southeast Asia (-1.1) are predicted any more precisely by the theory than are the Latin America and Caribbean cases. Fourth, even when adjusted for new insights gained from the unexpected transitions of Soviet bloc powers, the theory holds up well in Latin America. Deviations from the means of residuals for the new IPR index (Index of Power Resources and Structural Imbalance) was developed by Vanhanen in order to better explain the failure of his theory to predict the democratic transition in the former Soviet bloc countries. No such problems exist in Latin America. If one looks at Vanhanen's Table 4.1 it becomes clear that the IPRI for Latin America is appropriately far lower than the index for Europe and North America and also appropriately far higher than it is for sub-Saharan Africa. Thus, our intuitive sense of the cases matches quite closely Vanhanen's revised measure.

Despite these very strong arguments that favour the Vanhanen work, the task at hand is to detect its faults as they apply to the Latin American cases. These faults involve both errors of omission and errors of commission.

What has Vanhanen left out of his heroic effort to predict democracy world-wide? Any reading of his text will leave one with the clear impression that the focus of the work is heavily if not exclusively structural. The data presented tell us about many things. They give us information on education, agricultural class structure, concentration of non agricultural resources, etc. But these variables tell us little about the political culture of a given country. Since the initial work of Almond and Verba, political culture has been with us as a potentially important explanatory variable. Certainly Dahl's emphasis in *Polyarchy* on the beliefs of élites (especially political activists) has been taken very seriously by political scientists. More recently, Robert Putnam's (1993) study of Italy has linked the development of civic society to the emergence of a democratic political culture and given new life to the paradigm. Indeed, in a number of recent reviews, including that of David Laitin in the *APSR*, it has been argued that the study of democracy can no longer fail to include the political culture variable. While this is not the place to debate the utility of political culture as an explanatory variable, the absence of this data from Vanhanen's analysis makes it impossible to test directly its role in his 172 countries. It is important to note, of course, that the challenge of obtaining political culture data on such a large sample of nations is enormous, and even greater if one wishes to develop historical information. Putnam met that challenge for one country, Italy, and Ronald Inglehart (1988) has attempted to meet it for over twenty countries, but no researcher could be expected to gather data on 172 nations. The practical difficulties are real, but the lacunae in the research are equally real none the less.

A second omission is the absence of income distribution data. In some way, this is a problem similar to the one just mentioned, but one that is not nearly as complex. Labour force surveys exist for many nations, and income inequality data can be constructed from those surveys. The World Bank reports on many cases, and Edward Muller and I (1987) have attempted to expand the list with additional information. To Vanhanen's credit, he has included a surrogate measure, the concentration of non agricultural resources, but this measure is focused on private versus state ownership rather than distribution of income or wealth within the population. There is a great debate in the journals regarding the role of inequality in generating (or being a product of) regime type. The absence of this information in the Vanhanen data set makes it impossible for him to test the contribution of income distribution to democracy.

The absence of income distribution data is particularly significant for the Latin American cases. As a group, they are the countries in the world with the highest level of inequality in the distribution of income. Yet, within the region, there are countries like Costa Rica that have reduced their income inequality to reasonably low levels, yet right next door there is Honduras with perhaps the world's highest inequality in distribution. As a result, there is a lot that distinguishes these cases in terms of distribution. If we accept, as some have suggested, that income distribution is not merely a function of development as a strict interpretation of Kuznets' inverted U-curve would suggest, but is instead largely a product of policy decisions, then this variable becomes all the more important in Latin America.

One should hasten to add that these two omissions, while important, do not deprive the interested researcher from pursuing an inquiry with these variables added to the data set. One of the great virtues of Vanhanen's work is that it provides the raw data (and the sources) for each of his indicators. One could take his data, add the 'missing links', and do a reanalysis. The same point can be made for those critics who have challenged the statistical analysis itself. As Vanhanen points out in his text, some have called the statistical analysis naive. Indeed, I will critique him on some points in that regard in a moment. Yet, with the availability of his raw data in each of his publications, interested scholars can reanalyse his data with their technique of choice.

Errors of omission, both in terms of variables and analysis of data are flaws from which Vanhanen (or his followers) could recover. Of greater concern are errors of commission. These errors, too, could be remedied through inclusion of different data or recalculation of the methods utilized to produce indexes. But they presently lead Vanhanen to some potentially erroneous conclusions. It is important to focus on those.

Vanhanen claims that, 'the region of Latin America is geographically compact but culturally and ethnically heterogeneous'. While it is of course true that within the region there are countries that were colonies of Britain, France and the Netherlands, the overwhelming territorial area and population consists of former colonies of Iberia (Spain and Portugal). The overwhelming majority of the population of Latin America speaks Spanish or Portuguese, is Catholic in religion and shares a common experience of dependence and subordination to the Western hemisphere's global power, the United States. For all these regions, one would expect considerable homogeneity within this region on the democracy variable, a factor that Vanhanen does not emphasize. On the other hand, he is perfectly correct that within many of the nations of the region there are substantial ethnic minorities, especially the indigenous population and descendants of the former African slaves.

Vanhanen notes that in the 1970s he predicted the emergence of democracy in Latin America. As he states, 'The surprising victory of democracy in Latin America in the 1980s was not unexpected from the perspective of resource distribution, for IPR values were high enough to support democracy in nearly all countries'. Although that statement is true, it suggests that only via the IPR measure was democracy's emergence predictable, whereas to others, using other approaches, it was not. Vanhanen is quite correct that many Latin American experts were committed to the Bureaucratic–Authoritarian thesis proposed by O'Donnell, in which it was expected that these authoritarian regimes would last for a very long time since they had emerged out of increasing levels of economic development. Yet, those who examined data from the perspective of Lipset's classic thesis connecting economic and social development to democracy, would have concluded that democracy was very much a likely outcome. Indeed, in a direct application of the Lipset thesis, I found that with very few exceptions (Bolivia and Honduras) by the 1970s all Latin American nations had established the necessary (but not sufficient) conditions for the emergence of democratic rule (Seligson, 1987a; 1987b). These findings were based only upon two variables, GNP and literacy, and yet they replicated Vanhanen's far more complex multivariate IPR index. This raises the question of overdetermination in the Vanhanen approach; if one can come to the same conclusions with a far more parsimonious model, then the more complex model (and theory) is unwarranted.

A closer look at the Vanhanen measures reveal some troubling findings. He assigns Argentina an IPR of 33.4 and Uruguay 28.5, far and away the highest IPRs of any of the countries in Latin America. Indeed, these numbers nearly match those of Germany (42.4) and Switzerland (38.8). Yet, these are the countries that in the 1970s experienced the most violent breakdowns of democracy in all of Latin America with the exception of Chile. The military regimes that took power in those countries violated human rights at a frightful pace during the period of the so-called dirty war. In 1995 extensive revelations have emerged about the brutality of that war, in which hundreds if not thousands of still-alive political prisoners were tossed into the ocean from helicopters. True, the IPRs given in this volume are for 1993, but Vanhanen's earlier work also showed these countries to be at the top of the Latin American lists.

The values assigned to Argentina and Uruguay do not mesh well with the much lower value assigned to Costa Rica (20.0), the country nearly all experts agree is Latin America's strongest democracy. Indeed, in both objective and subjective ratings of democracy prepared by others, Costa Rica stands out. In the now classic Bollen (1980) index, Costa Rica was scored a 92, while Argentina received only a 53. In subjective ratings prepared every five years by Latin American experts, and formed into what has come to be known as the 'Fitzgibbon–Johnson Index', Costa Rica has been ranked number one for over twenty years, while Argentina has often been in the bottom tier of countries (Johnson, 1977). Something appears to be very wrong, then, with the IPR index with respect to these three countries, suggesting an underlying problem that might affect other countries as well.

What can account for this discrepancy? It does not emerge in Vanhanen's estimated degree of concentration (his Appendix 4), since each of the three countries has the same score (50). It is also not a factor in his measure of the index of family farms (Vanhanen's Appendix 3) since Costa Rica turns out to be higher, at 33 per cent, than Argentina (22 per cent) or Uruguay (27 per cent). I should note, however, that the subject of family farms is one to which I will return below. The discrepancy is also not a function of literacy, since each of these countries has literacy rates over 90 per cent. The large discrepancy emerges, instead, in the urbanization data (Appendix 2). Vanhanen shows, quite correctly, that Argentina and Uruguay are far more urban than Costa Rica. Argentina and Uruguay are both 86 per cent urban, non agricultural, while Costa Rica is only 47 per cent.

Vanhanen's thesis is that the higher the urban non agricultural population, the greater the chance for democracy. If this measure is used as a substitute for some measure of modernization and industrialization, then it makes sense. But in terms of theory, it does not. If true, it would suggest that countries that are basically rural and agricultural have little opportunity to become democratic. In fact, this contradicts Toqueville's image of America as well as the history of the United States. Furthermore, there is much literature that suggest that democracy in the US and Costa Rica are at least in part an outgrowth of the yeoman farmer. If so, then one would want to have more of those farmers, not fewer as the Vanhanen index would suggest.

In the IPR index for the three countries under consideration, the subcomponent labelled IOD (Index of Occupational Diversification) is where Argentina and Uruguay gain over Costa Rica. Argentina has an IOD of 88, Uruguay 86, but Costa Rica only 61.5. Because of this, Costa Rica lags badly behind the other two countries, yet we know its democracy is longer lived, more stable and deeper than that of Argentina and Uruguay. This suggests that this part of the IPR index is misleading and should be re-evaluated by Vanhanen.

Further difficulties emerge with this index. The case of Peru is particularly troubling. It has an index of 67.5, far higher than most countries in

Latin America, yet it experienced the most extensive guerrilla insurgency of any Latin American country in the 1990s. In addition, it was the one country to experience a complete breakdown of democracy as a result of an executive coup. Furthermore, the IPR index for Peru was 17.9, exceeding countries like Honduras, Mexico and Colombia, none of which have been seriously threatened with the overthrow of their systems.

Now I wish to return to the family farm issue. Vanhanen utilized the various World Census of Agriculture figures to develop his data. This certainly is the best source for the development of such an index, but its implementation by Vanhanen leaves some concerns. Consider the case of Costa Rica, once again, and compare it to El Salvador. Costa Rica scores thirty-three, while El Salvador scores thirty-six. In a recent article Seligson (1995) reviews the agrarian situation in El Salvador. By all accounts, for the year Vanhanen uses for El Salvador (1971), it was a country with one of Latin America's most extreme agrarian situations. Indeed, almost all analysts agree that the twelve-year civil war that broke out in 1980 was largely a function of the agrarian situation. It was only after the major land reforms of the early 1980s and the current post-civil war redistribution that El Salvador's land concentration has diminished. Yet, from the Vanhanen measure one would assume that the land tenure conditions in El Salvador were more favourable for democracy than those in Costa Rica. This discrepancy between the index and the reality again suggests that the index needs to be rethought.

One difficulty with the family farm index is that even though the World Census data used are the best that are available, they do have some serious problems. As Mark Edelman and I (Edelman and Seligson, 1994) have shown, census data can have a systematic bias, underrepresenting the largest farms and overrepresenting the smallest farms. We have demonstrated that in contrast, the land registry includes virtually all of the largest farms, but few of the smallest farms. This occurs because large land owners have the capability of paying the high costs of registering their property but are anxious to hide their ownership from the census takers for fear of expropriation by land reform agencies. On the other hand, small farmers do not have the economic resources to title their land, but use the census as a mechanism for obtaining some small measure of legitimacy of their claims. As a result of these biases in the two different sources, we argue that only the two sources combined can give us what we are looking for as a true measure of land distribution. In the case of El Salvador, the figures used by Vanhanen, no doubt, underrepresent the largest farms and therefore artificially increase the weight of the smaller farms in the census.

A further problem emerges in the case of Venezuela. There only 15 per cent of the farms meet Vanhanen's test. Yet, Venezuela established democracy in the late 1950s, decades before the current emergence of democratic regimes in Latin America. This suggests that either the index is wrong for

Venezuela, or that its utility in countries that are heavily urban and oil dependent is not as great as it is in other contexts.

A final concern is related to the IPRI index that was added to the Vanhanen approach to resolve the problem of the Eastern European cases. The central difficulty is his decision to combine that index with his IPR by adding a quarter of the value of the ISI. Why one-quarter? Why not one-half, or some other proportion? The decision seems to be entirely arbitrary and not based upon any theoretical considerations. Perhaps Vanhanen could go through an exercise in which he would examine the impact of including various proportions of ISI in the IPR after he has developed a theoretical explanation for each proportion.

CONCLUSIONS

In conclusion, the Vanhanen approach is one that we must all take very seriously. It is the most comprehensive data set that we have to date. At the same time, when looked at from the perspective of the Latin American region, troubling anomalies develop that suggest refinement of the measure is in order.

REFERENCES

Bollen, K. A. (1980) 'Issues in the measurement of political democracy', *American Sociological Review* 45, June: 387–8.

Dahl, R. A. (1971) *Polyarchy: Participation and Opposition*, New Haven and London: Yale University Press.

Edelman, M., and Seligson, M. A. (1994) 'Land inequality: A comparison of Census data and property records in twentieth-century Southern Costa Rica', *Hispanic American Historical Review* 73, 3: 445–91.

Inglehart, R. (1988) 'The renaissance of political culture', *American Political Science Review* 82, December: 1203–30.

Johnson, K. (1977) 'Research perspectives on the revised Fitzgibbon–Johnson Index of the image of political democracy in Latin America, 1945–1975', in J. W. Wilkie and K. Ruddle (eds) *Quantitative Latin American Studies: Methods and Findings*, Los Angeles: UCLA Latin American Center Publication.

Laitin, D. D. (1995), 'The Civic Culture', *American Political Science Review* 89, March: 168–73.

Muller, E. N., and Seligson, M. A. (1987) 'Insurgency and inequality', *American Political Science Review* 81, June: 425–51.

Putnam, R. D. (1993) *Making Democracy Work: Civic Traditions in Modern Italy*, Princeton: Princeton University Press.

Seligson, M. A. (1987a) 'Democratization in Latin America: The current cycle', in J. M. Malloy and M. A. Seligson (eds) *Authoritarians and Democrats: Regime Transition in Latin America*, Pittsburgh: University of Pittsburgh Press.

——(1987b) 'Development, democratization and decay: Central America at the crossroads', in J. M. Malloy and M. A. Seligson (eds) *Authoritarians and Democrats: Regime Transition in Latin America*, Pittsburgh: University of Pittsburgh Press.

——(1995) 'Thirty years of transformation in the agrarian structure of El Salvador, 1961–1991', *Latin American Research Review* 30, 3.

7 The democratic anomalies

Why some countries that have passed Vanhanen's democratic threshold are not democracies

Ilter Turan

INTRODUCTION

Is there a set of socio–economic factors which determine whether a society will be ruled by a politically democratic system? The question has always proved attractive to students of political development and policy makers. During the 1960s significant studies were conducted to uncover the socio-economic conditions which promoted the evolution of democratic systems. Charles F. Cnudde and Deane Neubauer's edited volume *Empirical Democratic Theory* summarized the scholarly achievements of the 1960s. As the optimism that the world was moving toward a greater number of democracies waned, so did interest in the empirical studies on the conditions of democracy.

The crumbling of the bipolar system, the disappearance of the Warsaw Pact, the demise of the Soviet Union stimulated once again hopes that democracies would come to prevail over the world. Although some new democracies have in fact emerged as a result of the change in the world system, there remain large sections of the world and many countries, that continue to be ruled by systems other than political democracy. It is in this context that Tatu Vanhanen's study of the socio–economic background conditions of political democracy comes at a relevant time.

Vanhanen is interested, in the final analysis, in the prospects for democracy in the world. He has attempted to develop a model which would make it possible for him to judge those prospects. His quantitative analysis shows that there are statistical correlations between his socio-economic variables and democratic regimes. Yet, there are a sufficient number of exceptions that some critical questions may be raised about his model as a means of explaining the presence and the prospects for the evolution of democratic systems.

My argument, which I shall elaborate in the following pages, raises the following points:

1 The path to democratic evolution is not linear, whereas the Vanhanen study tacitly assumes a unidirectional linear development.
2 The study leaves out a set of critical political and socio–political variables which appear to me to have significant explanatory powers as regards

whether a country evolves in a democratic direction or not. These include among others:

- whether the population of a country perceives itself to constitute a political community;
- whether a country has been under colonial domination;
- whether there are pressures in the international system supportive of democratic evolution;
- whether the interests of the power élites are served or seriously harmed by the introduction of democratic government.

I feel that we have to conceptualize studies of democratic evolution in a way which transcends assumptions of linearity and which integrates politics in a more comprehensive way into the analysis.

SOME METHODOLOGICAL CONSIDERATIONS

Tatu Vanhanen has done a formidable job in attempting to produce an empirically based model for the emergence of democratic political systems. I emphasize the word 'model' rather than 'theory' deliberately here because, while the model attempts to predict empirically the level at which one might expect democracy to become operative in a society, I am not convinced that it explains the process through which a democracy evolves.

Let me clarify what I mean. If explanation is taken to mean acounting for variance only in the statistical sense, then Vanhanen's model has explanatory powers. Yet, such an 'explanation', if it is one, does not give us a handle on the process through which a political system which could not be characterized as a democracy at some starting point, evolves into a democratic system at some later point. I think this is an important shortcoming for a very simple reason. There are a number of countries in the study, many of them located in the Middle East, Central Asia, North Africa, sub-Saharan Africa, and East and Southeast Asia which tend to deviate from the prediction that the model would offer us. More specifically, although the independent variables would lead us to expect that some countries would likely have democratic political systems, they, in fact, do not. The reverse is also occasionally true. Countries where one would not expect to find a democratic political system may have higher democratization scores, i.e. a more democratic system, than the indicators would lead us to predict. Such anomalies require explanations.

These deviations from the expected may derive from two major sources. First, they may occur because some other universal variables that affect the probability of democratic evolution, which have not been taken into account, are at work. Second, the deviations may emerge because there exist unique reasons in a particular country (a set of countries or a region of the world) that stand in the way of democratic evolution, although the universal forces which are supportive of democracy happen to be favouring such an evolution. To which source do we owe the presence of deviant cases?

In attempting an answer, we should follow the strategy which has been proposed some time ago by Przeworski and Teune. As shall be recalled, their argument was that in the conduct of comparisons, we should turn to variables which would have explanatory powers for all the units which are included in the comparison. Turning to unique explanations should be a step of last resort, a recourse which should be turned to only after the explanatory potential of the more universal variables had been exhausted (1970: 74–6). Said differently, we should try to minimize the unexplained variance, i.e. the residual, before turning to particularistic explanations.

The Przeworski–Teune argument may lead us to the question as to why region should constitute a variable along which countries should be grouped. The theoretical importance of region has to be spelled out clearly if we want to offer explanations which take region into account. I feel that grouping countries by region is defensible not on theoretical grounds, but on grounds of convenience. It may produce, on the other hand, a highly problematic result by concealing or leading us to ignore commonalties between countries which are not necessarily in the same region.

We can now move to the next question: In the case of countries in which the model would predict a democratic evolution because the 'democratic threshold' has been passed, but which in fact are not democracies, are there common explanatory factors which are not specific to a country (a specific set of countries or a region), that would help us understand the failure to democratic transition? Three regions (as defined by Vanhanen) in which there appear to be a higher incidence of non democratic regimes are:

1 North Africa, the Middle East and Central Asia;
2 sub-Saharan Africa; and
3 East and Southeast Asia.

It is also in these regions, especially the first, where we come to the problem of negative residuals; that is, countries that ought to be more democratic but are not. Why is this the case?

In his general attempt to account for regional differences, Vanhanen opts for the regional peculiarities argument. After recognizing the possibility that his indicators may have underestimated the level of democracy or exaggerated the degree of resource distribution in the case of countries which are found to be less democratic than expected, he goes on to say, 'However, it is more probable that a major part of regional differences is due to some regional factors not taken into account in my explanatory variables.' To the extent that some variables which are specific to a region can always be present, one cannot but agree with this suggestion. Yet, the explanation needs to be approached cautiously especially in light of the fact that North Africa, the Middle East and Central Asia are three separate regions of the world which are rarely grouped together. As already said, convenience may render such a grouping necessary but it is not a 'theoretical' reason.

In the search for universal (non region or country specific) variables which might help us understand why some countries are either not democracies or are not as democratic as they ought to be (or reducing the amount of 'unexplained variance' as statistically inclined researchers might choose to put it), we may turn to the experience of those countries that attempted to become democracies and failed irrespective of what part of the world they may be located in. In this way, we may not only be able to identify the factors which tend to undermine or even lead to the demise of a functioning democracy, but we may also develop some understanding of why democratic systems might be slow in evolving in some environments where economic variables which Vanhanen has used would lead us to expect democracy to obtain. It is possible that the conditions which contribute to the evolution of a democratic system may well be different to those factors which help sustain it. But, this is still a matter of debate, and should therefore not keep us from seeing if a variable which leads to the demise of democracy might also stand in the way of its evolution.

THE ANOMALOUS BUNCH

Let us list once again the regions of the world where, according to Vanhanen, what I shall call 'democratic anomalies' exist: (1) North Africa, the Middle East and Central Asia; (2) sub-Saharan Africa; (3) East and Southeast Asia. When one sees the list, one cannot but be struck by the fact that these are the very regions which had constituted the targets of European colonization and domination. Some were ruled directly or indirectly by colonial powers, others were given as mandates to major European powers, still others were conquered to become reluctant parts of a multi-national empire.

To appreciate how pervasive colonialism was in these regions, one needs to count the countries which had not been colonies in these regions. In the Middle East, North Africa and Central Asia group, there are twenty-nine countries, only six countries have not been direct colonies by a most generous interpretation including the Yemen, Egypt, Iran, Saudi Arabia, Turkey and Israel. Of these, only Turkey and Israel have histories of continued independence. Israel is a latecomer and transplant in the region. Turkey, on the other hand, has emerged following the collapse of a multi-ethnic empire which had fallen under extensive Western European influence. There are no countries which had not been colonies at one stage or another of their existence in sub-Saharan Africa with some possible reservations about South Africa and Liberia. And in East and Southeast Asia, Japan, Taiwan and Thailand are exceptions to what otherwise is a totally colonial past.

After the Second World War colonialism rapidly lost its legitimacy in the international community, a process which had already begun during the interwar period. As colonial empires were being dismantled, understandably, an attempt was made to build democracies in these newly emergent systems. Those countries that were divesting themselves of their former colonial rulers were, after all and for the most part, democracies. Furthermore, they felt that they constituted the 'free world' and tried to make the world 'safe for democracy'. One way to achieve that goal was to make sure that the countries coming into being would also be democracies.

But how would democracies come into being? The departing colonial power usually helped the newly independent country by setting up new institutions often including a constitution, an executive supported by a bureaucratic apparatus, a legislature and a court system before its departure. Some support was also extended afterwards. Then, there was economic assistance in which the United States was the principal provider. Each former colonial power, however, also carried out economic and technical assistance programmes in its former colonial possessions. Employing logic which is also implicitly adopted by Vanhanen, the proponents of economic assistance assumed that aid would produce urbanization, differentiation, literacy, exposure to mass media and other outcomes which would promote a democratic evolution. The relationship between economic development and democracy was seen to be linear. It was expected that as countries prospered economically, they would develop politically, i.e. in a democratic direction.

The hopes and aspirations regarding a democratic evolution were not borne out by developments. One by one, countries which appeared to have commenced on the path to democratic development terminated their experiment with democracy. In some cases, the end came by a military intervention, often preceded by social unrest or community strife. In other cases, traditional rulers were overthrown by a modernized military which found rulers as the major impediment to modernization. In still others, political leaders who had climbed to power by democratic means installed themselves into dictatorial permanence sometimes by using force but more often by usurping constitutional means such as elections and referendums.

If one is to describe the changing mood from unguarded optimism to moderate pessimism about the development of democracy in the newly emergent societies, s/he can call upon two books on political development. The first, the late Daniel Lerner's *The Passing of Traditional Society* (1958), drawing inferences from field research, offered a schematic explanation of the process by which developing countries would be making the transition to democratic government. Less than two decades later, Samuel Huntington in his *Political Order in Changing Societies* (1968), placed political order or institutionalization rather than democratic order as his key concept. Huntington pointed out that being governed rather than how to be governed was the critical problem for many a developing society.

Reviewing writings on the impediments to democratic evolution in developing societies, many variables may be extracted. Deegan, for example, in discussing those in the Middle East lists a number of them: 'weak institutionally; divided ethnically; tethered to authoritarian structures of government; lacking in unity; political legitimacy, tolerance of opposition; exploited by the external factor of the Cold War, and recently in thrall to fundamental religion' (Deegan 1994: 9). Space does not permit me to analyse all relevant variables. Rather, I have tried to put into groups those variables which I have felt to be significant. In the following pages, I will discuss these variables and how they may have hindered democratic evolution, although the Vanhanen variables should have promoted it. These are not region specific variables but, as my argument so far would imply, they are more likely to be found in parts of the world which have been targets of western colonialism or political domination.

THE LACK OF POLITICAL COMMUNITY AS AN IMPEDIMENT TO DEMOCRACY

In his well remembered article on 'Transitions to Democracy', Rustow (1970), echoing also the analysis of earlier scholars, suggested that in a democracy, there needed to be some consensus on the whole, the parts of which would compete against each other. The argument implied in this statement is that democracy may not be a suitable method for defining the political community. That it may constitute a means of managing conflict once the identity of the political community is established is quite another matter.

By political community, I mean a group of people who feel and/or accept that they should be living under the same government. In the analyses of the lack of a feeling of political community in a state, two factors are frequently mentioned as being dysfunctional: the artificiality of borders and the prevalence of other social organizations which claim the ultimate political loyalty of people. The two factors are in many instances interrelated. That is, borders are perceived to be artificial because they may cut across existing sociological or socio–political units. Alternatively, borders may bring together primordial groups which have not lived under the same administration before.

Let me use the example of Iraq to illustrate what I mean. When the Iraqi invasion of Kuwait was met by Operation Desert Storm culminating in the defeat of Saddam Hussein's armies, it was hoped that the Baathist dictatorship might be brought to an end, and a political democracy might be established in Iraq. To that end, the United States and some of her European allies searched for an opposition with whom it might be possible to co-operate in bringing democracy to that country. They soon discovered the hard reality of a society in which there appeared to be no consensus on the definition of political community. Various groups which were identified as Iraqi opposition were in fact representatives of smaller communities each distrusting others to an extent that it was not willing to take part in a common democratic movement that would require their co-operation. In fact, Saddam's tenure as a dictator owes much to the fragmented nature of the opposition. Sunni and Shia Arabs and Kurds have failed to develop a common or shared political identity which would allow them to compete within a political entity called Iraq. Hence, domination of one group over others by using the coercive instruments of the state to achieve integration has been the characteristic of the political system.

The lack of political community in Iraq has a history behind it. The current day Iraq is an entity which was created by the victors of the First World War in their efforts to divide up the spoils taken from the Ottoman Empire. No country called Iraq existed at the time. Three Ottoman provinces: Baghdad, Basrah and Mosul were united into a new unit called Iraq. In fact, in the secret arrangements made during the war Northern Iraq (Mosul) had initially been promised to France. It was later reclaimed by Great Britain which had succeeded in achieving military control of the area before France. France, on the other hand, was given compensation in the form of shares in oil from Mosul. Britain made Iraq into a kingdom in order to reward its chief Arab ally and client, the Sharif Hussein of Mecca, who served British interests during the war by leading an Arab revolt against their Turkish rulers. Faisal, the younger son of the Sharif was made the king.

The king came from the Hashemite family tracing its lineage to the prophet; and he had been a leader in the Arab nationalist revolt. With a king possessing such credentials, the royal regime was accorded some legitimacy by the subjects. But as it also proved to be the case in other British supported Middle Eastern kingdoms, the initial legitimacy gradually eroded as the royal rulers were forced to support such unpopular policies as fighting on Britain's side during the Second World War. In the case of the Iraqi kingdom, joining the Baghdad Pact against a rising tide of Arab nationalism constituted the occasion on which a *coup de grace* was inflicted on the increasingly unpopular regime in 1958 by a military leader, Brigadier Kasem. Neither Kasem nor others who first ousted him, then ousted each other from power through a series of *coups* were able to establish a stable basis of political legitimacy. Rulers relied on force to hold society together. Despite claiming to lead political organizations with Arab Nationalist ideologies, they staffed political and administrative positions not with believers in the cause, but with persons whom they trusted because of primordial linkages including family ties, lineage, tribal affiliation, being from the same town and belonging to the same religious sect.

Interestingly enough, earlier periods in Iraqi history might well have qualified it a democracy as defined by Vanhanen. Although the history of elections and parliamentary life in Iraq is chequered, it did exist during the period when Iraq was a kingdom and ruled by a traditional élite of rural and urban notables. As a new breed of military officers of lower class background, and rural or small town origins, subscribing ardently to

Arab nationalism ascended to the political stage, the consensus which had allowed for some competition between the traditional élites under the watchful eye of the royal house eroded. The regime was toppled by a military revolution in 1958. Then military interventions followed each other. Finally, under the rule of Saddam Hussein, the military dictatorship stabilized. The Iraqi experience is not unique. While no case is a replication of another, similar forces were clearly operative in the case of Syria and Egypt. But we need not limit ourselves to the Middle East: Nigeria went through the Biafra War trying to keep the Ibos within the federal system as its democracy crumbled; Zaire, then called the Belgian Congo, had to fight a secessionist war in Katanga shortly after its birth; in Uganda political power has changed hands through coups not elections; the mutual massacres of Hutus and Tutsis terminated the electoral process in Rwanda.

If we turn to the Central Asian republics, which have appeared on the world political scene only recently, we discover that none of these states correspond to a historical political entity (Helgesen 1994: 137). All contain populations which identify with their own kind in a neighbouring state, and all contain populations–which have been forcefully settled there at some point during Soviet rule, mostly during the Stalin era–who have not mixed in well with the local populations. Borders, sometimes drawn arbitrarily for administrative convenience, at other times drawn specifically with the intention of dividing politically difficult populations in order to rule them, proved problematical even before the demise of the Soviet Union (*cf.* Eickelman (ed.) 1993). For example, in 1989, in the Uzbek part of Ferghana Valley fighting broke out between Ahiska (Meskethian) Turks and Uzbeks in which no less than 120 people were killed. Ahiska Turks living across the Turkish border in Georgia had been driven East during the Second World War by Stalin, who suspected that their political loyalties might well lie with Turkey. Similarly, in 1990 in Osh, a Kyrgyz city in the northern tip of the Ferghana Valley, inter-communal strife between the Kyrgyz and the Uzbeks left 320 people dead (Sungur 1994: 230–1). Tajikistan is split between warring factions on the basis of regionalism (Helgesen 1994: 148). Turkmenistan is exposed to the danger of tribalism (Helgesen 1994: 148). One observer has counted eighteen border disputes of a serious nature in Central Asia (Sungur 1994: 231).

Integration, or holding the political community together, is one of the major concerns of political systems. If democratic competition is perceived to be destructive to 'national unity', or even seriously threatening it, the pressures which the Vanhanen variables may create in favour of democratization may be countered by pressures to preserve the community. It may also be that countries which have been more democratic at some point in the past when the pressures of break up or dismemberment were either non existent or not so intense, may evolve in less democratic directions despite the fact that they may have moved further along the economic indicators which promote the evolution of democracy.

Political units whose contemporary form has been determined more by colonizers than the indigenous populations are particularly vulnerable to non democratic rule. Having been imposed by outsiders or thus perceived, borders, ethnic, racial and other similar compositions of society, may easily be judged unfair, unjust, and therefore not legitimate. Attempts to change it by assimilating minorities, revising borders, and resort to similar means often undermine existing democratic arrangements or discourage the conduct of democratic experiments where none has been conducted before. This means that intensifying nationalism on the part of any of the major groups in a society tends to spell difficulty for democratic politics.

Clearly, a society can also try to cope with the challenges which we have been discussing here by employing means more appropriate to a political democracy. But, this presumes the presence of a democratic culture or a mind set which precedes the emergence of problems regarding the identity of the political community. Alternatively, democracy may be a long term outcome of interminable domestic struggles which become finally resolved by a 'grand compromise' (Rustow 1970). The incidence of such democratic evolution in the case of the developing world has, however, been scarce.

THE ROLE OF EXTERNAL FACTORS IN DEMOCRATIC EVOLUTION

The colonial political legacy

It has already been noted that, in the case of colonial possessions that later became independent countries, the colonial masters built some political institutions to which power was transferred. What these institutions were and whether they were democratic was determined to a great extent by (1) whether the colonial country itself was a political democracy; and (2) the conditions under which power was transferred to the indigenous government.

Whether the colonial country itself was a democracy is a condition which probably does not require extensive explanation. In most instances, European masters of a colony had developed a set of political and administrative institutions based on their own understandings of good and proper government. As they reconciled themselves to granting independence to former colonies, they took a set of preparatory measures. Since most of the colonial powers were political democracies, these included the preparation and the promulgation of a constitution, the opening of or the broadening of the representative basis of an existing legislature, the conducting of elections and similar steps. The democratic transition was facilitated by the fact that the indigenous political élites pressing for independence had also been trained in the political traditions of the mother country and were socialized into a set of values which resembled those of the élites of the latter. But, most importantly, in many instances starting out as a political democracy was a *sine qua non* of political independence. As Zubaida has aptly observed, democracy was a 'compulsory model supported by the new nationalist politicians and the retiring colonial administrators alike' (quoted in Owen 1993: 18).

In case the colonizer was not a political democracy, this being the case with former Portuguese and Soviet colonies, forces that favoured a democratic beginning were considerably less if not totally absent. This is clearly so in the Central Asian republics and Azerbaijan. These were all federal republics of the Soviet Union. They had all the political institutions which existed in a federal Soviet republic. They became independent as a result of the breakdown of the Union. No particular plans or preparations had been made for their breaking away; it was rather sudden. This meant that these countries all inherited the political institutions of the centrally administered, ideologically oriented one party state, as well as bureaucratic and political cadres socialized to that tradition. These constituted the major elements of a context within which the lack of rival political élites, the prevalence of economic conditions that could best be described as an emergency, and the existence of a not so well integrated ethnic mosaic that displayed explosive tendencies, all came together to produce regimes which, though legitimized by an electoral process, were not democratic.

The inference to be drawn from the above discussion is clear. Irrespective of where the regimes may stand today, colonies of European democracies were likely to have a more democratic start. Many among them, however, receded to non democratic forms of rule. Others were born non democracies from the beginning. Why? Earlier, we have alluded to the lack of political community argument as a challenge to the survival of democratic regimes. Now, we see that non democratic colonial masters are not likely to deliver democratic babies to the world, and babies born democratic do not necessarily remain democratic as time passes. Next, let us see how the way the baby was born may affect the chances of democratic birth and evolution.

The conditions under which power was transferred from a colonial country to an indigenous regime has also been important in shaping the regime of the new country. In cases where there was a prolonged struggle for independence, the political organization that led the independence movement usually assumed power as a single party. This was the case, for example, in Algeria with the FLN, the Neo-Destour in Tunisia and, to a lesser extent, with Istiqlal in Morocco. In any society where the Communist party assumed the leadership of an independence movement, a single party dictatorship was the inevitable outcome as demonstrated by the case of Vietnam and Kampuchea.

Sometimes, as in the case of Egypt which was not, strictly speaking, a colony but a protectorate of Great Britain, the initial moves to become more independent were led by men of a liberal nationalist and constitutionalist persuasion. During the interwar period, there were the beginnings of democratic development. But the exploitative behaviour of the British, totally subjugating the elected leadership to serve their interests, discredited so irreparably the credibility of the latter that a takeover by a military committee ending competitive politics in Egypt proved easy to effect. The British had not, in fact completed their withdrawal when the Revolutionary Command Council assumed political power.

Peaceful transitions to independence do not necessarily ensure that the newly emergent unit will be a democracy. This is contingent on other factors some of which we have discussed above. Anti-colonial wars and wars of independence, on the other hand, create a proclivity to one party systems.

The characteristics of the international system

The prevailing conditions in the international system also affect the evolution and the continuation of democratic systems. The ability of non democratic systems to retain themselves in power is not independent of how much value is accorded to having a democratic form of government and what kind of externally derived deprivations are to be endured, if any, by not having such a system. With this in mind, let us look at the post Second World War period. Although the Second World War was fought against totalitarian dictatorships in the name of democracy, the emergence of a highly competitive relationship between the American-led Western Bloc and the Soviet led Socialist Bloc brought matters of security to the fore, and rendered the promotion of democratic regimes a matter of secondary importance. For the next more than four decades, although the members of the Western Bloc continued to express a preference for democratic systems, non democratic systems were accorded as much recognition, economic and military assistance as political democracies. Furthermore, the existence of the Soviet Union, as one of the two major actors in the international system, both inspired and legitimized authoritarian regimes which promised economic development, particularly industrialization, to their citizens. It is only after the crumbling of the Warsaw Pact and the demise of the Soviet Union, culminating in the disappearance of the bipolar world that having a politically democratic regime has ascended in importance. Some non democratic leaders such as Zambia's Kaunda has chosen to democratize as a way of receiving support in his attempt to meet his country's economic difficulties. Others like Mobutu Sese Seko of Zaire, have made promises in the face of economic difficulties and strong domestic opposition, but have so far failed to live up to their promises. The Nigerian military government has even refused to relinquish to the winner of a national election.

In the Middle East, security concerns have prevailed over those pertaining to democratic government in the determination of super power foreign policies. For example, in analysing the link between Middle Eastern regimes and American foreign policy, Quandt questions:

At a time when democratic political movements seem to be gaining ground in many parts of the world, the Middle East appears to be a notable exception. Is this because the US is throwing its weight behind status quo, a status quo built around authoritarian political regimes of various sorts?

(Quandt 1993: 164)

Then, in explaining why the United States might have supported the *status quo*, he notes that oil was at stake, that Israel was involved, and that Soviet bids for influence were being countered (Quandt 1993: 165).

The role of the international system in influencing the domestic system is readily apparent in the case of Turkey, a country which has enjoyed democratic government since 1945–50 with three short interludes of military rule. In contrast to many of the examples we have been discussing here, Turkey has never been a colony. Beginning with the mid-eighteenth century, it has undergone comprehensive political and cultural modernization first under the Ottoman Empire and then under the Turkish Republic. During the empire, two attempts to introduce constitutional monarchy did not fare well since keeping the empire from disintegrating constituted the major concerns of governments during the late nineteenth and early-twentieth century. The Empire, nevertheless, came to an end at the end of the First World War. A popularly backed nationalist movement led mainly by Ottoman military officers succeeded in recovering territories which were still under Ottoman rule at the time of the signing of the Mudros Armistice but were occupied later by Allied Powers and established as a republic.

The political organization which had led the way in organizing the struggle transformed itself into a political party shortly before the declaration of the republic. It ruled the country as a single party until 1945, concentrating on policies of cultural modernization. Although Turkey did not participate in the Second World War, it was affected by it in many ways which generated forces which desired political change and the introduction of political competition. What is relevant for our purposes here, however, is the strong Russian pressure the country was exposed to regarding concessions on the status of the Turkish Straits and some territories on the Soviet border. These forced Turkey to move away from its neutral stance and draw closer to the Western Bloc. Thus, in addition to responding to the domestic forces promoting political change, the introduction of competitive politics was perceived as a way of gaining admission to the emerging Western Bloc, and ensuring Western protection of Turkey.

To conclude, whether a country has an operating democratic system is not just a product of domestic development but also one of both the broader international context and the specific set of relationships a country has with others. The end of colonialism, the emergence and the disappearance of the bipolar world and other international developments have influenced the internal processes of countries to produce pressures for or counter to a democratic evolution independent of their levels of socio–economic development.

THE POLITICAL ECONOMY OF DEMOCRATIC EVOLUTION

I have already referred in passing to the linear development assumption which was adopted by earlier students of the relationship between economic change and political development (by which usually democratic evolution was meant). Vanhanen's methodology is based on the same 'linearity of development' premise. Throughout the discussion we have come across some of the examples (of which there are many more) that indicate that countries which could have been classified as being democracies at a lower level of economic development, have 'receded' into being non democracies at a later period although their economic well-being may well have improved. Hence, there is an evident need for revision of the linearity of development assumption. I have already suggested two types of variables which might help us with the revision: the absence of a national political community, and the influences of the external context and relations of a country. There still remains another dimension, one which is related to the political economy of democratic evolution.

In a speech in which he contrasted the revolution with the previously existing political system in Egypt, and referring to the landowners and the pashas, Nasser remarked: 'They used this kind of democracy as an easy tool for the benefits of the feudal system. You have seen the feudalists gathering the peasants and driving them to the polling booths' (quoted in Owen 1993: 21). While Nasser is not remembered for his democratic achievements, his criticisms refer accurately to a problematic aspect of democratic practice in societies which got on the democratic bandwagon mainly through external impetus. The crux of the problem is that dominant élites will accept the mechanisms of political democracy only in so far as they can mobilize votes to keep themselves in power and their fundamental economic interests are not threatened. This means that if there already exists some kind of democratic structure, dominant élites will support it only to the extent it serves their ability to perpetuate their power, precisely the point Nasser was making. Alternatively, if domination is achieved through non democratic means, then the prevailing élites will try to foster an environment in which counter-élites are not allowed to flourish and organize, and challenge the dominant élites.

What are the socio–economic characteristics of societies in which there exists a dominant political élite which is reluctant to share power with other groups or relinquish it to a different configuration of groups in society? We may also pose the same question in a different way and ask: Is there a socio–economic structure in societies in which political competition is more likely to emerge and be sustained?

Let us start with the second way the question is asked. I think, in discussing the support for pluralism and competitive elections in society at large in the Arab Middle East, Roger Owen comments that 'in the Arab World, only Egypt seems to have had a sufficiently large and varied class of landowners, entrepreneurs and professionals to sustain this type of politics for a relatively long period of time, up to 1952' (Owen 1993: 36). In a broader sense, what Owen is referring to is the presence in a society of social classes that have sufficiently varied interests but are not so diametrically opposed that co-operation between them is totally ruled out. Lest I be misunderstood, let me point out that the existence of a socio–economic structure along the lines described above is not by itself sufficient guarantee that a democratic system will obtain where it did not exist or that it will survive where it does. As Roniger and Günes-Ayata note:

> Especially (but not only) in societies laden with social inequalities, public policies – whether distributive, regulative, or extractive – are potentially discretionary and thus open to clientelistic use and abuse.
> These trends stand, however, in dialectical confrontation with the dictates of democratization: access to power, participation, responsiveness by political élites to social demands.
> (Roniger and Günes-Ayata 1994: vii)

Nevertheless, other things being equal, both the emergence and the continuation of a political democracy may be considerably enhanced by the presence of such a structure.

Do those societies which would have been expected to be democracies but are not, differ in terms of their socio–economic structure from those which are? Both as regards countries which were colonies at some stage of their history, and those which were never colonies but were forced to modernize defensively, i.e. in the face of military defeat, the major cleavage in society often tends not to be socio–economic but cultural and political.

In the case of countries such as Russia and Turkey that fell under substantial Western European influence but which were never colonies, the rulers were the chief modernizers. There was a conscious decision to westernize society; neither society nor economy was left alone to develop autonomously at its own pace. They became the objects of state intervention and centrally run policies of development and transformation. This led to the growth of complex state mechanisms which were intended to direct and control change in almost every walk of life. It also led to the emergence of a political class, state élites, which dominated society. As sometimes happened, there also grew a class of entrepreneurs, but its prosperity generally depended on its willingness to extend co-operation to the state élites. The relations between state élites and society were almost in the nature of a command structure. The former, as modernizers, believed that they possessed a set of superior values which the masses should obediently accept. This hardly constituted a good beginning for democratization since state and society were not conceived as being on equal terms. Calls for democratization, under such circumstances, were interpreted simply as reactions and challenges to the state-led modernization.

There were similar problems in the former colonies and semi-colonies. During the colonial period, some groups such as traditional rulers and aristocrats co-operated with the colonial power to preserve their superior social and economic status in society. In other cases, some ethnic groups achieved a dominant position by collaborating with or working for colonial authorities. Finally, talented indigenous people were recruited to work for the administration or the military in the colonial system and became assimilated into the culture of the colonial power. These were the groups which initially assumed power after independence. After independence a symbiotic relationship developed between the colonial power and the political élites of the newly independent society. The colonial power usually extended economic and political support to the ruling élites and got their co-operative disposition in return. This turned out to be the case even in such societies as Algeria where a fierce war of independence had been fought against the French. But for more typical examples, one needs to look at the traditional regimes in the Middle East such as that of Iraq until 1958 and Jordan and Kuwait since their inception. Though not a colony, Saudi Arabia can also be cited here as representing a traditional regime whose authority has been persistently sustained by an outside power, the United States, against external and internal challenges in return for co-operating with the latter.

Vanhanen's Index of Occupational Differentiation and other variables do not capture cultural and political differences which may have a greater role in determining the chances of democratic evolution in a country than economically based differences alone.

Beblawi and Luciani have introduced another economic dimension to domination of society by a political élite. Inspired by their observations of the oil producing states of the Middle East, they argue that these are rentier states. By rentier state, they are referring to a state whose income derives from the extraction and the sale of oil, not from taxation of income generated by productive economic activity (Beblawi and Luciani 1987). Because the state acquires its income without the social transformation which usually accompanies productive economic activity, rentier states are spared the popular demands for political reform and participation. Rentier states, then, may appear to be economically well off, but they lack the social–economic structure which would promote politically democratic evolution.

In the societies which we have been looking at, the nature of the relationship between political élites and society is mainly a relationship of political power. Socio–economic relations, while also being important, are of a secondary order. Tatu Vanhanen's variables based on the socio–economic dimension alone, may fail to capture the role of the socio–political structure as an impediment to democratic evolution.

CONCLUSIONS

Vanhanen's study constitutes an outstanding attempt to relate some socio–economic background variables to the emergence and the continued existence of democratic political systems. He has managed to show us that a number of indicators, few in number (and a composite indicator built on them), are highly correlated with whether or not a country has a democratic political system. Vanhanen has also presented us with the puzzle that there are some societies where the socio–economic background variables would lead us to predict that there exists a democracy but where, in fact, there does not. Why? This necessitates the conduct of causal analysis. What I have tried to do in the preceding pages is to suggest some commonalities among the deviant cases, trying to explain why they might deviate from the prediction. I have further argued that it is important to understand the process through which the Vanhanen variables and others, including mine, operate to produce democratic outcomes. Expressed differently, I have tried to make a case that we should move from correlation to causality.

If an agenda is to be suggested for further research, it may be useful to conduct case studies, particularly of deviant cases. It is by studying them that we may better understand the limits of the validity and the applicability of our own general explanations for we know that *'Exceptio probat regulum'*.

REFERENCES

Beblawi, H. and Luciani, G. (1987) *The Rentier State*, London: Croom Helm.
Cnudde, C. F. and Neubauer, D. (eds) (1969) *Empirical Political Theory*, Chicago: Markham.
Deegan, H. (1994) *The Middle East and Problems of Democracy*, Boulder, Col.: Lynne Rienner.
Eickelman, D. F. (ed.) (1993) *Russia's Muslim Frontiers: New Directions in Cross-Cultural Analysis*, Bloomington: Indiana University Press.
Helgesen, M. M. (1994) 'Central Asia: Prospects for ethnic and nationalist conflict', in W. R. Duncan and G. P. Holman (eds) *Ethnic Nationalism and Regional Conflict: The Former Soviet Union and Yugoslavia*, Boulder, Col.: Westview Press.
Huntington, S. (1968) *Political Order in Changing Societies*, New Haven: Yale University Press.
Lerner, D. (1958) *The Passing of Traditional Society: Modernizing the Middle East*, Glencoe, Ill.: The Free Press.
Owen, R. (1993) 'The practice of electoral democracy in the Arab East and North Africa: Some lessons from nearly a century's experience', in E. Goldberg, R. Kasaba and J. Migdal (eds) *Rules and Rights in the Middle East*, Seattle: University of Washington Press.
Przeworski, A. and Teune, H. (1970) *The Logic of Comparative Social Inquiry*, New York: Wiley Interscience.
Quandt, W. B. (1993) 'American policy toward democratic political movements in the Middle East', in E. Goldberg, R. Kasaba and J. Migdal (eds) *Rules and Rights in the Middle East*, Seattle: University of Washington Press.
Roniger, L. and Günes-Ayata, A. (1994) 'Preface', in L. Roniger and A. Günes-Ayata (eds) *Democracy, Clientelism and Civil Society*, Boulder, Col.: Lynne Rienner.

Rustow, D. A. (1970) 'Transitions to democracy: Toward a dynamic model', *Comparative Politics* 2(3) 337–64.

Sungur, N. (1994) Ÿeniden Yapilanma Sürecinde Orto Asya Türk Cumhuriyetleri ve Gecis Dönemi Sorunlari, in B. E. Bohar (ed.) *Bagimsizligin ilk yillari: Azerbaycan, Kazakistan, Kirgista, Özbekistan, Turkmenistan,* Ankara: Kültür Bakanligi Yaymlari, No. 1723.

8 On statistical correlates of democratization and prospects of democratization in Africa

Some issues of construction, inference and prediction

Samuel Decalo

Tatu Vanhanen has set himself an ambitious and meritorious task in this book. One both central to current academic concerns in mainstream Political Science, and one that he is eminently qualified to undertake. The issues he addresses are not new – the prerequisites of democratization and the conditions that sustain democratic governance world-wide. But definitive, universally accepted answers to these questions, still persistently evade scholars. This is cogently attested to by the abundance of literature that has accumulated over several decades on the issue of democratization, the continued prevalence of such themes at national and international conferences, the academic mini-industry that still churns out research on these issues, and the sharp disagreements over matters of methodology, substance, variables, and detail, as well as of priority (i.e. 'stages of democratization' debate) among those continuing to plough these fertile academic fields.

It is not the function of this contribution to either assess or critique issues of basic statistical methodology, for which other scholars have been approached. Suffice it to say that though a regional specialist, empiricist, and more often than not micro-analyst, I am hardly averse to macro-statistical correlational work, and indeed look forward to the day when Vanhanen, or some other such scholar, will simplify my own academic travails by building more solid bridges between macro- and micro-analysis in African studies.

I also do not care to join in a debate in this context of Vanhanen's obviously appealing – but normative and deterministic – central assumption of democracy's etiology from 'a neo-Darwinian theory of evolution by natural selection' (Vanhanen 1995). Such an assumption (not a hypothesis) is extraneous to the quantitative analysis undertaken, and does not affect the correlations arrived at. Still, it does play a role, I suspect, in conditioning him *a priori* to assume, or expect, a universal quasi-uniform (historically inevitable?) political evolution of all societies towards democratic governance modalities through a progressive diffuseness of political power.

Though personally I may agree with the thesis and the one on which it rests (social diffuseness of power), the lessons of the failure of the equally appealing political development theory of the 1960s and 1970s should condition us not to assume evolution will win out. Darwin, after all, had many things to say about species that do not adapt! Only thirty years ago 'neo-Darwinian' evolutionary projections might confidently have predicted, and with requisite correlations, radically different (authoritarian) patterns of governance for the future. And even if the core assumptions that are laid down are inherently correct, with many countries likely to fail in democratization, the 'long run' could easily be a matter of many decades. I am not sure whether such long-term assumptions have more than speculative value, if only because variables extraneous to the issues being assessed may easily intervene to arrest diffuseness of power (even globally) or offer 'alternative' ways to democracy, which is, after all, to some degree a value-laden concept.

However that may be, in my own contribution I will first briefly outline how political and economic liberalization came to Africa, and the background against which democracy survives today, that should contribute to a qualitative contrast of the strains on the staying powers of the new political hybrids in Africa. At that stage I will turn to a few problems that arise in all statistical attempts to assess democratization in Africa.

Until the so-called 'winds of change' started sweeping the continent in 1989 there were really only two time-proved and full-fledged democracies in sub-Saharan Africa: Botswana and Mauritius, the latter also the only one to experience a change of government through elections. Another five or six, (e.g. Senegal and Côte d'Ivoire, were qualitatively judged by many (but hardly all) Africanists as relatively democratic, with the rest of the continent squarely in the authoritarian spectrum, though residing in a number of rubrics differently devised by scholars who cared to construct such typologies.

Democracy was by default (i.e. by virtue of its rarity on the continent), largely perceived as one extremity on a governance style continuum, if only to differentiate academically and pedagogically between a large number of clearly autocratic civilian and military regimes of various ideological hues, that were nevertheless different in their degree of hegemonic political dominance, intrusion and/or control of the economy, 'justifying' ideology if any, and civic and human abuses. There were after all, major differences – except to purists – between, for example, Amin's Uganda and Kerekou's People's Republic of Benin; between Habre's Chad and Ahidjo's Cameroon, though all were harshly authoritarian.

In like fashion, on the more benevolent side of the continua qualitative differences existed between, for example, Houphouet-Boigny's Côte d'Ivoire and Banda's Malawi. Many countries, however, either defied categorization, 'shifted' markedly from one monopolistic leader to another (e.g. Kenya under Kenyatta versus Kenya under Moi), or elicited quite diverse qualitative scholarly assessments. The best example of the latter instance may possibly have been Banda's reign in Malawi, judged by some as a paragon of 'responsible' if firm no-nonsense government, and by others as the epitome of harsh idiosyncratic rule perpetuating social inequities. For these and other reasons African Studies was replete with the various sub-jective rubrics and typologies, and differential assessment criteria that Van-hanen bemoans. Unfortunately, the nature of the current wave of 'democratization' in Africa and its possible temporal nature (Huntington 1991) empirically likewise calls for a number of non pure midway houses posing as they do the thorny problems of subjective assessments Vanhanen laments.

There were cogent country-specific reasons why only Botswana and Mauritius (which do not have widely diffused power) attained the distinc-tion of being the continent's only fully-fledged democracies. In-depth dis-cussion of these need not detain us, but one point is crucial. Despite substantial agreement among Africanists about the particular mix of vari-ables that made Botswana and Mauritius unique on the continent, no broader qualitative or quantitative extrapolations were feasible about the 'prerequisites of democracy' based on the experience of these two countries! Yet surely, in those days when democracy was very sharply set off in these two countries (unlike today where the democratic modality is crowded with look-alikes) some indicators or preconditions could have been arrived at? Not so. Whatever socio-economic variables were identified (primarily in Botswana, Mauritius being *sui generis*) as instrumental in producing demo-cratic governance, when found elsewhere, did not produce similar results. By way of illustration, the argument that Botswana's uniqueness stemmed from the ethnic homogeneity of the country (70 per cent of the population is of Tswana ethnicity, divided into seven clans) did not translate into a democratic ethos in Somalia, where 98 per cent of society in Somali; the much-lauded democratic virtues of Botswana's *kgotlas* (local village deci-sion-making bodies where every commoner had, in theory, the right to speak his mind), seen as building blocks of Botswana's national democratic ethos, when found in other countries, hardly affected national modalities. And so on.

When liberalization came to Africa it largely took scholars by surprise. In an influential article Huntington had argued in the mid-1980s that 'with few exceptions, the limits of democratic development in the world may well have been reached' (Huntington 1984: 218), supporting a thesis that the unique historical circumstances that had produced democracy in Europe 'will not occur again' (Tilly 1975: 81). Yet, a coalescence of a variety of external pressures and internal forces in Africa showed that the continent was more than ripe for change. For Africanists, what began to take place on the continent was nothing short of a revolutionary rearray of societal forces. And though pundits have since come out to proclaim the obvious inevitability of what eventually transpired (as with Kremlinologists), the totality of the change in Africa was not foreseeable in 1988.

The change that transpired was in all instances very reluctantly granted by incumbent élites with their backs virtually against the wall. In Africa there was no top-down Gorbachev-like reform process spinning out of control in directions originally not anticipated. Rather, in most cases liberalization came under the aegis of unconvinced and unrepentant autocratic political barons ruling morally, ideologically, and economically bankrupt states seething with a host of ethnic and economic grievances held by urban masses, civic leaders, and politically-bypassed societal influentials. The changed international scene had also robbed Afro-Marxist states of their ideological role model, requiring a re-array of power. All states lost their 'Cold War value' to fall prey to conditionalities for aid from global donor-agents and, for Francophone Africa, from France (Decalo 1992).

Only two leaders, Houphouet-Boigny and Bongo, in Côte d'Ivoire and Gabon respectively, saw the writing on the wall early, or heeded France's counsel, to mastermind early quasi-democratic power-sharing transformations that left their hegemony largely intact, partly because incipient opposition groups were not yet adequately organized. Other leaders, as in Benin and Congo, were driven into reforms by fiscal bankruptcy, collapsed banking sectors, and with literally no banknotes in state coffers to pay civil service payrolls already months in arrears, with their personal fate and security very much at stake. Others, as in Kenya, Malawi and Zambia, were likewise bulldozed by global donors to concede 'democracy' within the context of fiscal stress and societal tumult. (The 1990 demonstrations for multipartism in Lusaka saw crowds as large as those in Leipzig.) And still other regimes (Niger, Chad) were swept into liberalization by the spillover effect, since once the process began in the continent it acquired a momentum of its own.

External or financial pressures were not the sole vectors in the equation, though it is difficult to overestimate them. It was the coalescence of external and internal pressures that brought change in Africa. Internally, in many parts of Africa larger, much-transformed civil society had developed since independence. It had become marginalized by the major economic downslide of the continent in the 1980s, a function of global market forces for raw commodities, mismanagement of resources, and profligate spending on burgeoning civil services and state sectors, in Marxist and non Marxist states alike. It was the 'revolt' of civil society, aggravated by power barons entrenched within monolithic party systems and intent on ruling for ever, that spilled into urban city streets, paralyzing societal activity, that consummated the democratic revolution. However, in many other countries change was vigorously resisted despite external pressures and the revolt of civil society (as by General Abatcha in Nigeria); or 'democracy' was cosmetically adopted (by Mbasogo in Equatorial Guinea); or incumbent leaders held out with force of arms (as did General Eyadema in Togo, for eighteen months during which two-thirds of Lomé fled to Ghana), until a weary civil society accepted a power-sharing formula dictated by the incumbent. And in Algeria, political democracy promptly ushered in social autocracy (religious fundamentalism), that in turn brought about the roll-back of concessions granted earlier.

Change in Africa did not start automatically with the collapse of the Berlin Wall, 1989 being merely a conveniently accepted markpost. But external pressures for change in Africa during the 1980s related largely to economic reforms. Already by the early 1980s a more tightfisted French aid policy *vis-à-vis* Francophone Africa was visible. The World Bank, later to spell out political conditionalities (good government) for structural adjustment aid, had by the early 1980s adopted a tougher line on requisite economic changes for states queuing up for aid. Among the demands increasingly being made – to this day – were:

1 sharp cuts in bloated civil services, up to 50 per cent of which can be pruned without declines in social benefits, assuming efficiency and dispersal throughout the country;
2 economic privatization, to disencumber African public finances of debilitating annual fiscal drains, that even in mineral-rich states (Congo, Gabon, Nigeria) consume up to 50 per cent of revenues; and
3 the withdrawal of the state from both agrarian activities (state farms, plantations) and marketing boards (or fundamental reforms in the latter) that discriminate against rural producers' income (by up to 35 per cent) in favour of urban groups and projects stultifying agrarian growth and widening rural poverty.

Such economic liberalization was judged imperative for otherwise any new external funding would merely perpetuate fundamental economic flaws in Africa. By 1980 in many countries budgetary expenditures on civil services had reached 80 per cent; in seven states between 40 and 75 per cent of all salaried employment was in their civil services, while expenditures on public employment in an additional twenty countries was increasing at twice or more the pace of their economic growth, and foreign debt had reached stratospheric heights, all unsupportable burdens (Parfitt and Riley 1989). This was especially unacceptable since the vast majority of the state enterprises in Africa were deficitory, and civil services showed no sign of slowing their growth, since state patronage (public sector jobs) had become the functional equivalent of systemic legitimacy (Decalo 1990). What transpired in '1989' therefore, was the merger and forceful enunciation of external political and economic conditionalities on the part of donors of international aid, including the US (Butty 1991), within explosive internal settings. What is the situation today?

By 1995 the liberalization process had transformed much of the map of Africa. Without belittling the changes that have taken place in many states, the early optimism among many Africanists has been tempered. First, where power was ceded (for in many states – Gabon, Côte d'Ivoire, Togo, Kenya, Cameroon, Guinea, Ghana, Burkina Faso – authoritarian leaders re-emerged after competitive elections as born-again democrats), hegemonic power was only reluctantly relinquished, in a few instances with full expectations to bounce back to office in the future. Within the context of ethnic competitions that exist in many states, these are not prescriptions for democratic transition. Second, behind every political élite that ceded power, there are regions or ethnic groups that do not accept the idea of an 'electoral' loss of power. In some states 'expectations' even existed as to what region/ ethnic group 'should' next be in the saddle, based on the rotational principle. In Congo, for example, widespread feeling in the Far North existed that after Sassou-Nguesso it would be the Impfondo region's turn to control the presidency, since all others had already done so! With ethnic/regional patterns of voting the immutable building blocs of power, 'democracy' rules out sparsely populated Impfondo/and others) from ever being of political import, notwithstanding open political competition and electoral participation, and since 'diffusion of power' more affects the 'strong', not the weak, legitimate ethnic interests or basic rights cannot be necessarily assured. Despite this, as I will argue, this does not preclude perfectly acceptable democratic hybrids (human/civic rights, equity) from emerging.

Third, deeply intertwined with the above point, and enhancing its negative effects, are the conditions of scarcity that obtain in most of Africa: scarcity of money, resources, societal benefits, and ultimately, jobs. The societal groups that share the majority of these scarce resources have always been the civil service, armed forces and reigning politico-administrative class, while those seeking entry to the public trough are the burgeoning unemployed urban masses, including educated elements churned out in ever-larger numbers by the educational system. The chasm between scarcity and social expectations has made governance in most countries a harrowing experience punctuated by violent demonstrations, strikes, and power-grabs. State patronage has been used by leaders as social glue to cement to the Presidency the loyalty of ethnic and regional influentials; civil service (and parastatal sector) posts have been dispensed to university graduates, viewed as particularly volatile; and hence the fiscal bankruptcy of most states, both rich and poor, with little, if anything, left over for rural development or the masses, and the potential for destabilization – before and after 'democracy' – should rationalization of the public sector be attempted. Politics is a zero-sum game in Africa between the haves and the have-nots, with the stakes inordinately high – survival. Power-sharing, equity, regional even-handedness is difficult under such conditions.

Fourth, a significant number of states have not democratized at all, being in a social shambles (Somalia, Rwanda, Liberia); in transitional phases (Sierra Leone, Gambia, Lesotho); have successfully resisted pressures from within and without (Zaire, Nigeria); have only cosmetically adopted a semblance of competition and mass participation (Equatorial Guinea); or have by quasi-legitimate means (Kenya) or not so legal ones (Cameroon, Togo) returned former potentates to power, to continue oppressive policies with an 'electoral mandate'. The wide variety of 'transformations' that have taken place in Africa continue to pose problems to scholars (and not just to those statistically-oriented), qualitative or quantitative evaluations, today as in yesteryear.

Fifth, the political competition that has come about as a result of liberalization in Africa, has been in the majority of cases on the part of ethnic formations and narrow personalist parties, each geographically localized in 'historic' fiefdoms. (In most of Africa ethnic groups geographically localized, with the exception of modern capital cities.) While regional voting patterns, minority socio-cultural formations and 'independents' are familiar fare to comparativists, the extremely acute splinterization of political loyalties in Africa, transcending time and effects of modernization, is not. In Benin, a country of just over four million people and an electorate below two million, forty-one political parties registered once political space was allowed. A large number of single-member 'parties' secured representation in the legislature, with the largest party at the outset composed of only nine delegates. Through the formation of post-electoral alliances, something not fully expected, the splinterized national assembly was not reduced to chaos, suggesting possible solutions to some of the 'problems' currently being compiled. But percentage-wise the ethnic vote in the elections of the 1990s was virtually identical to that of 1960, illustrating the perpetuation of divisions in largely artificial countries (see Jackson and Rosberg 1985; 1986).

The same pattern has been repeated elsewhere where ethnicity remains a vital force. Over 110 political 'parties' emerged in Congo, though 'only' sixty-odd competed in the elections. Clearly, compared to the unipartyism of the past this is 'political competition'. But also clearly political systems where the building blocs of power are durable, acute, polarized and politicized ethnicity, led by irreplaceable leaders, are substantively different from systems of programmatic or ideological parties, as are systems of acute multipartyism, especially without strong centres. Conceptually both 'politics' and 'democracy' in such systems (and the problems of sustaining democracy as well as the integrity of the state itself) are quite different. Thus, whatever political hybrids currently exist on the continent may be temporary phenomena, since they are fragile and full of internal inconsistencies and tensions, but they may also survive as 'moderate democracies' because the Eurocentric alternative is simple not feasible. More vexing, the inordinately large number of exclusivist parties that compete for scarce resources, cannot *a priori* be assumed to ensure the survival of either civic or human rights (though they offer Vanhanen's requisite 'competition'), but paradoxically, the formation of coalitions and alliances may produce acceptable levels of protection of human/civil liberties. Possibly we are quantifying the African sample of the universe far too early.

Finally, despite the democratization of parts of Africa, little of long-term import has changed, or is likely to, on the economic front (Van de Walle 1994). The regimes that buckled to civil society and external pressures were bankrupt. They still are. Many are basically limping along thanks to small doses of international aid (that show no sign of significantly increasing) and through 'forgiveness' by European states of their national debts, even as they pile up new ones. Even the open elections in Congo and some other states could only take place after foreign funds were obtained. Fiscal short-falls, liquidity crises, payroll arrears continue in many countries, together with the same inevitable strikes and demonstrations.

Civil services have been pruned largely of 'phantom' workers (nonexistent personnel, whose paychecks had been pocketed by division heads); privatization and rationalization of state sectors has proceeded, but often at a snail's pace, except where enterprises have actually closed down under lock and key. For both policies entail dismissal of workers and concomitant potential for instability – that 'democracies' cannot quell as during the *ancien regime* via the armed forces! The closure of economically unmeritorious companies implies unemployment and trade unions (part of civil society) have fought many rearguard battles to save deficitory enterprises. In Congo the Lissouba government was for four years unable to effect the closure of a bank because 160-odd jobs were at stake, not to speak of other mammoth corporations that call for reorganization. Equally problematic has been privatization of deficitory but inherently viable former public enterprises, since interested foreign entrepreneurs insist on personnel cuts averaging 50 per cent of original manpower. That the pay-off can result in healthy industries – in Togo the bankrupt state steel mill was turned around financially in one year (Bergeron 1991) – is not an argument that sits well in societies with massive unemployment.

The World Bank had powerfully posited in 1989 the existence of a causal relationship between political democracy and meaningful and sustainable economic development in Africa, viewing the continent's economic crisis as a direct function of poor governance (The World Bank 1989). The link has hardly been visible in the half-decade since the democratic transformation began on the continent, unless growth rates of 2–4 per cent (barely keeping pace with population growth) in a handful of countries, can be deemed meaningful. Indeed, in recent years closer attention to the developmental experience of Southeast Asia's economic 'tigers' by the World Bank itself (World Bank 1993) seemingly suggests time-changing 'mixes' of authoritarianism within the context of efficient developmentally-minded regimes may be a better prescription for economic development.

The World Bank, and scholars, have also posited a relationship between free market economies and political democracy. Charles Lindblom most eloquently phrased the argument, when he noted:

> *only within market-oriented systems does political democracy arise.* Not all market-systems are democratic, but every democratic system is also a market-oriented system. Apparently, for reasons that are not wholly understood, political democracy has been unable to exist except when coupled with the market. An extraordinary proposition, it has so far held without exception.
>
> (Lindblom 1977: 116. Emphasis in the original.)

Though some other scholars (e.g. Dahl 1993) have suggested modifications of the formula, the basic relationship has not resulted in any perceivably positive advances in Africa, in either democratic governance or in economic development, much to the ultimate theoretical disarray in African Studies today.

How does the above overview of the democratization process and its limitations in Africa relate to the substantive aspects of Vanhanen's important study? Let me first note that there has always been, and probably always will be, an inevitable tension and tug-of-war between quantitative and qualitative studies; between the generalist and the specialist; the comparativist and the case-study expert. Indeed, such 'either/or' questions and issues, false, of course, in their supposed dichotomy, have for long been the anvil on which fresh graduate students have had their analytic skills honed, in American universities at least. I raise this issue directly in connection with the basic indicators of democracy proposed in this work. For, while as a comparativist I find little to quarrel with these and other statistical constructs, as an Africanist I have basic problems at the very outset with the trim approach to indicators of democracy and 'diffuseness of power' central to the study.

The two indicators of democracy that are proposed – indices of electoral participation and political competition – offer elegance in their simplicity, objectivity, and relative ease of quantification and, as is argued, they probably subsume many variables other scholars insist on including as measures, ingredients, or prerequisites of democracy. But not in much of the Third World. Despite the sound arguments for greater methodological rigour, and to be rid of subjective and evaluation bias, the indicators as they stand are highly Eurocentric, apart from the fact that the concept of democracy is to some extent itself value-laden. At a minimum they rest on conceptualizations of a neat, orderly retreat from political hegemony by élites who (subconsciously?) use rational choice theory to maximize future options and gains, in the context of large, quasi-modern, politically conscious electorates, with dedicated second-echelon leaders and a well developed civil society willing and able to mount the ramparts and fend off non democratic impulses.

But this is not the African context I have tried to portray above. In the African context neither 'democracy' nor 'measures of democracy' can necessarily be assumed to rest solely on indices of electoral participation and political competition, nor will diffuseness of power, as commonly understood, transpire, at least on the short term. There can be – and are – states that satisfy, to a greater or lesser extent, the suggested criteria, yet cannot be seen as democratic. There can be a multiplicity of parties (a boggling number, as indicated), and vigorous political competition (even fair, unrigged?) and significant levels of mass electoral participation, and a 'statistical' diffusion of power without what objective scholars would term a modicum of 'democracy'. Such hybrids are major improvements from their monolithic authoritarian civil or military antecedents, but are not democratic polities in the fullest sense of the word. There is as yet no 'second Botswana' on the continent.

On the other hand, if my gloomy, admittedly judgemental assessment that in most African states a meaningful diffuseness of power (a precondition of democracy, or sustainable democracy, according to Vanhanen) is unlikely to be arrived at, is much of the continent foredoomed to the absence of democracy? Not necessarily. One could argue democracy is not necessarily foreclosed (though gravely disadvantaged) in the absence of ingredients deemed vital elsewhere, for there is more to democracy than high levels of political competition, mass participation and diffuseness of power. One cannot be an absolutist, lest one's geographical scope of study needlessly narrows sharply. This is the reason for the persistent insistence by many scholars for 'additional' criteria for democracy (many subjectively arrived at, or quantifiable) that Vanhanen bemoans, that would allow for both absolutes, and ordinal rankings of the wide array of quasi- and not so quasi-democracies in Africa. At the minimum, from my perspective, an indicator of human rights/rule of law/press freedom needs to be added to efficiently separate out look-alikes.

By way of illustration three recent 'structural' examples of democratic transition may be briefly cited. In Congo, the country's first free elections (municipal, parliamentary and Presidential) since independence took place in 1992/93. Some 110 formations registered, sixty-odd competed in the elections in which there were high levels of electoral participation. Power today is shared in the national assembly, political alliances have emerged, and even political 'co-habitation' has taken place. An immense advance over the stultifying Marxist–Leninist northern military era of 1969–1991! But the basic political conflict (ethnic, regional, inter-generational, religious) continued until 1994 on the streets of Brazzaville, where over 1,000 have been killed. Rival youthful private militias ('Ninjas' and 'Zoulous' – witness the universalization/modernization effect of television that does not erode ethnic identity) clash across ethnic quarters; political murders intermittently take place; the former chief of staff (General Makoko) refused to recognize the new government; the old largely northern national army (a new one is being formed) remains loyal to ex-President General Sassou-Nguesso, who is now conceptually a northern warlord. Vanhanen alludes to these difficulties in Congo, lamenting the country's democratic prospects, but his assessment is based more on qualitative and subjective data, and not so much on the country's high levels of competition and participation.

Or witness Kenya, where with only 'normal' electoral aberrations (though with pre-election government-sponsored ethnic violence to illustrate multipartyism would lead to ethnic clashes!) Moi emerged victorious (due to a split opposition), to continue his heavy-handed rule, press censorship, and economic mismanagement of the country (Throup 1993). And what do we do with Togo, where though the legislative elections proceeded more or less in order, General Eyadema emerged 'victorious' in the 1993 Presidential contest – after an assassination attempt on the favourite, Gilchrist Olympio (son of the first President murdered by Eyadema in 1963), who was then barred from contesting the Presidency on a technicality. Togo's election, and new 'democracy', has been termed by some as 'flawed' but still valid. There has been mass political participation and political competition except for the Presidency. Democracy? Not really, but certainly power-sharing and a democratic 'whiff'. Subjective halfway houses are needed, a continuum to allow for the differentiation of the African existential universe.

Apart from reservations on the 'democracy' indices I only have space to make two cautionary remarks about all correlational analysis as it relates to Africa in general, and not necessarily to Vanhanen's. The issues, that are no doubt familiar to many readers, may be subsumed under (1) the unrelia-bility (or time-limited nature) of some supposedly fixed quantifiable data, that can taint all allegedly 'scientific' statistical analysis, and (2) the pre-sence of some variables (of necessity largely qualitative) that I regard as vital to any analysis, that are frequently ignored, a fact that has always been, to me, a central deficiency of much statistical work that purports to establish valid correlations.

The first point it is simply a cautionary reminder that some of the 'hardest' possible data in Africa, not to speak of less reliable ones, may in reality be extremely soft. I will only be able to refer to one kind, demo-graphic data, but note need be made that in many societies with porous borders and weak formal economies, much economic data is also very suspect, and that other 'indicators', such as 'number of doctors', may be really irrelevant since the vast majority of physicians practice in the capital city. Coming to demographics, however, I dare say no one really knows with any degree of certitude the actual population of half a dozen countries, while that of up to a dozen others are little more than (reliable or not so reliable) guestimates or projections from colonial-era data. I am not allud-ing here just to the enormous discrepancies in past Nigerian censuses, that tainted much 'per capita' data construct in former statistical efforts; or to the problem of dealing with countries with nomadic populations that cross international boundaries on transhumance patterns (Chad, Niger, Mali) sometimes included (or excluded) from official statistics of two countries; or to the underestimations in Mauritania of the black serfs of the Moors; or to lack of reliability of data about the Sahrawi Republic; sometimes included within Morocco's.

Even statistically-conscious countries present problems. In Gabon the variance between official Gabonese data and that published in UN manuals varies by 100 per cent; a similar variability in the demographics of the Central African Republic has been 'solved' not by census, but by Bangui splitting the difference between the UN's and its own data. During the murderous Nguema era in Equatorial Guinea over one third of the population fled the country (Decalo 1989), many not to return, since the current regime (now 'democratized') is headed by a clique of Nguema's former henchmen. But there is no reliable estimate of the country's current demography, which in the case of a country with a small population to start with and such a massive exodus is a serious problem. Congo's population, reliably estimated in 1990 (with the statistical office even projected demographic growth rates through the year 2005) was adjusted upwards by some 20 per cent when the Presidential elections took place in 1993!

Finally, the issue of some more or less qualitative constructs, may be of great value to purely statistical indicators in assessing democratization and its staying powers. One has to do with questions of political style, personality dynamics, motivations of African leaders. In my research on civil–military relations (Decalo 1990) I found such variables invariably extremely valuable as prime or supplemental predictors of intra-military corporate dynamics and civil–military relations. Politics is after all concerned with people in political contexts. To completely exclude the personal variable in political life because of intrinsic methodological difficulties, or the implicit subjectivity in its quantification, is outright hazardous. It results in overly mechanical approximations of the ingredients of complex, dynamic political processes, to the detriment of theory-building and predictive powers. This is especially true when dealing with relatively new polities without entrenched and legitimated structures, under hosts of socio-economic stresses – that allow personality variables and motivations wider scope of action.

I cannot at this juncture contribute a developed thesis on the centrality of political psychology insights on roles played by African political leaders in the transitions to democracy, or its sustainability. But there is more than adequate suggestive evidence that fieldwork analysts are aware of, to justify some exploration of this variable to the benefit of better-anchored under-standings of the dynamics of Africa's recent political transitions. There are documentable, personal reasons – that have nothing to do with structural attributes of states, that are the mill of much quantitative analysis – behind the varied responses, some reluctantly positive, others adamantly negative, of African leaders to democratization, that have, and will, play a role in determining its success or failure. The differential reactions to democratization of Kaunda and Eyadema, Moi and Houphouet-Boigny, are pregnant with implications that bear attention. General Kerekou's dignified accep-tance of electoral defeat in Benin; his constructive role in assuaging north-ern ethnic groups on their sense of 'loss' of power (to a southern President and assembly); his sanction (by supporting the rule of law) of the trial of a former ally, Major Tawes, for a coup bid aimed at reversing democracy, must be an ingredient that consolidated the transition in Cotonou, com-pared to Eyadema's negative role in next-door Lomé. If not undermined by subsequent socio-economic developments, a more democratic give-and-take political culture may emerge, in Benin, rather than in Togo.

Which leads to the final variable, political culture. The latter is more often utilized since a link, causal or not, has been posited between structural attributes of states, political culture and democratization (Inglehart 1988; 1990) though the directionality of the causality is at times disputed (Muller and Seligson 1994). The difficulties encountered in constructing reliable measures of civic and political culture for developed societies, are so immensely compounded within the context of non nation-states (Diamond 1993), that little work has occurred in African Studies specifically. Cursory analysis underscores that most African states contain weak civic and multiple political cultures. Complaints about non utilization of such data may thus be petty, and I am certainly not here addressing Vanhanen with a critique, but rather cautioning against gross generalizations. Differences in civic/political culture (however defined, quantified, and with whatever causality) are visible in comparative African studies. In the absence of real systematic research or hard data, only oblique references to the relevance of political culture have cropped up, merely suggesting that 'whatever it is, it is there and plays a role, however unclear!'

The goal of understanding precisely how democracy comes about, its minimal requisites, and what sustains it, is ambitious and full of pitfalls. The concerns of the globalist often tend to be reductionist, those of the regionalist maximalist. Possibly the two strains can only be married to the satisfaction of both by starting with maximalist all-inclusive positions, allowing time and the more thorough spread of quantifiable research in less developed regional studies to whittle down extraneous variables.

REFERENCES

Bergeron, I. (1991) 'Privatization through leasing: the Togo steel case', in R. Rama-murti and R. Vernon (eds) *Privatization and Control of State-Owned Enterprises*, Washington: The World Bank.

Butty, J. (1991) 'The democracy carrot', *West Africa*, 22 April.

Dahl, R. (1993) 'Why free markets are not enough', in L. Diamond and M. Plattner (eds) *Capitalism, Socialism and Democracy Revisited*, Baltimore: Johns Hopkins University Press.

Decalo, S. (1989) *Psychoses of Power: African Personal Dictatorships*, Boulder, Col.: Westview Press.

——(1990) 'Modalities of civil–military stability in Africa', *Journal of Modern African Studies* 28, 2.

——(1992) 'The process, prospects and constraints of democratization in Africa', *Africa Affairs* 91, 1.

Diamond, L. (ed.) (1993) *Political Culture and Democracy in Developing Countries*, Boulder, Col: Lynne Rienner.

Huntington, S. (1984) 'Will more countries become democratic?' *Political Science Quarterly* 99, 1.

——(1991) *The Third Wave: Democratization in the Late Twentieth Century*, Norman: University of Oklahoma Press.

Inglehart, R. (1988) 'The Renaissance of political culture', *American Political Science Review* 82, 3.

—— (1990) *Culture Shift in Advanced Industrial Society*, Princeton: Princeton University Press.

Jackson, R. and Rosberg, C. (1985) 'The marginality of African states', in G. Carter and P. O'Neara (eds) *African Independence: the First Twenty-five Years*, Bloomington: Indiana University Press.

—— (1986) 'Why Africa's weak states persist: The empirical and juridical in Statehood', in A. Kohli (ed.) *State and Development in the Third World*, Princeton: Princeton University Press.

Lindblom, C. (1977) *Politics and Markets*, New York: Basic Books.

Muller, E. and Seligson, M. (1994) 'Civic culture and democracy: the question of causal relationship', *American Political Science Review* 88, 3.

Parfitt, T. and Riley, S. (1989) *The African Debt Crisis*, London: Routledge.

Throup, D. (1993) 'Elections and political legitimacy in Kenya', *Africa* 63, 3.

Tilly, C. (1975) *The Formation of National States in Western Europe*, Princeton: Princeton University Press.

Van de Walle, N. (1994) 'Political liberation and economic policy reform in Africa', *World Development* 22, 4.

Vanhanen, T. (1995) *Prospects of democracy: 172 countries in the 1990s*, manuscript.

World Bank (1989) *Sub-Saharan Africa: from Crisis to Sustainable Development*, Washington: The World Bank.

—— (1993) *Southeast Asia*, Washington: The World Bank.

9 Some observations on prospects of democracy in the contemporary world
Africa's transition to a democratic governance system

John W. Forje

ANALYTICAL REFLECTION

The pioneering study of Tatu Vanhanen in the field of democratic prospects from a comparative political analysis perspective throws sufficient light on the merits and demerits of comparative governance especially between the established democracies and the transitional ones. The study builds on an expansion of scope along three distinctions, namely; first, the geographical scope which has shifted from an ethnocentric concentration on the established democracies of the western political systems to embracing the emerging non western style democracies of the so-called developing areas of Africa, Asia, and Latin America. Second, the broader intellectual focus which has equally been quite impressive as the expansion of the geographical horizons. Within the synthesis of this intellectual expansion, we see the abandonment of the emphasis of comparative political study on formal governmental institutions, legal rules and procedures and formal political ideologies to the pivotal embracement of political parties, pressure groups, voting behaviour, political socialization as crucial input ingredients in comparative political analysis. The third stage results from a marriage, holy or unholy, between geographical ethnocentricity and intellectual expansion; which has given birth to a kind of 'beyond frontier comparative' paradigm shift, that is, political analyses are no longer content with single-country studies analysis. Apparently their focus could be envisaged as stretching beyond national frontiers to a global commons comparative analytical study of political and governance systems.

This new emphasis has equally been triggered by post Second World War political developments and especially following the emergence of newly independent states on the global political landscape; and where the new emphasis on comparison has had profound impact. We now find ourselves caught in the dichotomy of 'developed and developing' politics. However, the yardstick for cross-national comparative studies draws heavily from the generic nature of politics as practised in the western democracies. Unfortunately, certain facets of the fundamental attributes and indicators of the western comparative dichotomy have not been fully

316 John W. Forje

established in the developing areas which blurs any form of comparative analysis.

The approach on cross-national comparative politics has greatly enriched our knowledge in the study of governance systems across the globe thus making it possible to critically and scientifically discuss the feasibility of looking at political activities as constituting a 'system' and 'functions' as general categories of political activities.

Apparently, conceptualization and a concern with the generic, the hall-mark of Vanhanen's pillars of research is bound to suffer certain defects following the shift from an ethnocentric to a cross-national comparative analytical approach. In other words, the indicators deployed by the author are good and valid as long as these indicators are used within the ethno-centric framework or time space. Once you move out of the ethnocentric space, certain pertinent traits must be duly considered. Scientifically, at least four distinct objectives can be realized from an analysis of two or more polities.

First, cross-polity comparison makes possible the construction of classi-fications, typologies and rankings. Second, cross-polity comparison yields a panoramic description of the universe of polities – for example, the extent to which certain traits prevail in a society; what overall qualitative general-izations can be made? and not least, the trends that can be discerned. Third, is the identification of uniformities of polity characteristics. Within the realm of this objective is to ascertain the ways in which certain polity characteristics cluster together making it possible for one to define and distinguish one type of polity from another. Equally important in this respect is to ascertain processes and behaviourial regularities that occur from one polity to another.

The four traits are well documented in this study. Sub-Saharan Africa presents the greatest challenge to any theory of comparative democratiza-tion as the region encompasses a complex mixture of Max Weber's classical distinctive typologies of:

1 the traditional polity;
2 the charismatic polity; and
3 the rational–legal polity, defined according to whether the authority wielded by the government is held to be justified and hence legitimate because
   (a) it is seen as continuation of the ancient and sanctified past;
   (b) it is wielded by a person who enjoys absolute personal devotion; and
   (c) it is exercised according to legally valid, rationally created rules.
                          (Weber 1947: 328; see also Almond and Verba 1965)

All factors involving the Notables, Old Bourgeoisie, Nationalist and New Intelligentsia.

My comments are not focused nor directed towards the three indicators of democracy – competition, participation and (the index of) democratization advanced by Vanhanen. Rather my comments are addressed to how these and other attributes without their firm institutionalization, particularly in the developing polities, make all statistical data meaningless. These attributes which constitute the pillars of democracy are currently missing on the political landscape of the African continent. Until they are functionally engraved in the political agenda of developing societies, we cannot arrive at a more comparable picture of statistical data impinging on the fundamentals of democracy in the emerging and old democracies.

In this respect, a conceptual framework construed on the synthesis of the structural–functional approach offers the most appropriate scientific explanation and analysis on how the continent has succeeded or continues to succeed or fail in its endeavours to institutionalize democratic governance systems in individual countries. The move from a non competitive to a semi-competitive politics through the death of the single-party and the rise of multi-party politics recently reinstated in some countries exacerbate how ruling regimes are ousted from authority by way of free elections. In chronological order, Benin, Cape Verde, São Tomé
and Príncipe, Zambia, Congo, Mali, Malawi, and eventually South Africa; and in countries where elections were won fraudulently by the incumbents as was the case of Cameroon's 1992 presidential elections and Togo's 1993 presidential elections.

A content analysis of the literature shows that colonial governmental tradition and post-colonial regimes were based upon autocracy, centralization and paternalism. In the last thirty-three years a process of 'hybridization' has occurred whereby external influences and internal dynamics have created a new totality in the democratization process. Thus, to comprehend the problems of the political situation in post-colonial Africa, the issue should be studied and analysed from the perspective of 'longue durée', a process of development that exhibits interruptions but is construed upon deeper structures of continuity. The legalization of 108 political parties in Cameroon in no way implies democracy and participation, rather, it is a continuation of the monolithic party system in a different form. However, the cherished values of democracy are knocking on the doors of the African society. There is no turning back to the old *status quo*. Change has to come to rid the continent of conflict, isolation, mistrust and instability.

CRITERIA FOR EVALUATING AFRICA'S DEMOCRATIC TRANSITION PROCESS

Democracy is usually measured in terms of a viable multi-party system, the separation of powers between the legislative, executive and judicial institutions of government, the rule of law through the setting up of constitutional and other legal norms, as well as adequate institutions for their enforcement, free and fair elections, freedom of the press, the general observance of human rights and freedoms. All these cardinal elements can and should be taken into account in the evaluation of the democratization process in the transition countries.

The non existence of these vital virtues retards the development and application of democracy in African countries. The very existence of these virtues highlights the fact that there is also a superior level where democracy becomes a state of mind, a way of living, both at the individual and collective scale; a model that permits society to function within the most fundamental parameters of governance. In short, the old democracies have attained a certain level of political culture; Africa has not. With a high level of political culture we can comfortably talk of the psychological mutations that affect both the individual and the collective social profile of people and stimulate their transformation from receivers of democracy into creators of democracy. The political culture attained in the western democracies shows that the possibilities of military coups in the United States, Britain, Canada, the Nordic countries, etc. are far remote when compared to the situation in Africa, where military coups in many cases are now a daily routine. In some of these countries, civilian regimes remain in office because of the unholy or holy alliance between them and the men in uniform.

Presently, the African countries are still attempting to begin the first stage of the democratic process – as receivers of democracy – hence, the political life as receiver cannot be compared to those of creators of democracy. Western countries can therefore be visualized as creators of democracy – they have attained a high status in the discipline. In the evaluation of the democratization process in Africa, it is imperative that due consideration be adequately directed to the following elements.

Each transition nation in its specific context

Just as many specific aspects of democratic system can be distinguished between American, British, Japanese, Swedish, Danish, French, etc. so also can we distinguish between the process of democratization in the African countries, for example, between former British and French colonies. The mentioned developed polities float in different forms of democracies. They do so because their internal social and political context, culture and tradition, including external factors in different ways, shaped their specific democratic profile. Different internal and external conditions have equally characterized the democratic evolution process of African countries; and this has to be taken into consideration in assessing the democratization process. Hence, morally and analytically, it is a mistake to label one country as a star-performer, and another as a late-comer or poor-performer without giving due consideration to each country's internal context, as well as the different amount of western economic and political support in the process of economic reform and democratization.

Dynamic indicators in the process of democratic reform

By and large, the success or failure in the process of democratic reformation or restructuring should not be judged in absolute terms – that is, by only concentrating on the absolute level of socio-economic exchange – but rather in relative ones – by equally looking at the time factor – or distance travelled in the process of democratic transition.

On the one hand, we can state that South Africa has taken a relatively short period, or come a long way on the 'democratic transition road'. It took off on the right path barely one year after the collapse of the apartheid system. So also was the shift of the baton from colonial administration to African majority rule in Ghana (1957), Nigeria (1960), Kenya (1964), etc. But events less than a decade later started to show the fragility of the governance system the colonial masters handed to their former colonies or, better still, how the Africans mismanaged the governance system. The principles of democratic governance were quickly replaced with ideological dogma and ethnic fanatism. What the future of the democratic process in South Africa will be is difficult to say now. One thing clear is that they can learn from the numerous mistakes of the rest of the African continent. In addition, the international political climate is much more favourable now than thirty years ago. The fear of communist infiltration in Africa and the collapse of the Cold War conflict are factors that put the evolving political situation in South Africa on a much better premise of success in the building of its internal political culture and governance system.

Generally, African countries like Nigeria, Ghana, Gambia, South Africa in the first years of political independence – i.e. in terms of the distance travelled on the path of democratization could be characterized as being remarkable. In the case of South Africa, if it keeps to the momentum of its dynamic take-off, it has a genuine chance to enter the group of frontrunners in the process of democratic reform.

On the other hand, contrasting Africa's democratic transition with that of the western countries, we observe that the former is relatively a newcomer to the game of democratic governance. Their distance travelled on the path of democratization is relatively short in comparison with the established democracies like Britain, USA, the Scandinavian countries, France, etc. Again, one can question why things have gone wrong in countries like Liberia and Ethiopia. These are countries that were not colonized like the rest of the African nations. They have not fared better, which again dismisses the scenario of 'distance travel' in a narrow sense. However, Africa is still in the early learning stages of the democratic game; but with the added advantage of learning from the failures or mistakes committed by the older democracies in their transition process. What can be questioned is whether they are learning from the mistakes of the older democracies.

Avoidance of wrong perceptions and biased categorization

Because of the failure of the nation-state, there is the common and constant tendency in the academic, mass media and political circles to propagate the idea or notion of certain countries being more capable of developing a genuine democratic governance system than others. Cultural, historical, geographic, economic and religious arguments, among others, have been advanced in supporting such theories. For example, given France's grip over the politics of its former colonies, unfortunately, the kind of genuine democratic governance, electoral transparence practised in France, has yet to be transferred to its former colonial satellites.

In this regard, the scenario of British indirect policies put its former colonies in a better position of realizing the benefits that go with democratic governance. Authoritarian backsliding will take some time in Francophone African countries. By logical consequences, domestic credentials may be hard to emerge in Francophone Africa, though Senegal's performances present some positive signals for a new dawn of democratic governance. Whether the Jacques Chirac regime will deliver the much needed political and economic leverage of disengagement leading to the birth of a new democratic governance system and political independence and freedom in Francophone Africa is still too early to speculate.

The criteria show that Africa stands on the threshold of a new political era, which calls for self-evaluation and self-understanding. It equally shows how complicated the issue of comparative analysis is and why certain inherent factors must be considered within the context and power of African politics and in the western social–political model, which is defined not only in the political and institutional framework of democracy but is connected to the other relevant aspects of western societies: prosperity and security. Thus, the process of post-independent African democratization encompasses a number of specific characteristics; namely:

1 escaping the pressure of dictatorial and monolithic systems, the need for freedom with responsibility, not freedom against the law, and the need for a new agenda of democratic education of the masses;
2 monolithicism has destroyed all forms of democratic governance and social coherence outside the party-state system, making a civil society to be non existent, giving rise to a kind of political and institutional vacuum, crisis of confidence in the governance system amongst others;
3 against the background of a crisis of confidence in the system, there is now a new feeling of insecurity, such as; internal political instability, social turmoil, economic difficulties, rise of ethnic violence in all forms, danger of the break-away of certain provinces amongst others.

Thus a newly reborn democratic governance system must be armed to deal precisely with these inherent convulsions of an unsettled political and economic order.

REINSTATING THE MISSING DIMENSION

A prerequisite for the prospects of genuine democracy in the region is the reinstating of certain crucial missing dimensions which constitute the fundamental conditions for sustainable democratization, namely, representation, accountability and participation (RAP).

All modalities for scientific analysis of voting habits, attitudes and forms of democratic behaviour in a governance system without people's access to RAP remains meaningless to the democratic governance system. This equally explains the failure of the Westminster or Elyseé models in the continent. First, from the beginning the colonial state was authoritarian and hierarchic by nature. Though the British and French administration, through their policy of indirect and direct rule, did tap into existing native authoritarian socio-political structures, neither of the systems gave existing African forms of governance a chance to survive or develop. It was only towards the tail end of the collapse of the colonial rule that *quasi* movements towards the introduction of a more democratic governance system went operational. Unfortunately, the length of time that remained to consolidate the democratic institutions was too short (see Diamond 1988; Cleaver 1992). The authoritarian nature of the colonial state had a direct effect on the emerging states in Africa that 'given the post-colonial state was an inheritor of the colonial entity's political, economic and social framework of rule, then it was not surprising that it would attempt to govern in the same way' (Haynes 1992), and with some nuances from the existing environment.

Second, under the colonial governance system, there was the absence of the development of a class of an independent economic basis; that is, no group could exert effective control over the state. It was a development that made the state essentially a haven where one could operate as one wished with impunity. The state at the same time provided the only opportunity for social mobility and prosperity. Consequently, competition became great, and this contributed to the erosion of the structural basis of the multi-party system. Thus the multi-party system became functionally ineffective (see Clapham 1992; Baylies and Settel 1992).

Finally, the rise and functioning of the political parties were focused towards a common goal – self-determination. But after the ascendency to independence, a great deal of dissension ensued, and a different political agenda emerged, which amounted to the consolidation of power into a few hands – or in some cases, a major party obtained the largest share of the votes in an election. This created the basis for the birth of the single-party state. It eventually eliminated opposition parties, which in turn minimised the participatory role of the citizens. A political culture failed to emerge from the very inception of the new states. The African single-party regime is singularly ill-equipped to deal openly with the various interest groups, and the more seriously it takes its role as single spokesman for the masses, the more difficult is the task. By rejecting the idea of bargaining with the various interest groups, the single-party regime fans civil disobedience, chaos and political instability. Thus the monolithic governance system is forced or obliged to rely on military or police force to maintain power. Generally, the single-party regime limits sharply the range of activities open to the various forms of political opposition and also the utility of these oppositions for the development of the political system as a whole. The sustainability of most civilian regimes depends on the coercion of the military into the party and governance system. Cameroon presents a typical example, hence the presence of the military on the streets in Cameroon unlike in a military ruled country, Nigeria, Sierra Leone, Gambia for example.

Political activities in the new states required more than the formal institutions of democracy – universal suffrage, the political party, and the elective legislature. A democratic form of participatory political system requires as well a political culture consistent with it. The nuances of the Western political culture transferred to the emerging states encountered serious difficulties – first the nature of the political culture itself, and second, the numerous problems confronting these new nation-states. This explains the great variation in the voting behaviour and in other indicators as shown by the statistical data depicting the issues of democracy in the region. It further highlights why the functionality of RAP is crucial in the development of a democratic political culture in Africa.

REPRESENTATION

Reverting to Abraham Lincoln's notion of 'government of the people', which implies representative governance, it equally requires concerted functional mechanisms to ensure a broad base representation of the population in the decision-making process. Thus an essential feature of representation is the sustainability of those in power. The masses must have at their disposal the ways and means through democratically conducted elections to oust the governors once the governed feel themselves dissatisfied with their pattern of governance. The sudden decline of the multi-party systems after independence eroded the basis for 'government of the people' through a free and fair democratic process. Thus the mechanisms of the monolithic authoritarian party system restricted the freedom of choice and representation. Hence in this respect, Lincoln's concept of democracy becomes a sham in the case of Africa. Contempt rather than respect for political adversaries laid the foundation for political violence and civil disobedience particularly during and after election periods.

Across the continent military governance system has been predominant. Nigeria, Ghana, Uganda, Chad and others have fluctuated between military and civilian administration. In a period of nine years, Benin experienced six *coups d'état*. The violence and state of emergencies that erupted after presidential elections in Algeria, Cameroon, Kenya, Ghana and in some other countries testify to either the alienation of the masses in the voting process or 'stolen victory' by the defeated ruling party. These are actions that destroy the basis for democracy and good governance. Even the peaceful establishment of single-party regimes in Cameroon, Senegal and Ivory Coast failed in terms of the sustainability of those in political command since it lacked the fundamental structural basis of representation by individual choices. In the same way one can equally argue that the institutions of post independence multi-party systems still implied one dominant party government, since the basis of the multi-party structure was nothing but an entrenched concentration and personalization of political power at the top and composed of specific ethnic blocs.

The introduction of the single-party state, even though it offered a higher voter turnout, also limited competitive choices among the voters. A high voter turnout under the monolithic party system should not be interpreted as 'representation', or government of the people, but rather as government against the people. Fear and reprisal and not ideological conviction forced people to vote. Any form of opposition towards the incumbent president or party leadership is perceived as subversive. Even under the multi-party system the incumbent leadership is never unseated anyway. Post independence political development has shown no functional differences between the single- and multi-party systems. There is little reason, if one argues from past experiences, to regard the re-introduction of multi-party systems as a panacea. What is required in the enhancement of the democratization process, is to open up and create adequate room for competitive choices and, of course, the mechanisms to unseat governments by democratic means. An opening of this kind will not only create conditions favouring the development of stable democracies, but it will equally give a different statistical reading and analysis from what has been presented in this study.

Over the years, Africa has experienced controversial elections – elections that have either limited people's choices or accepted stolen victories under the auspices of the judiciary system that is supposed to uphold and interpret the laws of the state without fear or favour. The case of Cameroon's 1992 presidential elections stands crystal clear in the violation of the inherent rights and role of the judiciary as a neutral referee for dispensing justice and for upholding the constitutionality of the nation (Forje 1993a; 1993b; see also Forje 1991a; 1991b). In this respect, the judiciary is a captive and weak institution operating on the orders of the executive branch of government.

Representation and free competitive choices presuppose the proper registration of voters, demarcation of constituencies, freedom of speech and association, an independent judiciary, and a comprehensive and concerted electoral law among others. There must be neutrality in the enforcement of the electoral laws. The registration of voters is an important aspect of the electoral system and democratization process. A list of voters is the quality, accuracy and safety, which guards against interference or tampering with the figures and the eventual falsification of the election results. Falsification of election results presents inaccurate electoral data. Very often these wrong data are used to paint the process of democratization under way in the continent. These data inhibit rather than contribute positively to the process of good governance in the region. Electoral data from the continent under the current governance system are inaccurate.

Finally, we should bear in mind that African nation states are societies where people have divergent political views based on the constellation of the ethnic groupings. Thus, in this crucial period of democratization, when a new wind of political change is blowing across each nation, people of the different sheds of political ideologies and ethnic diversity should have equal treatment and opportunities to express their opinions and to canvass for votes. The political environment in which elections and representation take place remains crucial to the democratic process. People are not allowed freely to choose among contending candidates and different ideological ideas. For that choice to be freely and fairly made, all contenders must have the chance to present and defend their ideological standings. Views from individuals and from a cross-section of the political spectrum must be accommodated and accounted for. This takes us to the second aspect – that of accountability and transparency.

ACCOUNTABILITY

The success of nation-building in the past has been jeopardized by its inability to be self-critical or self-examining, to conduct an honest and thorough self-evaluation, which should allow positive moves towards transparency. The doctrine of the separation of powers presupposes that the concept, 'government for the people', implies that those in power should equally be accountable to the governed or electors and be subjected to control at all times. The subjection to control enhances the existence of institutional 'checks and balances', a fundamental ingredient in democratic governance.

Both Jean Jacques Rousseau and de Montesquieu emphasized the need and notion of accountability. This is a missing dimension in African politics. Accountable government requires a judiciary separated from the executive. An independent and accessible judiciary should be regarded as one of the essential institutional pillars of modern democracy. Accountability itself refers to the obligation of a subordinate to be answerable to the super-ordinate in carrying out assigned duties and exercising discretionary powers. Accountability is supposed to make governments transparent, to emphasize and enhance governmental responsiveness and legitimacy and to improve policy implementation. Political parties are equally obliged to be accountable to their supporters and the nation.

It is regrettable that meaningful government and opposition benches are still absent from the political scenario of African countries. As a result of this absence, the process of democratization in the region has now reached a hopeless stage as mirrored by events in Burundi, Cameroon, Algeria, Congo, Ethiopia, Somalia, Nigeria, Zaire, Rwanda, South Africa, etc. The political environment is incompletely crystallized and dominated by contradictory factors – vertical linkages in the form of clientelism and ethnicity alongside horizontal groups in the nature of social classes, whose status is often nascent. The western democracies are stable because there is accountability and consensus on a broad range of issues. Accountability also opens avenues for patterns of orientations which enhance the 'psychic mobility' of the traditional man to think of himself like his western counterpart to see the social future and to seek out his own version of the better life, rather than passively accepting his heritage. South Africa's introduction of a Government of National Unity (GNU) stands out as the answer mitigating the apartheid undemocratic governance system. But the sustainability of GNU or the successful transition to majority party government structure will determine how democratically the New South Africa has fared well along the transitional road to genuine democratic governance. The degree of openness and level of debate concerning the new draft constitution for South Africa gives hope for a better start in the governance art as compared to the existing situation in most African countries. The mass participation of the people in the elections that sealed the apartheid governance system constitutes an acceptable frame of reference for voters, participation in future elections.

Since there is no accountability, the ruling regime has a free hand to do whatever it pleases. The act of non accountability is enhanced, since it is often claimed that physical violence in human relations is accommodated on a prodigious scale in Africa without offending customary values and norms. The events in Burundi, Liberia, Rwanda, and South Africa are manifestations of coercive power on the part of the ruling authority or ethnic group that happens to control the political and military machinery of the state. Accountability is equally required both within the parameters of the single and multi-party systems. The direction is towards more inclusive politics by introducing measures that extend societal participation in political decision-making. As a first step in that direction, the multi-party system remains a basic requirement for competitive politics, i.e. pluralism will produce greater accountability and, consequently, lead to the emergence of a democratic system. On the other hand, it could also be argued that single-party system, with scope for open debate and representation of minority interests, may actually be more democratic than a multi-party system in which there is only minimal public consultation and accountability. But in the absence of a political culture of participation and accountability, multi-party democracy is likely to remain confined to competition among the political élite to the exclusion of the masses.

PARTICIPATION

Participatory government implies 'government by the people', and not 'government against the people'. The custodians of political power (governors) are democratically bound not only to be substitutable and controlled but that people should participate equally in the political process. In most African states, the concept of basic democratic rights, i.e. the conditions for popular participation are grossly restricted. There is a total absence of the modalities for freedom of speech, peaceful assembly and expression of ideological and religious inclinations. There are no guarantees against the tyranny of either the minority or the majority, whichever one happens to control the machinery of political power.

In a democratically functional governance system, government by law implies that it is not the 'governor' but the society in its entirety that must approve the rules regulating the entire community. A prerequisite for this is a democratically elected legislative assembly: and the legislature must follow the will of the people. No one is more explicit on this issue than Gandhi: 'There goes my people. I must follow them because I am their leader'. Or in the words of the Aragon Nobility to King Philip of Spain: 'We, whose value as human beings is the same as yours, make you our king and Lord provided that you protect our freedoms, if not, you are no longer our King'. African legislators and leaders have shied away from this noble principle of democratic governance; partly perhaps through what Franz Fanon sees as the processes of double alienation – taking people's custom away from them first, reformulating these for the purpose of colonial rule and returning them to the people as if they were still their own – 'traditional' rule became autocratic (see de Gaay Fortman and Mikyo 1991).

Africa's transition in the global evolution of political and democratic governance systems requires a coherent and systematic analytical approach in order to put this evolution into proper perspective. While the traditions of parliamentary democracy, accountable administrative systems and respect for human rights are well established, particularly in certain western democracies, the situation is just the opposite in most African countries where totalitarian regimes triumph in the suppression of fundamental human rights.

The search for good governance has stimulated serious debates on what may be fashioned as the 'attracting and repelling' forces of democratic governance. The great divide within the academia as to what is 'democracy' and how it should be measured streamline the inconsistency in advancing a coherent theoretical approach to explaining the democratization process (see Lipset 1960; Lipset, *et al.* 1988; Huntington 1984; Sartori 1987). As a result, democracy has different meanings for different people, and the various participating forces exploit these divergencies to advance their political struggle for power resources. It is not surprising that the political systems of African states stretch from democracies to autocracies. Each of these systems in their different ways promote or limit the degree of the extensive competition and participation among citizens. It promotes or curtails the degree of civil and political liberties, and equally limits the checks and balances between the fundamental institutions of government.

Africa's transition to democratic governance fluctuates between these various forces and it is greatly influenced by the instrumentalities of colonial heritage. The footprints of this heritage remain many and varied. They have contributed to the rise of especially totalitarian regimes. The impediment to the emergence of a democratic governance system comes from an inappropriate blend of traditional cultural values and administrative rules with a distorted form of western political values, which were transferred to the colonies and which gave birth to a different kind of civic political culture. In this light, political culture is perceived as the specifically political orientations, the attitude towards the political system and its various parts, and the role of the individual within the system. Each system has certain functional problems which must be met if the system is to persist. Certain fundamental political beliefs and values, which enhance the rules of the game to ensure the functionality of the political system, are missing.

The missing identified elements of the African democratic ideology are: consent, accountability, limited government, representation, majority rule, minority rights, political opposition, and religious toleration, among others, and these leads to the absence of equality before the law, rights of juridical defence, equality of opportunity, freedom of thought, speech, press, and assembly, individual self-determination over a broad range of personal affairs. Since the patterns of social and political orientations are different between the western and non western democracies, so also are the findings presented by Vanhanen's study of democracy in the contemporary world. The prospects of democratization in Africa must find ways and means of containing issues such as pattern-maintenance and tension management; goal-attainment or goal-gratification and integration, which are concerned with the interaction of the units and individuals of the system to make it function coherently for the common good.

Furthermore, two fundamental problems that quickly emerge in the prospect for democracy hinge on the functional problems of social systems concerning the indicators of democracy and the comparability of political systems operating under different political systems. Apparently political scientists have not yet arrived at a consensus on what is democracy. Is it just government of the people, by the people and for the people, or does it presuppose also the existence of political rights and civil liberties? And what empirical indicators can be applied to measure the principal dimensions of democratization? Does applying the criteria of competition and the extent of participation give a clear picture on the entire problematics entangled with the issue of politics as a struggle for power and influence, or what Lasswell sees as 'the study of influence and the influential' (Lasswell 1958)? These and other related questions have to be seriously addressed before placing Africa's prospects in the democratization continuum process in its true perspectives.

Africa's prospects for democratization hinge upon the nature and structure of political resources as a mechanism of power incorporating the ways and means of inducing compliance, support, neutrality or non participation by other political actors. Equally vital in this connection are repelling attributes, political handicaps that permit disobedience, opposition, hostility, indifference, domination and rejection by other political actors as documented in the statistical analysis of the voting attitude and behaviour across many African countries in contrast to existing practices in most western democracies. All these factors contribute to the variations in the power of a particular type of political institution. They highlight the potential resources of power and weakness involved in the prospects for the democratization process in African countries. The potential strength and weakness, or in short resources and handicaps, stretch from information, social power, popularity, legitimacy, expertise, leadership skills, violence, to organization, economic power of office and management.

These are all varieties and complexities of the power base of the society which contribute or impede the democratization prospects of the country in question. Equally they help to determine whether the various institutions of the system, the presidency, parliament, electorate, the judiciary, political parties, pressure groups, etc. are too strong or too weak, and how they function within the system. If popular participation in elections represents a vital dimension of democracy, then it is equally essential to infer under what conditions these elections are conducted and how free and fair is the degree of participation ratio of the populace. Can institutions or political systems operating under different political environments be compared?

Take the case of Cameroon, where the virtues of democratic governance are denied to the people and political parties and other interest groups, where the use of the official mass media (radio, television, press) remains the prerogative of the ruling party, where press censorship and constant harrassment of opposition parties is the order of the day, where the citizens are restricted from registering for an election, where registration cards and registrars are manipulated so as to keep opposition members away from casting their votes, and where election results are manipulated so that the winning party attained 60 per cent of the votes in the ten provinces of the country. Compare this pathetic situation to that of open access and participation in all the democratic processes of the British, Swedish, Danish, Norwegian, etc. societies. The emerging political landscape in South Africa stands out in sharp contrast to the prevailing situation in Cameroon. The elections that sealed once and for all the inhuman apartheid governance system in South Africa was free and fair. This paved the way for the establishment of a united, democratic and non racial South Africa, at least for the time being. South Africa is today in a transition process to a new regional post-apartheid scenario. Given the potentially important post-apartheid role of a democratic South Africa in the development of the Southern African region, South Africa's democratization process cannot be seen in isolation from the broader international and regional contexts. During the past three to four years, many African countries have introduced democratic changes and policies, commonly referred to as Africa's second liberation. This was the result of both international pressure associated with development finance and assistance, and internal pressures, popular demands for more representative governments and improvement in the quality of life of the population. Second, the high degree of illiteracy prevalent in most African countries remains a fundamental impediment for the people to critically and objectively access the issues in questions. When people do not know, or are unaware of their rights, they are easily exposed to external manipulation either by coercion, persuasion, or inducements among others.

Claude Ake points out that one of the pernicious effects of adopting borrowed theories is that it breeds a top-down and highly centralized regime in economic, political and administrative spheres. As is inevitable, in a top-down process a handful of people virtually control decision-making. They affect the vast masses and come to exercise unequal and enormous power over their own people. Thus they create conditions in which a society ceases to be civil (Ake 1990). The cases of Algeria, Burundi, Cameroon, Somali, Rwanda, Liberia, and Zaire are examples. In addition, the media industry in Africa evolved in a culture in which governments largely concentrate their political power and control over civil society through control of information flow. Freedom of speech in all forms is denied to the people by the ruling party.

This brings to the forefront how various bodies and institutions (political parties, pressure groups, parliament, presidency, judiciary, etc.) exhibit their willingness to take on 'manifest and latent' functions to the working of the system. We further discover that various institutions of government and political party machinery remain untended flowerings from the soil of independence and popular government that inhibit the nurturing of political competitiveness and consensus, but that exacerbate dictatorial and totalitarian civil governance and military intervention.

CONCLUSIONS

Figures are static, and statistical data hide certain underlying descriptive explanatory factors within the polity. These salient factors must be distinguished according to how they relate to political, societal, or historical and geographical phenomena, how each of these distinctions aid or impede comparative politics in a developing polity, and how they place in proper perspective the prospects of democracy in Africa in relation to the rest of the world.

The underlying argument of my comments has been devoted to drawing three major analytical distinctions, namely:

1 The sociological perspectives, which have been contrasted with the non sociological perspectives. The former has stressed patterns in view of which political systems may be described, compared and explained with emphasis on a more appropriate perspective for comparative political governance system studies.
2 Descriptive–explanatory factors have been distinguished in relation to how they relate to political, societal, or historical and geographical phenomena.
3 Distinction between functional and causal analysis has been made.

These three inter-related distinctions enhance our knowledge of comparative politics and in analysing the various salient factors that entrench and group the continent as having a very harsh undemocratic political environment. Thus the existence of incremental coercion impedes all forms of genuine democracy and social integration to function and prosper properly. The indicators presented in the statistical analysis on the process of democratization in Africa should remain mainly as a form with less than the needed substance because of the gross absence of an enabling environment for the citizens to democratically participate in the process of 'government of the people, by the people and for the people', not against the people as is the current practice.

To begin with, the concluding remarks are that the statistical data on the prospects of democracy clearly indicate a serious challenge to the notion of interest aggregation, which in turn streamlines various stresses or crises being experienced in the society, namely: identity, legitimacy, penetration, participation, integration and distribution crisis, identified with the political modernization syndrome and sequences of development. In this respect, the most disturbing question is, what happens to a society when there is a broad demand for equality and participation, when there is a need for increased capacity or governmental capabilities, and when the processes of differentiation and specialization tend to become more acute (see Pye 1966)?

The presented statistical data and the preceding observations on emerging prospects of democracy in Africa show the existence of three degrees of political competitiveness underpinning the democratic process in the region: (1) competitive, (2) semi-competitive and (3) authoritarian (civilian and military regimes). Most African countries fall under authoritarian regime, and as a result of the new wind of change, are gradually moving towards semi-competitive as indicated during the past three years by the election results in Algeria, Benin, Cameroon, Congo, Kenya, Nigeria, and Zambia. This is an indication of the movement from the monolithic single-party system to multi-party politics, or a semi-competitive system in the making.

However, to say that South Africa's 1994 general elections leading to the formation of a Government of National Unity (GNU) has made the country enter the 'competitive stage' would be an exaggeration. We have to wait and see what happens after the end of the first term of the current legislative institution before drawing a conclusion. Nevertheless, it is a healthy sign in the right direction for competitive politics. In like manner, it is difficult to state whether the 1995 elections in Zimbabwe could be judged as competitive since it is alleged that opposition parties did not have access to the government-owned public media as did the ruling party. The elections were conducted in a free and calm environment; free in the sense that voters were not harrassed or prevented from actually casting their votes; and no major incidents occurred to disrupt the process. But to conclude that it was fair is a different issue. In no way can the elections be compared to the 1994 US Congressional elections where all competing parties had equal access to the media, public and private. Second, that the president and chiefs reserve the right to nominate thirty members to the legislative assembly makes a mockery of competitive election of parliamentarians.

Politics in Africa has yet to reach the stage where the constitution entrenches the ideals of a government of separated powers, or of a government of separated institutions sharing powers and to put an end to the abuse of powers. The western concept of democracy rests on the assumption of a heterogeneously structured society, a society that displays conflicts of interest. From this perspective, the core element is political legitimation, expressed in the right to a free vote and the institutions associated with it. A second feature being that of political competition. It is of vital importance that a society is not oriented in a streamlined way towards a particular goal but that conflicts are legitimate, that not only is the free playing-out of conflicts in the form of differing political ideas and the autonomous representation of interests made possible by the system, but the system itself is based on the regulated conflict and makes that conflict part of itself. These are the decisive elements, within whose configuration there are variants. There is the highly representation democracy of which the core elements are free elections, and the concomitant possibility for legitimation at any time to be withdrawn from those who hold power by those at whom power is targeted, as well as political competition through pluralism (Kremendahl 1994: 75).

A number of interpreting correlations become obvious from the statistical data presented. For example, that economic development, literacy and communication among others appears to cause and to sustain the actions and orientations patterns of constitutionalism and political competitiveness; the absence of these inhibits democratic governance. The challenge therefore is for the African polity to move from its present underdeveloped governance system to a developed one. For the past thirty-three years, the African polity has been under constant pressure to slide back to less complex and less competitive political forms; the mechanism for this has been the wildfire of the single authoritarian political party system that has devastated the political landscape of the continent and destroyed the aspirations of the people on the eve of political independence.

African polities are therefore under great pressure to advance to more appropriate, more complex and more competitive political forms, or what could be seen as the challenging elements of the convergence thesis of underdeveloped democratic governance polity. The statistical data for Africa *vis-à-vis* the rest of the world, especially the advanced democracies of the West, argue strongly in favour of a strong correlation between economic development, literacy and communication – i.e. the more economically and industrially developed its political system it will equally be subjected to increasing pressure to resemble the systems of the western democracies. To achieve this requires a movement towards a pluralistic society capable of engineering and securing the rule of law.

REFERENCES

Ake, C. (1990) 'The case for democracy', in *Beyond Autocracy*, Atlanta: Carter Center.

Almond, G. A. and Verba, S. (1965) *The Civic Culture*, Princeton: Princeton University Press.

Baylies, C. and Settel, M. (1992) 'The fall and rise of multiparty politics in Zambia', *Review of African Political Economy* 53, July: 75–91.

Clapham, Ch. (1992) 'Democratization in Africa: Obstacles and prospects', paper presented at the African Studies Association of the United Kingdom (ASAUK), conference on 'Order and disorder in Africa', Stirling, 8–10 September.

Cleaver, G. W. (1992) *The Movement Towards Democracy in Africa: Internal Dynamics or External Pressure?*, M.A. thesis, Coventry University Press.

Diamond, L. (1988) *Class, Ethnicity and Democracy in Nigeria*, Syracuse: Syracuse University Press.

Forje, J. W. (1991a) *Democracy and Democratization in Cameroon: A Case Study of a Rapidly Changing Political Landscape*, Yaounde: Institute of Human Sciences.

——(1991b) 'Advancing democracy and participation: Challenges for the future. The changing political landscape of Cameroon', Paper presented at the XIIth World Conference of the World Future Studies Federation, Barcelona, Spain, 17–21 September.

——(1993a) 'Coherence or chaos in our uncommon or common future', paper presented at the XIIIth World Conference of World Futures Studies Federation, Turku, Finland, 23–7 August.

——(1993b) *The Failure of the Nation-State and the Return to Functional Democracy in Cameroon*, Department of Politics, University of Buea.

Gaay Fortman, B. de, and Mikyo, A. (1991) 'A false start: Law and development in the framework of a colonial legacy', *ISS Working Paper*, Series No. 112, The Hague.

Haynes, J. (1992) 'The state, good governance and democracy in Africa', paper presented at the conference of the African Studies Association of the United Kingdom (ASAUK), Stirling, 8–10 September.

Huntington, S. P. (1984) 'Will more countries become democratic?', *Political Science Quarterly* 99(2): 193–218.

Kremendahl, H. (1994) 'The link between democracy and industrial modernization', in A. Geltent and H. Simon (eds) *Transformation in Central, Eastern, and South-Eastern Europe*, Documents of the International Conference, 17–19 June, Publication No. 18, Development and Peace Foundation, Germany.

Lasswell, H. (1958) *Politics: Who Gets What, When, How*, USA: Meridian Books.
Lipset, S. M. (1960) *Political Man: The Social Bases of Politics*, New York: Double-day.
Lipset, S. M., Linz, J. J., and Diamond, L. (1988) *Politics in Developing Countries: Africa*, Boulder, Col.: Lynne Rienner.
Pye, L. W. (1966) *Aspects of Political Development*, Boston: Little, Brown.
Sartori, G. (1987) *The Theory of Democracy Revised*, Chatham, NJ: Chatham House.
Weber, M. (1947) *The Theory of Social and Economic Organisations*, translated by A. M. Henderson and T. Parsons. New York: Oxford University Press.

10　Prospects of democracy in Oceania

John Henderson

What are the prospects for democracy in Oceania – that vast region of the Southern Pacific made up of widely scattered islands and the continent of Australia? Professor Vanhanen's important analysis provides an optimistic prediction that democracy will survive not just in the established democratic systems of Australia and New Zealand, but also in some of the world's newest, smallest, and poorest nations of the Pacific Island region. Indeed, he cites the island states as examples that democracy can flourish in the difficult circumstances that third world nations face, and is not necessarily restricted to the relatively wealthy nations. He concludes that Papua New Guinea, Vanuatu, Solomon Islands and Western Samoa have remained more democratic than might be expected from their resource base, and the experience of other non industrialized countries. His findings confirm other research which has demonstrated that in terms of the democratic and peaceful transfer of power, the Pacific Islands rate well (Fry 1983; Larmour 1983, 1994; Crocombe *et al.* 1992).

Professor Vanhanen defines democracy as 'a political system in which different groups are legally entitled to compete for power and in which institutional power holders are elected by the people and are responsible to the people'. He does not include the controversial area of human rights in his definition. This makes it easier to relate his definition to the Pacific Islands, where the cultures and traditions stress collective rather than individual rights.

In terms of this definition all Pacific Island states, with the exception of Tonga where the King still rules and Fiji whose constitution discriminates against the Indo-Fijian population, could arguably qualify as democracies. Western Samoa has only recently qualified in terms of the definition, with the granting of full universal suffrage in 1990. However, candidates must still possess a chiefly title – which, it could be argued, is a restriction on the freedom for all to compete for power. Many Western Samoans will argue that their traditional 'matai' system is, in fact, more democratic, because to hold a matai title one must gain the respect of the extended family group. It is interesting to note that the Samoan language does not contain a word for vote or democracy – but that consensus decision-making is deeply entrenched in the traditional political system (Lafoa'i 1992). Indeed, throughout the region indigenous politicians stress the importance of consensus, and tend to define 'democracy' in terms of the responsiveness of the political system to the people's needs and wishes. There is an increasing assertiveness in the questioning of the relevance of 'Western' notions of elections and opposition parties. (Lawson, 1993)

It is for this reason that regrettably I do not share Professor Vanhanen's optimism regarding the future of democracy in Oceania. My own analysis, based on extensive travel and research in the region, including many interviews with Pacific Island politicians, is that these small democracies will be under increasing threat during the next decade (see Henderson 1990). While most will seek to maintain the appearance of democratic systems, the trend towards promoting the superiority of traditional political systems will increasingly render the central features of democracy – the elected assembly of parliament – as little more than a facade necessary to maintain in order to attract foreign aid.

Nevertheless, it is true that to date the Pacific region does appear to be the exception to the general pattern of Third World post-independence politics in which inherited Western type political systems proved to be short lived. The military have taken over in just one country – Fiji in 1987. Even in this case the efforts to restore a democratic system appear to be much more successful than in most other Third World states which have experienced military takeovers. It is important to reflect on the reasons for this, and in what other respects the Pacific Island region is different from Africa, Asia or Central and Latin America.

But first I wish to stress that although my conclusions differ from Professor Vanhanen, I am impressed by the boldness – and importance – of his attempt to predict the future of democracy in 172 nations. He is doing what too few political scientists, who nevertheless claim to be social scientists, attempt: formulating a theory, and then subjecting it to rigorous testing. In this case Professor Vanhanen has gone one step further, and invited area specialists to comment on his findings. In doing so he is no doubt aware that his fellow political scientists who specialize in a particular region are unlikely to be sympathetic to his theory that the move towards democracy is generally uniform across time and cultures. After all the whole rationale for area studies is that there are 'special' features about a particular region which warrant separate study.

Nevertheless, I readily concede that Professor Vanhanen has made a convincing attempt to prove his central thesis – that the degree of democracy depends principally on the distribution of economic, intellectual and other power resources. However, while I support his goal of moving from general theory to making predictions (as this is what political science, if it is worthy of its name, should be about) I do not agree with several of his predictions relating to Pacific Island states. But before looking into these cases it is important to examine more closely just what constitutes the Oceania region, and what distinguishes it from other areas of the world.

THE REGION OF OCEANIA

Professor Vanhanen variously refers to the region as 'Australasia and the Pacific' and 'Oceania'. My preference is to use the term Oceania to embrace Australia, New Zealand and the Pacific Island states as it captures the major influence on the region – the vast Pacific Ocean. While small in population (approximately twenty-seven million) and numbers of independent or self governing states (sixteen), the region covers nearly one fifth of the globe. The term 'Australasia' should be avoided, as it implies domination by one state. When Australia and New Zealand are not included in the analysis, the reference should be to Pacific Island states.

Indeed the question must be asked: for the purposes of the analysis that Professor Vanhanen undertakes, should the economically developed and predominantly European 'settler' nations of Australia and New Zealand have been included with the small, and in many cases 'micro', states of the Pacific Islands? While instinctively I like to think of New Zealand as a Pacific Island state, and have sought to make the case for a Pacific identity based partly on the fact that the Polynesian people make up nearly a fifth of New Zealand's population (Henderson 1992), in economic terms New Zealand (and Australia) belong in the Europe and North America grouping. As Professor Vanhanen is seeking to make comparisons between regions, including those two developed states with five developing states, it is bound to distort results. In this case the composition helps explain why the region is more democratic in terms of the quantitative ratings than might be expected from a region made up mainly of Third World states. It is true that some of his other six regions also include both rich and poor nations (e.g. the twenty-eight states in the North Africa, Middle East and Central Asia region) but in those cases there are many more countries included in the region, which would minimize any distortions. The other small region, also containing just seven states is South Asia, which includes all developing countries. I nevertheless accept that Australia and New Zealand present real (and perhaps insurmountable) difficulties in any analysis based on geographic regions.

A more fundamental concern with the definition of the region is that it includes just seven of the regions thirteen fully independent states (a further two are self-governing). The main reason is that Professor Vanhanen uses the population level of 100,000 as the cut-off point for countries to be included in his study. But even under this criterion the Federated States of Micronesia (population 102,000) and Tonga (population 100,000) should have been included. The exclusion of Tonga is particularly important in terms of a study on democracy, as it remains, in essence, a feudal monarchy (see Campbell 1992; 1994; Afeaki 1983). Just nine of Tonga's parliament of thirty are elected by the people. A further nine are elected by the thirty noble families, and the King appoints the remaining twelve, which form his cabinet. The King retains autocratic powers, which would have given Tonga a zero rating on the 'index of democracy', and lowered the region's overall democratic rating. But there is a pro-democracy movement in Tonga, and the case is worthy of further consideration because I believe it may well become a democracy worthy of the name following the death of the present King (Hills 1993). It is interesting to note in terms of Professor Vanhanen's resource indicators that Tonga puts considerable emphasis on education, and has achieved near 100 per cent literacy.

The reason given for the 100,000 population criterion is both the difficulty of obtaining reliable data and (more importantly) that states under this figure will inevitably be highly dependent on larger states for economic, administrative and security support. It is assumed that this will mean that the political institutions of very small states will reflect more foreign than domestic influences. But much the same argument could be made for many larger, and dependent Third World states. For instance, within the Oceania region, it would be difficult to demonstrate that Kiribati (population 69,000) is more dependent on foreign assistance than the Solomon Islands (population 323,000).

While it is accepted that, having established a criterion, it is necessary to apply it uniformly in all regions, it nevertheless is worth noting that it may well have a distorting effect on regions with several micro-states. This is particularly the case in Oceania where the number of total states is small (just thirteen). The other states excluded from the study because of the population criterion, in addition to the Federated States of Micronesia, Tonga and Kiribati referred to earlier, are the Marshall islands (population 42,000), Nauru (9,000) and Tuvalu (9,000).

Within the Oceania region the population criterion has a further distorting effect of over-representing the Melanesian states (including Papua New Guinea, Solomon Islands, Vanuatu and Fiji), compared with just one Polynesian (Western Samoa), and no Micronesian states. (The fully independent Polynesian states not included are Tonga and Tuvalu. The four independent Micronesian states are Kiribati, Federated States of Micronesia, Marshall Islands and Nauru.) The criterion could have influenced the results as Melanesian culture is much more egalitarian in terms of politics and resource distribution (and, it could be argued democratic) than the more hierarchical chiefly Polynesian societies. (Micronesia contains a mixture of both types of political culture.)

WHAT IS DIFFERENT IN OCEANIA?

In view of Professor Vanhanen's finding that Oceania differs from other regions in terms of its democratic ratings an examination will first be made of some general points which may explain this difference. Attention will be focused on areas where the experience of Pacific Island politics gives rise to difficulties with some of the concepts and measurements used in the study. The following factors will be considered: the youthful nature of the population, the preponderance of small states, the weak state of political parties, the absence of the need to struggle for independence, the relatively recent achievement of that independence, the limited nature of military involvement in politics, and the general well-being of the region.

Professor Vanhanen calculates participation in the political system – one of his two key determinants of democracy – as the number of total votes calculated as a percentage of the total population rather than of those qualified to vote. He uses this formula because of the need to gain reliable data and to be compatible with his earlier research. However he acknowledges that this can be misleading in the case of developing countries whose populations tend to be concentrated in the younger age groups (who do not qualify to vote). This is particularly the case in the Pacific Islands, which have some of the world's highest birth rates. For instance, in the Solomon Islands, whose population is growing at the rate of 3.5 per cent annually, the percentage of the population under fifteen is 47.34 per cent – more than double the New Zealand figure of 23.08 per cent.

Competition is the second determinant of democracy used by Professor Vanhanen. As has been noted, Oceania contains several of the world's mircostates. The relationship between size and democracy, and particularly the competition factor, is both interesting and debatable. On the one hand it can be argued that only in very small states can direct democracy of the classical Greek city state model operate. But, as the experience of Pacific micro-states demonstrate, it is very difficult in such closely knit societies for genuine competition to occur. In small communities, where everyone knows each other, politics remains very much a family affair. Party politics is seen in negative terms as divisive, and counter to the Pacific Island tradition of consensus rather than competitive politics.

One of the consequences of small size and intimate politics in the Pacific Islands has been the failure of political parties to become established. Certainly there are few examples of parties with a mass base in the Pacific Island region – and they are becoming rarer. Parties defined by ideology are not relevant in societies where the clan or tribe defines one's identity. Parties are weak to the point of being non existent in some of the very small states. Often parties are little more than parliamentary factions formed after elections.

The absence of established political parties has consequences for the application of Professor Vanhanen's analysis, as his measurement of political competition – one of his two key variables for measuring the degree of democratization – is based on the level of party support as measured in terms of votes gained. For example, in Papua New Guinea (which has a better established party system than most of the very small states) at the last general election in 1992 the combined vote of the independent candidates was greater than that of the largest single party – the Pangu Pati. The reason was that many politicians wished to keep their party affiliation options open to the highest bidder after the election.

The means Professor Vanhanen uses for calculating 'competition' is by subtracting the percentage of the vote for the major party from 100 (thereby measuring the level of support for minor parties) is also open to questions. The assumption is that the higher the figure, the more democratic the country. But the calculation also measures the degree of fragmentation of the political system which can work against its effectiveness – including its ability to deliver representative government. In the case of Papua New Guinea the main Pangu Pati gained just 18 per cent of the vote in the 1992 General Election, followed closely by the 15 per cent vote for the People's Democratic Movement. Clearly when 'major' parties gain such a small percentage of the vote the result is likely to be political instability (as has been the case in Papua New Guinea), rather than effective democratic government. In the Solomon Islands the current government has suggested that, in order to avoid the instability created by fragmented political parties, legislation should be adopted restricting the number of parties to two.

It may well be that both upper and lower limits should be established for the competition element of the 'threshold of democracy'. Professor Vanhanen establishes a minimum vote level of 30 per cent for opposition parties to cross this threshold. In future studies it may also be wise to establish a maximum opposition vote – say 70 per cent (which would require the major governing party to establish at least 30 per cent of the popular vote).

The large number of parties, and their limited support, reflects the divided nature of Melanesian society. Professor Vanhanen sees the diverse nature of the culture highlighted by the more than 600 languages in Papua New Guinea and 60 in the Solomon Islands, as positive for democracy, because it prevents the establishment of a dominant political party based on a single ethnic group. But the cost in terms of the difficulty of maintaining national unity is tragically evident in the long and bitter struggle by the people of Bougainville to break away from Papua New Guinea.

The weak standing of political parties in the Pacific Island region raises the question of whether, as has been widely assumed, the establishment of political parties is an essential ingredient of a democratic political system. The competition demanded by party systems is seen as divisive – even subversive – and wasteful of the scarce talent in many Pacific Island states. From a Pacific Island perspective the consensus approach is more, not less, democratic as it allows for greater public involvement in the making of decisions. However Professor Vanhanen's analysis does not seek to measure the responsiveness of the elected representatives to the electorate. While consensus decision-making is, by its nature, impossible to measure objectively, it would be possible to include data on other indicators of the political systems responsiveness. For instance, frequency of elections and number of electors per representative could be measured (small states clearly rate well on this latter indicator) (Levine 1983).

One of the reasons why political parties have remained weak in Pacific Island states was the absence, in most cases, of the need to form mass nationalist parties of the African type to fight for independence. Most Pacific Island states did not struggle to end colonialism, but were pushed (or nudged) to accept independence by their colonial rulers. Where there were exceptions, such as in Vanuatu, nationalist parties did develop, but have weakened and split in recent years (Premdas and Steeves, 1989). The absence of the need for radical independence parties in the Pacific Islands explains much of the conservative nature of their politics, and the continued influence of traditional political leaders.

A further distinguishing characteristic of the region is the relative recent granting of independence. Although Western Samoa led the way by gaining independence in 1962, most Pacific Island states did not follow until the 1970s, and Vanuatu did not achieve independence until 1980. This means that it is only recently that a second post-independence generation of leaders is beginning to emerge, and having to face the growing disillusionment which inevitably sets in after the euphoria of newly gained independence has evaporated.

The relatively recent gaining of independence may help explain the general absence, with one notable exception, of military involvement in politics. It could be argued that insufficient time has elapsed for the civilian politicians to demonstrate their corruption and inability to govern – the justification often given for military takeovers. However, the main reason is the limited nature of the military forces in the region. It is no accident that the region's only coups occurred in 1987, and both in Fiji, where the region's strongest military force is established (Lawson 1991; Lal 1988).

It is, however, ironical that democracy has been most directly challenged in the Pacific Island region in the country with arguably the most advanced economy and, in Professor Vanhanen's terms, widest distribution of economic, knowledge and other power resources. Nevertheless, it can be argued that Fiji's comparatively speedy return to civilian rule and re-establishment of a parliamentary system, is supportive of Vanhanen's predictions. But a complete return to a democratic system will require changing the racial basis in the current constitution which guarantees the indigenous Fijian population a majority of the parliamentary seats, despite the fact that the Indo–Fijian population is approximately the same size (Lal 1993).

My own prediction is that the country most likely to face a military coup is Papua New Guinea, which also has significant military forces, but lacks the discipline and high morale of the Fiji forces (Dorney 1990; Hegarty 1989). A senior Papua New Guinea politician suggested to me that the military will take over in a 'quiet coup', by which he meant by default following the collapse of civilian government.

Tonga has a smaller military force, and military takeovers both in favour and in opposition to greater democracy have been suggested. Vanuatu has a para-military force whose loyalty has been put under severe test during the recent periods of political instability. The Solomons have recently announced plans to establish military forces to prevent the spill over of the PNGs' Bougainville problem into the Solomons. Western Samoa and the other island states have never established military forces – which would seem the best way of ensuring there will be no military coups. There is an important message here for aid donors: that giving military aid is likely to undermine rather than promote the security of small democratic states.

My own concern is that the challenge to existing democratic systems is unlikely to come directly from the military, but more indirectly through the re-assertion of traditional political systems. Western type constitutional systems will be maintained for the sake of appearances only. This pessimistic scenario points to one of the problems with Professor Vanhanen's analysis – that while it can measure voter participation and competition, it does not seek to assess, for instance, how effective a check parliament can be on the executive.

A further reason why Pacific Island politics may seem to have better democratic prospects than other developing areas is the general well-being of the region. By Third World standards, the region is relatively well off with 'knowledge' resources, as education is widely available to most young people. Although relatively poor in material resource terms, the generally benign climate and generosity of aid donors ensures that it would be rare indeed for any Pacific Islander to die of hunger or lack of housing. While the small size of the urban population limits opportunities, the subsistence type economy that is still widely practised takes care of basic human needs. Professor Vanhanen's estimation of 60 per cent of land under traditional tenure systems is too low for most island states.

What of the future? Professor Vanhanen predicts the survival of democracy throughout Oceania. My view is that democracy is likely to continue to be under threat in Fiji, be challenged in Papua New Guinea and possibly be in jeopardy in Vanuatu and the Solomon Islands, and under stress in Western Samoa. The remainder of this contribution will briefly examine the prospects for democracy in each of these countries in turn.

The racial bias of Fiji's constitution has been noted. This, together with the shift in the population balance in favour of the indigenous Fijians should ensure the circumstances of an Indo-Fijian dominated government that prompted the 1987 coups will not be repeated. However, should a coalition of political forces again appear to threaten Fijian paramountcy, there is little doubt that the military will again intervene. The current Prime Minister, Sitiveni Rabuka is the same man who – as a Colonel – led the 1987 coup. In the meantime the racially weighted constitution means that there has not been a full restoration of democratic government. Therein lies the problem. Fiji seeks the international respectability of being a democracy, but not at the price of real power sharing with its Indo-Fijian population. Ultimately, when forced to choose, the rights of indigenous peoples are rated more highly than democratic rights. It is a view that is widely accepted throughout the region – with the exception of Australia and New Zealand.

I have already identified Papua New Guinea as the country in the region most likely to be subjected to a military takeover. A military coup may be provoked by the widespread political corruption, the breakdown of law and order, or (and most likely) the military's concern for its own well-being and status. These factors have provoked earlier defiance by the military (and police) of the civilian government. But talk of a military coup has not turned into concerted action, in part because the divided nature of the country is reflected in the military. If a coup did occur, these internal divisions are likely to result in a series of counter-coups, as has occurred in some African countries.

The overthrow of democratic government in Papua New Guinea would raise questions about the relationship of democracy to economic resources. Papua New Guinea is potentially a very wealthy country, as it has very large natural resources – including minerals, gas and forestry. Its problem is the need to provide a stable political and administrative environment to enable commerce to flourish. This difficulty has its origins in the colonial boundaries, which grouped very diverse cultures together as one nation. It is a problem shared with other Melanesian states of the Solomon Islands and Vanuatu, which lack the advantages of Papua New Guinea's natural wealth.

Vanuatu's democratic system also faces an uncertain future. In addition to cultural differences, underlined by the more than 100 indigenous languages, the country remains divided between the dominant English- and minority French-speaking populations. This reflects Vanuatu's unhappy period of joint colonial rule between Britain and France. It was France's unwillingness to grant independence which gave rise to the nationalist movement in Vanuatu, and the domination of the nationalist party, the Vanuaaku Party for the first decade of independence. But in the past six years party politics has become more fragmented (and similar in this regard to Papua New Guinea).

Vanuatu does not have an army, but it does have a small para-military mobile force. To date this force has kept out of politics – including during the 1988 short-lived 'constitutional coup' when the Governor-General illegally swore into office a new Prime Minister. More recently politics has faced an uncertain future as the government is dominated by the French-speaking party, which is kept in power by a breakaway faction from the Vanuaaku Party. (The para-military forces are mainly from the English-speaking section of the population). Further political instability is inevitable, which provides an uncertain climate for a new democracy.

Solomon Island's politics has also been unstable, for much the same reasons as its Melanesian neighbours. In 1994, in a situation reminiscent of the 1988 Vanuatu crisis, the Governor-General swore into office a new Prime Minister despite the refusal of the incumbent to resign. If current plans to establish military forces eventuate there must be a risk of military intervention to end the instability. As with the other examples, the problem is likely to remain unless political parties become established.

Western Samoa is the most favourably placed of the Pacific Island states being considered to maintain the democratic system it inherited from New Zealand. But while the trappings of democracy – elections and parliament – remain, its effectiveness is likely to continue to decline. As in most Pacific Island states, Parliament seldom meets and when it does cannot provide any real check on the executive. This was proved by the current government's extension of its parliamentary term by two years. The legitimacy of Parliament has been undermined by widespread accusations of corruption, and mass marches on parliament in favour of restoring the powers of traditional leaders. While the 1990 move to universal suffrage ended the restriction of voting to the chiefs (the matai), it was motivated as much (or more) by the need to prevent the further splitting of matai titles, as by any commitment to the democratic principle of one person, one vote. The low turn out, and narrow passage of the referendum approving universal suffrage indicated a lack of any groundswell of support for democracy.

In conclusion, I should emphasize that, despite the problems listed above, the Pacific Island region remains a generally peaceful and caring group of countries enjoying a lifestyle and standard of living not found elsewhere in the Third World. Much of these advantages stem from the retention of their own cultures. As the island states' contact with the outside world expands, so too will its problems of political instability. The main crisis to date – the Fiji coups and the Bougainville crisis – have occurred in the countries which have been most affected by exposure to international economic pressures (mining in the case of Bougainville). The challenge ahead is how to marry the best features of traditional political systems – the emphasis on consensus decision-making – with the representative requirement of democracy. Especially in small countries, it is not difficult to understand why maintaining consensus assumes a higher priority than encouraging party competition. What is needed in addition to Professor Vanhanen's valuable framework of analysis is a measure of the effectiveness of government in meeting the needs and wishes of the people in whose name they rule.

REFERENCES

Afeaki, E. (1983) 'Tonga: The last Pacific kingdom', in R. Crocombe and A. Ali (eds) *Politics in Polynesia*, Suva: University of the South Pacific.

Campbell, I. C. (1992) *Island Kingdom: Tonga Ancient and Modern*, Christchurch: Canterbury University Press.

——(1994) 'The doctrine of accountability and the unchanging focus of power in Tonga', *Journal of Pacific History* 29: 81–94.

Crocombe, R., Neemia, U., Ravavu, A. and Von Busch, W. (1992) *Culture and Democracy in the South Pacific*, Suva: Institute for Pacific Studies.

Dorney, S. (1990) *Papua New Guinea: People, Politics and History Since 1975*, Milsons Pt., NSW: Random House.

Fry, G. (1983) 'Succession of government in the post-colonial states of the South Pacific', *Politics* 18, 1: 48–60.

Hegarty, D. (1989) *Papua New Guinea: At the Political Crossroads?*, Canberra: ANU.

Henderson, J., Blakely, R. and O'Brien, T. (1990) *Towards a Pacific Island Community*, Report of the South Pacific Review Group, Wellington: Government Printer.

—— (1992) 'Culture, ethnicity and political representation in New Zealand', in R. Crocombe, *et al. Culture and Democracy in the South Pacific*, Suva: University of the South Pacific.

Hills, R. (1993) 'Predicaments in Polynesia: Culture and constitutions in Western Samoa and Tonga', *Pacific Studies* 16, 4: 115–29.

Lafoa'i, I. (1992) 'Universal suffrage in Western Samoa: A political review', *Journal of Pacific History* 20, 3: 67–73.

Lal, B. V. (1988) *Power and Prejudice: The Making of the Fiji Crisis*, Wellington; NZIIA.

—— (1993) 'Chiefs and Indians: Elections and politics in contemporary Fiji', *The Contemporary Pacific* 5, 2: 275–301.

Larmour, P. (1983) *Solomon Politics*, Suva: U.S.P.

—— (1994) 'A foreign flower? Democracy in the South Pacific', *Pacific Studies* 17, 1: 45–77.

Lawson, S. (1991) *The Failure of Democratic Politics in Fiji*, New York: Oxford University Press.

—— (1993) 'The politics of tradition: Problems for political legitimacy and democracy in the South Pacific', *Pacific Studies*. 16, 2: 1–29.

Levine, S. (1983) *Pacific Power Maps: An Analysis of the Constitutions of Pacific Island Politics*, Honolulu: University of Hawaii.

Premdas, R. and Steeves, J. S. (eds) (1989) *Politics and Government in Vanuatu: From Colonial Unity to Post Colonial Disunity*, Townsville: James Cook University.

Bibliography

Abedeji, A. (1994) 'An alternative for Africa', *Journal of Politics* 5, 4: 119–32.
Africa Contemporary Record (1985–89), London: Rex Collings.
Africa Demos (1991–93), Atlanta, Georgia: The African Governance Program.
Africa Research Bulletin. Political, Social and Cultural Series (1985–93), Oxford: Basil Blackwell.
Africa South of the Sahara 1982–83 (1982), London: Europa Publications Ltd.
Ajami, I. (1978) *Agricultural Development in Iran.* Three articles, LTC Reprint 134, Madison: Land Tenure Center, University of Wisconsin.
Alexander, R. D. (1980) *Darwinism and Human Affairs*, London: Pitman Publishing.
Allison, L., Kukhianidze, A. and Matsaberidze, M. (1993) 'The Georgian election of 1992', *Electoral Studies* 12, 2: 174–9.
Almond, G. A. (1992) 'Democratization and "crisis, choice, and change"', American Political Science Association Annual meeting, 4 September, Chicago, Ill.
Anckar, D. (1994) 'Giganter och miniatyrer – arkitektoriska beröringspunkter', *Politiikka* 36, 2: 81–95.
Annuario Estadistico 1977 (1979), Caracas: Republica de Venezuela, Oficina Central de Estadistica e Informatica.
Arat, Z. F. (1991) *Democracy and Human Rights in Developing Countries*, Boulder, Col.: Lynne Rienner.
——(1994) 'Development of democracy, markets and the bourgeoisie', paper presented at the XVIth World Congress of the International Political Science Association, 21–5 August, Berlin.
ARB. See *Africa Research Bulletin.*
Arter, D. (1993) *The Politics of European Integration in the Twentieth Century*, Aldershot: Dartmouth.
Asian Recorder (1993).
Atta, D. V. (1991) 'First results of the "Stolypin" land reform in the RSFSR', *Report on the USSR* 3, 29: 20–23.
Ayubi, N. N. (1991) *Political Islam: Religion and Politics in the Arab World*, London and New York: Routledge.
——(1993) 'Is democracy possible in the Middle East?', paper presented at the ECPR Joint Sessions of Workshops, April 2–8, Leiden.
Bahgat, G. (1994) 'Democracy in the Arab world: An elitist approach', *International Relations* 12, 2: 49–60.
Bahout, J. (1993) 'Liban: Les élections législatives de l'été 1992', *Monde Arabe Maghreb/Machrek*, La documentation francaise, 139, Janv.-Mars: 53–84.
Banks, A. S. (1972) 'Correlates of democratic performance', *Comparative Politics* 4, 2: 217–30.

Banks, A. S. (1981) 'An index of socio-economic development 1869–1975', *The Journal of Politics* 43: 390–411.

——(ed.) (1990) *Political Handbook of the World: 1990*, Binghamton, NY: CSA Publications, State University of New York.

Banks, A. S., Carlip, V., DeWitt, R. P., and Overstreet, W. (eds) (1981) *Economic Handbook of the World: 1981*, New York: McGraw-Hill.

Baogang He (1994) 'Dilemmas of pluralist development and democratization in China', paper presented at the XVIth IPSA World Congress in Berlin, 21–5 August.

Baral, L. R. (1994) 'The return of party politics in Nepali', *Journal of Democracy* 5, 1: 121–33.

Barkan, J. D. (1993) 'Kenya: lessons from a flawed election', *Journal of Democracy* 4, 3: 85–99.

Barkow, J. H., Cosmides, L. and Tooby, J. (1992) *The Adapted Mind. Evolutionary Psychology and the Generation of Culture*, New York: Oxford University Press.

Bayart, J.-F. (1994) 'Republican trajectories in Iran and Turkey: a Tocquevillian reading', in G. Salamé (ed.) *Democracy without Democrats? The Renewal of Politics in the Muslim World*, London: I. B. Tauris Publishers.

BBC Summary of World Broadcasts (SWB) (issued by BBC monitoring) (1988–93) Parts 1–5, Reading: British Broadcasting Corporation.

Beetham, D. (1992) 'Liberal democracy and the limits of democratization', in D. Held (ed.) *Prospects for Democracy*, Political Studies 40, special issue, Norwich: Blackwell Publishers.

——(1993) 'Democracy: key principles and indices', paper presented at the ECPR Joint Sessions of Workshops, 2–8 April, Leiden.

Berg-Schlosser, D. (1989) 'Conditions of democracy in Third World countries', in *Democracy in the Modern World: Essays for Tatu Vanhanen*, Tampere: University of Tampere.

——(1993) 'Democratization in Africa – Conditions and prospects', paper presented at the ECPR Joint Sessions of Workshops, 2–8 April, Leiden.

Berg-Schlosser, D. and DeMeur, G. (1994), 'Conditions of democracy in interwar Europe: A Boolean test of major hypotheses', *Comparative Politics* 26, 3: 253–79.

Bertrand, T. F. M. and Puijenbroek, R. A. G. van (1987) 'The measurement of democracy in cross-national research: the construction of a scale', paper presented at the ECPR Joint Sessions of Workshops, 10–15 April, Amsterdam.

Betzig, L. L. (1986) *Despotism and Differential Reproduction: A Darwinian View of History*, New York: Aldine.

Blahó, A. (1994) *Russian Transition – Chinese Reforms. A Comparative View*, UNU World Institute for Development Economics Research (UNU/WIDER), Forssa: Printing House.

Blanchard, O. J. (1994) 'Transition in Poland', *The Economic Journal* 104, 426: 1169–77.

Blondel, J. (1990) *Comparative Government: An Introduction*, New York: Philip Allan.

——(1995) *Comparative Government: An Introduction*, 2nd edition, London: Prentice Hall/Harvester Wheatsheaf.

Bollen, K. A. (1979) 'Political democracy and the timing of development', *American Sociological Review* 44, 4: 572–87.

——(1980) 'Issues in the comparative measurement of political democracy', *American Sociological Review* 45, 3: 370–90.

——(1983) 'World system position, dependency, and democracy: the cross-national evidence', *American Sociological Review* 48, August: 468–79.

——(1990) 'Political democracy: Conceptual and measurement traps', *Studies in Comparative International Development* 25, 1: 7–27.

Bollen, K. A. and Grandjean, B. D. (1981) 'The dimension(s) of democracy: Further issues in the measurement and effects of political democracy', *American Sociological Review* 46, October: 651–9.

Bowen-Jones, H. (1980) 'Agriculture in Bahrain, Kuwait, Qatar, and UAE', in M. Ziwar-Daftari (ed.) *Issues in Development: The Arab Gulf States*, London: MD Research and Sciences Ltd.

Bremmer, I. and Welt, C. (1995) 'Kazakhstan's quandary', *Journal of Democracy* 6, 3: 139–54.

Bromley, S. (1993) 'Prospects for democracy in the Middle East', in D. Held (ed.) *Prospects for Democracy: North, South, East, West*, Oxford: Polity Press.

Brown, D. E. (1991) *Human Universals*, New York: McGraw-Hill.

Browne, C. (1989) *Economic Development in Seven Pacific Island Countries*, Washington, DC: International Monetary Fund.

Bruce, J. W. and Harrell, P. (1989) *Land Reform in the People's Republic of China 1978–1988*, Research paper, Wisconsin: Land Tenure Center, University of Wisconsin.

Brumberg, D. (1992) 'Algeria', *Africa Demos* 2, 3: 3, 16.

Bruun, K. (1969) 'Taloudellisen vallan ongelma', in K. Bruun and A. Eskola (eds) *Taloudellinen valta Suomessa*, Helsinki: Tammi.

Bulgarian Economic Review (1992) 'Government states its performance and intentions' 1, 8: 8–12 April.

Buultjens, R. (1978) *The Decline of Democracy: Essays on an Endangered Political Species*, Maryknall, N.Y.: Orbis Books.

Callaghy, T. (1994) 'Africa: Back to the future?', *Journal of Democracy* 5, 4: 133–45.

Cammack, P. (1994) 'Democratization and citizenship in Latin America', in G. Parry and M. Moran (eds) *Democracy and Democratization*, London and New York: Routledge.

Carlson, C. (1991) 'Turkmenistan: Inching towards democratization', *Report on the USSR* 3, 1: 235–6.

Carson, R. L. (1973) *Comparative Economic Systems*, New York: Macmillan.

Central Statistical Office of Finland (1988) *Presidential Election 1988*, Helsinki: Valtion painatuskeskus.

Chan, K. Ka-lok (1994) 'The Polish general election of 1993', *Issues and Studies* 30, 4: 74–109.

Chang Chen-pang (1994) 'The resurgence of the bourgeoisie in Mainland China', *Issues and Studies* 30, 5: 31–44.

Chazan, N. (1988) 'Ghana: problems of governance and the emergence of civil society', in L. Diamond *et al.* (eds) *Democracy in Developing Countries. Vol. 2. Africa*, Boulder, Col.: Lynne Rienner.

Chekharin, E. (1977) *The Soviet Political System Under Developed Socialism*, Moscow: Progress Publishers.

Chilcote, R. H. (1992) 'Southern European transitions in comparative perspective', in R. H. Chilcote *et al. Transitions from Dictatorship to Democracy*, New York: Crane Russak.

Chilcote, R. H., Hadjiyannis, S., López, F. A., Nataf, D. and Sammis, E. (1992) *Transitions from Dictatorship to Democracy: Comparative Studies of Spain, Portugal, and Greece*, New York: Crane Russak.

China, a Country Study (1988) DA Pam 550–60, Washington, DC: US Government Printing Office.

Clapham, C. (1993) 'Democratization in Africa: obstacles and prospects', paper presented at the ECPR Joint Sessions of Workshops, 2–8 April, Leiden.

Cloete, F. (1992) 'Between Scylla and Charybdis: Policy choices and the development of democracy in South Africa', in T. Vanhanen (ed.) *Strategies of Democratization*, Washington: Crane Russak.

CMEA. See Council for Mutual Economic Assistance.

Cohen, J. M., and Koehn, P. H. (1978) *Rural and Urban Land Reform in Ethiopia*, LTC Reprint No, 135. Madison: Land Tenure Center, University of Wisconsin.

Coleman, J. S. (1960/1964) 'Conclusion: The political systems of the developing areas', in G. A. Almond and J. S. Coleman (eds), *The Politics of the Developing Areas*, Princeton, NJ: Princeton University Press.

The Commonwealth Fact Sheet, Malta (1976), London: Commonwealth Institute.

Congressional Quarterly Weekly Report (1988).

Coppedge, M., and Reinicke, W. (1988) 'A scale of polyarchy', in R. D. Gastil *Freedom in the World: Political Rights and Civil Liberties 1987–1988*, New York: Freedom House.

——(1990) 'Measuring polyarchy', *Studies in Comparative International Development* 25, 1: 51–72.

Corney, J. (1993), 'A nuclear nation in trouble', *Time* No. 16, 19 April: 29.

Costa, E. F. (1993) 'Peru's presidential coup', *Journal of Democracy* 4, 1: 28–40.

Coulter, P. (1975) *Social Mobilization and Liberal Democracy: A Macroquantitative Analysis of Global and Regional Models*, Lexington, Massachusetts: Lexington Press.

Council for Mutual Economic Assistance (CMEA), Secretariat, (1979) *Statistical Yearbook of Member States of the Council for Mutual Economic Assistance*, London: IOC Industrial Press Ltd.

Cutright, P. (1963) 'National political development: measurement and analysis', *American Sociological Review* 28, 2: 253–64.

Cyprus: A Country Study (1980), Washington, DC: US Government Printing Office.

Cziffra, C. (1995) 'Microcosmic Mauritius', *IIAS Newsletter* 4: 11.

Dahl, R. A. (1971) *Polyarchy: Participation and Opposition*, New Haven: Yale University Press.

——(1982) *Dilemmas of Pluralist Democracy: Autonomy vs. Control*, New Haven: Yale University Press.

——(1985) *A Preface to Economic Democracy*, Chicago: The University of Chicago Press.

——(1989) *Democracy and its Critics*, New Haven and London: Yale University Press.

Daily News (1995), Sofia, Bulgaria.

Deasy, G. F., Griess, P. R., Miller, E. W. and Case, E. C. (1958) *The World's Nations: An Economic and Regional Geography*, Chicago: J. B. Lippincott Company.

Decalo, S. (1990) *Coups and Army Rule in Africa*, New Haven: Yale University Press.

——(1992) 'The process, prospects and constraints of democratization in Africa', *Africa Affairs* 91, 362: 7–35.

Deegan, H. (1993) *The Middle East and Problems of Democracy*, Milton Keynes: Open University Press.

Deutsch, K. W. (1961) 'Social mobilization and political development', *The American Political Science Review* 60, 3: 493–514.

Diamond, L. (1992) 'Economic development and democracy reconsidered', in G. Marks and L. Diamond (eds) *Reexamining Democracy: Essays in Honor of Seymour Martin Lipset*, London: Sage.

——(1994) 'Political culture and democracy' and 'Causes and effects', in L. Diamond (ed.) *Political Culture and Democracy in Developing Countries*, Boulder, Col.: Lynne Rienner.

Diamond, L. and Marks, G. (1992) 'Seymour Martin Lipset and the study of democracy', in G. Marks and L. Diamond (eds) *Reexamining Democracy: Essays in Honor of Seymour Martin Lipset*, London: Sage.

Diamond, L., and M. F. Plattner (eds) (1993) *The Global Resurgence of Democracy*, Baltimore and London: The Johns Hopkins University Press.

Diamond, L., Linz, J. J. and Lipset, S. M. (eds) (1988–9) *Democracy in Developing Countries*, 3 vols, Boulder, Col.: Lynne Rienner.
——(1990) *Politics in Developing Countries: Comparing Experiences with Democracy*, Boulder, Col.: Lynne Rienner.
Dickerman, C. W. and Bloch, P. C. (1991) *Land Tenure and Agricultural Productivity in Malawi*, LTC Paper, Wisconsin: Land Tenure Center, University of Wisconsin.
Dicklich, S. (1994) 'The democratization of Uganda under the NRM régime', paper presented at the XVIth IPSA World Congress in Berlin, 21–5 August.
Dix, R. H. (1994) 'History and democracy revisited', *Comparative Politics* 27, 1: 91–105.
Dobzhansky, T., Ayala, F. J., Stebbins, G. L. and Valentine, J. W. (1977) *Evolution*, San Francisco: W. H. Freeman and Company.
Dogan, M. (1994) 'Use and misuse of statistics in comparative research', in M. Dogan and A. Kazancigil (eds.) *Comparing Nations: Concepts, Strategies, Substance*, Oxford: Basil Blackwell.
Donelly, Sally B. (1995) 'Central Asia: Hardfisted democracy', *Time*, 15 May: 36.
dos Santos, T. (1993/1970) 'The structure of dependence', in M. A. Seligson and J. T. Passé-Smith (eds) *Development and Underdevelopment: The Political Economy of Inequality*, Boulder, Col.: Lynne Rienner Publishers.
Eastern Europe and the Commonwealth of Independent States 1992 (1992), London: Europa Publications Limited.
Eastern Europe and the Commonwealth of Independent States 1994 (1994), London: Europa Publications Limited.
Eckstein, S., Donald, G., Horton, D. and Carroll, T. (1978) *Land Reform in Latin America: Bolivia, Chile, Mexico, Peru, and Venezuela*, Staff Working Paper No. 275, Washington, DC: The World Bank.
L'economie Camerounaise (1977), Numéro speciál du bulletin de l'Afrique noire, Paris: Ediafric la documentation africaine.
The Economist (1994) 'Democracy and growth: Why voting is good for you', 27 August: 15–17.
The Economist Intelligence Unit (EIU) (1985) *The Economist Intelligence Review of Senegal, The Gambia, Guinea-Bissau, Cape Verde, Annual Supplement* (1985); *Indochina: Vietnam, Laos, Cambodia, Annual* (1985); *Indonesia, Annual* (1985), London: The Economist Publications.
Edwards, A. (1994) 'Democratization and qualified explanation', in G. Parry and M. Moran (eds) *Democracy and Democratization*, London and New York: Routledge.
Eibl-Eibesfeldt, I. (1984) *Die Biologie des menschlichen Verhaltens. Grundriss der Humanethologie*, Munich: Piper.
EIU. See The Economist Intelligence Unit.
Electoral Studies (1987–94).
El-Solh, R. (1993) 'Islamist attitudes towards democracy: a review of the ideas of Al-Ghazali, Al-Turbani and Amara', *British Journal of Middle Eastern Studies* 20, 1: 57–64.
Ethiopia. A Country Study (1981), Washington, DC: US Government Printing Office.
Etzioni-Halevy, E. (1992) 'The autonomy of élites and transitions from non democratic regimes: the cases of the Soviet Union and Poland', *Research in Political Sociology* 6: 257–76.
The Europa World Year Book (1991–4), London: Europa Publications Limited.
FAO (1966–70) *Report on the 1960 World Census of Agriculture*, vol. 1: a–c, Rome: Food and Agriculture Organization of the United Nations.
——(1973–80) *Report on the 1970 World Census of Agriculture*, Census bulletins numbers 1–29, Rome: Food and Agriculture Organization of the United Nations.

FAO (1981) *1970 World Census of Agriculture. Analyses and International Comparison of the Results*, Rome: Food and Agriculture Organization of the United Nations.

——(1983–9) *Report on the 1980 World Census of Agriculture. Results by Countries*, Census bulletins numbers 3–28, Rome: Food and Agriculture Organization of the United Nations.

——(1991) *Production Yearbook*, vol. 44, 1990, FAO Statistics Series No. 99, Rome: Food and Agriculture Organization of the United Nations.

——(1993) *Production Yearbook*, vol. 46, 1992, FAO Statistics Series No. 112, Rome: Food and Agriculture Organization of the United States.

The Far East and Australasia Yearbook 1991 (1991), London: Europa Publications Limited.

Fargues, P. (1994) 'Demographic explosion or social upheaval?', in G. Salamé (ed.) *Democracy without Demokrats? The Renewal of Politics in the Muslim World*, London: I. B. Tauris Publishers.

Der Fischer Weltalmanach 1989 (1988), Frankfurt: Fischer Taschenbuch Verlag.

Fitzmaurice, J. (1993) 'The Estonian elections of 1992', *Electoral Studies* 12, 2: 168–73.

Flanigan, W. and Fogelman, E. (1971) 'Patterns of political development and democratization: a quantitative analysis', in J. V. Gillespie and B. A. Nesvold (eds) *Macro-Quantitative Analysis. Conflict, Development, and Democratization*, Beverly Hills: Sage.

Fossedal, G. A. (1989) *The Democratic Imperative: Exporting the American Revolution*, New York: Basic Books.

Frank, A. G. (1967) *Capitalism and Underdevelopment in Latin America*, New York and London: Monthly Review Press.

Freedom House (1991) *Freedom in the World: Political Rights and Civil Liberties 1990–91*, New York: Freedom House.

——(1992) *Freedom in the World: Political Rights and Civil Liberties: 1991–92*, New York: Freedom House.

Friedrich, C. J. (1950) *Constitutional Government and Democracy*, revised edition, Boston: Ginn and Co.

Fukuyama, F. (1995) 'Confucianism and democracy', *Journal of Democracy* 6, 2: 20–33.

Fuller, E. (1990) 'Round Table coalition wins resounding victory in Georgian Supreme Soviet elections', *Report on the USSR* 2, 46: 13–16.

——(1991) 'The Georgian presidential elections', *Report on the USSR* 3, 23: 20–2. ; ;

Gardner, H. S. (1988) *Comparative Economic Systems*, Chicago: Dreyden Press.

Gastil, R. D. (1985) 'The past, present, and future of democracy', *Journal of International Affairs* 38, 2: 161–79.

——(1988) *Freedom in the World: Political Rights and Civil Liberties, 1987–1988*, New York: Freedom House.

——(1990) 'The comparative survey of freedom: Experiences and suggestions', *Studies in Comparative International Development* 25, 1: 25–50.

Girnius, S. (1991) 'Referendum in Lithuania', *Report on the USSR* 3, 13: 16–17.

Graham, N. A. and Edwards, K. L. (1984) *The Caribbean Basin to the Year 2000. Demographic, Economic, and Resource-Use Trends in Seventeen Countries. A Compendium of Statistics and Projections*, Boulder, Col.: Westview Press.

Greenvald, J. (1992) 'The hunt for a safe rouble', *Time* 138: No. 10, 9 March.

Griffin, C. E. (1993) 'Democracy in the Commonwealth Caribbean', *Journal of Democracy* 4, 2: 84–94.

Gurr, T. R. (1974) 'Persistence and change in political systems, 1800–1971', *The American Political Science Review* 68, 4: 1482–504.

Gurr, T. R., Jaggers, K. and Moore, W. H. (1990) 'The transformation of the western state: The growth of democracy, autocracy, and state power since 1800', *Studies in Comparative International Development* 25, 1: 73–108.

Haaland, G. (1986) 'Farming systems, land tenure and ecological balance in Bhután', paper presented at the Ninth European Conference on Modern South Asian Studies, 9–12 July, Heidelberg.

Haavio-Mannila, E., Dahlerup, D., Edvards, M., Gudmundsdóttir, E., Halsaa, B., Hernes, H. M., Hänninen-Salmelin, E., Sigmundsdóttir, B., Sinkkonen, S. and Skard, T. (1985) *Unfinished Democracy: Women in Nordic Politics*, Oxford: Pergamon Press.

Hadenius, A. (1992) *Democracy and Development*, Cambridge: Cambridge University Press.

——(1994) 'Assessing democratic progress in Africa', paper presented at the XVIth IPSA World Congress in Berlin, 21–5 August.

Hall, J. A. (1993) 'Consolidation of democracy', in D. Held (ed.) *Prospects for Democracy: North, South, East, West*, Oxford: Polity Press.

Haney, G. (1971) *Die Demokratie – Wahrheit, Illusionen und Verfälschungen*, Berlin: Staatsverlag der Deutschen Demokratischen Republik.

Hartlyn, J. (1989) 'Colombia: The politics of violence and accommodation', in L. Diamond, J. J. Linz, and S. M. Lipset (eds), vol. 4, *Democracy in Developing Countries: Latin America*, Boulder, Col.: Lynne Rienner.

Hawthorn, G. (1993) 'Sub-Saharan Africa', in D. Held (ed.) *Prospects for Democracy: North, South, East, West*, Oxford: Polity Press.

HDR. See UNDP, *Human Development Report*.

Held, C. C. (ed.) (1994) *Middle East Patterns: Places, Peoples, and Politics*, 2nd edition, Boulder, Col.: Westview Press.

Held, D. (1992) 'Democracy: from city-states to a cosmopolitan order', *Political Studies* 40 (special issue *Prospects for Democracy*), 10–39.

Held, D. (ed.) (1993) *Prospects for Democracy: North, South, East, West*, Oxford: Polity Press.

Hewitt, C. (1977) 'The effect of political democracy and social democracy on equality in industrial societies: A cross-national comparison', *American Sociological Review* 42, 2: 450–64.

Hine, D. (1987) 'Italian general election of 1987', *Electoral Studies* 6, 3: 267–70.

Horowitz, D. L. (1991) *A Democratic South Africa: Constitutional Engineering in a Divided Society*, Berkeley: University of California Press.

Hove, S. (1987) 'The Maltese general election of 1987', *Electoral Studies* 6, 3: 235–47.

Human Development Report. See UNDP.

Huntington, S. P. (1984) 'Will more countries become democratic?', *Political Science Quarterly* 99, 2: 193–218.

——(1991) *The Third Wave: Democratization in the Late Twentieth Century*, Norman and London: University of Oklahoma Press.

Hurst, C. E. (1979) *The Anatomy of Social Inequality*, St Louis: The C. V. Mosby Company.

Hyde-Price, A. G. V. (1994) 'Democratization in Eastern Europe: the external dimension', in G. Pridham and T. Vanhanen (eds) *Democratization in Eastern Europe: Domestic and International Perspectives*, London and New York: Routledge.

IFES (1991–4) *Elections Today. News from the International Foundation for Electoral Systems*, Washington, DC.

IMF (International Monetary Fund (1992a) *Economic Review. Armenia*. Washington, DC: International Monetary Fund.

——(1992b) *Economic Review. Common Issues and Interrepublic Relations in the Former USSR*, Washington, DC: International Monetary Fund.

Internationales Handbuch. Staaten der Welt von A–Z. Internationale Zusammenschlüsse und Organizationen (1987), Ravensburg: Munzinger-Archiv GmbH.

Inter-Parliamentary Union (1981–1994) *Chronicle of Parliamentary Elections and Developments* (1981–94), Geneva: International Centre for Parliamentary Documentation.

IPU. See Inter-Parliamentary Union.

Israel. A Country Study (1978), Washington, DC: US Government Printing Office.

Issues and Studies (1993–94), Taipei: Institute of International Relations.

Jackman, R. W. (1974) 'Political democracy and social equality: a comparative analysis', *American Sociological Review* 39, 1: 29–45.

Jackman, R. W. and Miller, R. A. (1995) 'Voter turnout in the industrial democracies during the 1980s', *Comparative Political Studies* 27, 4: 467–92.

Jackson, K. D. (1989) 'The Philippines: the search for a suitable democratic solution, 1946–1986', in L. Diamond *et al.* (eds) *Democracy in Developing Countries* vol. 3. Asia, Boulder, Col.: Lynne Rienner.

Janda, K. (1992) A book review 'The process of democratization: A comparative study of 147 states, 1980–1988', *Journal of Politics* 54, August: 928–30.

Japan Statistical Yearbook 1982 (1982), Japan: Statistical Bureau, Prime Minister's Office.

Journal of Democracy (1991–5), Baltimore, Md: Johns Hopkins University Press.

Kaimowitz, D. (1980) 'The organization of agricultural production in the Syrian Arab Republic', *Land Tenure Center Newsletter* 60: 3–6.

Kanté, B. (1994) 'Senegal's empty election', *Journal of Democracy* 5, 1: 96–108.

Karl, T. L. (1990) 'Dilemmas of democratization in Latin America', *Comparative Politics* 23, 1: 1–21.

—— (1995) 'The hybrid regimes of Central America', *Journal of Democracy* 6, 3: 72–86.

Kasfir, N. (1993) 'Elections in Kenya', *Africa Demos* 3, 2: 11, 13.

Kazancigil, A. (1991) 'Democracy in Muslim countries: Turkey in comparative perspective', *International Social Science Journal* 128: 343–60.

Keesing's Record of World Events (1985–95).

Kennedy, P. (1993) *Preparing for the Twenty-first Century*, London: Fontana Press.

Komarov, E. N. (1992) 'The emergence of a multiparty system in the Soviet Union', in T. Vanhanen (ed.) *Strategies of Democratization*, Washington: Crane Russak.

Koste, T. (1969) '20 perhettä', in K. Bruun and A. Eskola (eds) *Taloudellinen valta Suomessa*, Helsinki: Tammi.

Krämer, G. (1994) 'The integration of the integrists: a comparative study of Egypt, Jordan and Tunisia', in G. Salamé (ed.) *Democracy without Democrats? The Renewal of Politics in the Muslim World*, London: I. B. Tauris.

Kurian, G. T. (1987) *Encyclopedia of the the Third World*, 3rd edn, New York: Facts on File.

—— (1992) *Encyclopedia of the Third World*, 4th edn, New York: Facts on File.

Kuusela, K. (1994) 'The new electoral systems in Eastern Europe 1989–91', in G. Pridham and T. Vanhanen (eds) *Democratization in Eastern Europe*, London: Routledge.

Lakanwal, A. G. (1980) 'Implementation of democratic land reform in the Democratic Republic of Afghanistan', in *Agrarreformen und Agraraufbau in den Ländern Asiens, Afrikas und Lateinamerikas*, Leipzig: Institut für tropische Landwirtschaft, Karl-Marx-Universität, DDR.

Lakshman, W. D. (1980) *Income and Wealth Distribution in Sri Lanka: An Examination of Evidence Pertaining to Post-1960 Experience*, Tokyo: International Development Center of Japan.

Länder der Erde. Politisch-ökonomisches Handbuch (1981), 7. Auflage, Autorenkollektiv, Köln: Pahl-Rugenstein Verlag.

Land Tenure Center (1979) *Land Concentration in the Third World: Statistics on Number and Area of Farms Classified by Size of Farms* 28, Training and Methods Series, Madison: University of Wisconsin.

Lane, J-E. and Ersson, S. (1990) *Comparative Political Economy*, London and New York: Pinters.

——(1994) *Comparative Politics: An Introduction and New Approach*, Cambridge: Polity Press.

Latin American and Caribbean Review (1986), 7th edn, Essex: World of Information.

Leenders, R. (1993) 'Transitions from authoritarian rule in the Arab world', *Civil Society* 15, March: 17–18.

Lerner, D. (1968 [1958]) *The Passing of Traditional Society: Modernizing the Middle East*, New York: The Free Press.

Levine, D. H. (1989) 'Venezuela: The nature, sources, and future prospects of democracy', in L. Diamond, J. J. Linz, and S. M. Lipset (eds), vol. 4, *Democracy in Developing Countries: Latin America*, Boulder, Col.: Lynne Rienner.

Levy, D. C. (1989) 'Mexico: sustained civilian rule without democracy', in L. Diamond *et al.* (eds) *Democracy in Developing Countries: Latin America*, vol. 4, Boulder, Col.: Lynne Rienner.

Lewis, P. G. (1993) 'Democracy and its future in Eastern Europe', in D. Held (ed.) *Prospects for Democracy: North, South, East, West*, Oxford: Polity Press.

Lewis, W. A. (1965) *Politics in Western Africa*, London: Allen & Unwin.

Lijphart, A. (1980 [1977]) *Democracy in Plural Societies: A Comparative Exploration*, New Haven: Yale University Press.

Lindblom, C. E. (1977) *Politics and Markets: The World's Political-Economic Systems*, New York: Basic Books.

Linz, Juan J. (1990a) 'The perils of presidentialism', *Journal of Democracy* 1, 1: 59–69.

——(1990b) 'The virtues of parliamentarism', *Journal of Democracy* 1, 4: 84–91.

——(1990c) 'Democracia: Presidencialismo o parlamentarismo. Hace alguna diferencia?', in J. J. Linz *et al.* (eds) *Hacia una democracia moderna: La opcion parlamentaria*, Santiago, Chile: Ediciones Universidad de Chile.

Linz, J. J., Lijphart A., Valenzuela, A. and Godoy Arcaya, O. (eds) (1990) *Hacia una democracia moderna: La opcion parlamentaria*, Santiago, Chile: Ediciones Universidad de Chile.

Lipset, S. M. (1959) 'Some social requisites of democracy: economic development and political legitimacy', *The American Political Science Review* 53, 1: 69–105.

——(1960) *Political Man: The Social Bases of Politics*, New York: Doubleday.

——(1983) *Political Man: The Social Bases of Politics*, expanded and updated edition, London: Heinemann.

——(1994) 'The social requisites of democracy revisited', *American Sociological Review* 59, February: 1–22.

Lipset, S. M., Seong, K.-R. and Torres, J. C. (1993) 'A comparative analysis of the social requisites of democracy', *International Social Science Journal*, 136, May: 155–75.

Lorenz, K. Z. (1982) *The Foundations of Ethology: The Principal Ideas and Discoveries in Animal Behavior*, trans. K. Z. Lorenz and R. W. Kickert, New York: Simon and Schuster.

Lovenduski, J. (1986) *Women and European Politics: Contemporary Feminism and Public Policy*, Amherst: The University of Massachusetts Press.

Lucas, R. E. B. and Papanek, G. F. (eds) (1988) *The Indian Economy: Recent Development and Future Prospects*, Delhi: Oxford University Press.

Luciani, G. (1994) 'The oil rent, the fiscal crisis of the state and democratization', in G. Salamé (ed.) *Democracy without Democrats? The Renewal of Politics in the Muslim World*, London: I. B. Tauris Publishers.

McColm, R. B. (1992) 'The comparative survey of freedom 1991–1992: between two worlds', in Freedom House Survey Team, *Freedom in the World: Political Rights and Civil Liberties 1991–1992*, New York: Freedom House.

McDowall, D. (1984) *Lebanon: A Conflict of Minorities*, Report No. 61, London: Minority Rights Group.

McLeon, I. (1994) 'Democratization and economic liberalization: which is the chicken and which is the egg?', *Democratization* 1, 1: 27–40.

Malloy, J. M. (1987) 'The politics of transition in Latin America', in J. M. Malloy and M. A. Seligson (eds) *Authoritarians and Democrats: Regime Transition in Latin America*, Pittsburgh: University of Pittsburgh Press.

Maloney, C. (1995) 'Where did the Maldives people come from', *IIAS Newsletter*, 5, Summer: 33–4.

Manheim, J. B., and Rich, R. C. (1986) *Empirical Political Analysis: Research Methods in Political Science*, New York and London: Longman.

Mann, D. (1990) 'The RSFSR elections: The Congress of People's Deputies', *Report on the USSR* 2, 15: April 13.

Martin, G. and O'Reilley, J. (1993) 'Madagascar', *Africa Demos* 3, 2: 7–8.

Marquette, J. F. (1974) 'Social change and political mobilization in the United States: 1870–1960', *American Political Science Review* 68, 3: 1058–74.

Matiba, K. (1995) 'This brave woman who stood up to a cruel African regime', *The Mail*, 6 August: 28.

Mayr, E. (1982) *The Growth of Biological Thought: Diversity, Evolution, and Inheritance*, Cambridge, Mass: Harvard University Press.

——(1988) *Toward a New Philosophy of Biology: Observations of an Evolutionist*, Cambridge, Mass: Harvard University Press.

Marsden, K. and Bélot, T. (1988) *Private Enterprise in Africa: Creating a Better Environment*, World Bank Discussion Papers, Washington, DC: The World Bank.

Mbaku, J. M. (1994) 'Rent seeking and democratization strategies in Africa', *Internationales Afrikaforum* 30, 3: 274–89.

Merkl, P. H. (1993) 'Which are today's democracies?', *International Social Science Journal* 136, May: 257–70.

The Middle East and North Africa 1993 (1993), London: Europa Publications Limited.

Miller, D. (ed.) (1983) *A Pocket Popper*, Oxford: Fontana Paperbacks.

Mittwally, S. H. (1980) 'Sozialökonomische Aspekte der Nahrungsmittelproduktion in Ägypten', in *Agrarreformen und Agraraufbau in den Ländern Asien, Afrikas und Lateinamerikas*, Leipzig: V. Internationales Sommerseminar des Institutes für Tropische Landwirtschaft der Karl-Marx-Universität, DDR.

Mohnot, S. R. (1962) *Concentration of Economic Power in India*, Allahabad: Chaitanya Publishing House.

Moore, M. (1995) 'Democracy and development in cross-national perspective: A new look at the statistics', *Democratization* 2, 2: 1–19.

Morrison, D. G., Mitchell, R. C. and Paden, J. N. (1989) *Black Africa: A Comparative Handbook*, 2nd edn, London: Macmillan.

Muhlberger, S. and Paine, P. (1993) 'Democracy's place in world history', *Journal of World History* 4, 1: 23–45.

Muller, E. N. (1985) 'Dependent economic development, aid dependence on the United States, and democratic breakdown in the Third World', *International Studies Quarterly* 29, 4: 445–69.

Muller, E. N. (1993 [1984]) 'Financial dependence in the capitalist world economy and the distribution of income within states', in M. A. Seligson and J. T. Passé-Smith (eds) *Development and Underdevelopment: The Political Economy of Inequality*, Boulder, Col.: Lynne Rienner.

Muni, S. D. (1991) 'Patterns of democracy in South Asia', *International Social Science Journal* 128: 361–72.

Mushi, S. (1992) 'The long road to democracy in Tanzania', *Africa Demos* 2, 3: 10–11.

Ndue, P. N. (1994) 'Africa's turn toward pluralism', *Journal of Democracy* 5, 1: 45–54.

Needler, M. C. (1967) 'Political development and socio-economic development: the case of Latin America', *The American Political Science Review* 62, 3: 889–97.

Nellis, J. R. (1986) *Public Enterprises in sub-Saharan Africa*, World Bank Discussion Papers, Washington, DC: The World Bank.

Neubauer, D. E. (1967) 'Some conditions of democracy', *The American Political Science Review* 61, 4: 1002–9.

Niklasson, T. (1994) 'The Soviet Union and Eastern Europe, 1988–9: interactions between domestic change and foreign policy', in G. Pridham and T. Vanhanen (eds) *Democratization in Eastern Europe: Domestic and International Perspectives*, London and New York: Routledge.

Nohlen, D. and Nuscheler, F. (eds) (1982–3) *Handbuch der Dritten Welt*, vols. 2–8, Hamburg: Hoffmann und Campe.

Norton, A. R. (1995) 'The challenge of inclusion in the Middle East', *Current History: A Journal of Contemporary World Affairs* 94, 588: 1–6.

Nyrop, R. F., Benderly, B. L., Carter, L. N., Cover, W. W., Eglin, D. R., Kirchner, R. A., Moeller, P. W., Mussen, W. A., Pike, C. E. and Shinn, R-S. (1977) *Area Handbook for the Persian Gulf States*, DAPam. 550–185, Washington, DC: US Government Printing Office.

Obasanjo, O. (1993) 'Reclaiming Africa's democratic roots', *Choices: The Human Development Magazine* 2, 1: 18–21.

O'Donnell, G. A. (1973) *Modernization and Bureaucratic-Authoritarianism: Studies in South American Politics*, Berkeley: Institute of International Studies, University of California.

O'Donnell, G. A. and Schmitter, P. C. (1986) *Transitions from Authoritarian Rule: Tentative Conclusions about Uncertain Democracies*, Baltimore and London: The Johns Hopkins University Press.

O'Donnell, G., Schmitter, P. C. and Whitehead, L. (eds) (1986) *Transitions from Authoritarian Rule*, 4 vols, Baltimore and London: The Johns Hopkins University Press.

Olcott, M. B. (1993) 'Central Asia on its own', *Journal of Democracy* 4, 1: 92–103.

Olsen, M. E. (1968) 'Multivariate analysis of national political development', *American Sociological Review* 33, 5: 699–712.

Olson, M. (1993) 'Dictatorship, democracy, and development', *American Political Science Review* 87, 3: 567–76.

O'Regan, A. (1992) 'Return to sartorial eloquence? Lipset, Dahl, Huntington, and Skocpol and redemocratization', paper delivered at the 1992 Annual meeting of the American Political Science Association, 3–6 September, Chicago.

Owen, R. (1994) 'Socio-economic change and political mobilization: The case of Egypt', in G. Salamé (ed.) *Democracy without Democrats? The Renewal of Politics in the Muslim World*, London: I. B. Tauris Publishers.

Pacific Islands Monthly (1992).

Parekh, B. (1992) 'The cultural particularity of liberal democracy', in D. Held (ed.) *Prospects for Democracy*, Political Studies 40, special issue, Norwich: Blackwell Publishers.

Park, T. K., Baro, M. and Ngaido, T. (1991) *Conflicts over Land and the Crisis of Nationalism in Mauritania*, LTC Paper, Wisconsin: Land Tenure Center, University of Wisconsin.

Parry, G. and Moran, M. (1994) 'Democracy and democratization', in G. Parry and M. Moron (eds) *Democracy and Democratization*, London and New York: Routledge.

Pennock, J. R. (1979) *Democratic Political Theory*, Princeton, NJ: Princeton University Press.

People's Republic of China Year Book 1990/91 (1990), Beijing: PRC Year Book Ltd.

Perry, C. S. (1980) 'Political contestation in nations: 1960, 1963, 1967, and 1970', *Journal of Political and Military Sociology* 8, 2: 161–74.

Perthes, V. (1994) 'The private sector, economic liberalization, and the prospects of democratization: The case of Syria and some other Arab countries', in G. Salamé (ed.) *Democracy without Democrats? The Renewal of Politics in the Muslim World*, London: I. B. Tauris Publishers.

Pinkney, R. (1993) *Democracy in the Third World*, Milton Keynes: Open University Press.

Popper, K. (1983) *Objective Knowledge: An Evolutionary Approach*, revised edition, Oxford: Clarendon Press.

——(1992) *In Search of a Better World: Lectures and Essays from Thirty Years*, London and New York: Routledge.

Poppovic, M. and Pinheiro, P. S. (1995) 'How to consolidate democracy? A human rights approach', *International Social Science Journal* 143, March: 75–89.

Potter, D. (1993) 'Democratization in Asia', in D. Held (ed.) *Prospects for Democracy*, Oxford: Polity Press.

Prevost, G. (1994) 'Nicaragua under Chamorro–democratization or a retreat from mass participation', paper presented at the IPSA World Congress in Berlin, 21–5 August.

Pride, R. A. (1970) *Origins of Democracy: A Cross-National Study of Mobilization, Party Systems, and Democratic Stability*, Beverly Hills: Sages.

Prybyla, J. (1992) 'China's economic dynamos', *Current History: A World Affairs Journal* 91: No. 566.

Pryde, J. (1994) 'Kyrgyzstan: the trials of independence', *Journal of Democracy* 5, 1: 109–20.

Pryor, F. L. (1988a) *Income Distribution and Economic Development in Madagascar: Some Historical Statistics*, World Bank Discussion Papers, Washington, DC: The World Bank.

——(1988b) *Income Distribution and Economic Development in Malawi: Some Historical Statistics*, World Bank Discussion Papers, Washington, DC: The World Bank.

Ramsay, J. (1991) *Global Studies. Africa*, 4th edn, Connecticut: The Dushkin Publishing Group.

Report to the Pyithu Hluttaw on the Financial, Economic and Social Conditions of the Socialist Republic of the Union of Burma for 1978–79 (1978), Rangoon: Ministry of Planning and Finance.

Republic of China Yearbook 1991–92 (1991), Taipei: Kwang Hwa Publishing Company.

Reynolds, A. (1995) 'Constitutional engineering in Southern Africa', *Journal of Democracy* 3, 2: 86–99.

Reyntjens, F. (1995) *Burundi: Breaking the Cycle of Violence*, London: Minority Rights Group.

Riddell, J. C. and Dickerman, C. (1986) *Country Profiles of Land Tenure: Africa 1986*, Madison: Land Tenure Center, University of Wisconsin.

Riggs, F. W. (1994) 'Bureaucracy: A profound puzzle for presidentialism', in A. Farazmand (ed.) *Handbook of Bureaucracy*, New York: Marcel Dekker.

——(1995) 'Ethnonational conflicts and viable constitutionalism', unpublished first draft.

Roland, G. (1994) 'On the speed and sequencing of privatisation and restructuring', *The Economic Journal* 104, 426: 1158–68.

Rowen, H. S. (1995) 'The tide underneath the "Third Wave"', *Journal of Democracy* 6, 1: 52–64.

Roy, O. (1994) 'L'Asie centrale et le national-soviétisme', *Cahiers Internationaux de Sociologie* 96, Janvier-Juin: 177–89.

Russett, B. M. (1968) 'Inequality and instability: the relation of land tenure to politics', in R. A. Dahl and D. E. Neubauer (eds) *Readings in Modern Political Analysis*, Englewood Cliffs, NJ: Prentice-Hall.

Russett, B. M., Alker, H. R., Deutsch, K. W. and Lasswell, H. D. (1964) *World Handbook of Political and Social Indicators*, New Haven: Yale University Press.

Rustow, D. W. (1970) 'Transition to democracy: Toward a dynamic model', *Comparative Politics* 8, 2: 337–64.

Samatar, S. S. (1991) *Somalia: a Nation in Turmoil*, London: Minority Rights Group.

San, G. (1992) 'The economic development and international co-operation of Taiwan, ROC', paper presented at the Sino-American-European Conference on Contemporary China in Taipei, Taiwan, Republic of China, 16–22 August.

Sancton, T. A. (1987) 'Democracy's fragile flower spreads its roots', *Time* 130, 28: 10–11.

Sartori, G. (1987) *The Theory of Democracy Revisited*, Chatham, NJ: Chatham House Publishers.

——(1995) 'How far can free government travel?', *Journal of Democracy* 6, 3: 101–111.

Saward, M. (1993) 'Democratic theory and indices of democratization', paper presented at the ECPR Joint Sessions of Workshops, 2–8 April, Leiden.

Schroeder, G. E. (1990) 'Nationalities and the Soviet economy', in L. Hajda and M. Beissinger (eds) *The Nationalities Factor in Soviet Politics and Society*, Boulder, Col.: Westview Press.

Seligson, M. A. (1987a) 'Democratization in Latin America: the current cycle', in J. M. Malloy and M. A. Seligson (eds) *Authoritarians and Democrats: Regime Transition in Latin America*, Pittsburgh: University Press of Pittsburgh.

——(1987b) 'Development, democratization, and decay: Central America at the crossroads', in J. M. Malloy and M. A. Seligson (eds) *Authoritarians and Democrats: Regime Transition in Latin America*, Pittsburgh: University Press of Pittsburgh.

——(1988) 'Economic development and democracy in Latin America', paper presented at the IPSA World Congress in Washington, 28 August–1 September.

Seligson, M. A. and Passé-Smith, J. T. (eds) (1993) *Development and Underdevelopment: The Political Economy of Inequality*, Boulder, Col.: Lynne Rienner.

Shah, S. (1984) 'Bhutan economy has been slow to modernize, but development plan envisages rapid growth', *IMF Survey*, 20 February.

Sharma, D. (1992) 'God bless the coalition'. *Pacific Islands Monthly* 62, 1: 12–14.

Shelton, V. (1993) 'Namibia', *Africa Demos* 3, 2: 6–7.

Shin, D. C. (1994) 'On the third wave of democratization: A synthesis and evaluation of recent theory and research', *World Politics* 47, 1: 135–70.

Short, R. P. (1984) 'The role of public enterprises: An international statistical comparison', in R. H. Floyd, C. S. Gray and R. P. Short (eds) *Public Enterprise in Mixed Economies: Some Macroeconomic Aspects*, Washington, DC: IMF.

Shrestha, J. B. (1982) 'Industrial development of Nepal', in *Occasional Papers. Series Four*, Varanasi: Centre for the Study of Nepal, Department of Political Science, Banaras Hindu University.

Shukla, S. K. (1994) 'World's largest democracy on trial – Problems in Indian democracy', paper presented at the IPSA World Congress in Berlin, 21–5 August.

Slider, D. (1990) 'The Soviet Union', *Electoral Studies* 9, 4: 295–302.
Smith, A. K. (1969) 'Socio-economic development and political democracy: a causal analysis', *Midwest Journal of Political Science* 30, 1: 95–125.
Smolar, A. (1994) 'A communist comeback?', *Journal of Democracy* 5, 1: 70–84.
Soares, G. A. D. (1988) 'Economic development and democracy in Latin America', paper presented at the IPSA World Congress in Washington, 28 August–1 September.
Socor, V. (1991) 'Moldavia resist pressure and boycotts', *Report on the USSR* 3, 13: 9–14.
Sorensen, G. (1993) *Democracy and Democratization: Processes and Prospects in a Changing World*, Boulder, Col.: Westview Press.
Statistical Abstract of Iceland (1967), Statistics of Iceland, II, 40, Reykjavik.
Statistical Abstract of Latin America (1990) James W. Wilkie (ed.), vol. 28, Los Angeles: UCLA Latin American Center Publications.
SWB. See *BBC Summary of World Broadcasting*.
Taagepera, R. (1990) 'The Baltic states', *Electoral Studies* 9, 4: 303–11.
Tadesse, Z. (1991) 'Beyond authoritarian rule', *Africa Demos* 1, 5: 5.
The Taiwan Development Experience And Its Relevance To Other Countries (1988), Taipei: Kwang Hwa Publishing Co.
Taylor, S. (1993) 'Ethiopia', *Africa Demos* 3, 2: 4, 8.
Third World Guide 93/94: Facts, Figures, Opinions (1993), Instituto del Tercer Mundo, Santafé de Bogotá, DC: Panamericana Formas e Impresos.
Time (1986).
Tolz, V. (1994) 'Russia's parliamentary elections: What happened and why', *RFE/RL Research Report*, vol. 3, No. 2, 14 January, Radio Free Europe, Radio Liberty.
Topornin, B., and Machulsky, E. (1974) *Socialism and Democracy: A Reply to Opportunists*, Moscow: Progress Publishers.
Tordoff, W. (1994) 'Political liberalization and economic reform in Africa', *Democratization* 1, 1: 100–115.
Tucker, S. and Smith, K. (1993) 'Burundi', *Africa Demos* 3, 2: 3, 10.
Turan, I. (1991) 'Islamic resurgence and politics: a comparative framework', paper presented at the IPSA World Congress in Buenos Aires, 21–25 July.
UNDP (the United Nations Development Programme) (1990–4) *Human Development Report*, years 1990–4, New York: Oxford University Press.
Unesco (1990–94) *Statistical Yearbook*, years 1990–4, Paris: Unesco.
United Nations (1993) *Statistical Yearbook 1990/1991*, New York: United Nations.
Vanhanen, T. (1963) *Poliittisen vaikutusvallan jakaantuminen Intiassa* (Distribution of political power in India), Licentiate's dissertation, Tampere: University of Tampere.
——(1968) *Puolueet ja pluralismi*, with English Summary *Parties and Pluralism*, Porvoo: Werner Söderström Osakeyhtiö.
——(1971) *Dependence of Power on Resources: A Comparative Study of 114 States in the 1960's*, Jyväskylä: University of Jyväskylä, Institute of Social Science Publications.
——(1975) *Political and Social Structures, Part 1: American Countries, 1850–1973*, Tampere: Institute of Political Science, University of Tampere (Research reports No. 38).
——(1977a) *Political and Social Structures: European Countries 1850–1974*, Ann Arbor: Published for Finnish Political Science Association by University Microfilms International.
——(1977b) *Political and Social Structures: Asian and Australasian Countries 1850–1975*, Ann Arbor: Published for Centre for the Study of Developing Societies, Delhi, by University Microfilms International.

——(1979) *Power and the Means of Power: A Study of 119 Asian, European, American, and African States, 1850–1975*, Ann Arbor: Published for Centre for the Study of Developing Societies, Delhi, by University Microfilms International.

——(1982) *The Roots of Democracy: India Compared with its Neighbours*, Hong Kong: Asian Research Service.

——(1984a) *The Emergence of Democracy: A Comparative Study of 119 States, 1850–1979*, Helsinki: The Finnish Society of Sciences and Letters.

——(1984b) 'Yhteiskunnallinen valta ja päätöksenteko', in *Mies – nainen – ihminen: Tieteen näkemyksiä sukupuolten eroista ja tasa-arvosta*, Helsinki: Opetusministeriö, Valtion painatuskeskus.

——(1990a) *The Process of Democratization: A Comparative Study of 147 States, 1980–88*, New York: Crane Russak.

——(1990b) 'Strategies of Democratization', paper presented at the XIth World Conference of the World Futures Studies Federation, 27–31 May, Budapest.

——(1990c) 'How to consolidate democracy by means of social and political architecture?', paper presented at the ECPR Joint Sessions of Workshops, 2–7 April, Bochum.

——(1991a) 'Structural imbalance as an explanation for the collapse of hegemonic regimes in Eastern Europe', paper presented at the ECPR Joint Sessions of Workshops, 22–8 March, University of Essex.

——(1991b) *Politics of Ethnic Nepotism: India as an Example*, New Delhi: Sterling Publishers.

——(1991c) 'Institutional strategies of democratization', paper presented at the XVth World Congress of the International Political Science Association, 21–5 July, Buenos Aires.

——(1992a) 'Social constraints of democratization' and 'Conclusion', in T. Vanhanen (ed.) *Strategies of Democratization*, Washington: Crane Russak.

——(1992b) *On the Evolutionary Roots of Politics*, New Delhi: Sterling Publishers.

——(1993) 'Construction and use of an index of democracy', in D. G. Westendorff and D. Ghai (eds) *Monitoring Social Progress in the 1990s*, Aldershot: Avebury.

Vanhanen, T. and Kimber, R. (1994) 'Predicting and explaining democratization in Eastern Europe', in G. Pridham and T. Vanhanen (eds) *Democratization in Eastern Europe: Domestic and International Perspectives*, London: Routledge.

Viro vuosikirja 1993.

Waller, M. (1994) 'Voice, choice and loyalty: democratization in Eastern Europe', in G. Parry and M. Moron (eds) *Democracy and Democratization*, London and New York: Routledge.

Wallerstein, I. (1982/1974) 'The rise and future demise of the world capitalist system: Concepts for comparative analysis', in R. Falk, S. S. Kim and S. H. Mendlovitz (eds) *Studies on a Just World Order. Volume I. Toward a Just World Order*, Boulder, Col.: Westview Press.

——(1993 [1975]) 'The present state of the debate on world inequality', in M. A. Seligson and J. T. Passé-Smith (eds) *Development and Underdevelopment: The Political Economy of Inequality*, Boulder, Col.: Lynne Rienner.

Ward, M. (1971) *The Role of Investment in the Development of Fiji*, Cambridge: University Press.

Waterbury, J. (1994) 'Democracy without democrats? The potential for political liberalization in the Middle East', in G. Salamé (ed.) *Democracy without Democrats? The Renewal of Politics in the Muslim World*, London: I. B. Tauris Publishers.

Wekkin, G. D., Whistler, D. E., Kelley, M. A. and Maggiotto, A. (eds) (1993) *Building Democracy in One-Party Systems: Theoretical Problems and Cross-Nation Experiences*, Westport, Connecticut: Praeger.

Wesson, R. (ed.) (1988) *Democracy: A World Survey 1987*, New York: Praeger.

Whistler, D. E. (1993) 'The mainstream democratic vision', in G. D. Wekkin *et al.* (eds.) *Building Democracy on One-Party Systems,* Westport, Connecticut: Praeger.

Whitehead, L. (1993) 'The alternatives to "liberal democracy": a Latin American perspective', in D. Held (ed.) *Prospects for Democracy,* Oxford: Polity Press.

Winham, G. R. (1970) 'Political development and Lerner's theory: Further test of a causal model', *American Political Science Review* 64, 3: 810–18.

Womack, B. (1992) 'Political reform in China in the 1980s: a comparative communist perspective', in T. Vanhanen (ed.) *Strategies of Democratization,* Washington: Crane Russak.

Woodward, P. (1994) 'Democracy and economy in Africa: the optimists and the pessimists', *Democratization* 1, 1: 116–32.

World Atlas of Agriculture. Volume 1. Europe, USSR, Asia Minor, (1969), *Volume 2. Asia and Oceania,* (1970), *Volume 3. Americas,* (1970), *Volume 4. Africa,* (1976), Committee for the World Atlas of Agriculture, Novara: Instituto Geografico De Agostini.

World Bank (1988) *Social Indicators of Development 1988,* Baltimore and London: The Johns Hopkins University Press.

——(1992) *Social Indicators of Development 1991–92,* Baltimore and London: The Johns Hopkins University Press.

World Development Report (1991–4), Published for the World Bank, New York: Oxford University Press.

The World Factbook 1991–92 (1992), Central Intelligence Agency, Washington: Brassey's (US) Inc.

Worldmark Encyclopedia of the Nations (1984) vols 1–4, 6th edn, New York: Worldmark Press.

Wu, J. J. (1993) 'The ROC's Legislative Yuan election of December 1992', *Issues and Studies* 29, 1: 119–21.

Index

Afghanistan 75, 125–7; expected to remain a non democracy in the near future 126; ethnic civil war 125

Africa 8, 33, 47–8, 65–6, 73, 127–41, 302–13, 315–32, 335; *see also* sub-Saharan Africa

Ake, C. 329

Albania 75, 104, 108, 293; democratic system expected to survive 108

Algeria 92, 122, 298, 304, 323, 325, 329–30; IPR value predicts democratization 122; Islamic Salvation Front 122

Almond, G. A. 278

alternative explanatory factors 6, 8, 11, 14–15, 18–21, 99–101, 118, 157, 161–2, 288–9; colonial background 161, 292–4; external factors 154, 161, 166–7, 294–5; historical legacies 161; income distribution 279; local factors 142, 153, 160–1, 167; political culture 20, 161, 278, 313; random factors 157; regional factors 100–3, 285–6; *see also* unexplained variation

alternative theoretical explanations for democracy 3, 5, 10–26, 156; bureaucratic-authoritarian model 11, 280; Dahl's conditions of democracy 14; dependency theory 11, 13, 21; development paradigm (Lerner-Lipset model) 10–12, 21, 75–6, 156, 280; Diamond, Linz and Lipset's factors for democratic development 15; Diamond's human development hypothesis 12–13, 21, 77–9, 156; Gastil's diffusion theory 11, 17–18; Hadenius' requisites of democracy 18–19; Huntington's arguments 15–17;

Olson's theoretical arguments 19–20; resource distribution or evolutionary theory 21–6; Rustow's stages of democratization 21; Whistler's balance of forces theory 19; *see also* studies of democracy and democratization

Anckar, D. 153

Angola 75; democratization not yet expected 135

anomalies 158–9; Seligson on 280–3; Turan on democratic anomalies 284–99

Antigua and Barbuda 61

Arabs 66, 128; Arab countries 66, 118–19, 121–4, 127; Arab nationalism 290–1

Arat, Z. A. 18, 30; Arat's index of 'democraticness' correlated with Vanhanen's ID 40; index of 'democraticness' 32

area specialists 7–9; *see also* Decalo, Forje, Henderson, Seligson, Turan

Argentina 8, 114, 116; democratic institutions predicted to survive 114; Seligson on 280–1

Aristotle 10

Armenia 61, 110–11; democratic system predicted to survive 111

Australia 66, 151–3, 334, 336, 342; predicted to continue as a democracy 152

Australasia and the Pacific *see* Oceania

Austria 164

authoritarian regimes 4, 28, 36–7, 58, 114–19, 122, 125–6, 128, 131–5, 137–8, 148–9, 175, 294, 310, 326–7, 330; military governments 136, 147–8, 280, 322–3; single-party states 321–23